BARRON'S
STUDENTS' #1 CHOICE

PASS KEY

TO THE

TOEFL *

TEST OF ENGLISH AS A FOREIGN LANGUAGE

Fourth Edition

Pamela J. Sharpe, Ph.D.
The Ohio State University

BARRON'S EDUCATIONAL SERIES, INC.

To my former students
at home and abroad

© Copyright 2001 by Barron's Educational Series, Inc.

Prior editions © Copyright 1999, 1996, 1994 by Barron's Educational
Series, Inc.

All rights reserved.
No part of this book may be reproduced
in any form, by photostat, microfilm, xerography,
or any other means, or incorporated into any
information retrieval system, electronic or
mechanical, without the written permission
of the copyright owner.

Material in this book was adapted from
Barron's *How to Prepare for the TOEFL*,
10th Ed., by Pamela J. Sharpe, Ph.D. © Copyright 2001
by Barron's Educational Series, Inc.

All inquiries should be addressed to:
Barron's Educational Series, Inc.
250 Wireless Boulevard
Hauppauge, New York 11788
http://www.barronseduc.com

Library of Congress Catalog Card No. 00-060856
International Standard Book No. 0-7641-7435-5

Library of Congress Cataloging-in-Publication Data

Sharpe, Pamela J.
    Pass key to the TOEFL / Pamela J. Sharpe.—4th ed.
        p. cm.
    "Material in this book was adapted from Barron's How to prepare for
the TOEFL, 10th ed., by Pamela J. Sharpe"—T.p. verso.
    ISBN 0-7641-7435-5 (book & compact audio disk)
    1. Test of English as a Foreign Language—Study guides. 2. English
language—Textbooks for foreign speakers. 3. English language—
Examinations—Study guides. I. Sharpe, Pamela J. Barron's how to
prepare for the TOEFL. II. Title.
PE1128 .S523 2001
428'.0076—dc21   00-060856

CONTENTS

INTRODUCTION

QUESTIONS AND ANSWERS CONCERNING THE TOEFL

REVIEW OF SECTION 1: LISTENING

REVIEW OF SECTION 2: STRUCTURE

REVIEW OF SECTION 3: READING

REVIEW OF WRITING ESSAYS

TOEFL MODEL TESTS

ANSWER KEYS FOR THE TOEFL REVIEW EXERCISES AND MODEL TESTS

EXPLANATORY ANSWERS FOR THE TOEFL MODEL TESTS

SCORE ESTIMATES   421

TRANSCRIPT FOR THE LISTENING SECTIONS OF THE TOEFL MODEL TESTS   427

To the Student

Barron's *Pass Key to the TOEFL* is the concise version of the classic *Barron's How to Prepare for the TOEFL*. Small enough to put in your purse, backpack, or book bag, this convenient book can always be in the right place when you have a few minutes to study—on the bus, while you wait for an appointment, or on break at work or school.

This concise version, *Pass Key to the TOEFL*, can be used to prepare for both the Supplemental Paper-Based TOEFL and for the Computer-Based TOEFL. To make this book smaller, less expensive, and more convenient to carry with you, we have included four Model Tests in the book and the audio for two Model Tests on the compact disk. The larger version of this book, *Barron's How to Prepare for the TOEFL*, includes eight Model Tests. The CD-ROM that supplements the book includes the audio and the computer screens for Computer-Assisted Model Tests as well as a Computer-Adaptive Model Test.

Ideally, you would use these two books for two different purposes. You would use this book, *Pass Key to the TOEFL*, to take the best advantage of your time while you are away from your computer or when you don't want to carry heavy materials. You would use the larger version of this book, *Barron's How to Prepare for the TOEFL*, and the CD-ROM that supplements it, when you have access to your computer.

Study thoughtfully, and take the TOEFL with confidence. It may well be the most important examination of your academic career. And this book can be an essential pass key to your success.

To the Teacher

Rationale for a TOEFL Preparation Course

Although *Barron's Pass Key to the TOEFL* may be perceived as a self-study guide for students who were preparing to take the TOEFL, in the years since its first publication, I have received letters from ESL teachers around the world who are using the book successfully for classroom study. In fact, in recent years, many special courses have been developed within the existing ESL curriculum to accommodate TOEFL preparation.

I believe that these TOEFL preparation courses respond to three trends within the profession. First, there appears to be a greater recognition on the part of many ESL teachers that student goals must be acknowledged and addressed. For the engineer, the business person, the doctor, or the preuniversity student, a satisfactory score on the TOEFL is one of the most immediate goals; for many, without the required score, they cannot continue their professional studies or obtain certification to practice their professions. They may have other language goals as well, such as learning to communicate more effectively or improving their writing, but these goals do not usually exert the same kinds of pressure that the required TOEFL score does.

Second, teachers have recognized and recorded the damaging results of test anxiety. We have all observed students who were so frightened of failure that they have performed on the TOEFL at a level far below that which their performance in class would have indicated. The standardized score just didn't correspond with the score in the gradebook. In addition, teachers have become aware that for some students, the TOEFL represents their first experience in taking a computer-assisted test. The concepts of working within time limits, marking on a screen, and guessing to improve a score are often new and confusing to students, and they forfeit valuable points because they must concentrate on unfamiliar procedures instead of on language questions.

Third, teachers have observed the corresponding changes in student proficiency that have accompanied the evolutionary changes in ESL syllabus design. Since this book was first written, we have moved away from a grammatical syllabus to a notional functional syllabus, and at this writing, there seems to be growing interest in a content-based syllabus. Viewed in terms of what has actually happened in classrooms, most of us have emphasized the teaching of functions and meaning and de-emphasized the teaching of forms. As we did so, we noticed with pride the improvement in student fluency and with dismay the corresponding loss of accuracy. Some of our best, most fluent students received disappointing scores on the test that was so important to them.

Through these observations and experiences, teachers have concluded that (1) students need to work toward their own goals, (2) students need some time to focus on accuracy as well as on fluency, and (3) students need an opportunity to practice taking a standardized test in order to alleviate anxiety and develop test strategies. With the introduction of the Computer-Based TOEFL, the opportunity to gain experience taking a computer-assisted model test has also become important to student confidence and success. In short, more and more teachers have begun to support the inclusion of a TOEFL preparation course in the ESL curriculum.

Organization of a TOEFL Preparation Course

Organizing a TOEFL preparation course requires that teachers make decisions about the way that the course should be structured and the kinds of supplementary materials and activities that should be used.

Structuring

Some teachers have suggested that each review section in this book be used for a separate class; they are team teaching a TOEFL course. Other teachers direct their students to the language laboratory for independent study in listening comprehension three times a week, checking on progress throughout the term; assign reading and vocabulary study for homework; and spend class time on structure and writing. Still other teachers develop individual study plans for each student based on previous TOEFL part scores. Students with high listening and low reading scores concentrate their efforts in reading labs, while students with low listening and high reading scores spend time in listening labs.

Materials and Activities

Listening. Studies in distributive practice have convinced teachers of listening comprehension that a little practice every day for a few months is more valuable than a lot of practice concentrated in a shorter time. In addition, many teachers like to use two kinds of listening practice—intensive and extensive. Intensive practice consists of listening to problems like those in the review of listening in this book.

By so doing, the student progresses from short conversations through longer conversations to mini-talks, gaining experience in listening to simulations of the TOEFL examination. Extensive practice consists of watching a daytime drama on television, listening to a local radio program, or auditing a class. Creative teachers everywhere have developed strategies for checking student progress such as requiring a summary of the plot or a prediction of what will happen the following day on the drama; a one-sentence explanation of the radio program, as well as the name of the speaker, sponsor of the program, and two details; a copy of student notes from the audited class.

Structure. Of course, the focus in a review of structure for the TOEFL will be on form. It is form that is tested on the TOEFL. It is assumed that students have studied grammar prior to reviewing for the TOEFL, and that they are relatively fluent. The purpose of a TOEFL review then is to improve accuracy. Because accuracy is directly related to TOEFL scores and because the scores are tied to student goals, this type of review motivates students to pay attention to detail that would not usually be of much interest to them.

Among ESL teachers, the debate rages on about whether students should over see errors in grammar. But many teachers have recognized the fact that students *do* see errors all the time, not only in the distractors that are used on standardized tests like the TOEFL and teacher-made tests like the multiple-choice midterms in their grammar classes, but also in their own writing. They argue that students must be able to recognize errors, learn to read for them, and correct them.

The student preparing for the TOEFL will be required not only to recognize correct answers but also to eliminate incorrect answers, or distractors, as possibilities. The review of structure in this book supports recognition by alerting students to avoid certain common distractors. Many excellent teachers take this one step further by using student compositions to create personal TOEFL tests. By underlining four words or phrases in selected sentences, one phrase of which contains an incorrect structure, teachers encourage students to reread their writing. It has proven to be a helpful transitional technique for students who need to learn how to edit their own compositions.

Reading. One of the problems in a TOEFL preparation course is that of directing vocabulary study. Generally, teachers feel that encouraging students to collect words and develop their own word lists is the best solution to the problem of helping students who will be faced with the dilemma of responding to words from a possible vocabulary pool of thousands of words that may appear in context in the reading section. In this way, they will increase their vocabularies in an ordered and productive way, thereby benefiting even if none of their new words appears on the test that they take. Activities that support learning vocabulary in context are also helpful.

In order to improve reading, students need extensive practice in reading a variety of material, including newspapers and magazines as well as short excerpts from textbooks. In addition, students need to check their comprehension and time themselves carefully. Many teachers are using preparation books for the General Education Degree (GED) in special reading labs for students preparing for the TOEFL. Books such as *Barron's How to Prepare for the GED* contain passages at about the same level as those on the TOEFL and include comprehension questions after each passage. Teachers report that passages on natural science, social science, and general interest only should be assigned because literature passages often require that the student read and interpret poetry and plays, and these literary readings do not appear on the TOEFL. Again, it is well to advise students of the advantages of distributed practice. They should be made aware that it is better to read two passages every day for five days than to read ten passages in one lab period.

It is also necessary for students who are preparing for the Computer-Based TOEFL to practice reading from a computer screen. The skill of scrolling through text is different from the skill of reading a page in a book. To succeed on the TOEFL and after the TOEFL, students must develop new reading strategies for texts on screens. An English encyclopedia on CD-ROM is an inexpensive way to provide students with a huge amount of reading material from all the nonfiction content areas tested on the TOEFL. By reading on screen, students gain not only reading comprehension skills but also computer confidence.

Writing. There are many excellent ESL textbooks to help students improve their writing. Because the TOEFL limits the topics to opinion, persuasion, and argument, some teachers tend to emphasize these types of topics in composition classes.

The extensive list of writing topics published in the *Information Bulletin* for the Computer-Based TOEFL offers teachers an opportunity to use actual TOEFL topics in class. In order to help students organize their thoughts, the topics can be used as conversation starters for class discussion. In this way, students will have thought about the topics and will have formed an opinion before they are presented with the writing task on the TOEFL.

It is also a good idea to time some of the essays that students write in class so that they can become accustomed to completing their work within thirty minutes.

Although teachers need to develop grading systems that make sense for their teaching situations, the scoring guide that is used for the essay on the TOEFL is general enough to be adapted for at least some of the assignments in an ESL composition class. By using the guide, teachers can inform students of their progress as it relates to the scores that they can expect to receive on the essay they will write for the TOEFL.

Networking with ESL Teachers

One of the many rewards of writing is the opportunity that it creates to exchange ideas with so many talented colleagues. At conferences, I have met ESL teachers who use or have used one of the previous editions of this book; through my publisher, I have received letters from students and teachers from fifty-two nations. This preface and many of the revisions in this new edition were included because of comments and suggestions from those conversations and letters.

Thank you for your ideas. I hope that by sharing we can help each other and thereby help our students more. Please continue corresponding by mail or by e-mail.

Pamela Sharpe
1406 Camino Real
Yuma, Arizona 85364
sharpe@teflprep.com

Acknowledgments

It is with affection and appreciation that I acknowledge my indebtedness to the late Dr. Jayne C. Harder, Director of the English Language Institute of the University of Florida, who initiated me into the science of linguistics and the art of teaching English as a foreign language.

I am also very grateful to my parents, Robert and Lilly Sharpe, for their enthusiastic encouragement during the preparation of the manuscript and for their assistance in typing and proofreading each of the previous editions; to the late Tom Clapp, for the maturity and confidence that I gained from our marriage; to Carole Berglie of Barron's Educational Series, Inc., for her insights and guidance in seeing the first edition of the manuscript through to publication; and to all of the editors at Barron's for their contributions to later editions.

I was particularly fortunate to be reunited for the fourth edition with the outstanding editor for the third edition, Marcy Rosenbaum, and the talented production manager for the third edition, Debby Becak, whose suggestions and designs, both large and small, improved every chapter and contributed to make this the best edition yet. I also recognize and appreciate the significant effort by my research assistant, Kathy Telford, who proved to be an invaluable member of the team for her skillful proofreading and attention to the important details in the writing process.

With the assistance of Judy Peterson and the cooperation of Roxanne Nuhaily at the English Language Program, University of California, San Diego, the items for the Computer-Adaptive Model Test were field tested; with the collaboration of Dr. Sherri McCarthy-Tucker, the items were analyzed and calibrated; in consultation with Karen McNiel and Dr. Jean Zukowski-Faust, a review of the reading level for the revised reading comprehension passages was completed, and a number of items were substantially improved.

Finally, I would like to say a special thank you to my husband, John T. Osterman, for the unconditional love, the daily interest in and support for my writing career, and the best chapter in my life story.

Permissions

With the permission of Mr. Frank Berlin, Sexton Educational Programs, New York, explanations for several of the listening comprehension problems have been adapted from previous work by the author.

With the permission of Educational Testing Service, the test instructions contained in this publication for the various sections of TOEFL have been reprinted from the *Information Bulletin* for the *Computer-Based TOEFL*. The granting of this permission does not imply endorsement by ETS or the TOEFL program of the contents of this publication as a whole or of the practice questions that it contains. Since the types of questions in TOEFL and the instructions pertaining to them are subject to change, candidates who register to take TOEFL should read carefully the edition of the *Information Bulletin* that will be sent to them free of charge with their registration material.

Timetable for the TOEFL

TIMETABLE FOR THE SUPPLEMENTAL PAPER-BASED TOEFL
Total Time: 3 hours

Section 1 (40 Minutes)	Listening Comprehension	50 Questions
Section 2 (25 Minutes)	Structure and Written Expression	40 Questions
Section 3 (55 Minutes)	Reading Comprehension	50 Questions
TWE (30 Minutes)	Essay	1 Question

TIMETABLE FOR THE COMPUTER-BASED TOEFL
Total Time: 4.5 hours

Tutorial (Untimed)	Computer Skills	7 Tutorials
Section 1 (40–60 Minutes)	Listening	30–50 Questions
Section 2: Part One (15–20 Minutes)	Structure	20–25 Questions
Break (5 Minutes)		
Section 3 (70–90 Minutes)	Reading	44–55 Questions
Section 2: Part Two (30 Minutes)	Essay	1 Question

Note: Actual times will vary in accordance with the time the supervisor completes the preliminary work and begins the actual test. The time for the tutorial will vary from one person to another. Format and numbers of questions will also vary from one test to another. This timetable is a good estimate.

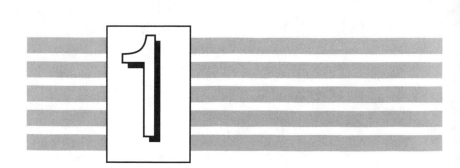

INTRODUCTION

Study Plan for the TOEFL

Many students do not prepare for the TOEFL. They do not even read the *Information Bulletin* that they receive from Educational Testing Service along with their registration forms. You have an advantage. Using this book, you have a study plan.

Barron's TOEFL Series

There are three books in the Barron's TOEFL series to help you prepare for the Test of English as a Foreign Language. Each book has a different purpose.

Barron's Practice Exercises for the TOEFL. A book for learners at an intermediate level who need preview and practice for the TOEFL. It includes a general preview of the TOEFL examination, a review of the most frequently tested problems, and almost one thousand exercises. Two separate cassette tapes accompany the book to give you practice in listening comprehension. You may have used *Barron's Practice Exercises for the TOEFL* before using this book.

Barron's How to Prepare for the TOEFL. A book for learners at high intermediate and advanced levels who need review and practice for the TOEFL. It includes questions and answers about the TOEFL examination, a detailed review for each section of the examination, practice exercises, and eight model tests similar to the actual TOEFL examination. Several sets of additional materials are available to supplement this book, including a separate package of cassette tapes and a separate package of audio compact disks. The book may be accompanied by compact disks for audio only or a CD-ROM for use with a computer. A computer-adaptive test like that of the Computer-Based TOEFL is found on the CD-ROM.

Barron's Pass Key to the TOEFL. A pocket-sized edition of *Barron's How to Prepare for the TOEFL.* It is for high intermediate and advanced learners who need review and practice for the TOEFL and want to be able to carry a smaller book with them. It includes questions and answers about the TOEFL examination, basic tips on how to prepare for the TOEFL, and four model tests from *Barron's How to Prepare for the TOEFL.* One audio compact disk accompanies the book to give you practice in listening to two model tests.

More About This Book

In preparing to take the TOEFL or any other language examination, it is very important to review the language skills for each section of the examination and to have an opportunity to take model tests that are similar to the actual examination.

Reviewing will help you recall some of the language skills you have studied in previous classes and other books. Taking model tests will give you the experience of taking a TOEFL before you take the actual examination.

Remember, the purpose of the book is to provide you with a concise review of the language skills for each section of the TOEFL examination and to provide you with opportunities to take model tests similar to the actual TOEFL examination.

By studying this book, you should renew and sharpen your skills, increase your speed, and improve your score.

Planning to Take the TOEFL

Study Plan I—For Intermediate Level Learners
- First, use *Barron's Practice Exercises for the TOEFL* to begin your TOEFL preparation.
- Then use this book, *Barron's Pass Key to the TOEFL* for preparation at times when you do not have a computer available.
- Also use *Barron's How to Prepare for the TOEFL* with the CD-ROM for practice on computer-assisted tests.

Study Plan II—For High Intermediate Level or Advanced Learners
- Use *Barron's How to Prepare for the TOEFL* with the CD-ROM for practice on computer-assisted tests.
- Use *Barron's Pass Key to the TOEFL* for preparation at times when you do not have a computer available.

Study Plan III—For Advanced Learners
- Use this book, *Barron's Pass Key to the TOEFL* for the most concise study plan.

A Ten-Week Calendar

Week One
- Read Chapter 2, "Questions and Answers Concerning the TOEFL."
- Write TOEFL Services for a copy of the *Information Bulletin*.
- Register for your test date.

Week Two
- Study Chapter 3, "Review of Section 1: Listening."
- Take the Listening Section of Model Test 1: Computer-Assisted TOEFL, and follow directions for marking in the book.
- Refer to the Answer Key in Chapter 8 and the Explanatory Answers in Chapter 9.
- Refer to Chapter 11 "Transcript for the Listening Sections of the TOEFL Model Tests."

Week Three
- Begin Chapter 4, "Review of Section 2: Structure," the Patterns.
- Complete the Practice Exercises, and refer to the Answer Key in Chapter 8.
- Mark the Problems that you need to review again.

Week Four
- Continue Chapter 4, "Review of Section 2: Structure," the Style Problems.
- Complete the Practice Exercises, and refer to the Answer Key in Chapter 8.
- Mark the Problems that you need to review again.

Week Five
- Study Chapter 5, "Review of Section 3: Reading."
- Complete the Practice Exercises and refer to the Answer Key in Chapter 8.

Week Six
- Take the Structure and Reading sections of Model Test 1: Computer-Assisted TOEFL, and follow directions for marking in the book.
- Write the essay at the end of Model Test 1.
- Refer to the Answer Key in Chapter 8 and the Explanatory Answers in Chapter 9.

Week Seven

- Take all three sections of Model Test 2: Computer-Assisted TOEFL, and follow directions for marking in the book.
- Write the essay at the end of Model Test 2.
- Refer to the Answer Key in Chapter 8 and the Explanatory Answers in Chapter 9.

Week Eight

- Take all three sections of Model Test 3: Computer-Assisted TOEFL, and follow directions for marking in the book.
- Write the essay at the end of Model Test 3.
- Refer to the Answer Key in Chapter 8 and the Explanatory Answers in Chapter 9.

Week Nine

- Take all three sections of Model Test 4: Computer-Assisted TOEFL.
- Write the essay at the end of Model Test 4.
- Refer to the Answer Key in Chapter 8 and the Explanatory Answers in Chapter 9.

Week Ten

- Study all the Problems that you have marked in the Review Chapters.
- Review all the errors that you have made on the Model Tests.

Adjusting the Calendar

Ideally, you will have ten weeks to prepare for the TOEFL. But, if you have a shorter time to prepare, follow the plan in the same order, adjusting the time to meet your needs.

If you have taken the TOEFL before, you already know which section or sections are difficult for you. Look at the part scores on your score report. If your lowest score is on Section 1, Listening, then you should spend more time reviewing Section 1. If your lowest score is on Section 2 or Section 3, then you should spend more time reviewing them.

For additional Model Tests and for practice marking your answers on a computer, use the larger version of this book, *Barron's How to Prepare for the TOEFL* and the CD-ROM that supplements it.

Plan for Preparation

To improve your scores the most, follow this plan:

- *First,* concentrate on listening, structure, writing, and reading, instead of on vocabulary. Your score will improve, because when you are engaged in listening and reading, you are practicing skills that you can apply during the examination regardless of the content of the material. When you are reviewing structure, you are studying a system that is smaller than that of vocabulary, and, like the skills of listening and reading, has the potential for application on the TOEFL that you take. Many of the structures that you study will probably appear on the examination. But when you review lists of vocabulary, even very good lists, you may study hundreds of words and not find any of them on the examination. This is so because the system is very large. There are thousands of possible words that may be tested.

- *Second,* spend time preparing every day for at least an hour instead of sitting down to review once a week for seven hours. Even though you are studying for the same amount of time, research shows that daily shorter sessions produce better results on the test.

- *Finally,* do not try to memorize questions from this or any other book. The questions on the test that you take will be very similar to the questions in this book, but they will not be exactly the same.

What you should try to do as you use this and your other books is learn how to apply your knowledge. Do not hurry through the practice exercises. While you are checking your answers to the model tests, *think* about the correct answer. Why is it correct? Can you explain the answer to yourself before you check the explanatory answer? Is the question similar to others that you have seen before?

Plan for Additional Preparation

Although this book should provide you with enough review material, some of you will want to do more in order to prepare for the TOEFL. Suggestions for each section follow.

- *To prepare for Section 1,* Listening, listen to radio and television newscasts and weather reports, television documentaries, lectures on educational television stations, and free lectures sponsored by clubs and universities. Attend movies in English. Try to make friends with speakers of American English and participate in conversations.

- *To prepare for Section 2,* Structure, use an advanced grammar review book. If you are attending an English course, do not stop attending.

- *To prepare for Section 3,* Reading, read articles in English newspapers and magazines, college catalogs and admissions materials, travel brochures, and entries that interest you from American and English encyclopedias. Try to read a variety of topics—American history, culture, social science, and natural science.

- *To prepare for the essay,* Writing, refer to the TOEFL *Information Bulletin* for the Computer-Based TOEFL or visit the TOEFL web site at *www.toefl.org.* Actual essay topics for the TOEFL are listed in the TOEFL *Bulletin* and on the web site.

A Good Start

Learn to relax. If you start to panic in the examination room, close your eyes and say "no" in your mind. Tell yourself, "I will not panic. I am prepared." Then take several slow, deep breaths, letting your shoulders drop in a relaxed manner as you exhale.

Concentrate on the questions. Do not talk. Concentrate your attention. Do not look at anything in the test room except the answers that correspond to the question you are working on.

Do not think about your situation, the test in general, your score, or your future. If you do, force yourself to return to the question.

If you do not understand a problem and you do not have a good answer, do your best. Then stop thinking about it. Be ready for the next problem.

Do not cheat. In spite of opportunity, knowledge that others are doing it, desire to help a friend, or fear that you will not make a good score, *do not cheat.*

On the TOEFL, cheating is a very serious matter. If you are discovered, your test will not be scored. Legal action may be taken by Educational Testing Service (ETS).

Suggestions for Success

Your attitude will influence your success on the TOEFL examination. You must develop patterns of positive thinking. To help in developing a positive attitude, memorize the following sentences and bring them to mind after each study session. Bring them to mind when you begin to have negative thoughts.

I know more today than I did yesterday.
I am preparing.
I will succeed.

Remember, some tension is normal and good. Accept it. Use it constructively. It will motivate you to study. But don't panic or worry. Panic will cause loss of concentration and poor performance. Avoid people who panic and worry. Don't listen to them. They will encourage negative thoughts.

You know more today than you did yesterday.
You are preparing.
You will succeed.

QUESTIONS AND ANSWERS CONCERNING THE TOEFL

The TOEFL is the Test of English as a Foreign Language.

Almost one million students from 180 countries register to take the TOEFL every year at test centers throughout the world. Some of them do not pass the TOEFL because they do not understand enough English. Others do not pass it because they do not understand the examination.

The following questions are commonly asked by students as they prepare for the TOEFL. To help you, they have been answered here.

TOEFL Programs

What is the purpose of the TOEFL?

Since 1963 the TOEFL has been used by scholarship selection committees of governments, universities, and agencies such as Fulbright, the Agency for International Development, AMIDEAST, Latin American Scholarship Program, and others as a standard measure of the English proficiency of their candidates. Now some professional licensing and certification agencies also use TOEFL scores to evaluate English proficiency.

The admissions committees of more than 2,400 colleges and universities in the United States and Canada require foreign applicants to submit TOEFL scores along with transcripts and recommendations in order to be considered for admission. Some colleges and universities in other English-speaking countries also require the TOEFL for admissions purposes.

Many universities use TOEFL scores to fulfill the foreign language requirement for doctoral candidates whose first language is not English.

Which TOEFL testing programs are available now?

Three TOEFL testing programs are available—the Supplemental Paper-Based TOEFL, the Computer-Based TOEFL, and the Institutional TOEFL. The Supplemental Paper-Based TOEFL and the Computer-Based TOEFL programs are the official administrations. The Institutional TOEFL is not an official administration.

What is the Computer-Based TOEFL program?

The Computer-Based TOEFL (CBT) was introduced July, 1998, in the United States, Canada, Latin America, Europe, Australia, Africa, the Middle East, and a limited number of Asian nations. In October, 2000, the CBT was introduced in all other Asian countries, with the exception of the People's Republic of China, where it will be given for the first time in 2002–2003, completing the worldwide phase-in of the Computer-Based TOEFL. A list of test centers established for the purpose of administering the Computer-Based TOEFL program appears in the free TOEFL *Information Bulletin* available from TOEFL Services, or on the TOEFL web site. Be sure that you request the TOEFL *Information Bulletin* for the Computer-Based TOEFL program.

What is the Supplemental Paper-Based TOEFL program?

The Supplemental Paper-Based TOEFL program is a paper and pencil version of the TOEFL that was reintroduced on a temporary basis to replace mobile computer-based testing in a few remote areas. Visit the TOEFL web site at *www.toefl.org/infobull.html* for a list of the areas where the Supplemental Paper-Based TOEFL is currently being offered. If you cannot use the web site, you can check at one of the United States Information Service (USIS) offices in your country for an *Information Bulletin for Supplemental TOEFL Administrations.*

What is the Institutional TOEFL program?

More than 1,200 schools, colleges, universities, and private agencies administer the Institutional TOEFL. The Institutional TOEFL is the same length, format, and difficulty as the Supplemental Paper-Based TOEFL, but the dates and the purposes of the Institutional TOEFL are different from those of the official TOEFL.

The dates for the Institutional TOEFL usually correspond to the beginning of an academic session on a college or university calendar.

The Institutional TOEFL is used for admission, placement, eligibility, or employment only at the school or agency that offers the test.

If you plan to use your scores for a different college, university, or agency, you should take one of the official TOEFL tests, either the Supplemental Paper-Based TOEFL or the Computer-Based TOEFL.

How can I order an *Information Bulletin?*

There are four ways to order a TOEFL *Information Bulletin.*

download	*www.toefl.org/infobull.html*
phone	1-609-771-7100
FAX	1-609-771-7500
mail	TOEFL Services
	P.O. Box 6151
	Princeton, NJ 08541-6151
	U.S.A.

Many schools also have copies of the *Information Bulletin* in their counseling centers.

Be sure that you request the correct TOEFL *Information Bulletin* for your test. Ask for either the Computer-Based *Information Bulletin* or the *Information Bulletin for Supplemental TOEFL Administrations.*

It is correct to limit your correspondence to two sentences. For example:

REQUEST FOR THE TOEFL *INFORMATION BULLETIN*

(write your address here)

(write the date here)

TOEFL Services
P.O. 6151
Princeton, NJ 08541-6151
U.S.A.

Dear TOEFL Representative:

Please send me a copy of the TOEFL *Information Bulletin* for the (write Computer-Based TOEFL or Supplemental Paper-Based TOEFL here).

Thank you for your attention.

Sincerely yours,

(write your name here)

The TOEFL *Information Bulletin* is often available overseas in U.S. embassies and advising offices of the United States Information Service, binational centers, IIE and AMIDEAST Counseling Centers, Fulbright offices, and ETS Regional Registration Centers, as well as in Sylvan Technology Centers.

May I choose to take the Computer-Based TOEFL or the Supplemental Paper-Based TOEFL?

When the Computer-Based TOEFL is phased in for the area where you will take your TOEFL, you must take the Computer-Based TOEFL. All Paper-Based TOEFL tests will be replaced.

The TOEFL web site lists the areas where the Supplemental Paper-Based TOEFL has been reintroduced on a temporary basis.

Which language skills are tested on the TOEFL?

In general, the same four language skills are tested in all TOEFL programs. Listening, structure, writing, and reading are tested in three separate sections:

Section 1   Listening
Section 2   Structure/Writing
Section 3   Reading

There are some differences in the types of questions used to test the language skills, however. Charts that outline the differences between the Computer-Based TOEFL and the Supplemental Paper-Based TOEFL are printed at the beginning of each Review Chapter in this book.

On the Computer-Based TOEFL, the essay counts as 50 percent of the total score for Section 2.

Does the TOEFL have a composition section?

Computer-Based TOEFL

The Computer-Based TOEFL has a Writing section. On the Writing section and on the TWE (Test of Written English), you must write a short essay on an assigned topic.

The essay should be about 300 words long. The topic is typical of academic writing requirements at colleges and universities in

North America. You have 30 minutes to finish writing. Both the Writing section and the TWE are described in greater detail in Chapter 6 of this book.

Supplemental Paper-Based TOEFL

The Paper-Based TOEFL does not have a composition section, but if you take the TOEFL in August, October, December, February, or May, you will also take the TWE.

Are all the TOEFL tests the same length?

Computer-Based TOEFL

The forms for the Computer-Based TOEFL vary in length. Some items are for research purposes and are not scored. Scored items are selected by the computer, based on the level of difficulty and the number of correct responses from previous items. Difficult items are worth more points than average or easy items.

Supplemental Paper-Based TOEFL

All of the forms for the Paper-Based TOEFL are the same length.

How does the Supplemental Paper-Based TOEFL and the Institutional TOEFL compare with the Computer-Based TOEFL?

The Supplemental Paper-Based TOEFL and the Institutional TOEFL are different from the Computer-Based TOEFL not only because it is a different experience to take a test with a pencil and paper as compared with a computer but also because the test designs are different. The Supplemental Paper-Based TOEFL and the Institutional TOEFL are linear tests. This means that all the questions appear in a row, and everyone receives the same questions. The Computer-Based TOEFL has two sections, Listening and Structure, that are computer-adaptive. This means that only one question appears on the screen, and everyone does not receive the same questions. Everyone begins with a question of average difficulty. If you answer it correctly, you are given a more difficult question. If you answer it incorrectly, you are given an easier question. You receive more points for answering difficult questions correctly than you do for answering average or easy questions correctly.

For a more detailed comparison of the Paper-Based TOEFL with the Computer-Based TOEFL, please refer to the charts at the beginning of each Review Chapter in this book.

Is the Computer-Based TOEFL fair?

The Computer-Based TOEFL is fair because the computer is constantly adjusting the selection of items based on your responses. It allows you to achieve that maximum number of points that you are capable of based on your English language proficiency. In addition, everyone receives the same test content and the same proportion of question types—multiple-choice and computer-assisted.

What if I have little experience with computers?

There is a Tutorial at the beginning of the Computer-Based TOEFL to help you become familiar with the computer before you begin your test. In the Tutorial, you will review how to use a mouse, how to scroll, and how to answer all the question types on the test.

If you would like to work through the Tutorial before the day of your Computer-Based TOEFL, you can request a CD-ROM Sampler from ETS. In the United States and Canada, call 1-800-446-3319. From other countries, call 1-619-771-7243. Or, if you have access to the web, you can use the Sampler by visiting the TOEFL web site at *http://www.toefl.org*. There are also a few samples of the Tutorial in the TOEFL *Information Bulletin*.

Registration

How do I register for the TOEFL?

Computer-Based TOEFL

There are three ways to register for the Computer-Based TOEFL. If you plan to pay by credit card—VISA, MasterCard, or

American Express—you may register by phone. Call Candidate Services at 1-800-468-6335, or phone your Regional Registration Center. The phone numbers for the regional centers are listed in the TOEFL *Information Bulletin*. If you plan to pay by check, money order, or credit card, you may register by mail. To arrange a test in the United States, Canada, Puerto Rico, or a U.S. territory, return the voucher request form in your *Information Bulletin*, along with your registration fee to TOEFL Services in Princeton, New Jersey. There is a mailing label provided in the *Information Bulletin*. To arrange a test in all other locations where the Computer-Based TOEFL is offered, return the International Test Scheduling Form to your Regional Registration Center. There are mailing labels provided in the TOEFL *Information Bulletin*. Be sure to sign the form and include your registration fee.

You will be asked to choose two days of the week and two months of the year as well as two test centers. If there are no appointments available on the dates you have requested, you will be assigned a date close to the request you have made.

Supplemental Paper-Based TOEFL

The *Information Bulletin for Supplemental TOEFL Administrations* has a registration form in it. Using the directions in the TOEFL *Information Bulletin*, fill out the form and mail it to the TOEFL Registration Office. Be sure to sign the form and include your registration fee.

Institutional TOEFL

The school, college, university, or agency that administers the Institutional TOEFL should have registration forms available. Fees vary.

The school, college, university, or agency will return your registration form and the registration fee to TOEFL Services along with the forms and fees of all of the other applicants for the Institutional Testing.

When should I register for the TOEFL?

If you are taking the TOEFL as part of the application process for college or university admission, plan to take the test early enough for your score to be received by the admission office in time to be considered with your application. Usually, a test date at least two months before the admission application deadline allows adequate time for your scores to be considered with your admission application.

Test centers often receive more requests than they can accommodate on certain dates. Try to schedule your appointment by phone or mail at least a month before the date you prefer to take the TOEFL, especially in October, November, December, April, and May.

What are the fees for the TOEFL?

Computer-Based TOEFL

In the United States, the registration fee is $110 U.S. The fee may be paid by check, credit card, money order, bank draft, or U.S. postal money order. In Canada, the fee is $118.

In other countries, the registration fee was originally advertised as $125 U.S., but TOEFL Services is now offering the Computer-Based TOEFL worldwide at $110 U.S. Because of rates of exchange, the actual cost may vary from one country to another. For exact fees in local currency, and options for payment, refer to the TOEFL *Information Bulletin*.

Supplemental Paper-Based TOEFL

The fee for the Supplemental Paper-Based TOEFL is $75 U.S.

Which credit cards will be accepted?

Only MasterCard, VISA, and American Express may be used to pay for TOEFL registration fees and services.

May I pay by check or money order?

In order to pay for the Supplemental Paper-Based TOEFL by check or money order, include payment with your registration form.

In order to pay for the Computer-Based TOEFL by check or money order, you should complete a voucher request form and mail it to the TOEFL Office with your payment. There is a special form and envelope in the middle of the *Information Bulletin for the Computer-Based TOEFL* for this purpose, or you can find these materials on the TOEFL web site. You will receive a CBT voucher by return mail.

Which currencies will be accepted?

Payments at the current exchange rate for the U.S. dollar may be made in the following currencies:

Australian Dollar	German Mark	Norwegian Krone
Austrian Schilling	Hong Kong Dollar	Portuguese Escudo
Belgian Franc	Irish Pound	Saudi Riyal
British Pound	Italian Lira	Singapore Dollar
Danish Krone	Japanese Yen	Spanish Peseta
Euro Dollar	Netherlands Guilder	Swedish Krona
Finnish Markka	New Zealand Dollar	Swiss Franc
French Franc		

Is there a fast way to send mail to the TOEFL Office?

For the fastest delivery, use the express courier delivery address:

TOEFL Services (25-Q-310)
Distribution and Receiving Center
225 Phillips Blvd
Ewing, NJ 08628-7435
U.S.A.

Will Educational Testing Service (ETS) confirm my registration?

Computer-Based TOEFL

If you register for the Computer-Based TOEFL, you will receive an appointment confirmation number. If you do not receive an appointment confirmation number, or if you lose your appointment confirmation number, call 1-800-GOTOEFL (1-800-468-6335) in the United States or call your Regional Registration Center outside the United States. The phone numbers for Regional Registration Centers are listed in the TOEFL *Information Bulletin*.

Supplemental Paper-Based TOEFL

If you register for the Paper-Based TOEFL, you will receive an admission ticket. Your admission ticket is your confirmation.

You must complete the ticket and take it with you to the test center on the day of the test along with your passport.

If you have not received the admission ticket two weeks before the date of your TOEFL test, call TOEFL Services or call your local representative. The phone numbers for local representatives are listed in the TOEFL *Information Bulletin*.

May I change the date or cancel my registration?

Computer-Based TOEFL

In the United States, Canada, Puerto Rico, and U.S. territories, call Candidate Services at 1-800-468-6335. Be sure to call by noon, three business days before the date of your appointment, or you will not receive a partial reimbursement of your registration fee. If you want to choose a different date, you may be asked to pay a rescheduling fee of $40 in the U.S. or $42 in Canada.

In all other locations, call your Regional Registration Center by noon, five business days before the date of your appointment, or you will not receive a partial reimbursement of your registration fee. If you want to choose a different date, you may be asked to pay a rescheduling fee of $40.

You must provide your appointment confirmation number when you call. You will be given a cancellation number.

Supplemental Paper-Based TOEFL

Test date changes and cancellations are not permitted for the Paper-Based TOEFL; however, you may receive absentee credit. If you do not take the Paper-Based TOEFL, write "absentee credit" across your admission ticket and send it to TOEFL Services. It must arrive within sixty days of your test date for you to receive $10 cash or $10 credit toward registration for a different date.

May I give my appointment to a friend?

Appointments cannot be reassigned or exchanged among friends.

How should I prepare the night before the TOEFL?

Don't go to a party the night before you take your TOEFL examination. But don't try to review everything that you have studied in this book either. By going to a party, you will lose the opportunity to review a few problems that may add valuable points to your TOEFL score. But by trying to review everything, you will probably get confused, and you may even panic.

Select a limited amount of material to review the night before you take the TOEFL.

And remember, you are not trying to score 100 percent on the TOEFL examination. No one knows everything. If you answer 75 percent of the questions correctly, you will receive an excellent score.

May I register on the day of the TOEFL?

Registration of candidates on the day of the TOEFL is permitted for the CBT only, but most of the time there is no space for candidates not pre-registered for that day.

Test Administration

Where are the test centers?

The most recent listing of the test centers for TOEFL administrations worldwide is found in the current *Information Bulletin* or on the TOEFL web site.

What kind of room will be used for the TOEFL?

Computer-Based TOEFL

Rooms used for the Computer-Based TOEFL are small. They are like the study areas in a library or a language laboratory. There are usually only six to fifteen students at individual computer stations. Each student has a headset. It is a good idea to wear clothing that allows you to adjust to warm or cold room temperatures.

Supplemental Paper-Based TOEFL

The rooms vary greatly from one test site to another. Rooms used for the Paper-Based TOEFL tend to be large. The seats are usually school desks. It is a good idea to wear clothing that allows you to adjust to warm or cold room temperatures.

What should I take with me to the examination room?

Computer-Based TOEFL

Take your appointment confirmation number and your official identification.

You will not need a watch because the computer screen has a clock face on it. Books, dictionaries, tape recorders, cellular phones, pagers, highlighters, pens, and notes are not permitted in the examination room. Some centers will have lockers for you to store your possessions, but it is really better not to take with you anything that you cannot take into the examination room.

Supplemental Paper-Based TOEFL

Take three sharpened number two pencils with erasers on them, your admission ticket, and photo identification form. In addition to your photo identification, you must have official identification with you.

It would be helpful to take a watch, although most examination rooms will have clocks. Books, dictionaries, tape recorders, cellular phones, pagers, highlighters, pens, and notes are not permitted in the examination room.

What kind of identification is required?

Computer-Based TOEFL

In the United States, only your valid passport will be accepted. In other countries, your valid passport is still the best identification, but if you do not have a passport, you may refer to the TOEFL *Information Bulletin* for special directions.

Your photograph will be taken at the test center and reproduced on all official score reports sent to institutions. Your identification will be checked against the new photograph. In addition, all Computer-Based TOEFL sessions will be videotaped.

Be sure to use the same spelling and order of your name on your registration materials or phone registration, the Test Center log that you will sign when you enter the test area, the forms on the computer screens, and any correspondence that you may have with TOEFL Services, Candidate Services, or other local representatives.

Supplemental Paper-Based TOEFL

The test center supervisor will not admit you if you do not have official identification. In the United States, only your valid passport will be accepted. The supervisor will not allow you to enter with an expired passport or a photocopy of your passport. In other countries, your valid passport is still the best identification, but if you do not have a passport, you may refer to the TOEFL *Information Bulletin* for special directions.

Be sure that your photo identification and your passport picture look like you do on the day of the examination. If not, you may not be admitted to the examination room.

Be sure to use the same spelling and order of your name on your registration materials, admission ticket, answer sheet, and any correspondence that you may have with either TOEFL Services or your Regional Registration Center.

Will I sign a confidentiality statement?

Before you begin the Computer-Based TOEFL, you will be asked to sign a confidentiality statement. You will agree to keep confidential the content of all test questions. The purpose of this procedure is to protect the security of the test.

Where should I sit?

You will be assigned a seat. You may not select your own seat.

It is usually better not to sit with friends anyway. You may find yourself looking at friends instead of concentrating on your test materials. You may even be accused of cheating if it appears that you are communicating in some way.

What if I am late?

Report to the test center thirty minutes before the appointment time for your TOEFL. You will need a half hour to check in. If you arrive late, you may not be admitted, and your fee may not be refunded.

How long is the testing session of the TOEFL?

Computer-Based TOEFL

The time for the Computer-Based TOEFL will vary, depending on your familiarity with computers. There is a computer Tutorial at the beginning of the session for those who need some practice using the computer before taking the Computer-Based TOEFL. In general, the Computer-Based TOEFL takes four hours, including the Tutorial. When you finish, you may leave the room quietly.

Supplemental Paper-Based TOEFL

The total time for the testing session of the Paper-Based TOEFL is two hours. Since the instructions are not included as part of the timed sections, the actual time that you will spend in the examination room will be about three hours. When the TWE is given with the TOEFL, the total time will be about three and one half hours. When you finish, you must sit quietly until the supervisor dismisses the group.

How much time do I have to complete each of the sections?

It is wise to work as rapidly as possible without compromising accuracy. Check the timetable for the TOEFL on page xiv.

Are breaks scheduled during the TOEFL?

Computer-Based TOEFL

There is a ten-minute break scheduled during the Computer-Based TOEFL. It usually occurs between the Structure and the Reading sections.

Supplemental Paper-Based TOEFL

There are no breaks scheduled during the Paper-Based TOEFL.

Is there a place to eat lunch at the test centers?

Some of the testing centers are conveniently located near restaurants, but many, especially the mobile centers, are not. You may want to take a snack with you to eat before or after your test.

How can I complain about a test administration?

If you feel that the test situation was not fair, you have a right to register a complaint. Within three days of the date of the test, write a letter to Test Administration Services. The phone number is 1-609-771-7100. Mention the date of your test, the city, and the country. Explain why you feel that the test was not fair.

Examination

What kinds of questions are found on the TOEFL?

Computer-Based TOEFL
The majority of the questions on the Computer-Based TOEFL are multiple-choice. There are also some other types of questions on the Computer-Based TOEFL. These questions will have special directions on the screen. You will have many examples of them in the Model Tests in this book.

Supplemental Paper-Based TOEFL
All the questions on the Paper-Based TOEFL are multiple-choice.

How do I answer the test questions?

Computer-Based TOEFL
When you are presented with a multiple-choice question, read the four possible answers on the screen, point the arrow and click beside the answer that you choose. The oval will change from white to black. When you are presented with other types of questions, follow the directions on the screen.

Supplemental Paper-Based TOEFL

Read the four possible answers in your test book, and mark the corresponding space on the answer sheet, which will be provided for you at the test center.

How do I mark the answers?

Computer-Based TOEFL

Before the examination begins, you will have an opportunity to practice marking the answers to questions on the computer screen. The Tutorial will include all the different types of questions on the Computer-Based TOEFL.

MARKING THE ANSWER SCREEN: COMPUTER-BASED TOEFL

One question is shown on the computer screen. One answer is marked on the screen.

Example

Directions: Click on the one word or phrase that best completes the sentence.

The United States is a country in

- ○ South America
- ○ Central America
- ● North America
- ○ Antarctica

Time   Help Answer Confirm Next

Supplemental Paper-Based TOEFL

Before the examination begins, the supervisor will explain how to mark the answer sheet. Be sure to fill in the space completely.

MARKING THE ANSWER SHEET: SUPPLEMENTAL PAPER-BASED TOEFL

One question is shown in the test book. One answer is marked on the answer sheet.

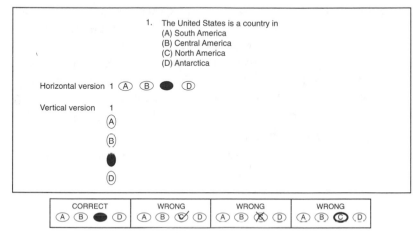

May I make notes in the test book or on the scratch paper?

Computer-Based TOEFL

There is no test book for the Computer-Based TOEFL. All of the questions and the answer options are presented on the computer screen. You may not use the scratch paper for your essay to make notes for any other section of the test.

Supplemental Paper-Based TOEFL

You are not allowed to make marks in your test book for the Supplemental Paper-Based TOEFL. You may not underline words or write notes in the margins of the test book. It is considered cheating.

May I change an answer?

Computer-Based TOEFL

On the first two sections of the Computer-Based TOEFL, Listening and Structure, you can change your answer by clicking on the new answer. You can change your answer as many times as you wish, until you click on the **Confirm Answer** button. When you click on **Confirm Answer**, you move to the next question, and you cannot go back to a previous question. On the third section of the Computer-Based TOEFL, Reading, you can change your answer as many times as you wish. You may go on to the next question and back to the previous questions. The CD-ROM that supplements this book will provide you with practice in choosing and changing answers on the computer screen.

Supplemental Paper-Based TOEFL

You may erase an answer on the answer sheet if you do so carefully and completely. Stray pencil marks may cause inaccurate scoring by the test-scoring machine.

If I am not sure of an answer, should I guess?

Computer-Based TOEFL

Try to answer every question. Your score will be based not only on the difficulty of the questions but also on the number of questions answered.

Supplemental Paper-Based TOEFL

If you are not sure of an answer, you should guess. The number of incorrect answers is not subtracted from your score. Your score is based on the number of correct answers only.

Do not mark more than one answer for each question. Do not leave any questions blank on your answer sheet.

How should I guess?

Computer-Based TOEFL

In the first two sections, Listening and Structure, eliminate the incorrect answers, then guess, but do not use a "guess answer" to finish these sections quickly. You will receive a lower score for random guessing.

On the third section, Reading, try to manage your time so that you can finish all of the questions, but if you have only a minute or two left, try to answer all of the remaining questions. Use a "guess answer."

Pace yourself so that you can finish as much of the test as possible. On the first two sections, Listening and Structure, you will be scored based on the number of questions answered, the number of correct answers you have submitted, and the level of difficulty of the questions that you have answered. On the third section, Reading, you will be scored on the number of questions you have answered, and the number of correct answers you have submitted.

Supplemental Paper-Based TOEFL

First, eliminate all of the possibilities that you know are NOT correct. Then, if you are almost sure of an answer, guess that one.

If you have no idea of the correct answer for a question, choose one letter and use it for your "guess" answer throughout the entire examination.

The "guess" answer is especially useful for finishing a section quickly. If the supervisor tells you to stop working on a section before you have finished it, answer all of the remaining questions with the "guess" answer.

What should I do if I discover that I have marked my answers incorrectly?

Computer-Based TOEFL

It is not possible to mark your screen incorrectly because the computer program will present only one question on each screen. If you change your mind after you have confirmed a response on the Listening or Structure sections, the computer will not allow you to return to a previous question on these two sections, and you will not be able to change the answer that you have confirmed.

As you see, it is very important to be sure of the answer before you click on **Confirm Answer**.

Supplemental Paper-Based TOEFL

Do not panic. Notify the supervisor immediately.

If you have marked one answer in the wrong space on the answer sheet, the rest of the answers will be out of sequence. Ask for time at the end of the examination to correct the sequence. The TOEFL test supervisor may or may not allow you to do this.

To save time finding the number on the answer sheet that corresponds to the problem you are reading, to avoid mismarking, and to save space on your desk, use your test book as a marker on your answer sheet. As you advance, slide the book down underneath the number of the question that you are marking on the answer sheet.

May I choose the order of the sections on my TOEFL?

You may not choose the order. Listening, Structure, and Reading are tested in that order. The essay is written last. When you have finished with a section, you may not work on any other section of the test.

What if I cannot hear the tape for the Listening section?

Computer-Based TOEFL

You will have your own headset for the Computer-Based TOEFL. Before the Listening section begins, you will have an opportunity to adjust the volume yourself. Be careful to adjust the volume when you are prompted to do so. If you wait until the test begins, you cannot adjust it.

Supplemental Paper-Based TOEFL

It is the responsibility of the supervisor for the Paper-Based TOEFL to make sure that everyone is able to hear the tape. If you cannot hear it well, raise your hand and ask the supervisor to adjust the volume.

May I keep my test?

TOEFL Services makes copies of TOEFL tests available for purchase. Visit the TOEFL web site for more information.

If you try to keep or copy TOEFL tests, the TOEFL Office may take legal action.

What can I do if I do not appear to take the test?

Computer-Based TOEFL

There is a $60 refund, if you cancel your test five business days before the date of your appointment.

Supplemental Paper-Based TOEFL

If you do not appear to take the test, you have a right to request a partial refund. If you enter the examination room, you cannot request a partial refund. You must make your request within sixty days of the date of the TOEFL test. Ask for "absentee credit" when you write to the TOEFL Office. The refund is $10.

Score Reports

How is my TOEFL scored?

Computer-Based TOEFL

Total Computer-Based TOEFL scores range from 0 to 300.

First, each of the three sections of the TOEFL is graded on a scale from 0 to 30. Then the scores from the three sections are added together. Finally, the sum is multiplied by 10 and divided by 3.

For example, the following scores were received on the three sections:

Listening	23
Structure and Writing	25
Reading	27
	75

$75 \times 10 = 750 \div 3 = 250$ Total TOEFL Score

Supplemental Paper-Based TOEFL

Total Paper-Based TOEFL scores range from 310 to 677.

First, each of the three sections of the TOEFL is graded on a scale from 31 to 68. Then the scores from the three sections are added together. Finally, the sum is multiplied by 10 and divided by 3.

For example, the following scores were received on the three sections:

Listening Comprehension	52
Structure and Written Expression	48
Vocabulary and Reading Comprehension	50
	150

$150 \times 10 = 1500 \div 3 = 500$ Total TOEFL Score

How do I interpret my score?

There are no passing or failing scores on the TOEFL. Each agency or university will evaluate the scores according to its own requirements. Even at the same university, the requirements may vary for different programs of study, levels of study (graduate or undergraduate), and degrees of responsibility (student or teaching assistant).

The following summary of admissions policies are typical of U.S. universities, assuming, of course, that the applicant's documents other than English proficiency are acceptable.

TYPICAL ADMISSIONS POLICIES OF AMERICAN UNIVERSITIES

Paper-Based TOEFL Score	Policy	Computer-Based TOEFL Score
650 or more	admission assured for graduate students	280 or more
600–649	admission assured for undergraduate students	250–279
550–599	admission probable for graduate students	213–249
500–549	admission probable for undergraduate students	173–212
450–499	individual cases reviewed	133–172
449 or less	referral to English language program probable	132 or less

Refer to the TOEFL *Information Bulletin* or web site for a detailed chart of percentile ranks for total TOEFL scores. This will help you interpret your score relative to the scores of others taking the examination.

How do the scores on the Supplemental Paper-Based TOEFL compare with those on the Computer-Based TOEFL?

A concordance table is a table that shows comparisons. A concordance table for the Paper-Based TOEFL and the Computer-Based TOEFL has been mailed to all institutions that use TOEFL scores for admissions decisions. A copy of the concordance table is printed in the TOEFL *Information Bulletin* and posted on the TOEFL web site.

A shorter version of the table follows:

Paper-Based TOEFL	Computer-Based TOEFL
677	300
650	280
600	250
550	213
500	173
450	133
400	97

If I score very poorly on one part of the TOEFL, is it still possible to receive a good total score?

If you feel that you have done very poorly on one part of a section, do not despair. You may receive a low score on one part of a section and still score well on the total examination if your scores on the other parts of that section and the other sections are good.

When can I see my scores?

Computer-Based TOEFL

After you complete your Computer-Based TOEFL, you can view your estimated score on the screen. You will be able to see section scores for both Listening and Reading, as well as for the multiple-choice part of the Structure section, but the essay, which is included as half of the Structure score, will not have been graded. The estimated score that you will see shows a total score range based on a very poorly written essay or on a very well written essay. For example, your score range might be 150–220.

You are entitled to five copies of your test results, including one personal copy for yourself and four official score reports.

Your official scores for all sections will be mailed to you about two to five weeks after you take your Computer-Based TOEFL, but you will have a very good idea how you performed on the test after you see the estimate.

Supplemental Paper-Based TOEFL

You are entitled to four copies of your test results, including one personal copy for yourself and three official score reports.

You will receive your copy about five weeks after you take the test.

Scores are not available by phone for the Supplemental Paper-Based TOEFL.

How can I know my scores sooner?

If your essay is typed instead of handwritten, your scores will be mailed sooner. If you would like to know your score on the same day that the report is mailed, you may use the TOEFL phone service. Using a touch-tone phone, call the TOEFL Office, and you will hear prompts to enter your appointment number, your test date, your date of birth, and a credit card number. The fee to hear your scores by phone is $10, plus any long-distance charges that apply.

To call toll-free from the United States or Canada, touch 1-888-TOEFL-44, which is 1-888-863-3544. To call with long distance charges from all other locations, touch 1-609-771-7267.

What can I do if I question my score report?

Computer-Based TOEFL

The *Information Bulletin for the Computer-Based TOEFL* includes a request form to arrange for your essay to be rescored by two graders who have not seen it previously. The fee for this service is $50.

Supplemental Paper-Based TOEFL

Occasionally, the computer will score an answer sheet incorrectly because of the way you have marked it. If you feel your score is much, much lower than you expected, you have a right to request that your answer sheet be hand scored.

Two people will score your answer sheet independently. If their results are different from that of the computer, your score will be changed. The cost of this service is $20 for the TOEFL and $45 for the TWE. You must make your request within six months of the date of the test.

To make a request, write a letter to TOEFL Services.

May I cancel my scores?

Computer-Based TOEFL

Before you view your scores, you may cancel them. If you do, they will not be sent to any institutions or to you. You will not know how you performed. If you view your scores, you may not cancel them. You will then choose four institutions to receive your score report. All of this is arranged by responding to questions on the computer screen.

Supplemental Paper-Based TOEFL

If you do not want your Paper-Based TOEFL scores to be reported, you have a right to cancel them. To cancel your test scores, you must complete the score cancellation section of your TOEFL answer sheet, or you must write, e-mail, call, or fax TOEFL Services. If a signed request is received at TOEFL Services within seven days of the date of the test, your scores will not be reported.

How will the agencies or universities of my choice be informed of my score?

Computer-Based TOEFL

Two weeks after the testing, your official score reports will be forwarded directly to the agencies and/or universities that you designated on the information section on the computer screen on the day of the examination.

Personal copies of score reports are not accepted by institutions without confirmation by TOEFL Services. Scores more than two years old are not considered valid.

Supplemental Paper-Based TOEFL

Five weeks after the testing, your official score reports will be forwarded directly to the agencies and/or universities that you designated on an information section at the top of the TOEFL answer sheet on the day of the examination.

You may send your personal copy to an institution or agency, but the score will probably have to be confirmed by an official at TOEFL Services before you can be admitted. Scores more than two years old cannot be reported or verified.

How can I send additional reports?

Computer-Based TOEFL

There is a form in the TOEFL *Information Bulletin* that you can use to have official score reports sent to institutions that were not listed on your computer screen. In addition, the TOEFL Office provides a telephone service for additional score reports. To use the service, you will need a touch-tone phone. You will be asked for your appointment confirmation number, a credit card number, your test date, and both the institution and department codes for the schools you wish to add to your score report list. You will use the numbers on your touch-tone phone to enter the numbers for all of the dates and codes.

The fee for this service is $12 per call, and $12 for each report.

Supplemental Paper-Based TOEFL

There is a form in the TOEFL *Information Bulletin* that you can use to have official score reports sent to institutions that were not listed on your answer sheet.

You may also request official score reports by phone. To use this service, you must have your admission ticket, a credit card, and a touch-tone phone. Call 1-609-771-7267 from six in the morning to ten at night, New York time. The fee for this service is a $12 charge to your credit card per call, an $11 charge per score report, plus a charge to your telephone bill for the long distance call. Official score reports will be mailed three days after your telephone request.

May I take the TOEFL more than one time?

Computer-Based TOEFL

You may not take the Computer-Based TOEFL more than once a month. For example, if you take the Computer-Based TOEFL in July, you must wait until August to take it again.

Supplemental Paper-Based TOEFL

You may take the Paper-Based TOEFL as many times as you wish in order to score to your satisfaction.

If I have already taken the TOEFL, how will the first score or scores affect my new score?

TOEFL scores are considered to be valid for two years. If you have taken the TOEFL more than once, but your first score report is dated more than two years ago, TOEFL Services will not report your first score.

If you have taken the TOEFL more than once in the past two years, TOEFL Services will report the score for the test date you request on your score request form.

Is there a direct correspondence between proficiency in English and a good score on the TOEFL?

There is not always a direct correspondence between proficiency in English and a good score on the TOEFL. Many students who are proficient in English are not proficient in how to approach the examination. That is why it is important to prepare by using this book.

What is the relationship between my score on the Model Tests in this book and my score on the TOEFL?

It is not possible to calculate an exact TOEFL score from a score that you might receive on a Model Test in this book. This is so because the actual TOEFL examination has a wider variety of problems.

The Model Tests in this book have been especially designed to help you improve your total TOEFL score by improving your knowledge of the types of problems that most often appear on the TOEFL. These problem types are repeated throughout the Model Tests so that you will have practice in recognizing and answering them.

By improving your ability to recognize and correctly answer those types of problems that most often appear on the TOEFL, you will improve your total TOEFL score.

Can I estimate my TOEFL score after I have prepared, using this book?

To estimate your TOEFL score, use the Score Estimates on pages 423–426 of this book.

Will I succeed on the TOEFL?

You will receive from this book what you give to this book. The information is here. Now, it is up to you to devote the time and effort. Thousands of other students have succeeded by using this book. You can be successful, too.

Updates

Visit the TOEFL web site at **www.toefl.org** or my web site at **www.teflprep.com** for the latest information about the TOEFL.

This web site helps students and professionals prepare for the Test of English as a Foreign Language (TOEFL®). You are invited to practice with the types of questions that appear on the TOEFL, visit the TEFL Prep Center Bookstore, and ask Dr. Pamela Sharpe questions about her books. The TEFL Prep Center web site also has information about scholarships and news about the TOEFL.

Welcome	The Practice Page	The TEFL Center Bookstore	TOEFL News	Scholarship Opportunities	Dear Dr. Sharpe

If you are not seeing images or if the page is loading improperly, you may want to use these links to download Netscape Navigator or Internet Explorer, available at no cost.

REVIEW OF SECTION 1: LISTENING

Overview of the Listening Section

QUICK COMPARISON
PAPER-BASED TOEFL AND COMPUTER-BASED TOEFL
SECTION 1

Paper-Based TOEFL Listening Comprehension	Computer-Based TOEFL Listening
There are fifty questions—thirty on Part A; twenty on Parts B and C.	There are between thirty and fifty questions.
There are three types of questions—short conversations; longer conversations and class discussions; mini-talks and lectures.	There are three types of questions—short conversations; longer conversations and class discussions; mini-talks and lectures.
The three types of questions are presented in three separate parts. Part A has short conversations; Part B has long conversations and class discussions; Part C has mini-talks and lectures.	The three types of questions are presented in three sets. The first set has short conversations; the second set has longer conversations and class discussions; the third set has lectures.
Everyone taking the TOEFL answers the same questions.	The computer selects questions based on your level of language proficiency.
The test administrator plays a tape and adjusts the volume.	You have a headset to listen to the audio. You can adjust the volume before the test begins.

There are no pictures or visual cues.	Each short conversation begins with a picture to provide orientation. There are several pictures and visual cues with each longer conversation and lecture.
You hear the questions, but they are not written out for you to read.	The questions are written out on the computer screen for you to read while you hear them.
Everyone taking the TOEFL proceeds at the same pace. You cannot pause the tape.	You may control the pace by choosing when to begin the next conversation or lecture.
The section is timed. At the end of the tape, you must have completed the section.	The section is timed. A clock on the screen shows the time remaining for you to complete the section.
You may not replay any of the conversations or lectures.	You may not replay any of the conversations or lectures.
All of the questions are multiple-choice.	Most of the questions are multiple-choice, but some of the questions have special directions.
Every question has only one answer.	Some of the questions have two answers.
You answer on a paper answer sheet, filling in ovals marked (A), (B), (C), and (D).	You click on the screen in the oval that corresponds to the answer you have chosen, or you follow the directions on the screen.

You can return to previous questions, erase, and change answers on your answer sheet.

You cannot return to previous questions. You can change your answer before you click on **Confirm Answer**. After you click on **Confirm Answer**, you will see a screen that notifies you to get ready to listen to the next conversation or lecture. You cannot go back.

You may not take notes.

You may not take notes.

Review of Problems and Questions for the Listening Section

This Review can be used to prepare for both the Supplemental Paper-Based TOEFL and the Computer-Based TOEFL. For the most part, the same types of problems are tested on both the Paper-Based TOEFL and the Computer-Based TOEFL; however, questions on Informal Conversations and Tours are found only on the Paper-Based TOEFL and are not addressed in this book.

Most of the questions on both the Paper-Based TOEFL and the Computer-Based TOEFL are multiple-choice. Some of the questions on the Computer-Based TOEFL are computer-assisted. The computer-assisted questions have special directions on the screen.

Although the computer-assisted questions in this book are numbered, and the answer choices are lettered A, B, C, D, the same questions on the CD-ROM that accompanies the book are not numbered and lettered. You need the numbers and letters in the book to refer to the Answer Key, the Explanatory Answers, and the Transcript for the Listening section. On the CD-ROM, you can refer to other chapters by clicking on the screen. The questions on the CD-ROM that is available to supplement this book are like those on the Computer-Based TOEFL.

Types of Problems in Short Conversations

Details

Details are specific facts stated in a conversation.

In some short conversations, you will hear all of the information that you need to answer the problem correctly. You will NOT need to draw conclusions.

When you hear a conversation between two speakers, you must remember the details that were stated.

EXAMPLE

Man: Front desk. How may I help you?
Woman: I'd like to arrange a wake-up call for tomorrow
              morning at seven o'clock, please.

Narrator: When does the woman want to get up tomorrow?
Answer: Seven o'clock in the morning.

Idiomatic expressions

Idiomatic expressions are words and phrases that are character-istic of a particular language with meanings that are usually different from the meanings of each of the words used alone.

In some short conversations, you will hear idiomatic expres-sions, such as "to kill time," which means to wait.

When you hear a conversation between two speakers, you must listen for the idiomatic expressions. You will be expected to recog-nize them and restate the idiom or identify the feelings or attitudes of the speaker.

It will help you if you study a list of common idioms as part of your TOEFL preparation.

EXAMPLE

Man:	I'm single. In fact, I've never been married.
Woman:	No kidding!

Narrator:	What does the woman mean?
Answer:	She is surprised by the man's statement.

3   Suggestions

A *suggestion* is a recommendation.

In some short conversations, you will hear words and phrases that make a suggestion, such as "you should," "why don't you," or "why not."

When you hear the words and phrases that introduce a suggestion, you must be able to recognize and remember what the speaker suggested, and who made the suggestion.

EXAMPLE

Woman:	Do you know if there is a Lost and Found on campus? I left my book bag in this room earlier, and it's gone.
Man:	Too bad. Look, why don't you check with your teacher first? Maybe someone in your class turned it in.

Narrator:	What does the man suggest that the woman do?
Answer:	Ask her teacher about the book bag.

4   Assumptions

An *assumption* is a statement accepted as true without proof or demonstration.

In some short conversations, an assumption is proven false, and the speaker or speakers who had made the assumption express surprise.

When you hear a conversation between two speakers, you must be able to recognize remarks that register surprise, and draw conclusions about the assumptions that the speaker may have made.

EXAMPLE

Woman: Let's just e-mail our response to Larry instead of calling.

Man: *Larry* has an e-mail address?

Narrator: What had the man assumed about Larry?
Answer: He would not have an e-mail address.

5 Predictions

A *prediction* is a guess about the future based on evidence from the present.

In some short conversations, you will be asked to make predictions about the future activities of the speakers involved.

When you hear a conversation between two speakers, you must listen for evidence from which you may draw a logical conclusion about their future activities.

EXAMPLE

Man: Could you please book me on the next flight out to Los Angeles?

Woman: I'm sorry, sir. Continental doesn't fly into Los Angeles. Why don't you try Northern or Worldwide?

Narrator: What will the man probably do?
Answer: He will probably get a ticket for a flight on Northern or Worldwide Airlines.

6   Implications

Implied means suggested, but not stated. In many ways, implied conversations are like prediction conversations.

In some short conversations, you will hear words and phrases or intonations that will suggest how the speakers felt, what kind of work or activity they were involved in, or where the conversation may have taken place.

When you hear a conversation between two speakers, you must listen for information that will help you draw a conclusion about the situation.

EXAMPLE

Woman: Where's Anita? We were supposed to go to the library to study.

Man: Well, here is her coat, and her books are over there on the chair.

Narrator: What does the woman imply about Anita?

Answer: Anita has not left for the library yet.

7   Problems

A *problem* is a situation that requires discussion or solution.

In some short conversations, you will hear the speakers discuss a problem.

When you hear a discussion between two speakers, you must be able to identify what the problem is. This may be more difficult because different aspects of the problem will also be included in the conversation.

EXAMPLE

Woman:	It only takes two hours to get to New York, but you'll have a six-hour layover between flights.
Man:	Maybe you could try routing me through Philadelphia or Boston instead.
Narrator:	What is the man's problem?
Answer:	His flight connections are not very convenient.

8   Topics

A *topic* is a main theme in a conversation or in a piece of writing.

In some short conversations, the speakers will discuss a particular topic.

When you hear a conversation, you must be able to identify the main topic from among several secondary themes that support the topic.

EXAMPLE

Man:	Tell me about your trip to New York.
Woman:	It was great! We saw the Statue of Liberty and the Empire State Building and all of the tourist attractions the first day, then we saw the museums the second day and spent the rest of the time shopping and seeing shows.
Narrator:	What are the man and woman talking about?
Answer:	The woman's trip.

Types of Problems in Longer Conversations

9   Academic Conversations

Academic conversations are conversations between students and professors or other academic personnel on a college or university campus.

In some longer conversations, you will hear an academic conversation between two speakers.

When you hear a conversation, you must be able to summarize the main ideas. You may also be asked to recall important details.

EXAMPLE

Marcy:	Do you have a minute, Dr. Peterson?
Dr. Peterson:	Sure. Come on in, Marcy. What's the problem?
Marcy:	Well, I'm not sure. I got this letter, and I don't understand it very well.
Dr. Peterson:	Let's see it.
Marcy:	It's from the Financial Aid Office. Are they going to cancel my student aid?
Dr. Peterson:	I would hope not. Hmmmn. Oh, I see. Here's what happened. You are only registered for three hours next semester.
Marcy:	That's true, but I plan to register for another class during open registration. I heard about a new environmental science course, and I'm waiting for it to be assigned a sequence number.
Dr. Peterson:	Well, then, you don't have a problem. You see, the terms of your grant require that you take at least six hours per semester.
Marcy:	I know, but I've never gotten a letter before.
Dr. Peterson:	I think it's a new procedure. Don't worry about it. Just be sure to sign up for at least three more hours before the beginning of the semester.
Marcy:	Thanks, Dr. Peterson. I'm really glad you were in your office today.
Question:	What is Marcy's problem?
Answer:	She has received a letter from the Financial Aid Office.
Question:	Why did Marcy receive a letter?
Answer:	She did not register for six hours this semester.
Question:	What had Marcy planned to do?
Answer:	Register for three more hours during open registration.

Question:	How does Marcy feel when she leaves Dr. Peterson's office?
Answer:	Relieved.

Types of Problems in Talks and Lectures

10   Class Discussions

Class discussions are conversations that occur in classrooms.

In some talks, you will hear a class discussion between two, three, or more speakers.

When you hear a discussion, you must be able to summarize the important ideas. You will usually NOT be required to remember small details.

It will help you to audit some college classes.

EXAMPLE

Miss Richards:	Good morning. My name is Miss Richards, and I'll be your instructor for Career Education 100. Before we get started, I'd appreciate it if you would introduce yourselves and tell us a little bit about why you decided to take this class. Let's start here. . . .
Bill:	I'm Bill Jensen, and I'm a sophomore this term, but I still haven't decided what to major in. I hope that this class will help me.
Miss Richards:	Good, I hope so, too. Next.
Patty:	I'm Patty Davis, and I'm majoring in foreign languages, but I'm not sure what kind of job I can get after I graduate.
Miss Richards:	Are you a sophomore, too, Patty?
Patty:	No. I'm a senior. I wish I'd taken this class sooner, but I didn't know about it until this term.

Miss Richards: Didn't your advisor tell you about it?
Patty: No. A friend of mine took it last year, and it helped her a lot.

Miss Richards: How did you find out about the course, Bill?
Bill: The same way Patty did. A friend of mine told me about it.

Question: In what class does this discussion take place?
Answer: Career Education.

Question: What are the two students talking about?
Answer: They are introducing themselves.

Question: Why is the woman taking the course?
Answer: To help her find a job after graduation.

Question: How did the students find out about the course?
Answer: From friends who had taken it.

11 Academic Talks

Academic talks are short talks that provide orientation to academic courses and procedures.

In some talks, you will hear academic talks on a variety of college and university topics.

When you hear a talk, you must be able to summarize the main ideas. You must also be able to answer questions about important details. You will usually not be asked to remember minor details.

EXAMPLE

Since we'll be having our midterm exam next week, I thought I'd spend a few minutes talking with you about it. I realize that none of you has ever taken a class with me before, so you really don't know what to expect on one of my exams.

First, let me remind you that I have included a very short description of the midterm on the syllabus that you received at the beginning of the semester. So you should read that. I also recommend that you organize and review your notes from all of our class sessions. I'm not saying that the book is unimportant, but the notes should help you to identify those topics that we covered in greatest detail. Then, you can go back to your book and reread the sections that deal with those topics. I also suggest that you take another look at the articles on reserve in the library. They have information in them that is not in the book, and although we didn't talk much about them in class, I do feel that they are important, so you can expect to see a few questions from the articles on the exam. Oh, yes, I almost forgot. Besides the twenty-five objective questions, there will be five essay questions, and you must choose three.

EXAMPLE

Question: What does the speaker mainly discuss?
Answer: The midterm exam.

Question: When will the students take the exam?
Answer: Next week.

Question: According to the professor, what should the students do to prepare?
Answer: Study their notes, the articles on reserve, and appropriate sections of the book.

Question: What is the format of the exam?
Answer: Twenty-five objective questions and five essay questions.

12   Lectures

Lectures are short talks that provide information about academic subjects. They are like short lectures that might be heard in a college classroom.

In some talks, you will hear academic information in a short lecture.

When you hear a lecture, you must be able to summarize the important ideas. You must also be able to answer questions that begin with the following words: *who, what, when, where, why?*

It will help you to listen to documentary programs on radio and television. Programs on educational broadcasting networks are especially helpful. Listen carefully. Ask yourself questions to test your ability to remember the information.

EXAMPLE

Ernest Hemingway began his writing career as an ambitious young American newspaperman in Paris after the first World War. His early books, including *The Sun Also Rises,* were published in Europe before they were released in the United States.

Hemingway always wrote from experience rather than from imagination. In *Farewell to Arms,* published in 1929, he recounted his adventures as an ambulance driver in Italy during the war. In *For Whom the Bell Tolls,* published in 1940, he retold his memories of the Spanish Civil War.

Perhaps more than any other twentieth-century American writer, he was responsible for creating a style of literature. The Hemingway style was hard, economical, and powerful. It lured the reader into using imagination in order to fill in the details.

In 1952, Hemingway published *The Old Man and the Sea,* a short, compelling tale of an old fisherman's struggle to haul in a giant marlin that he had caught in the Gulf of Mexico. Some critics interpreted it as the allegory of man's struggle against old age; others interpreted it as man against the forces of nature. This book was the climax of Hemingway's career. Two years later he was awarded the Nobel Prize for literature.

Question:	What theme did Hemingway use for many of his books?
Answer:	War.

Question:	What was the Hemingway style?
Answer:	Short and powerful.

Question:	What prize did Hemingway win after he wrote *The Old Man and the Sea?*
Answer:	The Nobel Prize for literature.

Question:	What advice would Hemingway probably give to other writers?
Answer:	Write from experience about things you have seen and people you have known.

TYPES OF QUESTIONS

Multiple-Choice Questions

Paper-Based TOEFL

1. What theme did Hemingway use for many of his books?
   (A) War
   (B) Romance
   (C) Travel
   (D) Sports

2. What was the Hemingway style?
   (A) Long descriptions
   (B) Imaginative details
   (C) Short sentences
   (D) Difficult symbolism

3. What prize did Hemingway win after he wrote *The Old Man and the Sea?*
   (A) The Nobel Prize for literature
   (B) The European Prize for best book of 1952
   (C) The Lifetime Achievement Award for literature
   (D) The American Newspapers Prize for young writers

4.   What advice would Hemingway probably give to other writers?
   (A) Write for a newspaper before you begin writing novels
   (B) Create your own style of literature
   (C) Write from experience about things you have seen and
       people you have known
   (D) Travel in order to meet interesting people

Answer Sheet

1. ● Ⓑ Ⓒ Ⓓ
2. Ⓐ Ⓑ ● Ⓓ
3. ● Ⓑ Ⓒ Ⓓ
4. Ⓐ Ⓑ ● Ⓓ

Computer-Based TOEFL

What theme did Hemingway use for many of his books?
   ● War
   ○ Romance
   ○ Travel
   ○ Sports

What was the Hemingway style?
   ○ Long descriptions
   ○ Imaginative details
   ● Short sentences
   ○ Difficult symbolism

What prize did Hemingway win after he wrote *The Old Man
and the Sea?*
   ● The Nobel Prize for literature
   ○ The European Prize for best book of 1952
   ○ The Lifetime Achievement Award for literature
   ○ The American Newspapers Prize for young writers

What advice would Hemingway probably give to other writers?
   ○ Write for a newspaper before you begin writing novels
   ○ Create your own style of literature
   ● Write from experience about things you have seen and
     people you have known
   ○ Travel in order to meet interesting people

Computer-Assisted Questions

Two-Answer Questions. On some of the computer-assisted questions, you will be asked to select two answers. Both answers must be correct to receive credit for the question.

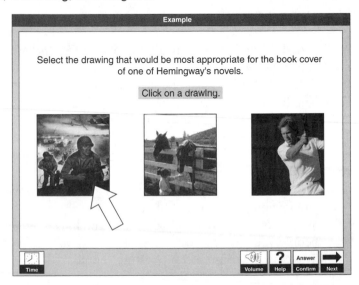

Visual Questions. On some of the computer-assisted questions, you will be asked to select a visual. The visual may be a picture, a drawing, or a diagram.

Sequencing Questions. On some of the computer-assisted questions, you will be asked to sequence events in order. The events could be historical events or the steps in a scientific process.

All answers must be sequenced correctly to receive credit for the question.

Example

The professor briefly describes Hemingway's life as an author. Summarize the biographical data by putting the events in order.

Click on a sentence. Then click on the space where it belongs.
Use each sentence only once.

Hemingway wrote about his experiences as an ambulance driver during the war

Hemingway published *The Old Man and the Sea*

Hemingway received the Nobel Prize for literature

Hemingway was a newspaper reporter in Paris

1 | Hemingway was a newspaper reporter in Paris

2 |

3 |

4 |

Time   Volume   Help ?   Answer Confirm   Next ➡

Classification Questions. On some of the computer-assisted questions, you will be asked to classify information by organizing it in categories.

Example

How did Hemingway use his experiences in different novels?
Click on a sentence. Then click on the space where it belongs.
Use each sentence only once.

He was fishing in the Gulf of Mexico.

He was driving an ambulance in Italy.

He was working as a newspaper reporter in Paris.

The Sun Also Rises	*Farewell to Arms*	*The Old Man and the Sea*
		He was fishing in the Gulf of Mexico.

Time   Volume   Help ?   Answer Confirm   Next ➡

Computer Tutorial for the Listening Section

In order to succeed on the Computer-Based TOEFL, you must understand the computer vocabulary used for the test, and you must be familiar with the icons on the computer screens that you will see on the test. First, review the vocabulary. Then study the computer screens in this Tutorial.

Testing Tools: Vocabulary, Icons, and Keys

General Vocabulary for the Computer-Based TOEFL

Mouse	A small control with one or two buttons on it.	
Mouse Pad	A rectangular pad where you move the *mouse*.	
Arrow	A marker that shows you where you are moving on the computer screen. Move the *mouse* on the *mouse pad* to move the **Arrow** on the screen.	

Click   To depress the button on the *mouse* is to **Click** the *mouse*. **Click** the *mouse* to make changes on the computer screen.

Icon   A small picture or a word or a phrase in a box. Move the *arrow* to the **Icon** and *click* on the **Icon** to tell the computer what to do.

Icons for the Computer-Based TOEFL

Dismiss   An example of an *icon*. *Click* on **Dismiss**
Directions   **Directions** to tell the computer to remove the directions from the screen.

Oval   The *icon* beside the answers for the multiple-choice test questions. Move the *arrow* to the **Oval** and *click* on one of the **Ovals** to choose an answer.

Next   An example of an *icon*. To see the next question on the screen, *click* on **Next** first and then *click* on **Confirm Answer**.

Confirm   An example of an *icon*. *Click* on **Confirm**
Answer   **Answer** after you *click* on **Next** to see the next
                 question on the screen. Remember, *click* on
                 Next, **Confirm Answer** in that order.

Help   An example of an *icon*. *Click* on the question
                 mark to see a list of the *icons* and directions for
                 the section.

Time   An *icon* of a clock in the bottom left corner of the
                 screen. *Click* on the clock face to hide or show
                 the time you have left to finish the section of the
                 test you are working on. Five minutes before the
                 end of each section of the test, the clock will
                 appear automatically. Remember, the time
                 appears in numbers at the top of the screen,
                 not on the clock face. You cannot use the clock
                 during the recording.

Specific Vocabulary for Section 1

Volume   One additional *icon* at the bottom of the screen in
                 the Listening section. *Click* on **Volume** to go to a
                 screen with an *up arrow* and a *down arrow*. *Click*
                 on the *up arrow* to make the recording louder.
                 Click on the *down arrow* to make the recording
                 softer. Remember, you can change the volume
                 while the speaker is giving directions, but not
                 after the directions have concluded.

COMPUTER SCREENS FOR THE COMPUTER-BASED TOEFL

View the name of the section

1 View the number of the question on the screen
2 View the total number of questions in thesection

When finished reading directions click on the icon below

Dismiss Directions

1 Click to go to another screen
2 See the first question

1 Click to see the time remaining
2 View the time in minutes and seconds
3 Click again to remove the time

1 Click to go to another screen
2 Click on the directions for the section or the explanations of the icons

1 Click first
2 Click second to mark a final answer and go to the next question

TIP: When the icons are black, you can click on them. When they are gray, they are not functioning. For example, **Confirm Answer** is gray until you click on **Next**. Then **Confirm Answer** is black. Remember the order to click on these two icons.

Computer Screens for Section 1

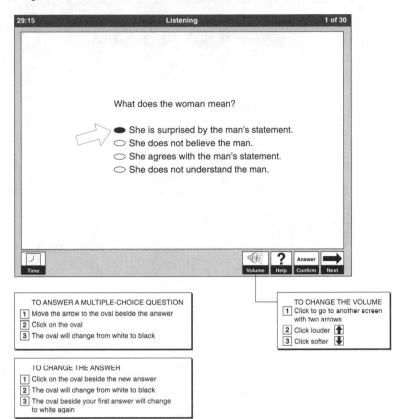

TIP: Most of the questions on the Computer-Based TOEFL are multiple-choice. When you learn to move the arrow to the oval and click on the oval, you will be able to answer most of the questions.

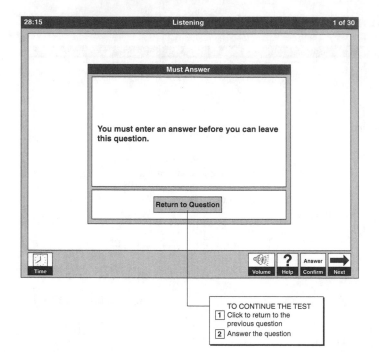

TIP: When you do not answer a question, or when you do not confirm your answer, this screen appears. You can spend a lot of time returning to questions that you have not answered. Don't skip questions in the Listening and Structure sections.

Simulations for Section 1

In order to prepare for the experience that you will have on the Computer-Based TOEFL, use the CD-ROM that supplements the larger version of this book; *Barron's How to Prepare for the TOEFL*. Locate the Listening section on the Model Tests. The computer will simulate features of the Listening section on the Computer-Based TOEFL. These Model Tests are computer-assisted.

As part of your study plan, be sure to review all of the questions in all of the Model Tests. Use the Explanatory Answers on the CD-ROM or on pages 377–420. Finally, take the Cumulative Model Test on the CD-ROM. This test is computer-adaptive, which means that the computer will select questions for you at your level of language proficiency.

If you choose not to purchase the larger version of this book, or you do not have a computer, you can still simulate some of the features of the Computer-Based TOEFL. In Section 1 of the Model Tests in Chapter 7, the questions are written out for you to read while you listen to them. This is different from the Paper-Based TOEFL. Instead of the CD-ROM, you may be using either an audio compact disk or a cassette. Pause the tape or compact disk occasionally to give yourself more control of the time for each question. But be careful not to pause too often or you will not be able to complete all of the questions within the total time allowed for the section.

Advice for the Listening Section: Computer-Based TOEFL

Be sure to adjust the volume before you begin. Before you begin the Listening section, you will have an opportunity to adjust the volume on your headset. Be sure to do it before you dismiss the directions and begin the test. After the test has begun, you may not adjust the volume.

Do not let the visuals of people distract you from listening to the short conversations. We all respond in different ways to pictures. If you become too involved in looking at the pictures, you may pay less attention to the recording. For the most part, the pictures of people are for orientation to the short conversation. After you look briefly at the picture, give your full concentration to the conversation. If you take the Model Tests on the CD-ROM that supplements the larger version of this book, *Barron's How to Prepare for the TOEFL*, first practice by watching the screen during the short conversation and then by closing your eyes or looking away during the conversation. Find the best way for you to listen to this part of the test.

Focus on the visuals of objects, art, specimens, maps, charts, and drawings in the talks. In general, the pictures of people are for orientation to the talks, whereas the visuals of objects, art, specimens, maps, charts, and drawings support the meaning of the talks. Do not focus on the pictures of people. Do focus on the other visuals that appear during the talks. They could reappear in a question. When you take the Model Tests, practice selective attention.

Disregard the pictures of the lecturer and the students, and be alert to the other visuals.

Be sure to read the question while you are hearing it. The questions will be shown on the screen while you are hearing them. If you find that it is to your advantage to close your eyes or look away during the short conversations, be sure to give your full attention to the screen again while the question is being asked. During the questions for longer conversations and talks, watch the screen carefully. By using the Model Tests, you will be able to develop a rhythm for interacting with the screen that is to your advantage.

REVIEW OF SECTION 2:
STRUCTURE

Overview of the Structure Section

QUICK COMPARISON
PAPER-BASED TOEFL AND COMPUTER-BASED TOEFL
SECTION 2

Paper-Based TOEFL Structure and Written Expression	*Computer-Based TOEFL Structure*
There are two types of questions—incomplete sentences and sentences with underlined words and phrases.	There are two types of questions—incomplete sentences and sentences with underlined words and phrases.
The two types of questions are presented in separate parts. Part A has incomplete sentences, and Part B has sentences with underlined words and phrases.	The two types of questions are presented at random in one continuous section. You may see two incomplete sentences, one sentence with underlined words and phrases, another incomplete sentence, and so forth.
There are forty questions—fifteen on Part A and twenty-five on Part B.	There are between twenty and twenty-five questions.
All of the questions are multiple-choice.	All of the questions are multiple-choice.
Everyone taking the TOEFL answers the same questions.	The computer will select questions based on your level of proficiency.
Every question has only one answer.	Every question has only one answer.

You have twenty-five minutes to complete the section.

You may control the pace by choosing when to begin the next question, but the section is timed. A clock on the screen shows the time remaining for you to complete the section.

You answer on a paper answer sheet, filling in ovals marked (A), (B), (C), and (D).

You click on the screen either in the oval or on the underlined word or phrase.

You can return to previous questions, erase, and change answers on your answer sheet.

You cannot return to previous questions. You can change your answer before you click on **Confirm Answer**. After you click on **Confirm Answer**, you will see the next question. You cannot go back.

The score on Section 2 is not combined with the score on the essay in the Test of Written English (TWE).

The score on Section 2 is combined with the score on the essay in the Writing section.

Review of Problems and Questions for the Structure Section

This Review can be used to prepare for both the Supplemental Paper-Based TOEFL and the Computer-Based TOEFL. For the most part, the same types of problems are tested on both the Paper-Based TOEFL and the Computer-Based TOEFL. All of the questions on both the Paper-Based TOEFL and the Computer-Based TOEFL are multiple-choice. Computer-assisted questions have special directions.

Strategies and Symbols for Review

Strategies

How will this Review of Structure help you?

It won't teach you every rule of English grammar, but it will provide you with a review of the problems in structure and written expression that are most commonly tested on the TOEFL.

Use this review to study and to check your progress. Follow three easy steps for each problem.

1. *Review the generalization.* First, read the explanation and study the word order in the chart. Then, close your eyes, and try to see the chart in your mind.
2. *Study the examples.* Focus on the examples. First, read them silently, noting the difference between the correct and incorrect sentences. Then, read the underlined parts of the correct sentences aloud.
3. *Check your progress.* First, complete the exercise. Each exercise has two questions—one similar to Part A and the other similar to Part B on the Structure and Written Expression section of the TOEFL. Then, check your answers, using the Answer Key in Chapter 8 of this book.

If you are studying in an English program, use this review with your grammar book. After your teacher presents a grammar rule in class, find it in this review (see pages 75–160). Refer to the generalization, study the examples, and check your progress by completing the exercise.

When you go to your next grammar class, you will be more prepared. When you go to your TOEFL examination, you will be more confident. With preparation, you can succeed in school and on the TOEFL.

Symbols

In order for you to use the patterns and rules of style in this review, you must understand five kinds of symbols.

Abbreviations. An abbreviation is a shortened form. In the patterns, five abbreviations, or shortened forms, are used: *S* is an abbreviation for *Subject,* *V* for *Verb,* *V Ph* for *Verb Phrase,* *C* for *Complement,* and *M* for *Modifier.*

Small Letters. Small letters are lowercase letters. In the patterns, a verb written in small (lowercase) letters may not change form. For example, the verb *have* may not change to *has* or *had* when it is written in small letters.

Capital Letters. Capital letters are uppercase letters. In the patterns, a verb written in capital (uppercase) letters may change form. For example, the verb *HAVE* may remain as *have,* or may change to *has* or *had,* depending upon agreement with the subject and choice of tense.

Parentheses. Parentheses are curved lines used as punctuation marks. The following punctuation marks are parentheses: ( ). In the patterns, the words in parentheses give specific information about the abbreviation or word that precedes them. For example, *V (present)* means that the verb in the pattern must be a present tense verb. *N (count)* means that the noun in the pattern must be a countable noun.

Alternatives. Alternatives are different ways to express the same idea. In the patterns, alternatives are written in a column. For example, in the following pattern, there are three alternatives:

had would have could have	participle

The alternatives are *had, would have,* and *could have.* Any one of the alternatives may be used with the participle. All three alternatives are correct.

PATTERNS

Patterns are the parts of a sentence. In some books, *patterns* are called *structures.* In *patterns,* the words have the same order most of the time.

Some of the most important patterns are summarized in this review section. Remember, the generalizations in the charts and explanations for each pattern refer to the structure in the examples. There may be similar structures for which these generalizations are not appropriate.

Missing Main Verb

Remember that every English sentence must have a subject and a main verb.

S	V	
The sound of the dryer	bothers	my concentration

Avoid using an -*ing* form, an infinitive, an auxiliary verb, or another part of speech instead of a main verb.

EXAMPLES

INCORRECT: The prettiest girl in our class with long brown hair and brown eyes.

CORRECT: The prettiest girl in our class has long brown hair and brown eyes.

INCORRECT: In my opinion, too soon to make a decision.

CORRECT: In my opinion, it is too soon to make a decision.

INCORRECT: Do you know whether the movie that starts at seven?

CORRECT: Do you know whether the movie that starts at seven is good?

or

Do you know whether the movie <u>starts</u> at seven?

INCORRECT: Sam almost always a lot of fun.
  CORRECT: Sam <u>is</u> almost always a lot of fun.

INCORRECT: The book that I lent you having a good bibliography.
  CORRECT: The book that I lent you <u>has</u> a good bibliography.

EXERCISES

Part A: Choose the correct answer.

Arizona _____ a very dry climate.
  (A) has
  (B) being
  (C) having
  (D) with

Part B: Choose the incorrect word or phrase and correct it.

Venomous snakes <u>with</u> <u>modified</u> teeth connected to
                       (A) 疑 必 後

<u>poison glands</u> <u>in which</u> the venom <u>is secreted</u> and stored.
      (B)   (C)   (D)

Verbs that Require an Infinitive in the Complement

Remember that the following verbs require an <u>infinitive</u> for a verb in the complement.

[in'finitiv]
從

agree	decide	hesitate	need	refuse
appear	demand	hope	offer	seem
arrange	deserve	intend	plan	tend
ask	expect	learn	prepare	threaten
claim	fail	manage	pretend	wait
consent	forget	mean	promise	want

许 承诺 默认
同意

S	V	C (infinitive)	M
We	had planned	to leave	day before yesterday

Avoid using an *-ing* form after the verbs listed. Avoid using a verb word after *want*.

EXAMPLES

INCORRECT:	He wanted speak with Mr. Brown.
CORRECT:	He <u>wanted</u> <u>to speak</u> with Mr. Brown.

INCORRECT:	We demand knowing our status.
CORRECT:	We <u>demand</u> <u>to know</u> our status.

INCORRECT:	I intend the inform you that we cannot approve your application.
CORRECT:	I <u>intend</u> <u>to inform</u> you that we cannot approve your application.

INCORRECT:	They didn't plan buying a car.
CORRECT:	They didn't <u>plan</u> <u>to buy</u> a car.

INCORRECT:	The weather tends improving in May.
CORRECT:	The weather <u>tends</u> <u>to improve</u> in May.

EXERCISES

Part A: Choose the correct answer.

One of the least effective ways of storing information is learning _____ it.

(A) how repeat
(B) repeating
(C) to repeat
(D) repeat

Part B: Choose the incorrect word or phrase and correct it.

Representative democracy seemed <u>evolve</u> <u>simultaneously</u>
                             (A)   (B)

<u>during</u> the eighteenth and nineteenth centuries in Britain,
(C)

Europe, and <u>the United States</u>.
            (D)

PROBLEM 3

Verbs that Require an *-ing* Form in the Complement

Remember that the following verbs require an *-ing* form for a verb in the complement:

admit	enjoy	recall
appreciate	finish	recommend
avoid	keep	regret
complete	mention	risk
consider	miss	stop
delay	postpone	suggest
deny	practice	tolerate
discuss	quit	understand

S	V	C (-ing)	M
He	enjoys	traveling	by plane

Avoid using an infinitive after the verbs listed.

Forbid may be used with either an infinitive or an *-ing* complement, but *forbid from* is not idiomatic.

EXAMPLES

INCORRECT:	She is considering not to go.
CORRECT:	She is <u>considering</u> not <u>going</u>.
INCORRECT:	We enjoyed talk with your friend.
CORRECT:	We <u>enjoyed</u> <u>talking</u> with your friend.
INCORRECT:	Hank completed the writing his thesis this summer.
CORRECT:	Hank <u>completed</u> <u>writing</u> his thesis this summer.
INCORRECT:	I miss to watch the news when I am traveling.
CORRECT:	I <u>miss</u> <u>watching</u> the news when I am traveling.
INCORRECT:	She mentions stop at El Paso in her letter.
CORRECT:	She <u>mentions</u> <u>stopping</u> at El Paso in her letter.

EXERCISES

Part A: Choose the correct answer.

Strauss finished _____ two of his published compositions before his tenth birthday.

(A) written
(B) write
(C) to write
(D) writing

Part B: Choose the incorrect word or phrase and correct it.

<u>Many</u> people have stopped <u>to smoke</u> <u>because</u> they are afraid
  (A)   (B)   (C)

that it <u>may be</u> harmful to their health.
      (D)

[handwritten notes:]
appreciate doing sth   deny doing sth
regret doing sth
tolerate doing sth
admit doing sth
postpone doing sth

4 Verb Phrases that Require an *-ing* Form in the Complement

Remember that the following verb phrases require an *-ing* form for a verb in the complement:

approve of	*do not mind*	*keep on*
be better off	*forget about*	*look forward to*
can't help	*get through*	*object to*
count on	*insist on*	*think about*
		think of

S	V Ph	C (-ing)	M
She	forgot about	canceling	her appointment

Avoid using an infinitive after the verb phrases listed. Avoid using a verb word after *look forward to* and *object to*. *(Refer to pages 81 and 82 for more on verb words.)*

Remember that the verb phrase *BE likely* does not require an *-ing* form but requires an infinitive in the complement.

EXAMPLES

INCORRECT: She is likely knowing.
CORRECT: She is likely to know.

INCORRECT: Let's go to the movie when you get through to study.
CORRECT: Let's go to the movie when you get through studying.

INCORRECT: We can't help to wonder why she left.
CORRECT: We can't help wondering why she left.

INCORRECT: I have been looking forward to meet you.
CORRECT: I have been looking forward to meeting you.

INCORRECT: We wouldn't mind to wait.
CORRECT: We wouldn't mind waiting.

EXERCISES

Part A: Choose the correct answer.

Many modern architects <u>insist on</u> _____ materials native
to the region that will blend into the surrounding landscape.

    (A) use
    (B) to use
    (C) the use
    (D) using

Part B: Choose the incorrect word or phrase and correct it.

During Jackson's administration, those <u>who</u> did not approve of
                                      (A)

<u>permit</u> common people in the White House <u>were shocked</u> by
  (B)   (C)

the president's insistence that they <u>be invited</u> into the mansion.
                                       (D)

PROBLEM 5   Irregular Past Forms

Remember that past forms of the following irregular verbs are
not the same as the participles:

Verb Word	Past Form	Participle
be	was/were	been
beat	beat	beaten
become	became	become
begin	began	begun

Verb Word	*Past Form*	*Participle*
bite	*bit*	*bitten*
blow	*blew*	*blown*
break	*broke*	*broken*
choose	*chose*	*chosen*
come	*came*	*come*
do	*did*	*done*
draw	*drew*	*drawn*
drink	*drank*	*drunk*
drive	*drove*	*driven*
eat	*ate*	*eaten*
fall	*fell*	*fallen*
fly	*flew*	*flown*
forget	*forgot*	*forgotten*
forgive	*forgave*	*forgiven*
freeze	*froze*	*frozen*
get	*got*	*gotten or got*
give	*gave*	*given*
go	*went*	*gone*
grow	*grew*	*grown*
hide	*hid*	*hidden*
know	*knew*	*known*
ride	*rode*	*ridden*
run	*ran*	*run*
see	*saw*	*seen*
shake	*shook*	*shaken*
show	*showed*	*shown*
shrink	*shrank*	*shrunk*
sing	*sang*	*sung*
speak	*spoke*	*spoken*
steal	*stole*	*stolen*
swear	*swore*	*sworn*
swim	*swam*	*swum*
take	*took*	*taken*
tear	*tore*	*torn*
throw	*threw*	*thrown*
wear	*wore*	*worn*
weave	*wove*	*woven*
withdraw	*withdrew*	*withdrawn*
write	*wrote*	*written*

S	V (past)	M
The concert	began	at eight o'clock

Avoid using a participle instead of a past for simple past statements.

EXAMPLES

INCORRECT: They done it very well after they had practiced.
  CORRECT: They <u>did</u> it very well after they had practiced.

INCORRECT: Before she run the computer program, she had checked it out with her supervisor.
  CORRECT: Before she <u>ran</u> the computer program, she had checked it out with her supervisor.

INCORRECT: We eat dinner in Albuquerque on our vacation last year.
  CORRECT: We <u>ate</u> dinner in Albuquerque on our vacation last year.

INCORRECT: My nephew begun working for me about ten years ago.
  CORRECT: My nephew <u>began</u> working for me about ten years ago.

INCORRECT: I know that you been forty on your last birthday.
  CORRECT: I know that you <u>were</u> forty on your last birthday.

EXERCISES

Part A: Choose the correct answer.

Before the Angles and the Saxons _____ to England, the Iberians had lived there.
(A) coming
(B) come
(C) came
(D) did come

Part B: Choose the incorrect word or phrase and correct it.

When Columbus <u>seen</u> the New World, he <u>thought</u> that he
     (A)   (B)

<u>had reached</u> the East Indies <u>by way of</u> a Western route.
   (C)   (D)

PROBLEM 6

Factual Conditionals—Absolute, Scientific Results

Remember that *absolute conditionals* express scientific facts. *Will* and a verb word expresses the opinion that the result is absolutely certain.

CONDITION			RESULT		
If	S	V (present) ,	S	V (present)	
If	a catalyst	is used ,	the reaction	occurs	more rapidly

or

CONDITION			RESULT		
If	S	V (present) ,	S	will	verb word	
If	a catalyst	is used ,	the reaction	will	occur	more rapidly

Avoid using *will* and a verb word instead of the present verb in the clause beginning with *if*. Avoid using the auxiliary verbs *have*, *has*, *do*, and *does* with main verbs in the clause of result.

EXAMPLES

INCORRECT: If water freezes, it has become a solid.
CORRECT: <u>If water freezes, it becomes</u> a solid.
            or
      <u>If water freezes, it will become</u> a solid.

INCORRECT: If children be healthy, they learn to walk at about eighteen months old.
CORRECT: <u>If children are</u> healthy, <u>they learn</u> to walk at about eighteen months old.

or

If <u>children</u> <u>are</u> healthy, <u>they</u> <u>will learn</u> to walk at about eighteen months old.

INCORRECT: If orange blossoms are exposed to very cold temperatures, they withered and died.

CORRECT: If <u>orange blossoms</u> <u>are exposed</u> to very cold temperatures, <u>they</u> <u>wither and die</u>.

or

If <u>orange blossoms</u> <u>are exposed</u> to very cold temperatures, <u>they</u> <u>will wither and die</u>.

INCORRECT: If the trajectory of a satellite will be slightly off at launch, it will get worse as the flight progresses.

CORRECT: If <u>the trajectory</u> of a satellite <u>is</u> slightly off at launch, <u>it</u> <u>gets</u> worse as the flight progresses.

or

If <u>the trajectory</u> of a satellite <u>is</u> slightly off at launch, <u>it</u> <u>will get</u> worse as the flight progresses.

INCORRECT: If light strikes a rough surface, it diffused.

CORRECT: If <u>light</u> <u>strikes</u> a rough surface, <u>it</u> <u>diffuses</u>.

or

If <u>light</u> <u>strikes</u> a rough surface, <u>it</u> <u>will diffuse</u>.

EXERCISES

Part A: Choose the correct answer.

If water is heated to 212 degrees F. _____ as steam.

(A) it will boil and escape

(B) it is boiling and escaping

(C) it boil and escape

(D) it would boil and escape

Part B: Choose the incorrect word or phrase and correct it.

If a <u>live sponge is broken</u> into pieces, each piece <u>would turn</u>

         (A)   (B)

into a new sponge <u>like</u> <u>the original one</u>.

         (C)   (D)

Factual Conditionals—Probable Results for the Future

Remember that *will* and a verb word expresses the opinion that the results are absolutely certain. In order of more to less probable, use the following modals: *will, can, may.*

If	S	V (present)		,	S	will can may	verb word	
If	we	find	her address	,	we	will	write	her

S	will can may	verb word		if	S	V (present)	
We	will	write	her	if	we	find	her address

Avoid using the present tense verb instead of a modal and a verb word in the clause of result.

EXAMPLES

INCORRECT: If you put too much water in rice when you cook it, it got sticky.

CORRECT: If <u>you put</u> too much water in rice when you cook it, <u>it will get</u> sticky.

or

<u>It will get</u> sticky <u>if you put</u> too much water in rice when you cook it.

INCORRECT: If they have a good sale, I would have stopped by on my way home.

CORRECT: If <u>they have</u> a good sale, <u>I will stop</u> by on my way home.

or

<u>I will stop</u> by on my way home <u>if they have</u> a good sale.

INCORRECT:	We will wait if you wanted to go.
CORRECT:	<u>We</u> <u>will wait</u> <u>if</u> <u>you</u> <u>want</u> to go.

or

<u>If</u> <u>you</u> <u>want</u> to go, <u>we</u> <u>will wait</u>.

INCORRECT:	If you listen to the questions carefully, you answer them easily.
CORRECT:	<u>If</u> <u>you</u> <u>listen</u> to the questions carefully, <u>you</u> <u>will answer</u> them easily.

or

<u>You</u> <u>will answer</u> them easily <u>if</u> <u>you</u> <u>listen</u> to the questions carefully.

INCORRECT:	If we finished our work a little early today, we'll attend the lecture at the art museum.
CORRECT:	<u>If</u> <u>we</u> <u>finish</u> our work a little early today, <u>we'll attend</u> the lecture at the art museum.

or

<u>We'll attend</u> the lecture at the art museum <u>if</u> <u>we</u> <u>finish</u> our work a little early today.

EXERCISES

Part A: Choose the correct answer.

If services are increased, taxes _____.
(A) will probably go up
(B) probably go up
(C) probably up
(D) going up probably

Part B: Choose the incorrect word or phrase and correct it.

If you don't register before the last day of regular registration,
         (A)   (B)
you paying a late fee.
      (C)   (D)

Contrary-to-Fact Conditionals—Change in Conditions *Unless*

Remember that there is a subject and verb that determines the change in conditions after the connector *unless*.

S	V	unless	S	V	
Luisa	won't return	unless	she	gets	a scholarship

Avoid deleting *unless* from the sentence; avoid deleting either the subject or the verb from the clause after *unless*.

EXAMPLES

INCORRECT:	I can't go I don't get my work finished.
CORRECT:	I can't go <u>unless</u> <u>I</u> <u>get</u> my work finished.
INCORRECT:	They are going to get a divorce unless he stopping drugs.
CORRECT:	They are going to get a divorce <u>unless</u> <u>he</u> <u>stops</u> taking drugs.
INCORRECT:	You won't get well unless you are taking your medicine.
CORRECT:	You won't get well <u>unless</u> <u>you</u> <u>take</u> your medicine.
INCORRECT:	Dean never calls his father unless needs money.
CORRECT:	Dean never calls his father <u>unless</u> <u>he</u> <u>needs</u> money.
INCORRECT:	We can't pay the rent unless the scholarship check.
CORRECT:	We can't pay the rent <u>unless</u> <u>the scholarship check</u> <u>comes</u>.

EXERCISES

Part A: Choose the correct answer.

Football teams don't play in the Super Bowl championship
_____ either the National or the American Conference.
(A) unless they win
(B) but they win
(C) unless they will win
(D) but to have won

Part B: Choose the incorrect word or phrase and correct it.

Usually <u>boys</u> cannot <u>become</u> Boy Scouts <u>unless completed</u>
  (A)   (B)   (C)
<u>the fifth grade</u>.
  (D)

/skaʊt/

they complete

9

unless + 后跟一般现在式.
不能跟 将来时.

Importance—Subjunctive Verbs

Remember that the following verbs are used before *that* and the
verb word clause to express importance.

ask	*propose* /prəˈpəʊz/ 申请，提案 议划 求婚
demand	*recommend*
desire	*request*
insist	*require*
prefer	*suggest*
	urge /ɜːdʒ/ 冲动, 驱策 力劝

S	V	that	S	verb word	
Mr. Johnson	prefers	that	she	speak	with him personally

Avoid using a present or past tense verb instead of a verb word.
Avoid using a modal before the verb word.

Note: The verb *insist* may be used in non-subjunctive patterns in the past tense. For example: *He* insisted *that I* was *wrong*.

EXAMPLES

INCORRECT: The doctor suggested that she will not smoke.
  CORRECT: The doctor <u>suggested</u> that she not <u>smoke</u>.

INCORRECT: I propose that the vote is secret ballot.
  CORRECT: I <u>propose</u> that the vote <u>be</u> secret ballot.

INCORRECT: The foreign student advisor recommended that she studied more English before enrolling at the university.
  CORRECT: The foreign student advisor <u>recommended</u> that she <u>study</u> more English before enrolling at the university.

INCORRECT: The law requires that everyone has his car checked at least once a year.
  CORRECT: The law <u>requires</u> that everyone <u>have</u> his car checked at least once a year.

INCORRECT: She insisted that they would give her a receipt.
  CORRECT: She <u>insisted</u> that they <u>give</u> her a receipt.

EXERCISES

Part A: Choose the correct answer.

Less moderate members of Congress are insisting that changes in the Social Security System _____ made.
  (A) will
  (B) are
  (C) being
  (D) be

Part B: Choose the incorrect word or phrase and correct it.

<u>Many</u> architects prefer that a dome <u>is used</u> to roof buildings that
  (A)   (B)   *be used*
need <u>to conserve</u> <u>floor space</u>.
         (C)   (D)

10 Importance—Impersonal Expressions

Remember that the following adjectives are used in impersonal expressions.

essential /i'senʃəl/ n 要素，本质，要点，精髓适
imperative /im'porativ/ adj 命就的，绝对义要的
important
necessary

it is	adjective	infinitive	
It is	important	to verify	the data

or

it is	adjective	that	S	verb word	
It is	important	that	the data	be	verified

Avoid using a present tense verb instead of a verb word. Avoid using a modal before the verb word.

EXAMPLES

INCORRECT: It is not necessary that you must take an entrance examination to be admitted to an American university

CORRECT: It is not necessary to take an entrance examination to be admitted to an American university.

or

It is not necessary that you take an entrance examination to be admitted to an American university.

INCORRECT: It is imperative that you are on time.
CORRECT: It is imperative to be on time.

>   *or*
> It is imperative <u>that</u> <u>you</u> <u>be</u> on time.

INCORRECT: It is important that I will speak with Mr. Williams
              immediately.

  CORRECT: <u>It is important</u> <u>to speak</u> with Mr. Williams
              immediately.

>   *or*
> <u>It is important</u> <u>that</u> <u>I</u> <u>speak</u> with Mr. Williams
> immediately.

INCORRECT: It is imperative that your signature appears on your
              identification card.

  CORRECT: <u>It is imperative</u> <u>to sign</u> your identification card.

>   *or*
> <u>It is imperative</u> <u>that</u> <u>your signature</u> <u>appear</u> on your
> identification card.

INCORRECT: It is essential that all applications and transcripts are
              filed no later than July 1.

  CORRECT: <u>It is essential</u> <u>to file</u> all applications and transcripts no
              later than July 1.

>   *or*
> <u>It is essential</u> <u>that</u> <u>all applications and transcripts</u> <u>be</u>
> filed no later than July 1.

EXERCISES

Part A: Choose the correct answer.

It is necessary _____ the approaches to a bridge, the road
design, and the alignment in such a way as to best
accommodate the expected traffic flow over and under it.

   (A) plan
   (B) to plan
   (C) planning
   (D) the plan

Part B: Choose the incorrect word or phrase and correct it.

It is essential that vitamins <u>are</u> supplied either by foods <u>or</u>
                                  (A)   (B)
<u>by supplementary tablets</u> for normal growth <u>to occur</u>.
                    (C)   (D)

11 Purpose—Infinitives

Remember that an infinitive can express purpose. It is a short form of *in order to*.

S	V	C	infinitive (purpose)	
Laura She	jogs takes	 vitamins	to stay to feel	fit better

Avoid expressing purpose without the word *to* in the infinitive. Avoid using *for* instead of *to*.

EXAMPLES

INCORRECT: Wear several layers of clothing for keep warm.
  CORRECT: Wear several layers of clothing <u>to keep</u> warm.

INCORRECT: David has studied hard the succeed.
  CORRECT: David has studied hard <u>to succeed</u>.

INCORRECT: Don't move your feet when you swing for play golf well.
  CORRECT: Don't move your feet when you swing <u>to play</u> golf well.

INCORRECT: Virginia always boils the water twice make tea.
  CORRECT: Virginia always boils the water twice <u>to make</u> tea.

INCORRECT: Wait until June plant those bulbs.
  CORRECT: Wait until June <u>to plant</u> those bulbs.

EXERCISES

Part A: Choose the correct answer.

In the Morrill Act, Congress granted federal lands to the states
_____ agricultural and mechanical arts colleges.

   (A) for establish
   (B) to establish
   (C) establish
   (D) establishment

Part B: Choose the incorrect word or phrase and correct it.

Papyrus <u>was used</u> <u>for to make</u> not only paper <u>but also</u> sails,
       (A)   (B)   (C)

baskets, <u>and</u> clothing.
     (D)

12   Passives—Word Order

Remember that in a passive sentence the actor is unknown or not important. The subject is not the actor.

Passive sentences are also common in certain styles of scientific writing.

S	BE	participle	
State University	is	located	at the corner of College and Third

Avoid using a participle without a form of the verb BE.

EXAMPLES

INCORRECT: My wedding ring made of yellow and white gold.
CORRECT: My wedding ring <u>is made</u> of yellow and white gold.
                   (It is the *ring*, not the person who made the ring, that
                   is important.)

INCORRECT: If your brother invited, he would come.
CORRECT: If your brother <u>were invited</u>, he would come.
            (It is your *brother*, not the person who invited him,
            that is important.)

INCORRECT: Mr. Wilson known as Willie to his friends.
CORRECT: Mr. Wilson <u>is known</u> as Willie to his friends.
            (It is *Mr. Wilson*, not his friends, that is important.)

INCORRECT: References not used in the examination room.
CORRECT: References <u>are not used</u> in the examination room.
            (It is *references*, not the persons using them, that are
            important.)

INCORRECT: Laura born in Iowa.
CORRECT: Laura was <u>born</u> in Iowa.
            (It is *Laura*, not her mother who bore her, that is
            important.)

EXERCISES

by

Part A: Choose the correct answer.

In the stringed instruments, the tones _____ by playing a
bow across a set of strings that may be made of wire or gut.
   (A) they produce
   (B) producing
   (C) are produced
   (D) that are producing

Part B: Choose the incorrect word or phrase and correct it.

<u>Work</u> <u>is</u> often <u>measure</u> in units <u>called</u> foot pounds.
 (A) (B)   (C)   (D)

by meaning

13 Belief and Knowledge—Anticipatory *It*

Remember that an anticipatory *it* clause expresses belief or knowledge. Anticipatory means before. Some *it* clauses that go before main clauses are listed below:

It is believed
It is hypothesized /haɪˈpɒθɪsaɪz/ 假设
It is known
It is said
It is thought
It is true
It is written

Anticipatory *it*	that	S	V	
It is believed	that	all mammals	experience	dreams

Avoid using an *-ing* form, a noun, or an infinitive instead of a subject and verb after an anticipatory *it* clause.

EXAMPLES

INCORRECT: It is hypothesized that the subjects in the control group not to score as well.

CORRECT: It is hypothesized that the subjects in the control group will not score as well.

INCORRECT: It is generally known that she leaving at the end of the year.

CORRECT: It is generally known that she is leaving at the end of the year. ○ 限构句.

INCORRECT: It is said that a buried treasure near here.

CORRECT: It is said that a buried treasure was hidden near here.

INCORRECT: It is believed that a horseshoe bringing good luck.
  CORRECT: <u>It is believed</u> that <u>a horseshoe</u> <u>brings</u> good luck.

INCORRECT: It is thought that our ancestors building this city.
  CORRECT: <u>It is thought</u> that <u>our ancestors</u> <u>built</u> this city.

EXERCISES

Part A: Choose the correct answer.

_____ Giant Ape Man, our biggest and probably one of
our first human ancestors, was just about the size of a male
gorilla. /ɡoˈrilə / 大猩猩
  (A) It is believed that
  (B) That it is
  (C) That is believed
  (D) That believing

Part B: Choose the incorrect word or phrase and correct it.

<u>That it is believed</u> that <u>most of the earthquakes</u> in the world
        (A)   (B)
occur <u>near</u> <u>the youngest</u> mountain ranges—the Himalayas, the
        (C)   (D)
Andes, and the Sierra Nevadas.

14 Predictions—*Will Have* + Participle

Remember that *will have* followed by a participle and a future
adverb expresses a prediction for a future activity or event.

adverb (future)	S	will	have	participle	
By the year 2010,	researchers	will	have	discovered	a cure for cancer

Avoid using *will* instead of *will have*.

EXAMPLES

INCORRECT: You will finished your homework by the time the movie starts.

CORRECT: You <u>will</u> have <u>finished</u> your homework <u>by the time the movie starts</u>.

INCORRECT: Jan will left by five o'clock.

CORRECT: Jan <u>will</u> have <u>left</u> <u>by five o'clock</u>.

INCORRECT: Before school is out, I have returned all of my library books.

CORRECT: <u>Before school is out</u>, I <u>will</u> have <u>returned</u> all of my library books.

INCORRECT: We have gotten an answer to our letter by the time we have to make a decision.

CORRECT: We <u>will</u> have <u>gotten</u> an answer to our letter <u>by the time we have to make a decision</u>.

INCORRECT: Before we can tell them about the discount, they will bought the tickets.

CORRECT: <u>Before we can tell them</u> about the discount, they <u>will</u> have <u>bought</u> the tickets.

EXERCISES

Part A: Choose the correct answer.

By the middle of the twenty-first century, the computer _____ a necessity in every home.

(A) became
(B) becoming
(C) has become
(D) will have become

Part B: Choose the incorrect word or phrase and correct it.

It is believed that <u>by 2010</u> immunotherapy <u>have succeeded</u> in
      (A)   (B)   (C)
<u>curing</u> a number of serious illnesses.
  (D)

15 Missing Auxiliary Verb—Active

Remember that some main verbs require auxiliary verbs.

	BE	-*ing*	
Mom	is	watering	her plants

	HAVE	participle	
Mom	has	watered	her plants

	MODAL	verb word	
Mom	should	water	her plants

Avoid using -*ing* forms without BE, participles without HAVE, and verb words without modals when -*ing*, a participle, or a verb word function as a main verb.

EXAMPLES

INCORRECT: The party is a surprise, but all of her friends coming.
CORRECT: The party is a surprise, but all of her friends <u>are coming</u>.

INCORRECT: She read it to you later tonight.
CORRECT: She <u>will read</u> it to you later tonight.

INCORRECT: The sun shining when we left this morning.
CORRECT: The sun <u>was shining</u> when we left this morning.

INCORRECT: We gone there before.
CORRECT: We <u>have gone</u> there before.

INCORRECT: I can't talk with you right now because the doorbell ringing.
CORRECT: I can't talk with you right now because the doorbell <u>is ringing</u>.

EXERCISES

Part A: Choose the correct answer.

The giraffe survives in part because it _____ the vegetation in the high branches of trees where other animals have not grazed.
   (A) to reach
   (B) can reach
   (C) reaching
   (D) reach

Part B: Choose the incorrect word or phrase and correct it.

According to some scientists, the earth losing its outer
   (A)   (B) (C)
atmosphere because of pollutants.
                (D)

PROBLEM

16   Missing Auxiliary Verb—Passive

Remember that the passive requires an auxiliary BE verb.

S	BE		participle
The plants		are	watered
The plants	have	been	watered
The plants	should	be	watered

Avoid using a passive without a form of BE.

EXAMPLES

INCORRECT: The phone answered automatically.
   CORRECT: The phone is answered automatically.

INCORRECT: They have informed already.
  CORRECT: They <u>have been</u> informed already.

INCORRECT: These books should returned today.
  CORRECT: These books <u>should be</u> returned today.

INCORRECT: The plane delayed by bad weather.
  CORRECT: The plane <u>was</u> <u>delayed</u> by bad weather.

INCORRECT: My paper has not typed.
  CORRECT: My paper <u>has</u> not <u>been</u> <u>typed</u>.

EXERCISES

Part A: Choose the correct answer.

Hydrogen peroxide _____ as a bleaching agent because it
effectively whitens a variety of fibers and surfaces.

(A) used
(B) is used
(C) is using
(D) that it uses

Part B: Choose the incorrect word or phrase and correct it.

If a rash <u>occurs</u> within twenty-four hours <u>after taking</u> a new
            (A)   (B)
<u>medication</u>, the treatment <u>should discontinued</u>.
      (C)   (D)

17 Object Pronouns after Prepositions

Remember that personal pronouns used as the object of a
preposition should be object case pronouns.

	preposition	pronoun (object)
I would be glad to take a message	for	her

Remember that the following prepositions are commonly used with object pronouns:

among	*of*
between	*to*
for	*with*
from	

Avoid using a subject pronoun instead of an object pronoun after a proposition.

EXAMPLES

INCORRECT: The experiment proved to my lab partner and I that prejudices about the results of an investigation are often unfounded.

CORRECT: The experiment proved <u>to</u> my lab partner and <u>me</u> that prejudices about the results of an investigation are often unfounded.

INCORRECT: Of those who graduated with Betty and he, Ellen is the only one who has found a good job.

CORRECT: Of those who graduated <u>with</u> Betty and <u>him</u>, Ellen is the only one who has found a good job.

INCORRECT: Among we men, it was he who always acted as the interpreter.

CORRECT: <u>Among us</u> men, it was he who always acted as the interpreter.

INCORRECT: The cake is from Jan, and the flowers are from Larry and we.

CORRECT: The cake is from Jan, and the flowers are <u>from</u> Larry and <u>us</u>.

INCORRECT: Just between you and I, this isn't a very good price.

CORRECT: Just <u>between</u> you and <u>me</u>, this isn't a very good price.

EXERCISES

Part A: Choose the correct answer.

Since the Earth's crust is much thicker under the continents, equipment would have to be capable of drilling through 100,000 feet of rock to investigate the mantle _____.

    (A) beneath them
    (B) beneath their
    (C) beneath its
    (D) beneath they

Part B: Choose the incorrect word or phrase and correct it.

According to Amazon legends, men <u>were forced</u> to do all of the
                                    (A)   (B)

household tasks for the women warriors <u>who</u> governed and
                                                  (C)

protected the cities <u>for they</u>.
                    (D)

Relative Pronouns that Refer to Persons and Things

Remember that *who* is used to refer to persons, and *which* is used to refer to things.

	someone	who	
She is	the secretary	who	works in the international office

Avoid using *which* instead of *who* in reference to a person.

	something	which	
This is	the new typewriter	which	you ordered

Avoid using *who* instead of *which* in reference to a thing.

EXAMPLES

INCORRECT: The people which cheated on the examination had to leave the room.

CORRECT: The people who cheated on the examination had to leave the room.

INCORRECT: There is someone on line two which would like to speak with you.

CORRECT: There is someone on line two who would like to speak with you.

INCORRECT: Who is the man which asked the question?
CORRECT: Who is the man who asked the question?

INCORRECT: The person which was recommended for the position did not fulfill the minimum requirements.

CORRECT: The person who was recommended for the position did not fulfill the minimum requirements.

INCORRECT: The student which receives the highest score will be awarded a scholarship.

CORRECT: The student who receives the highest score will be awarded a scholarship.

EXERCISES

Part A: Choose the correct answer.

Charlie Chaplin was a comedian _____ was best known for his work in silent movies.
- (A) who
- (B) which
- (C) whose
- (D) what

Part B: Choose the incorrect word or phrase and correct it.

Absolute zero, the temperature at *who* whom all substances have

(A)   (B)

zero thermal energy and thus, the lowest possible temperatures,

(C)

is unattainable in practice.

(D)

19 Count Nouns

Remember that *count nouns* have both singular and plural forms. Plural numbers can precede *count nouns* but not *noncount* nouns.

There are several categories of *count nouns* that can help you organize your study. Some of them are listed here.

1. Names of persons, their relationships, and their occupations:
   one boy   *two boys*
   one friend   *two friends*
   one student   *two students*

2. Names of animals, plants, insects:
   one dog   *two dogs*
   one flower   *two flowers*
   one bee   *two bees*

3. Names of things with a definite, individual shape:
   one car   *two cars*
   one house   *two houses*
   one room   *two rooms*

4. Units of measurement:
   one inch   *two inches*
   one pound   *two pounds*
   one degree   *two degrees*

5. Units of classification in society:

one family	*two families*
one country	*two countries*
one language	*two languages*

6. Containers of noncount solids, liquids, pastes, and gases:

one bottle	*two bottles*
one jar	*two jars*
one tube	*two tubes*

7. A limited number of abstract concepts:

one idea	*two ideas*
one invention	*two inventions*
one plan	*two plans*

Number (plural)	Noun (count-plural)
sixty	years

Avoid using a singular *count noun* with a plural number.

EXAMPLES

INCORRECT:	We have twenty dollar left.
CORRECT:	We have <u>twenty dollars</u> left.
INCORRECT:	I hope that I can lose about five pound before summer.
CORRECT:	I hope that I can lose about <u>five pounds</u> before summer.
INCORRECT:	Several of the people in this class speak three or four language.
CORRECT:	Several of the people in this class speak <u>three or four languages</u>.
INCORRECT:	The temperature has risen ten degree in two hours.
CORRECT:	The temperature has risen <u>ten degrees</u> in two hours.
INCORRECT:	The teacher has ordered two book, but they aren't in at the bookstore.
CORRECT:	The teacher has ordered <u>two books,</u> but they aren't in at the bookstore.

EXERCISES

Part A: Choose the correct answer.

A desert receives less than twenty-five _____ of rainfall every year.
  (A) centimeter
  (B) a centimeter
  (C) centimeters
  (D) of centimeters

Part B: Choose the incorrect word or phrase and correct it.

<u>In 1950</u> it was <u>naively</u> predicted that <u>eight or ten computers</u>
  (A)   (B)   (C)
would be sufficient <u>to handle</u> all of the scientific and business
                    (D)
needs in the United States.

20 Noncount Nouns

Remember that *noncount* nouns have only one form. They are used in agreement with singular verbs. The word *the* does not precede them.

There are categories of *noncount* nouns that can help you organize your study. Some of them are listed here.

1. Food staples that can be purchased in various forms:
   bread
   meat
   butter

2. Construction materials that can change shape, depending on what is made:
   wood
   iron
   grass

3. Liquids that can change shape, depending on the shape of the container:
   oil
   tea
   milk

4. Natural substances that can change shape, depending on natural laws:
   steam, water, ice
   smoke, ashes
   oxygen

5. Substances with many small parts:
   rice
   sand
   sugar

6. Groups of things that have different sizes and shapes:
   clothing   *(a coat, a shirt, a sock)*
   furniture   *(a table, a chair, a bed)*
   luggage   *(a suitcase, a trunk, a box)*

7. Languages:
   Arabic
   Japanese
   Spanish

8. Abstract concepts, often with endings *-ness*, *-ance*, *-ence*, *-ity*:
   beauty
   ignorance
   peace

9. Most *-ing* forms:
   learning
   shopping
   working

noun (noncount)	verb (singular)	
Friendship	is	important

Avoid using *the* before a *noncount* noun. Avoid using a plural verb with a noncount noun.

EXAMPLES

INCORRECT: The happiness means different things to different people.
  CORRECT: <u>Happiness</u> means different things to different people.

INCORRECT: Toshi speaks the Japanese at home.
  CORRECT: Toshi speaks <u>Japanese</u> at home.

INCORRECT: Bread are expensive in the grocery store on the corner.
  CORRECT: <u>Bread is</u> expensive in the grocery store on the corner.

INCORRECT: I like my tea with the milk.
  CORRECT: I like my tea with <u>milk</u>.

INCORRECT: If you open the door, airs will circulate better.
  CORRECT: If you open the door, <u>air</u> will circulate better.

EXERCISES

Part A: Choose the correct answer.

_____ at 212 degrees F. and freezes at 32 degrees F.
(A) Waters boils
(B) The water boils
(C) Water boils
(D) Waters boil

Part B: Choose the incorrect word or phrase and correct it.

<u>The religion</u> attempts <u>to clarify</u> mankind's <u>relationship</u> with a
       (A)   (B)   (C)
<u>superhuman power</u>.
       (D)

Nouns with Count and Noncount Meanings

Remember that some nouns may be used as *count* or as *non-count* nouns depending on their meanings. Materials and abstract concepts are *noncount* nouns, but they may be used as *count* nouns to express specific meanings.

Count noun	Specific meaning	Noncount noun	General meaning
an agreement agreements	an occasion or a document	agreement	abstract concept all agreements
a bone bones	a part of a skeleton	bone	construction material
a business businesses	a company	business	abstract concept all business transactions
a cloth cloths	a piece of cloth	cloth	construction material
a decision decisions	an occasion	decision	abstract concept all decisions
an education educations	a specific person's	education	abstract concept all education
a fire fires	an event	fire	material
a glass glasses	a container	glass	construction material
a history histories	a historical account	history	abstract concept all history
an honor honors	an occasion or an award	honor	abstract concept all honor
a language languages	a specific variety	language	abstract concept all languages
a life lives	a specific person's	life	abstract concept all life
a light lights	a lamp	light	the absence of darkness

a noise	a specific	noise	abstract concept
noises	sound		all sounds
a pain	a specific	pain	abstract concept
pains	occasion		all pain
a paper	a document	paper	construction
papers	or sheet		material
a pleasure	a specific	pleasure	abstract concept
pleasures	occasion		all pleasure
a silence	a specific	silence	abstract concept
silences	occasion		all silence
a space	a blank	space	the universe
spaces			
a stone	a small rock	stone	construction
stones			material
a success	**an achievement**	success	abstract concept
successes			all success
a thought	an idea	thought	abstract concept
thoughts			all thought
a time	a historical period	time	abstract concept
times	or moment		all time
a war	a specific war	war	the general act of war
wars			all wars
a work	an artistic creation	work	employment
works			abstract concept
			all work

	a document	
I have	a paper	due Monday

	construction material	
Let's use	paper	to make the present

Avoid using *count* nouns with specific meanings to express the general meanings of *noncount* nouns.

EXAMPLES

INCORRECT: Dr. Bradley will receive special honor at the graduation.

CORRECT: Dr. Bradley will receive <u>a special honor</u> at the graduation.
(an award)

INCORRECT: She needs to find a work.

CORRECT: She needs to find <u>work</u>.
(employment)

INCORRECT: My neighbor dislikes a noise.

CORRECT: My neighbor dislikes <u>noise</u>.
(all sounds)

INCORRECT: We need glass for the juice.

CORRECT: We need <u>a glass</u> for the juice.

or

We need <u>glasses</u> for the juice.
(containers)

INCORRECT: A war is as old as mankind.

CORRECT: <u>War</u> is as old as mankind.
(the act of war)

EXERCISES

Part A: Choose the correct answer.

It is generally believed that an M.B.A. degree is good preparation for a career in _____.

(A) a business
(B) business
(C) businesses
(D) one business

Part B: Choose the incorrect word or phrase and correct it.

<u>A space</u> <u>is</u> the last frontier for <u>man</u> <u>to conquer</u>. /kɔ́ŋkɔ/
(A)   (B)   (C)   (D)   征服，获胜

22 Noncount Nouns that Are Count Nouns in Other Languages

Remember, many nouns that are *count* nouns in other languages may be *noncount* nouns in English. Some of the most troublesome have been listed for you on the following page.

advice	homework	money	poetry
anger	ignorance	music	poverty
courage	information	news	progress
damage	knowledge	patience	
equipment	leisure	permission	
fun	luck		

	Ø	Noun (noncount)
Did you do your		homework?

Avoid using *a* or *an* before *noncount* nouns.

EXAMPLES

INCORRECT: Do you have an information about it?
CORRECT: Do you have <u>information</u> about it?

INCORRECT: Counselors are available to give you an advice before you register for your classes.
CORRECT: Counselors are available to give you <u>advice</u> before you register for your classes.

INCORRECT: George had a good luck when he first came to State University.
CORRECT: George had good <u>luck</u> when he first came to State University.

INCORRECT: A news was released about the hostages.
CORRECT: <u>News</u> was released about the hostages.

INCORRECT: Did you get a permission to take the placement test?
CORRECT: Did you get <u>permission</u> to take the placement test?

EXERCISES

Part A: Choose the correct answer.

Fire-resistant materials are used to retard _____ of
modern aircraft in case of accidents.

    (A) a damage to the passenger cabin
    (B) that damages to the passenger cabin
    (C) damage to the passenger cabin
    (D) passenger cabin's damages

Part B: Choose the incorrect word or phrase and correct it.

A progress has been made toward finding a cure for AIDS.
  (A)   (B)   (C) (D)

23 Singular and Plural Expressions of Noncount Nouns

Remember that the following singular and plural expressions are idiomatic:

a piece of advice	two pieces of advice
a piece of bread	two pieces of bread
a piece of equipment	two pieces of equipment
a piece of furniture	two pieces of furniture
a piece of information	two pieces of information
a piece of jewelry	two pieces of jewelry
a piece of luggage	two pieces of luggage
a piece of mail	two pieces of mail
a piece of music	two pieces of music
a piece of news	two pieces of news
a piece of toast	two pieces of toast
a loaf of bread	two loaves of bread
a slice of bread	two slices of bread
an ear of corn	two ears of corn
a bar of soap	two bars of soap

a bolt of lightning   two bolts of lightning
a clap of thunder   two claps of thunder
a gust of wind   two gusts of wind

突然一声 *响* *雷声;打雷* *狂风*

	a	singular	of	noun (noncount)
A folk song is	a	piece	of	popular music

	number	plural	of	noun (noncount)
I ordered	twelve	bars	of	soap

Avoid using the noncount noun without the singular or plural idiom to express a singular or plural.

EXAMPLES

INCORRECT: A mail travels faster when the zip code is indicated on the envelope.

CORRECT: A piece of mail travels faster when the zip code is indicated on the envelope.

INCORRECT: There is a limit of two carry-on luggages for each passenger.

CORRECT: There is a limit of two pieces of carry-on luggage for each passenger.

INCORRECT: Each furniture in this display is on sale for half price.
CORRECT: Each piece of furniture in this display is on sale for half price.

INCORRECT: I'd like a steak, a salad, and a corn's ear with butter.
CORRECT: I'd like a steak, a salad, and an ear of corn with butter.

INCORRECT: The Engineering Department purchased a new equipment to simulate conditions in outer space.

CORRECT: The Engineering Department purchased a new piece of equipment to simulate conditions in outer space.

<u>**EXERCISES**</u>

Part A: Choose the correct answer.

Hybrids have one more _____ per plant than the other varieties.

(A) corns
(B) ear of corn
(C) corn ears
(D) corn's ears

Part B: Choose the incorrect word or phrase and correct it.

<u>A few</u> tiles on *Skylab* <u>were</u> the only <u>equipments</u> that failed
  (A)   (B)   (C)

a pieces of equipment

<u>to perform</u> well in outer space.
  (D)

24   Infinitive and *-ing* Subjects

Remember that either an infinitive or an *-ing* form may be used as the subject of a sentence or a clause.

S (infinitive)		V	
To read	a foreign language	is	even more difficult

S (*-ing*)		V	
Reading	quickly and well	requires	practice

Avoid using a verb word instead of an infinitive or an *-ing* form in the subject. Avoid using *to* with an *-ing* form.

EXAMPLES

INCORRECT: To working provides people with personal satisfaction as well as money.

CORRECT: <u>To work</u> provides people with personal satisfaction as well as money.

or

<u>Working</u> provides people with personal satisfaction as well as money.

INCORRECT: The sneeze spreads germs.

CORRECT: <u>To sneeze</u> spreads germs.

or

<u>Sneezing</u> spreads germs.

INCORRECT: Shoplift is considered a serious crime.

CORRECT: <u>To shoplift</u> is considered a serious crime.

or

<u>Shoplifting</u> is considered a serious crime.

INCORRECT: The rest in the afternoon is a custom in many countries.

CORRECT: <u>To rest</u> in the afternoon is a custom in many countries.

or

<u>Resting</u> in the afternoon is a custom in many countries.

INCORRECT: To exercising makes most people feel better.

CORRECT: <u>To exercise</u> makes most people feel better.

or

<u>Exercising</u> makes most people feel better.

EXERCISES

Part A: Choose the correct answer.

_____ trees is a custom that many people engage in to celebrate Arbor Day.

(A) The plant
(B) Plant
(C) Planting
(D) To planting

Part B: Choose the incorrect word or phrase and correct it.

Spelling

Spell correctly is easy with the aid of a number of
(A)   (B)
word processing programs for personal computers.
        (C)   (D)

nominal

Nominal *That* Clause

方词性从何

Remember that sometimes the subject of a verb is a single noun. Other times it is a long noun phrase or a long noun clause.

One example of a long noun clause is the *nominal that* clause. Like all clauses, the *nominal that* clause has a subject and verb. The *nominal that* clause functions as the main subject of the main verb which follows it.

Nominal *that* clause S	V	
That vitamin C prevents colds	is	well known

EXAMPLES

INCORRECT: That it is that she has known him for a long time
              influenced her decision.
  CORRECT: <u>That she has known him for a long time</u> influenced
              her decision.

INCORRECT: It is that we need to move is sure.
  CORRECT: <u>That we need to move</u> is sure.

INCORRECT: Is likely that the library is closed.
  CORRECT: <u>That the library is closed</u> is likely.

INCORRECT: She will win is almost certain.
  CORRECT: <u>That she will win</u> is almost certain.

INCORRECT: That is not fair seems obvious.
  CORRECT: <u>That it is not fair</u> seems obvious.

EXERCISES

That + 引导句子.

Part A: Choose the correct answer.

_____ migrate long distances is well documented.
  (A) That it is birds
  (B) That birds
  (C) Birds that
  (D) It is that birds

Part B: Choose the incorrect word or phrase and correct it.

That it is the moon influences only one kind of tide is not
     (A)   (B)
generally known.
   (C)   (D)

affect

influence on

Noncount Nouns with Qualifying Phrases—*The*

Remember, *the* is used with count nouns. You have also learned that *the* can be used before an *-ing* noun that is followed by a qualifying phrase.

In addition, *the* can be used before a noncount noun with a qualifying phrase.

The	noncount noun	Qualifying Phrase	
The	art	of the Middle Ages	is on display

EXAMPLES

INCORRECT:	Poetry of Carl Sandburg is being read at the student union on Friday.
CORRECT:	The poetry of Carl Sandburg is being read at the student union on Friday.

INCORRECT:	Poverty of people in the rural areas is not as visible as that of people in the city.
CORRECT:	The poverty of people in the rural areas is not as visible as that of people in the city.

INCORRECT:	Science of genetic engineering is not very old.
CORRECT:	The science of genetic engineering is not very old.

INCORRECT:	History of this area is interesting.
CORRECT:	The history of this area is interesting.

INCORRECT:	Work of many people made the project a success.
CORRECT:	The work of many people made the project a success.

EXERCISES

Part A: Choose the correct answer.

_____ of Country-Western singers may be related to old English ballads.
(A) The music
(B) Music
(C) Their music
(D) Musics

Part B: Choose the incorrect word or phrase and correct it.

the philosophy

Philosophy of the ancient Greeks has been preserved in the
   (A)   (B)
scholarly writing of Western civilization.
     (C)   (D)

No Meaning *Not Any*

Remember that *no* means *not any*. It may be used with a singular or plural count noun or with a noncount noun.

no	noun (count singular) noun (count plural)	verb (singular) verb (plural)
No	tree	grows above the tree line
No	trees	grow above the tree line

no	noun (noncount)	verb (singular)	
No	art	is	on display today

Avoid using the negatives *not* or *none* instead of *no*. Avoid using a singular verb with a plural count noun.

EXAMPLES

INCORRECT: There is not reason to worry.
  CORRECT: There is <u>no reason</u> to worry.

INCORRECT: None news is good news.
  CORRECT: <u>No news</u> is good news.

INCORRECT: We have not a file under the name Wagner.
  CORRECT: We have <u>no file</u> under the name Wagner.

INCORRECT: None of cheating will be tolerated.
  CORRECT: <u>No cheating</u> will be tolerated.

INCORRECT: Bill told me that he has none friends.
  CORRECT: Bill told me that he has <u>no friends</u>.

EXERCISES

Part A: Choose the correct answer.

At Woolworth's first five-and-ten-cent store, _____ more than a dime.

(A) neither items cost
(B) items not cost
(C) items none costing
(D) no item cost

Part B: Choose the incorrect word or phrase and correct it.

Some religions <u>have none</u> deity but <u>are</u> philosophies that
            (A)   (B)   (C)

function <u>instead of religions</u>.
         (D)

28   *Almost All of the* and *Most of the*

Remember that *almost all of the* and *most of the* mean all except a few, but *almost all of the* includes more.

almost all (of the) most (of the)	noun (count—plural)	verb (plural)	
Almost all (of the) Most (of the)	trees in our yard trees	are are	oaks oaks

almost all (of the) most (of the)	noun (noncount)	verb (singular)
Almost all (of the) Most (of the)	art by R. C. Gorman art by R. C. Gorman	is expensive is expensive

Avoid using *almost without all* or *all of the*. Avoid using *most of* without *the*.

EXAMPLES

INCORRECT: Almost the states have a sales tax.
  CORRECT: Almost all of the states have a sales tax.
                or
             Almost all states have a sales tax.
                or
             Most of the states have a sales tax.
                or
             Most states have a sales tax.

INCORRECT: Most of teachers at State University care about their students' progress.
  CORRECT: Almost all of the teachers at State University care about their students' progress.
                or
             Almost all teachers at State University care about their students' progress.

or

Most of the teachers at State University care about their students' progress.

or

Most teachers at State University care about their students' progress.

INCORRECT: My cousin told me that most of people who won the lottery got only a few dollars, not the grand prize.

CORRECT: My cousin told me that almost all of the people who won the lottery got only a few dollars, not the grand prize.

or

My cousin told me that almost all people who won the lottery got only a few dollars, not the grand prize.

or

My cousin told me that most of the people who won the lottery got only a few dollars, not the grand prize.

or

My cousin told me that most people who won the lottery got only a few dollars, not the grand prize.

INCORRECT: Most the dictionaries have information about pronunciation.

CORRECT: Almost all of the dictionaries have information about pronunciation.

or

Almost all dictionaries have information about pronunciation.

or

Most of the dictionaries have information about pronunciation.

or

Most dictionaries have information about pronunciation.

INCORRECT: Is it true that most Americans watches TV every night?

CORRECT: It is true that almost all of the Americans watch TV every night?

or

Is it true that <u>almost all</u> Americans watch TV every night?

or

Is it true that <u>most of the</u> Americans watch TV every night?

or

Is it true that <u>most</u> Americans watch TV every night?

EXERCISES

Part A: Choose the correct answer.

_____ fuel that is used today is a chemical form of solar energy.

(A) Most (of *the*)
(B) The most
(C) Most
(D) Almost the *all*

Part B: Choose the incorrect word or phrase and correct it.

all
<u>Almost</u> the plants <u>known to us</u> are made up of
 (A)   (B)

a great many <u>cells</u>, specialized <u>to perform</u> different tasks.
       (C)   (D)

29   Nouns that Function as Adjectives

Remember that when two nouns occur together, the first noun describes the second noun; that is, the first noun functions as an adjective. Adjectives do not change form, singular or plural.

	noun	noun
All of us are foreign	language	teachers

Avoid using a plural form for the first noun even when the second noun is plural. Avoid using a <u>possessive form</u> for the first noun.

借用   access.

EXAMPLES

INCORRECT: May I borrow some notebooks paper?
CORRECT: May I borrow some <u>notebook paper</u>?

INCORRECT: All business' students must take the Graduate
            Management Admission Test.
CORRECT: All <u>business students</u> must take the Graduate
            Management Admission Test.

INCORRECT: I forgot their telephone's number.
CORRECT: I forgot their <u>telephone number</u>.

INCORRECT: There is a sale at the shoes store.
CORRECT: There is a sale at the <u>shoe store</u>.

INCORRECT: Put the mail on the hall's table.
CORRECT: Put the mail on the <u>hall table</u>.

EXERCISES

Part A: Choose the correct answer.

_____ is cheaper for students who maintain a B average
because they are a better risk than average or below-average
students.
   (A) Automobile's insurance
   (B) Insurance of automobiles
   (C) Automobile insurance
   (D) Insurance automobile

Part B: Choose the incorrect word or phrase and correct it.

Sex's education is instituted to help the student <u>understand</u> the
   (A)   (B)
process of maturation, <u>to eliminate anxieties</u> <u>related</u> to
                              (C)   (D)
development, to learn values, and to prevent disease.

PROBLEM 30 Hyphenated Adjectives

Remember that it is common for a number to appear as the first in a series of hyphenated adjectives. Each word in a hyphenated adjective is an adjective and does not change form, singular or plural.

	a	adjective	—	adjective	noun
Agriculture 420 is	a	five	—	hour	class

a	adjective	—	adjective	—	adjective	noun	
A	sixty	—	year	—	old	employee	may retire

Avoid using a plural form for any of the adjectives joined by hyphens even when the noun that follows is plural.

EXAMPLES

INCORRECT: A three-minutes call anywhere in the United States costs less than a dollar when you dial it yourself.

CORRECT: A three-minute call anywhere in the United States costs less than a dollar when you dial it yourself.

INCORRECT: They have a four-months-old baby.

CORRECT: They have a four-month-old baby.

INCORRECT: Can you make change for a twenty-dollars bill?

CORRECT: Can you make change for a twenty-dollar bill?

INCORRECT: A two-doors car is cheaper than a four-doors model.

CORRECT: A two-door car is cheaper than a four-door model.

INCORRECT: I have to write a one-thousand-words paper this weekend.

CORRECT: I have to write a one-thousand-word paper this weekend.

<u>**EXERCISES**</u>

Part A: Choose the correct answer.

The evolution of vertebrates suggests development from a very simple heart in fish to a _____ in man.
(A) four-chamber heart
(B) four-chambers heart
(C) four-chamber hearts
(D) four-chamber's heart

Part B: Choose the incorrect word or phrase and correct it.

The MX <u>is</u> a <u>four-stages</u> rocket with <u>an 8000</u>-mile range,
    (A)   (B)   (C)
<u>larger than</u> that of the Minuteman.
    (D)

31   Cause-and-Result—So

Remember that *so* is used before an adjective or an adverb followed by *that*. The *so* clause expresses cause. The *that* clause expresses result.

CAUSE				RESULT			
S	V	so	adverb adjective	that	S	V	
She	got up	so	late	that	she	missed	her bus
The music	was	so	loud	that	we	couldn't talk	

Avoid using *as* or *too* instead of *so* in clauses of cause. Avoid using *as* instead of *that* in clauses of result.

PATTERNS/PROBLEM 31   129

EXAMPLES

INCORRECT:	He is so slow as he never gets to class on time.
CORRECT:	He is <u>so slow that</u> he never gets to class on time.

INCORRECT:	This suitcase is as heavy that I can hardly carry it.
CORRECT:	This suitcase is <u>so heavy that</u> I can hardly carry it.

INCORRECT:	We arrived so late as Professor Baker had already called the roll.
CORRECT:	We arrived <u>so late that</u> Professor Baker had already called the roll.

INCORRECT:	He drives so fast as no one likes to ride with him.
CORRECT:	He drives <u>so fast that</u> no one likes to ride with him.

INCORRECT:	Preparing frozen foods is too easy that anyone can do it.
CORRECT:	Preparing frozen foods is <u>so easy that</u> anyone can do it.

EXERCISES

Part A: Choose the correct answer.

Oil paints are _____ they have become the most popular painter's colors.

(A) so versatile and durable that
(B) so versatile and durable than
(C) such versatile and durable as
(D) such versatile and durable

Part B: Choose the incorrect word or phrase and correct it.

By the mid nineteenth century, land was such expensive in
        (A)   (B)
large cities that architects began to <u>conserve</u> space <u>by designing</u>
                        (C)   (D)
skyscrapers.

32   Exact Similarity—*the Same as* and *the Same*

Remember that *the same as* and *the same* have the same meaning, but *the same as* is used between the two nouns compared, and *the same* is used after the two nouns or a plural noun.

noun		the same as	noun
This coat	is	the same as	that one

noun		noun		the same
This coat	and	that one	are	the same

noun (plural)		the same
These coats	are	the same

Avoid using *to* and *like* instead of *as*. Avoid using *the same* between the two nouns compared.

EXAMPLES

INCORRECT: That car is almost the same like mine.
CORRECT: That car is almost <u>the same as</u> mine.
                    or
              That car and mine are almost <u>the same</u>.

INCORRECT: My briefcase is exactly the same that yours.
CORRECT: My briefcase is exactly <u>the same as</u> yours.
                    or
              My briefcase and yours are exactly <u>the same</u>.

INCORRECT: Is your book the same to mine?
CORRECT: Is your book <u>the same as</u> mine?
                    or

Are your book and mine <u>the same</u>?

INCORRECT: Are this picture and the one on your desk same?
  CORRECT: Are this picture and the one on your desk <u>the same</u>?

or

Is this picture <u>the same as</u> <u>the one</u> on your desk?

INCORRECT: The teacher gave Martha a failing grade on her
             composition because it was the same a composition
             he had already read.
  CORRECT: The teacher gave Martha a failing grade on her
             composition because it was <u>the same as</u> <u>a</u>
             <u>composition</u> he had already read.

or

The teacher gave Martha a failing grade on her
composition because it and a composition he had
already read were <u>the same</u>.

_____   *the same as* 后 连接 东西.

EXERCISES

Part A: Choose the correct answer.

Although we often use "speed" and "velocity" interchangeably,
in a technical sense, "speed" is not always _____
"velocity."

(A) alike
(B) the same as
(C) similar
(D) as

Part B: Choose the incorrect word or phrase and correct it.

When two products are <u>basically</u> <u>the same as</u>, <u>advertising</u> can
                (A)   (B)   (C)

<u>influence</u> the public's choice.
(D)

33 General Similarity—*Like* and *Alike*

Remember that *like* and *alike* have the same meaning, but *like* is used between the two nouns compared, and *alike* is used after the two nouns or a plural noun.

noun		like	noun
This coat	is	like	that one

noun		noun		alike
This coat	and	that one	are	alike

noun (plural)		alike
These coats	are	alike

Avoid using *as* instead of *like*. Avoid using *like* after the two nouns compared.

n + like + n
n + n + alike

EXAMPLES

INCORRECT: The weather feels as spring.
  CORRECT: The weather feels like spring.

INCORRECT: These suits are like.
  CORRECT: This suit is like that suit.
                    or
             These suits are alike.

INCORRECT: Your recipe for chicken is like to a recipe that my
             mother has.
  CORRECT: Your recipe for chicken is like a recipe that my
             mother has.
                    or
             Your recipe for chicken and a recipe that my mother
             has are alike.

INCORRECT: I want to buy some shoes same like the ones I have on.

CORRECT: I want to buy some shoes <u>like</u> the ones I have on.

or

The shoes I want to buy and the shoes I have on are <u>alike</u>.

INCORRECT: Anthony and his brother don't look like.

CORRECT: Anthony doesn't look <u>like</u> his brother.

or

Anthony and his brother don't look <u>alike</u>.

EXERCISES

Part A: Choose the correct answer.

Although they are smaller, chipmunks are _____ most other ground squirrels.

(A) like to
(B) like as
(C) like
(D) alike

Part B: Choose the incorrect word or phrase and correct it.

<u>The first</u> living structures <u>to appear</u> on Earth thousands of years
   (A)   (B)

<u>ago</u> were <u>alike</u> viruses.
(C)   (D) *like*   *alike? 能作表语.*

34   General Difference—*to Differ from*

Remember that *differ* is a verb and must change forms to agree with the subject.

	DIFFER	from	
This one	differs	from	the rest

Avoid using BE with *differ*. Avoid using *than*, *of*, or *to* after *differ*.

differ be different from

EXAMPLES

INCORRECT: Sharon is different of other women I know.
CORRECT: Sharon is different from other women I know.
or
Sharon differs from other women I know.

INCORRECT: Do you have anything a little different to these?
CORRECT: Do you have anything a little different from these?
or
Do you have anything that differs a little from these?

INCORRECT: The campus at State University different from that of City College.
CORRECT: The campus at State University differs from that of City College.
or
The campus at State University is different from that of City College.

INCORRECT: Jayne's apartment is very differs from Bill's even though they are in the same building.
CORRECT: Jayne's apartment is very different from Bill's even though they are in the same building.
or
Jayne's apartment differs from Bill's even though they are in the same building.

INCORRECT: Customs differ one region of the country to another.
CORRECT: Customs differ from one region of the country to another.
or
Customs are different from one region of the country to another.

EXERCISES

Part A: Choose the correct answer.

Modern blimps like the famous Goodyear blimps _____
the first ones in that they are filled with helium instead of
hydrogen.
  (A) differ from
  (B) different from
  (C) is different from
  (D) different

Part B: Choose the incorrect word or phrase and correct it.

Crocodiles <u>different from</u> alligators in that they have
    (A)   (B)

<u>pointed snouts</u> and long lower teeth that stick out when their
      (C)

mouths <u>are closed</u>.
        (D)

Comparative Estimates— Multiple Numbers

Remember that the following are examples of multiple numbers:

half	*four times*
twice	*five times*
three times	*ten times*

	multiple	as	much many	as	
Fresh fruit costs	twice	as	much	as	canned fruit
We have	half	as	many	as	we need

Avoid using *so* instead of *as* after a multiple. Avoid using *more than* instead of *as much as* or *as many as*. Avoid using the multiple after *as much* and *as many*.

EXAMPLES

INCORRECT: This one is prettier, but it costs twice more than the other one.

CORRECT: This one is prettier, but it costs <u>twice as much as</u> the other one.

INCORRECT: The rent at College Apartments is only half so much as you pay here.

CORRECT: The rent at College Apartments is only <u>half as much as</u> you pay here.

INCORRECT: Bob found a job that paid as much twice as he made working at the library.

CORRECT: Bob found a job that paid <u>twice as much as</u> he made working at the library.

INCORRECT: The price was very reasonable; I would gladly have paid three times more than he asked.

CORRECT: The price was very reasonable; I would gladly have paid <u>three times as much as</u> he asked.

INCORRECT: We didn't buy the car because they wanted as much twice as it was worth.

CORRECT: We didn't buy the car because they wanted <u>twice as much as</u> it was worth.

EXERCISES

Part A: Choose the correct answer.

After the purchase of the Louisiana Territory, the United States had _____ it had previously owned.
   (A) twice more land than
   (B) two times more land than
   (C) twice as much land as
   (D) two times much land than

Part B: Choose the incorrect word or phrase and correct it.

With American prices for sugar at three times <u>as much the</u>
                                                      (A)

world price, manufacturers <u>are</u> beginning <u>to use</u> fructose
                             (B)   (C)

blended with pure sugar, <u>or</u> sucrose.
                          (D)

*his prices as much as the
    less.*

36

Comparative Estimates—*More Than* and *Less Than*

Remember that *more than* or *less than* is used before a specific number to express an estimate that may be a little more or a little less than the number.

	more than	number	
Steve has	more than	a thousand	coins in his collection

	less than	number	
Andy has	less than	a dozen	coins in his pocket

Avoid using *more* or *less* without *than* in estimates. Avoid using *as* instead of *than*.

EXAMPLES

INCORRECT: More one hundred people came to the meeting.

CORRECT: <u>More than one hundred</u> people came to the meeting.

INCORRECT: We have lived in the United States for as less than seven years.

CORRECT: We have lived in the United States for <u>less than seven</u> years.

INCORRECT:	The main library has more as one million volumes.
CORRECT:	The main library has <u>more than one million</u> volumes.

INCORRECT:	A new shopping center on the north side will have five hundred shops more than.
CORRECT:	A new shopping center on the north side will have <u>more than five hundred</u> shops.

INCORRECT:	There are most than fifty students in the lab, but only two computers.
CORRECT:	There are <u>more than fifty</u> students in the lab, but only two computers.

EXERCISES

Part A: Choose the correct answer.

In the Great Smoky Mountains, one can see _____ 150 different kinds of trees.
(A) more than   *as many as*
(B) as much as
(C) up as
(D) as many to

Part B: Choose the incorrect word or phrase and correct it.

Pelé <u>scored</u> <u>more as</u> *than* 1280 goals <u>during his career</u>, <u>gaining</u> a
    (A)   (B)   (C)
reputation as <u>the best</u> soccer player of all time.
         (D)

37   Comparative Estimates—*As Many As*

Remember that *as many as* is used before a specific number to express an estimate that does not exceed the number.

	as many as	number	
We should have	as many as	five hundred	applications

Avoid using *as many* instead of *as many as*. Avoid using *much* instead of *many* before a specific number.

Note: Comparative estimates with *as much as* are also used before a specific number that refers to weight, distance, or money. For example, *as much as* ten pounds, *as much as* two miles, or *as much as* twenty dollars.

EXAMPLES

INCORRECT: We expect as much as thirty people to come.
CORRECT: We expect <u>as many as</u> <u>thirty</u> people to come.

INCORRECT: There are as many fifteen thousand students attending summer school.
CORRECT: There are <u>as many as</u> <u>fifteen thousand</u> students attending summer school.

INCORRECT: The children can see as much as twenty-five baby animals in the nursery at the zoo.
CORRECT: The children can see <u>as many as</u> <u>twenty-five</u> baby animals in the nursery at the zoo.

INCORRECT: Many as ten planes have sat in line waiting to take off.
CORRECT: <u>As many as</u> <u>ten</u> planes have sat in line waiting to take off.

INCORRECT: State University offers as much as two hundred major fields of study.
CORRECT: State University offers <u>as many as</u> <u>two hundred</u> major fields of study.

EXERCISES

Part A: Choose the correct answer.

It has been estimated that _____ one hundred thousand men participated in the gold rush of 1898.
  (A) approximate
  (B) until
  (C) as many as
  (D) more

Part B: Choose the incorrect word or phrase and correct it.

It is generally accepted that the common cold <u>is caused</u> <u>by</u>
                                                      (A)   (B)
<u>as much as</u> forty <u>strains</u> of viruses <u>that</u> may be present in the air
   (C)   (D)
at all times.

PROBLEM 38

Degrees of Comparison—Superlative Adjectives

Remember that superlatives are used to compare more than two.

	the	most (least) adjective (two + syllables) adjective -est (one syllable) adjective -est (two + syllables ending in -er)
An essay test is	the	most difficult
An essay test is	the	hardest
An essay test is	the	trickiest

Avoid using a comparative -er form when three or more are compared.

EXAMPLES

INCORRECT: She is more prettier than all of the girls in our class.
CORRECT: She is <u>the prettiest</u> of all of the girls in our class.

INCORRECT: New York is the larger of all American cities.
CORRECT: New York is <u>the largest</u> of all American cities.

INCORRECT: Of all of the candidates, Alex is probably the less qualified.
CORRECT: Of all of the candidates, Alex is probably <u>the least qualified</u>.

INCORRECT: Although there are a number of interesting findings, a most significant results are in the abstract.
CORRECT: Although there are a number of interesting findings, <u>the most significant</u> results are in the abstract.

INCORRECT: In my opinion, the more beautiful place in Oregon is Mount Hood.
CORRECT: In my opinion, <u>the most beautiful</u> place in Oregon is Mount Hood.

EXERCISES

Part A: Choose the correct answer.

The blue whale is _____ known animal, reaching a length of more than one hundred feet.

(A) the large
(B) the larger
(C) the largest
(D) most largest

Part B: Choose the incorrect answer and correct it.

The <u>more</u> important theorem of all in plane geometry <u>is</u>
(A) (B)   (C)
<u>the</u> Pythagorean Theorem.
(D)

39 Degrees of Comparison—Irregular Adjectives

Remember that some very common adjectives have irregular forms. Some of them are listed here for you.

Adjective	Comparative— to compare two	Superlative— to compare three or more
bad	worse	the worst
far	farther	the farthest
	further	the furthest
good	better	the best
little	less	the least
many	more	the most
much	more	the most

	irregular comparative	than	
This ice cream is	better	than	the other brands

	irregular superlative	
This ice cream is	the best	of all

Avoid using a regular form instead of an irregular form for these adjectives.

EXAMPLES

INCORRECT: The lab is more far from the bus stop than the library.
CORRECT: The lab is <u>farther from</u> the bus stop than the library.
or
The lab is <u>further from</u> the bus stop than the library.

INCORRECT: The badest accident in the history of the city

occurred last night on the North Freeway.

CORRECT: The worst accident in the history of the city occurred last night on the North Freeway.

INCORRECT: These photographs are very good, but that one is the better of all.

CORRECT: These photographs are very good, but that one is the best of all.

INCORRECT: Please give me much sugar than you did last time.

CORRECT: Please give me more sugar than you did last time.

INCORRECT: This composition is more good than your last one.

CORRECT: This composition is better than your last one.

EXERCISES

Part A: Choose the correct answer.

_____ apples are grown in Washington State.

(A) Best
(B) The most good
(C) The best
(D) The better

Part B: Choose the incorrect word or phrase and correct it.

Because a felony is more bad than a misdemeanor, the
  (A)   (B)

punishment is more severe, and often includes a jail sentence
           (C)

as well as a fine.
  (D)

40   Double Comparatives

Remember that when two comparatives are used together, the first comparative expresses cause and the second comparative expresses result. A comparative is *more* or *less* with an adjective, or an adjective with *-er*.

CAUSE				RESULT			
The	comparative	S	V,	the	comparative	S	V
The	more	you	review,	the	easier	the patterns	will be

Avoid using *as* instead of *the*. Avoid using the **incorrect** form *lesser*. Avoid omitting *the*. Avoid omitting *-er* from the adjective.

EXAMPLES

INCORRECT: The more you study during the semester, the lesser you have to study the week before exams.

CORRECT: The more you study during the semester, the less you have to study the week before exams.

INCORRECT: The faster we finish, the soon we can leave.
CORRECT: The faster we finish, the sooner we can leave.

INCORRECT: The less one earns, the lesser one must pay in income taxes.

CORRECT: The less one earns, the less one must pay in income taxes.

INCORRECT: The louder he shouted, less he convinced anyone.
CORRECT: The louder he shouted, the less he convinced anyone.

INCORRECT: The more you practice speaking, the well you will do it.

CORRECT: The more you practice speaking, the better you will do it.

EXERCISES

Part A: Choose the correct answer.

It is generally true that the lower the stock market falls,
_____.

(A) higher the price of gold rises
(B) the price of gold rises high
(C) the higher the price of gold rises
(D) rises high the price of gold

Part B: Choose the incorrect word or phrase and correct it.

The higher the solar activity, <u>the intense</u> <u>the auroras</u> or polar
                               (A)   (B)
light displays in the skies <u>near</u> <u>the Earth's geomagnetic poles</u>.
                             (C)   (D)

41 Illogical Comparatives—General Similarity and Difference

Remember that comparisons must be made with logically comparable nouns. You can't compare *the climate* in the North with *the South*. You must compare *the climate* in the North with *the climate* in the South.

Remember that *that of* and *those of* are used instead of repeating a noun to express a logical comparative. An example with *different from* appears below.

noun (singular)		different	from	that	
Football in the U.S.	is	different	from	that	in other countries

noun (plural)		different	from	those	
The rules	are	different	from	those	of soccer

Avoid omitting *that* and *those*. Avoid using *than* instead of *from* with *different*.

EXAMPLES

INCORRECT: The food in my country is very different than that in
              the United States.

CORRECT: The food in my country is very <u>different from</u> <u>that</u> in
              the United States.

INCORRECT: The classes at my university are very different from
              State University.

CORRECT: The classes at my university are very <u>different from</u>
              <u>those</u> at State University.

INCORRECT: The English that is spoken in Canada is similar to the
              United States.

CORRECT: The English that is spoken in Canada is <u>similar to</u>
              <u>that</u> of the United States.

INCORRECT: Drugstores here are not like at home.
CORRECT: Drugstores here are not <u>like</u> <u>those</u> at home.

INCORRECT: The time in New York City differs three hours from
              Los Angeles.

CORRECT: The time in New York City <u>differs</u> three hours <u>from</u>
              <u>that</u> of Los Angeles.

在新地方。用介词. at , in .
高某介地方， 用 "of"

EXERCISES

Part A: Choose the correct answer.

One's fingerprints are _____.

    (A) different from those of any other person

    (B) different from any other person

    (C) different any other person

    (D) differs from another person

Part B: Choose the incorrect word or phrase and correct it.

Perhaps the colonists were <u>looking for</u> a climate <u>like England</u>,
                      (A)   (B)

like England's

when they decided <u>to settle</u> the North American continent
                      (C)

<u>instead of</u> the South American continent.
    (D)

illogical comparasion.

42 ## Addition—*Besides*

Remember that *besides* means in addition to. *Beside* means *near*.

excep means exclusive

besides	noun adjective	
Besides	our dog,	we have two cats and a canary
Besides	white,	we stock green and blue

	beside	noun
We sat	beside	the teacher

Avoid using *beside* instead of *besides* to mean *in addition*.

EXAMPLES

beside is different from besides.

INCORRECT: Beside Marge, three couples are invited.
  CORRECT: <u>Besides</u> Marge, three couples are invited.

INCORRECT: Beside Domino's, four other pizza places deliver.
  CORRECT: <u>Besides</u> Domino's, four other pizza places deliver.

INCORRECT: To lead a well-balanced life, you need to have other
       interests beside studying.
  CORRECT: To lead a well balanced life, you need to have other
       interests <u>besides</u> studying.

INCORRECT: Beside taxi service, there isn't any public
       transportation in town.
  CORRECT: <u>Besides</u> taxi service, there isn't any public
       transportation in town.

INCORRECT: Janice has lots of friends beside her roommate.
  CORRECT: Janice has lots of friends <u>besides</u> her roommate.

EXERCISES

Part A: Choose the correct answer.

_____ a mayor, many city governments employ a city manager.
- (A) Beside
- (B) Besides
- (C) And
- (D) Also

Part B: Choose the incorrect word or phrase and correct it.

To receive a degree from an American university, one must take
   (A)

many courses beside those in one's major field.
     (B)   (C)   (D)

43   Cause—*Because of* and *Because*

Remember that *because of* is a prepositional phrase. It introduces a noun or a noun phrase. *Because* is a conjunction. It introduces a clause with a subject and a verb.

	because	S	V
They decided to stay at home	because	the weather	was bad
or			
	because of	noun	
They decided to stay at home	because of	the weather	

Avoid using *because of* before a subject and verb. Avoid using *because* before a noun which is not followed by a verb.

EXAMPLES

INCORRECT: Classes will be canceled tomorrow because a national holiday.

CORRECT: Classes will be canceled tomorrow because it is a national holiday.

or

Classes will be canceled tomorrow <u>because of</u> <u>a national holiday</u>.

INCORRECT:	She was absent because of her cold was worse.
CORRECT:	She was absent <u>because</u> her cold was worse.

or

She was absent <u>because of</u> her cold.

INCORRECT:	John's family is very happy because his being awarded a scholarship.
CORRECT:	John's family is very happy <u>because</u> <u>he has been</u> <u>awarded</u> a scholarship.

or

John's family is very happy <u>because of</u> his being <u>awarded</u> a scholarship.

INCORRECT:	She didn't buy it because of the price was too high.
CORRECT:	She didn't buy it <u>because</u> <u>the price was</u> too high.

or

She didn't buy it <u>because of</u> the <u>price</u>.

INCORRECT:	It was difficult to see the road clearly because the rain.
CORRECT:	It was difficult to see the road clearly <u>because</u> <u>it was</u> <u>raining</u>.

or

It was difficult to see the road clearly <u>because of</u> the rain.

EXERCISES

Part A: Choose the correct answer.

_____ in the cultivation of a forest, trees need more careful planning than any other crop does.

(A) Because the time and area involved
(B) For the time and area involving
(C) Because of the time and area involved
(D) As a cause of the time and area involved

Part B: Choose the incorrect word or phrase and correct it.

because

Many roads and railroads <u>were built</u> in the 1880s <u>because of</u> the
             (A)   (B)   (C)

industrial cities needed a network <u>to link</u> them with sources of
                                (D)

supply.

44   Correlative Conjunctions—Inclusives *not only . . . but also*

Remember that *not only . . . but also* are correlative conjunctions. They are used together to include two parallel structures (two nouns, adjectives, verbs, adverbs).

	not only	parallel structure	but also	parallel structure
One should take	not only	cash	but also	traveler's checks
Checks are	not only	safer	but also	more convenient

Avoid using *only not* instead of *not only.* Avoid using *but* instead of *but also.*

Avoid using the incorrect pattern:

not only	parallel structure	but	parallel structure	also
not only	cash	but	traveler's checks	also
not only	safer	but	more convenient	also

EXAMPLES

INCORRECT: The program provides only not theoretical classes but also practical training.

CORRECT: The program provides <u>not only</u> theoretical classes <u>but also</u> practical training.

INCORRECT: The new models are not only less expensive but more efficient also.

CORRECT: The new models are <u>not only</u> less expensive <u>but also</u> more efficient.

INCORRECT: The objective is not to identify the problem but also to solve it.

CORRECT: The objective is <u>not only</u> to identify the problem <u>but also</u> to solve it.

INCORRECT: Not only her parents but her brothers and sisters also live in Wisconsin.

CORRECT: <u>Not only</u> her parents <u>but also</u> her brothers and sisters live in Wisconsin.

INCORRECT: To complete his physical education credits, John took not only swimming also golf.

CORRECT: To complete his physical education credits, John took <u>not only</u> swimming <u>but also</u> golf.

EXERCISES

Part A: Choose the correct answer.

Amniocentesis can be used not only to diagnose fetal disorders _____ the sex of the unborn child with 95 percent accuracy.

(A) but determining
(B) but also determining
(C) but to determine
(D) but also to determine

Part B: Choose the incorrect word or phrase and correct it.

The deadbolt is the best lock for entry doors because it is not only
          (A)   (B)   (C)
inexpensive but installation is easy.
               (D)

Future Result—*When*

Remember that *when* introduces a clause of condition for future result.

RESULT		CONDITION		
S	V (present) V (will + verb word)	when	S	V (present)
The temperature The temperature	drops will drop	when when	the sun the sun	sets sets

Avoid using *will* instead of a present verb after *when*.

EXAMPLES

INCORRECT: I will call you when I will return from my country.
CORRECT: I will call you <u>when</u> I <u>return</u> from my country.

INCORRECT: Marilyn plans to work in her family's store when she
              will get her M.B.A.
CORRECT: Marilyn plans to work in her family's store <u>when she
            gets</u> her M.B.A.

INCORRECT: He will probably buy some more computer software
              when he will get paid.
CORRECT: He will probably buy some more computer software
            <u>when</u> he <u>gets</u> paid.

INCORRECT: She will feel a lot better when she will stop smoking.
CORRECT: She will feel a lot better <u>when she stops</u> smoking.

INCORRECT: When Gary will go to State University, he will be a
              teaching assistant.
CORRECT: <u>When Gary goes</u> to State University, he will be a
            teaching assistant.

EXERCISES

Part A: Choose the correct answer.

Bacterial spores germinate and sprout _____ favorable
conditions of temperature and food supply.

(A) when encountering of
(B) when they encounter
(C) when they will encounter
(D) when the encounter of

Part B: Choose the incorrect word or phrase and correct it.

In <u>most states</u> insurance agents <u>must pass</u> an examination
    (A)   (B)
<u>to be licensed</u> when they <u>will complete</u> their training.
   (C)   (D)

46   Indirect Questions

Remember that question words can be used as conjunctions.
Question words introduce a clause of indirect question.
Question words include the following:

who	why
what	how
what time	how long
when	how many
where	how much

S	V	question word	S	V
I	don't remember	what	her name	is

V	S		question word	S	V
Do	you	remember	what	her name	is?

Avoid using *do*, *does*, or *did* after the question word. Avoid using the verb before the subject after the question word.

EXAMPLES

INCORRECT: I didn't understood what did he say.
  CORRECT: I didn't understand <u>what</u> <u>he</u> <u>said</u>.

INCORRECT: Do you know how much do they cost?
  CORRECT: Do you know <u>how much</u> <u>they</u> <u>cost</u>?

INCORRECT: I wonder when is her birthday.
  CORRECT: I wonder <u>when</u> <u>her birthday</u> <u>is</u>.

INCORRECT: Could you please tell me where is the post office?
  CORRECT: Could you please tell me <u>where</u> <u>the post office</u> <u>is</u>?

INCORRECT: Can they tell you what time does the movie start?
  CORRECT: Can they tell you <u>what time</u> <u>the movie</u> <u>starts</u>?

EXERCISES

Part A: Choose the correct answer.

Recently, there have been several outbreaks of disease like Legionnaire's syndrome, and doctors don't know _____.
   (A) what is the cause
   (B) the cause is what
   (C) is what the cause
   (D) what the cause is

Part B: Choose the incorrect word or phrase and correct it.

In Ground Control Approach, <u>the air traffic controller</u> <u>informs</u>
                                          (A)   (B)
the pilot how far <u>is the plane</u> from <u>the touchdown point</u>.
                        (C)   (D)

47   Negative Emphasis

Remember that negatives include phrases like *not one, not once, not until, never, never again, only rarely*, and *very seldom*. Negatives answer the question, *how often?* They are used at the beginning of a statement to express emphasis. Auxiliaries must agree with verbs and subjects.

negative	auxiliary	S	V	
Never	have	I	seen	so much snow

Avoid using a subject before the auxiliary in this pattern.

EXAMPLES

INCORRECT: Never again they will stay in that hotel.
  CORRECT: Never again will they stay in that hotel.

INCORRECT: Only rarely an accident has occurred.
  CORRECT: Only rarely has an accident occurred.

INCORRECT: Very seldom a movie can hold my attention like this one.

  CORRECT: Very seldom can a movie hold my attention like this one.

INCORRECT: Not one paper she has finished on time.
  CORRECT: Not one paper has she finished on time.

INCORRECT: Not once Steve and Jan have invited us to their house.

  CORRECT: Not once have Steve and Jan invited us to their house.

EXERCISES

Part A: Choose the correct answer.

Not until the Triassic Period _____.
    (A) the first primitive mammals did develop
    (B) did the first primitive mammals develop
    (C) did develop the first primitive mammals
    (D) the first primitive mammals develop

Part B: Chose the incorrect word or phrase and correct it.

Only rarely wins the same major league baseball team the
  (A)   (B)
World Series two years in a row.
             (C)   (D)

48   Duration—*For* and *Since*

Remember that *for* is used before a quantity of time. *For* expresses duration. *For* answers the question, *how long?* *Since* is used before a specific time. *Since* expresses duration too, but *since* answers the question, *beginning when?*

Remember that a quantity of time may be several days—a month, two years, etc. A specific time may be Wednesday, July, 1960, etc. You will notice that the structure *HAVE* and a participle is often used with adverbs of duration.

S	HAVE	participle		for	quantity of time
She	has	been	in the U.S.	for	six months

S	HAVE	participle		since	specific time
She	has	been	in the U.S.	since	June

Avoid using *for* before specific times. Avoid using *before* after HAVE and a participle.

EXAMPLES

INCORRECT: Mary has been on a diet since three weeks.
  CORRECT: Mary has been on a diet <u>for</u> three weeks.

INCORRECT: She has been living here before April.
  CORRECT: She has been living here <u>since</u> April.

INCORRECT: We haven't seen him since almost a year.
  CORRECT: We haven't seen him <u>for</u> almost a year.

INCORRECT: We have known each other before 1974.
  CORRECT: We have known each other <u>since</u> 1974.

INCORRECT: He has studied English since five years.
  CORRECT: He has studied English <u>for</u> five years.

EXERCISES

Part A: Choose the correct answer.

Penguins, the most highly specialized of all aquatic birds, may live _____ twenty years.
  (A) before
  (B) since
  (C) for
  (D) from

Part B: Choose the incorrect word or phrase and correct it.

Because national statistics on crime have only been kept
Smaller <u>for 1930,</u> <u>it</u> is not possible <u>to make</u> judgments about crime
   (A)   (B)   (C)
<u>during the early years</u> of the nation.
        (D)

49   Generalization—*As a Whole* and *Wholly*

Remember that *as a whole* means generally. *Wholly* means completely. *As a whole* is often used at the beginning of a sentence or a clause. *Wholly* is often used after the auxiliary or main verb.

generally as a whole	S	V	
As a whole	the news	is	correct

S	V	completely wholly	
The news	is	wholly	correct

Avoid using *wholly* instead of *as a whole* at the beginning of a sentence or clause to mean generally. Avoid using *as whole* instead of *as a whole*.

EXAMPLES

INCORRECT: Wholly, we are in agreement.
  CORRECT: <u>As a whole,</u> we are in agreement.
             (generally)

INCORRECT: The house and all of its contents was as a whole consumed by the fire.
  CORRECT: The house and all of its contents was <u>wholly</u> consumed by the fire.
             (generally)

INCORRECT: The teams are not rated equally, but, wholly, they are evenly matched.
  CORRECT: The teams are not rated equally, but, <u>as a whole,</u> they are evenly matched.
             (generally)

INCORRECT: Wholly, Dan's operation proved to be successful.
  CORRECT: <u>As a whole,</u> Dan's operation proved to be successful.
                    (generally)

INCORRECT: As whole, people try to be helpful to tourists.
  CORRECT: <u>As a whole,</u> people try to be helpful to tourists.
                    (generally)

EXERCISES

Part A: Choose the correct answer.

_____ the Gulf Stream is warmer than the ocean water
surrounding it.
  (A) Wholly
  (B) Whole
  (C) As a whole
  (D) A whole as

Part B: Choose the incorrect word or phrase and correct it.

Although <u>there are</u> exceptions, <u>as whole</u>, the male of the bird
                (A)   (B)
species is <u>more</u> <u>brilliantly</u> colored.
                (C)   (D)

50 Sentences and Clauses

Remember that a main clause, also called an independent
clause, can function as a separate sentence. A subordinate clause,
also called a dependent clause, must be attached to a main clause.
A dependent clause is often marked with the clause marker *that.*

SENTENCE		
Main Clause (Sentence)	Clause Marker - - - - - - - - - - - Dependent Clause	
We were glad	that	the box came

Avoid using the clause marker with dependent clauses as sentences. Avoid using the clause marker *that* with a sentence that has no dependent clause following it.

EXAMPLES

INCORRECT:	Utensils and condiments that are found on the table by the door.
CORRECT:	<u>Utensils and condiments</u> <u>are found</u> on the table by the door.
INCORRECT:	During final exam week, that the library when opening all night.
CORRECT:	During final exam week, <u>the library</u> <u>is open</u> all night.
INCORRECT:	The weather that is very rainy this time of year.
CORRECT:	<u>The weather</u> <u>is</u> very rainy this time of year.
INCORRECT:	All of the dorms that are located on East Campus.
CORRECT:	All of the <u>dorms</u> <u>are located</u> on East Campus.
INCORRECT:	During our vacation, that we suspended the newspaper delivery.
CORRECT:	During our vacation, <u>we</u> <u>suspended</u> the newspaper delivery.

EXERCISES

Part A: Choose the correct answer.

Of all the cities in Texas, _____.
- (A) that San Antonio is probably the most picturesque
- (B) San Antonio is probably the most picturesque
- (C) probably San Antonio the most picturesque
- (D) the most picturesque probably that San Antonio

Part B: Choose the incorrect word or phrase and correct it.

<u>Thunder</u> <u>that</u> is audible from distances as far away <u>as</u> ten <u>miles</u>.
  (A)   (B)   (C)   (D)

STYLE

Style is a general term that includes elements larger than a single grammatical pattern or structure. In most grammar books, *style* means *sentence structure*—that is, how the parts of a sentence relate to each other.

Some of the most important elements of style are summarized in this review section.

Point of View—Verbs

In all patterns, maintain a point of view, either present or past.

Avoid changing from present to past tense, or from past to present tense in the same sentence.

EXAMPLES

INCORRECT: He was among the few who want to continue working on the project.

CORRECT: He <u>is</u> among the few who <u>want</u> to continue working on the project.

or

He <u>was</u> among the few who <u>wanted</u> to continue working on the project.

INCORRECT: It is an accepted custom for a man to open the door when he accompanied a woman.

CORRECT: It <u>is</u> an accepted custom for a man to open the door when he <u>accompanies</u> a woman.

or

It <u>was</u> an accepted custom for a man to open the door when he <u>accompanied</u> a woman.

INCORRECT: She closed the door and hurries away to class.

CORRECT: She <u>closes</u> the door and hurries away to class.

or

She <u>closed</u> the door and <u>hurried</u> away to class.

INCORRECT: We receive several applications a day and with them had been copies of transcripts and degrees.

CORRECT: We <u>receive</u> several applications a day and with them <u>are</u> copies of transcripts and degrees.

or

We <u>received</u> several applications a day and with them <u>were</u> copies of transcripts and degrees.

INCORRECT: Mr. Davis tried to finish his research, but he found only part of the information that he needs.

CORRECT: Mr. Davis <u>tries</u> to finish his research, but he <u>finds</u> only part of the information that he <u>needs</u>.

or

Mr. Davis <u>tried</u> to finish his research, but he <u>found</u> only part of the information that he <u>needed</u>.

EXERCISES

Part A: Choose the correct answer.

The first transistor was basically a small chip made of germanium onto one surface of which two pointed wire contacts _____ side by side.

    (A) are made
    (B) made
    (C) were made
    (D) making

Part B: Choose the incorrect word or phrase and correct it.

<u>Because</u> early balloons were at the mercy of <u>shifting</u> winds,
    (A)   (B)
they <u>are</u> not considered a practical means of transportation
     (C)
<u>until the 1850s</u>.
      (D)

Point of View—Verbs and Adverbs

In all patterns, avoid using past adverbs with verbs in the present tense.

EXAMPLES

INCORRECT: Between one thing and another, Charles does not finish typing his paper last night.

CORRECT: Between one thing and another, Charles <u>did</u> not finish typing his paper <u>last night</u>.

INCORRECT: In 1990, according to statistics from the Bureau of Census, the population of the United States is 250,000,000.

CORRECT: <u>In 1990,</u> according to statistics from the Bureau of Census, the population of the United States <u>was</u> 250,000,000.

INCORRECT: We do not receive mail yesterday because it was a holiday.

CORRECT: We <u>did</u> not receive mail <u>yesterday</u> because it <u>was</u> a holiday.

INCORRECT: Mary does not finish her homework in time to go with us to the football game yesterday afternoon.

CORRECT: Mary <u>did</u> not finish her homework in time to go with us to the football game <u>yesterday afternoon</u>.

INCORRECT: Although there are only two hundred foreign students studying at State University in 1990, there are more than five hundred now.

CORRECT: Although there <u>were</u> only two hundred foreign students studying at State University <u>in 1990,</u> there are more than five hundred now.

EXERCISES

Part A: Choose the correct answer.

Iron _____ for weapons and tools in the Bronze Age
following the Stone Age.
   (A) is generally used
   (B) generally used
   (C) was generally used
   (D) used generally

Part B: Choose the incorrect word or phrase and correct it.

The Nineteenth Amendment to the Constitution gives women
          (A)   (B)
the right to vote in the elections of 1920.   *gave*.
          (C)   (D)

3   Agreement—Modified Subject and Verb

In all patterns, there must be agreement of subject and verb.
Avoid using a verb that agrees with the modifier of a subject
instead of with the subject itself.

EXAMPLES

INCORRECT: His knowledge of languages and international
                 relations aid him in his work.

CORRECT: His knowledge of languages and international
             relations aids him in his work.

INCORRECT: The facilities at the new research library, including
                 an excellent microfilm file, is among the best in the
                 country.

CORRECT: The facilities at the new research library, including
             an excellent microfilm file, are among the best in the
             country.

INCORRECT:	All trade between the two countries were suspended pending negotiation of a new agreement.
CORRECT:	All <u>trade</u> between the two countries <u>was</u> suspended pending negotiation of a new agreement.

INCORRECT:	The production of different kinds of artificial materials are essential to the conservation of our natural resources.
CORRECT:	The <u>production</u> of different kinds of artificial materials <u>is</u> essential to the conservation of our natural resources.

INCORRECT:	Since the shipment of supplies for our experiments were delayed, we will have to reschedule our work.
CORRECT:	Since the <u>shipment</u> of supplies for our experiments <u>was</u> delayed, we will have to reschedule our work.

EXERCISES

Part A: Choose the correct answer.

Groups of <u>tissues</u>, each with its own <u>function</u>, _____ in the human body.

    (A) it makes up the organs
    (B) make up the organs
    (C) they make up the organs
    (D) makes up the organs

Part B: Choose the incorrect word or phrase and correct it.

The Zoning Improvement Plan, <u>better known as</u> zip codes,
                              (A)

<u>enable</u> postal clerks <u>to speed</u> the routing of <u>an</u> ever-increasing
  (B)   (C)   (D)
volume of mail.

4 Agreement—Subject with Appositive and Verb

Remember that there must be agreement of subject and verb. An appositive is a word or phrase that follows a noun and defines it. An appositive usually has a comma before it and a comma after it.

In all patterns, avoid using a verb that agrees with words in the appositive after a subject instead of with the subject itself.

EXAMPLES

INCORRECT: The books, an English dictionary and a chemistry text, was on the shelf yesterday.

CORRECT: The books, an English dictionary and a chemistry text, were on the shelf yesterday.

INCORRECT: Three swimmers from our team, Paul, Ed, and Jim, is in competition for medals.

CORRECT: Three swimmers from our team, Paul, Ed, and Jim, are in competition for medals.

INCORRECT: Several pets, two dogs and a cat, needs to be taken care of while we are gone.

CORRECT: Several pets, two dogs and a cat, need to be taken care of while we are gone.

INCORRECT: State University, the largest of the state-supported schools, have more than 50,000 students on main campus.

CORRECT: State University, the largest of the state-supported schools, has more than 50,000 students on main campus.

INCORRECT: This recipe, an old family secret, are an especially important part of our holiday celebrations.

CORRECT: This recipe, an old family secret, is an especially important part of our holiday celebrations.

EXERCISES

Part A: Choose the correct answer.

Cupid, one of the ancient Roman gods, _____.
   (A) were a little winged child
   (B) representing as a little winged child
   (C) was represented as a little winged child
   (D) a little winged child

Part B: Choose the incorrect word or phrase and correct it.

Columbus, Ohio, the capital of the state, <u>are</u> not only <u>the largest</u>
(A)   (B)
city in Ohio <u>but also</u> a typical metropolitan area, often <u>used</u> in
(C)   (D)
market research.

Agreement—Verb-Subject Order

There and *here* introduce verb-subject order. The verb agrees
with the subject following it.

there	V	S
There	are	the results of the election

here	V	S
Here	is	the result of the election

Avoid using a verb that does not agree with the subject.

168   REVIEW OF SECTION 2: STRUCTURE

EXAMPLES

INCORRECT:	There was ten people in line already when we arrived.
CORRECT:	There <u>were</u> <u>ten people</u> in line already when we arrived.

INCORRECT:	There have been very little rain this summer.
CORRECT:	There <u>has been</u> <u>very little rain</u> this summer.

INCORRECT:	Here are their house.
CORRECT:	Here <u>is</u> <u>their house</u>.

INCORRECT:	There has been several objections to the new policy.
CORRECT:	There <u>have been</u> <u>several objections</u> to the new policy.

INCORRECT:	I think that there were a problem.
CORRECT:	I think that there <u>was</u> <u>a problem</u>.

EXERCISES

Part A: Choose the correct answer.

In a suspension bridge _____ that carry one or more flexible cables firmly attached at each end.

- (A) there is two towers on it
- (B) there are two towers
- (C) two towers there are
- (D) towers there are two

Part B: Choose the incorrect word or phrase and correct it.

There is about 600 schools <u>in the United States</u> that <u>use</u> the
  (A)   (B)   (C)
Montessori method <u>to encourage</u> individual initiative.
                       (D)

6   Agreement—Noun and Pronoun

In all patterns, there must be agreement of noun and pronoun.

Avoid using a pronoun that does not agree in number with the noun to which it refers.

EXAMPLES

INCORRECT: If you want to leave a message for Mr. and Mrs. Carlson, I will be glad to take them.

CORRECT: If you want to leave <u>a message</u> for Mr. and Mrs. Carlson, I will be glad to take <u>it</u>.

INCORRECT: Al is interested in mathematics and their applications.

CORRECT: Al is interested in <u>mathematics</u> and <u>its</u> applications.

INCORRECT: It is easier to talk about a problem than to resolve them.

CORRECT: It is easier to talk about <u>a problem</u> than to resolve <u>it</u>.

INCORRECT: Although their visas will expire in June, they can have it extended for three months.

CORRECT: Although <u>their visas</u> will expire in June, they can have <u>them</u> extended for three months.

INCORRECT: In spite of its small size, these cameras take very good pictures.

CORRECT: In spite of <u>their</u> small size, <u>these cameras</u> take very good pictures.

Exercises

Part A: Choose the correct answer.

A college bookstore that sells used textbooks stocks
_____ along with the new ones on the shelf under the
course title.

(A) its
(B) their
(C) a
(D) them

Part B: Choose the incorrect word or phrase and correct it.

Magnesium, <u>the lightest</u> of our structural metals, has an
             (A)

important place <u>among</u> common engineering materials
           (B)

<u>because of</u> <u>their</u> weight.
  (C)   (D)

7   Agreement—Subject and Possessive Pronouns

In all patterns, there must be agreement of subject pronoun and possessive pronouns that refer to the subject.

Subject Pronouns	Possessive Pronouns
I	my
you	your
he	his
she	her
it	its
we	our
you	your
they	their

Remember that *it* refers to a small baby. Avoid using *it's* instead of *its* as a possessive pronoun. *It's* means *it is*.

EXAMPLES

INCORRECT: Those of us who are over fifty years old should get their blood pressure checked regularly.

CORRECT: <u>Those of us</u> who are over fifty years old should get <u>our</u> blood pressure checked regularly.

INCORRECT: Our neighbors know that when they go on vacation, we will get its mail for them.

CORRECT: Our neighbors know that when <u>they</u> go on vacation, we will get <u>their</u> mail for them.

INCORRECT: A mother who works outside of the home has to prepare for emergencies when she cannot be there to take care of your sick child.

CORRECT: A mother who works outside of the home has to prepare for emergencies when <u>she</u> cannot be there to take care of <u>her</u> sick child.

INCORRECT: Wine tends to lose their flavor when it has not been properly sealed.

CORRECT: Wine tends to lose <u>its</u> flavor when <u>it</u> has not been properly sealed.

INCORRECT: Optional equipment on a car can add several hundred dollars to it's resale value when you trade it in.

CORRECT: Optional equipment on a car can add several hundred dollars to <u>its</u> resale value when you trade <u>it</u> in.

EXERCISES

Part A. Choose the correct answer.

The television programs we allow _____ to watch influence their learning.
   (A) a children
   (B) our children
   (C) our child
   (D) their childs

Part B: Choose the incorrect word or phrase and correct it.

Although maple trees are <u>among</u> the most colorful varieties
                              have (A)

in the fall, they lose <u>its</u> leaves <u>sooner than</u> oak trees.
  (B)   (C)   (D)

Verbal Modifiers— *-ing* and *-ed* Forms

-ing forms and *-ed* forms may be used as verbals. Verbals function as modifiers.

An introductory verbal modifier with *-ing* or *-ed* should immediately precede the noun it modifies. Otherwise, the relationship between the noun and the modifier is unclear, and the sentence is illogical.

Avoid using a noun immediately after an introductory verbal phrase which may not be logically modified by the phrase.

EXAMPLES

INCORRECT: After graduating from City College, Professor Baker's studies were continued at State University, where he received his Ph.D. in English.

CORRECT: <u>After graduating</u> from City College, <u>Professor Baker</u> continued his studies at State University, where he received his Ph.D. in English.

INCORRECT: Returning to her room, several pieces of jewelry were missing.

CORRECT: <u>Returning</u> to her room, <u>she</u> found that several pieces of jewelry were missing.

INCORRECT: Having been delayed by heavy traffic, it was not possible for her to arrive on time.

CORRECT: <u>Having been delayed</u> by heavy traffic, <u>she</u> arrived late.

INCORRECT: Accustomed to getting up early, the new schedule
              was not difficult for him to adjust to.

  CORRECT: <u>Accustomed to getting up</u> early, <u>he</u> had no difficulty
              adjusting to the new schedule.

INCORRECT: After finishing his speech, the audience was invited
              to ask questions.

  CORRECT: <u>After finishing</u> his speech, <u>he</u> invited the audience to
              ask questions.

EXERCISES

[handwritten: ing 是表术、主动. ed "表小、被动]

Part A: Choose the correct answer.

_____ air traffic controllers guide planes through
conditions of near zero visibility.

    (A) They talk with pilots and watch their approach on radar,
    (B) Talking with pilots and watching their approach on radar,
    (C) Talk with pilots and watch their approach on radar,
    (D) When they talked with pilots and watched their approach
       on radar,

Part B: Choose the incorrect word or phrase and correct it.

[handwritten: designing]

Have designed his own plane, *The Spirit of St. Louis*, Lindbergh
     (A)

<u>flew</u> from Roosevelt Field in New York across the ocean <u>to</u> Le
  (B)   (C)

Bourget Field <u>outside Paris</u>.
         (D)

Verbal Modifiers—Infinitives of Purpose to Introduce Instructions

[handwritten: 不定词]

An infinitive that expresses purpose may be used as an introductory verbal modifier. Remember that a verb word follows the infinitive. The verb word expresses a manner to accomplish the purpose.

Avoid using a noun or *to* with an *-ing* form instead of the infinitive of purpose. Avoid using an *-ing* form or a passive construction after an introductory verbal modifier.

EXAMPLES

INCORRECT: To protect yourself from dangerous exposure to the sun's rays, using a sunscreen.

CORRECT: <u>To protect</u> yourself from dangerous exposure to the sun's rays, <u>use</u> a sunscreen.

INCORRECT: Prepare for the TOEFL, study thirty minutes every day for several months.

CORRECT: <u>To prepare</u> for the TOEFL, <u>study</u> thirty minutes every day for several months.

INCORRECT: In order to take advantage of low air fares, to buy your tickets well in advance.

CORRECT: In order <u>to take advantage</u> of low air fares, <u>buy</u> your tickets well in advance.

INCORRECT: To taking action pictures, always use a high-speed film.

CORRECT: <u>To take</u> action pictures, always <u>use</u> a high-speed film.

INCORRECT: The send letters and packages from the United States overseas, use Global Mail or DHL Delivery.

CORRECT: <u>To send</u> letters and packages from the United States overseas, <u>use</u> Global Mail or DHL Delivery.

EXERCISES

Part A: Choose the correct answer.

To relieve pressure in the skull, _____ into the blood.
   (A) you will inject a strong solution of pure glucose
   (B) to inject a strong solution of pure glucose
   (C) a strong solution of glucose will inject purely
   (D) inject a strong solution of pure glucose

Part B: Choose the incorrect word or phrase and correct it.

To estimate how much <u>it will cost</u> <u>to build</u> a home, <u>finding</u> the
                        (A)   (B)   (C)

total square footage of the house and multiply <u>by cost</u> per
                                                    (D)

square foot.

10   Parallel Structure—In a Series

In all patterns, ideas of equal importance should be expressed
by the same grammatical structure.

Avoid expressing ideas in a series with different structures.

EXAMPLES

INCORRECT: Jane is young, enthusiastic, and she has talent.
CORRECT: Jane is <u>young,</u> <u>enthusiastic,</u> and <u>talented.</u>

INCORRECT: We learned to read the passages carefully and
                 underlining the main ideas.
CORRECT: We learned to <u>read</u> the passages carefully and
                 <u>to underline</u> the main ideas.

INCORRECT: The duties of the new secretary are to answer the
                 telephone, to type letters, and bookkeeping.
CORRECT: The duties of the new secretary are <u>to answer</u> the
                 telephone, <u>to type</u> letters, and <u>to do</u> the bookkeeping.

INCORRECT: The patient's symptoms were fever, dizziness, and
                 his head hurt.
CORRECT: The patient's symptoms were <u>fever,</u> <u>dizziness,</u> and
                 <u>headaches.</u>

INCORRECT: Professor Williams enjoys teaching and to write.
CORRECT: Professor Williams enjoys <u>teaching</u> and <u>writing.</u>

EXERCISES

Part A: Choose the correct answer.

In a hot, sunny climate, man acclimatizes by eating less, drinking more liquids, wearing lighter clothing, and _____.

    (A) skin changes that darken

    (B) his skin may darken

    (C) experiencing a darkening of the skin

    (D) darkens his skin

Part B: Choose the incorrect word or phrase and correct it.

The aims of the European Economic Community are to
eliminate tariffs between member countries; developing
    (A)   (B)
common policies for agriculture, labor, welfare, trade, and
transportation; and to abolish trusts and cartels.
    (C)   (D)

PROBLEM 11

Parallel Structure—After Correlative Conjunctions

Remember that ideas of equal importance are introduced by correlative conjunctions:

both . . . and
not only . . . but also

Avoid expressing ideas after correlative conjunctions with different structures.

EXAMPLES

INCORRECT:	She is not only famous in the United States but also abroad.
CORRECT:	She is famous not only <u>in the United States</u> but also <u>abroad</u>.
INCORRECT:	The exam tested both listening and to read.
CORRECT:	The exam tested both <u>listening</u> and <u>reading</u>.
INCORRECT:	He is not only intelligent but also he is creative.
CORRECT:	He is not only <u>intelligent</u> but also <u>creative</u>.
INCORRECT:	Flying is not only faster but also it is safer than traveling by car.
CORRECT:	Flying is not only <u>faster</u> but also <u>safer</u> than traveling by car.
INCORRECT:	John registered for both Electrical Engineering 500 and to study Mathematics 390.
CORRECT:	John registered for both <u>Electrical Engineering</u> 500 and <u>Mathematics</u> 390.

EXERCISES

Part A: Choose the correct answer.

Both historically and _____, Ontario is the heartland of Canada.

(A) in its geography
(B) geographically
(C) also its geography
(D) geography

Part B: Choose the incorrect word or phrase and correct it.

The cacao bean <u>was cultivated</u> <u>by the Aztecs</u> not only to drink
             (A)   (B)

<u>but also</u> <u>currency</u>.
   (C)   (D)

12 Redundancy—Unnecessary Phrases

In all patterns, prefer simple, direct sentences to complicated, indirect sentences. Find the Subject-Verb-Complement-Modifier, and determine whether the other words are useful or unnecessary.

S	V	C	M
Lee	learned	English	quickly

Avoid using an adjective with such phrases as *in character* or *in nature*.

Avoid using the redundant pattern instead of an adverb such as *quickly.*

in a	adjective	manner
in a	quick	manner

EXAMPLES

INCORRECT: The key officials who testified before the Senate committee responded in a manner that was evasive.

CORRECT: The key officials who testified before the Senate committee responded evasively.

INCORRECT: Mr. Davis knows a great deal in terms of the condition of the situation.

CORRECT: Mr. Davis knows a great deal about the situation.

INCORRECT: It was a problem which was very difficult in character and very delicate in nature.

CORRECT: The problem was difficult and delicate.

INCORRECT: The disease was very serious in the nature of it.

CORRECT: The disease was very serious.

INCORRECT: Mary had always behaved in a responsible manner.

CORRECT: Mary had always behaved responsibly.

EXERCISES

Part A: Choose the correct answer.

Waitresses and waiters who serve _____ deserve at least a 20 percent tip.
   (A) in a courteous manner
   (B) courteously
   (C) with courtesy in their manner
   (D) courteous

Part B: Choose the incorrect word or phrase and correct it.

Hummingbirds move <u>their</u> wings so <u>rapid a way</u> that they

                   (A)   (B)

appear <u>to be hanging</u> <u>in the air</u>.

         (C)   (D)

13 Redundancy—Repetition of Words with the Same Meaning

In all patterns, avoid using words with the same meaning consecutively in a sentence.

EXAMPLES

INCORRECT: The money that I have is sufficient enough for my needs.

CORRECT: The money that I have is <u>sufficient</u> for my needs

INCORRECT: Bill asked the speaker to repeat again because he had not heard him the first time.

CORRECT: Bill asked the speaker <u>to repeat</u> because he had not heard him the first time.

INCORRECT: The class advanced forward rapidly.

CORRECT: The class <u>advanced</u> rapidly.

INCORRECT: She returned back to her hometown after she had finished her degree.

CORRECT: She <u>returned</u> to her hometown after she had finished her degree.

INCORRECT: I am nearly almost finished with this chapter.

CORRECT: I am <u>nearly</u> finished with this chapter.

or

I am <u>almost</u> finished with this chapter.

EXERCISES

Part A: Choose the correct answer.

Famous for his _____ punctuation, typography, and language, Edward Estlin Cummings published his collected poems in 1954.

   (A) new innovations for

   (B) innovations in

   (C) newly approached

   (D) innovations newly approached in

Part B: Choose the incorrect word or phrase and correct it.

The idea of a submarine is <u>an old ancient one</u>, dating from
                                    (A)

<u>as early as</u> <u>the fifteenth century</u> when Drebbel and Da Vinci
   (B)   (C)

<u>made</u> preliminary drawings.
  (D)

14 Redundancy—Repetition of Noun by Pronoun

In all patterns, avoid using a noun and the pronoun that refers to it consecutively in a sentence. Avoid using a pronoun after the noun it refers to, and *that*.

EXAMPLES

INCORRECT: My teacher he said to listen to the news on the radio in order to practice listening comprehension.

CORRECT: <u>My teacher</u> <u>said</u> to listen to the news on the radio in order to practice listening comprehension.

INCORRECT: Steve he plans to go into business with his father.

CORRECT: <u>Steve</u> <u>plans</u> to go into business with his father.

INCORRECT: My sister she found a store that imported food from our country.

CORRECT: <u>My sister</u> <u>found</u> a store that imported food from our country.

INCORRECT: Hospitalization that it covers room, meals, nursing, and additional hospital expenses such as lab tests, X-rays, and medicine.

CORRECT: <u>Hospitalization</u> <u>covers</u> room, meals, nursing, and additional hospital expenses such as lab tests, X-rays, and medicine.

INCORRECT: Anne she wants to visit Washington, D.C., before she goes home.

CORRECT: <u>Anne</u> <u>wants</u> to visit Washington, D.C., before she goes home.

EXERCISES

Part A: Choose the correct answer.

A perennial is _____ for more than two years, such as trees and shrubs.

(A) any plant that it continues to grow

(B) any plant it continuing to grow

(C) any plant that continues to grow

(D) any plant continuing growth

Part B: Choose the incorrect word or phrase and correct it.

Advertising it provides most of the income for magazines,
           (A)   (B)   (C)

newspapers, radio, and television in the United States today.
                                            (D)

15   Transitive and Intransitive Verbs— *Raise* and *Rise*

A transitive verb is a verb that takes a complement. An intransitive verb is a verb that does not take a complement.

The following pairs of verbs can be confusing. Remember that *raise* is a transitive verb; it takes a complement. *Rise* is an intransitive verb; it does not take a complement.

Transitive		
Verb word	*Past*	*Participle*
raise	raised	raised

Intransitive		
Verb word	*Past*	*Participle*
rise	rose	risen

Remember that *to raise* means to move to a higher place or to cause to rise. *To rise* means to go up or to increase.

Raise and rise are also used as nouns. A *raise* means an increase in salary. A *rise* means an increase in price, worth, quantity, or degree.

S	RAISE	C	M
Heavy rain Heavy rain	raises raised	the water level of the reservoir the water level of the reservoir	every spring last week

S	RISE	C	M
The water level The water level	rises rose		when it rains every spring when it rained last week

EXAMPLES

INCORRECT: The cost of living has raised 3 percent in the past year.

CORRECT: The cost of living has risen 3 percent in the past year.

INCORRECT: The flag is risen at dawn by an honor guard.

CORRECT: The flag is raised at dawn by an honor guard.
(An honor guard raises the flag.)

INCORRECT: Kay needs to rise her grades if she wants to get into graduate school.

CORRECT: Kay needs to raise her grades if she wants to get into graduate school.

INCORRECT: The landlord has risen the rent.

CORRECT: The landlord has raised the rent.

INCORRECT: The smoke that is raising from that oil refinery is black.

CORRECT: The smoke that is rising from that oil refinery is black.

rise vi   raise vt

EXERCISES

Part A: Choose the correct answer.

The average elevation of the Himalayas is twenty thousand feet, and Mount Everest _____ to more than twenty-nine thousand feet at its apex.

(A) raises
(B) rises
(C) roses
(D) arises

Part B: Choose the incorrect word or phrase and correct it.

When the temperature is <u>risen</u> to <u>the burning point</u> without a
                    (A)   (B)
source of escape <u>for the heat</u>, spontaneous combustion <u>occurs</u>.
           (C)   (D)

16   Transitive and Intransitive Verbs— *Lay* and *Lie*

Remember that *lay* is a transitive verb; it takes a complement. *Lie* is an intransitive verb; it does not take a complement.

Transitive		
Verb word	*Past*	*Participle*
lay	laid	laid

Intransitive		
Verb word	*Past*	*Participle*
lie	lay	lain

Remember that *to lay* means to put, to place, or to cause to lie. *To lie* means to recline or to occupy a place.

The past form of the verb *to lie* is *lay*.

S	LAY	C	M
The postman	lays	the mail	on the table every day
The postman	laid	the mail	on the table yesterday

S	LIE	C	M
He	lies		on the sofa to rest every day after work
He	lay		on the sofa to rest yesterday after work

EXAMPLES

INCORRECT: Her coat was laying on the chair.

CORRECT: Her coat was lying on the chair.

INCORRECT: I have lain your notebook on the table by the door so that you won't forget it.

CORRECT: I have laid your notebook on the table by the door so that you won't forget it.

INCORRECT: Key West lays off the coast of Florida.

CORRECT: Key West lies off the coast of Florida.

INCORRECT: Why don't you lay down for awhile?

CORRECT: Why don't you lie down for awhile?

INCORRECT: Linda always forgets where she lies her glasses.

CORRECT: Linda always forgets where she lays her glasses.

EXERCISES

Part A: Choose the correct answer.

The geographic position of North America, _____ in the early days of the European settlement.

(A) laying between the Atlantic and the Pacific Oceans, isolating it

(B) isolating it as it laid between the Atlantic and the Pacific Oceans

(C) lying between the Atlantic and the Pacific Oceans, isolated it

(D) isolating it between the Atlantic and the Pacific Oceans as it was layed

Part B: Choose the incorrect word or phrase and correct it.

Melanin, a pigment that <u>lays</u> under the skin, <u>is</u> responsible for
　　　　　　　　　　　(A)　　　　　　　(B)
skin color, including the variations that <u>occur</u> <u>among</u> different
　　　　　　　　　　　　　　　　　　(C)　　(D)
races.

17 Transitive and Intransitive Verbs— *Set* and *Sit*

Remember that *set* is a transitive verb; it takes a complement. *Sit* is an intransitive verb; it does not take a complement.

Transitive		
Verb word	*Past*	*Participle*
set	set	set

Intransitive		
Verb word	*Past*	*Participle*
sit	sat	sat

Remember that *to set* means to put, to place, or to cause to sit. *To sit* means to occupy a place on a chair or a flat surface.

S	SET	C	M
The students	set	the lab equipment	on the table every class
The students	set	the lab equipment	on the table last class period

S	SIT	C	M
The equipment	sits		on the table every class
The equipment	sat		on the table last class period

EXAMPLES

INCORRECT:	Please sit the telephone on the table by the bed.
CORRECT:	Please <u>set the telephone</u> on the table by the bed.

INCORRECT:	Won't you set down?
CORRECT:	Won't <u>you sit</u> down?

INCORRECT:	Their house sets on a hill overlooking a lake.
CORRECT:	Their <u>house sits</u> on a hill overlooking a lake.

INCORRECT:	Let's sit your suitcases out of the way.
CORRECT:	Let's <u>set your suitcases</u> out of the way.

INCORRECT:	Terry has set there waiting for us for almost an hour.
CORRECT:	<u>Terry has sat</u> there waiting for us for almost an hour.

EXERCISES

Part A: Choose the correct answer.

When Jacqueline Kennedy was first lady, she collected many beautiful antiques and _____ them among the original pieces in the White House.

(A) sat
(B) set
(C) sit
(D) sits

Part B: Choose the incorrect word or phrase and correct it.

Hyde Park, the family estate <u>of Franklin D. Roosevelt,</u> <u>sets</u> on
                                        (A)   (B)
top of a bluff <u>overlooking</u> <u>the Hudson River</u>.
                   (C)   (D)

sits

18   Similar Verbs—*Make* and *Do*

Verb word	Past	Participle
do	*did*	*done*

Verb word	Past	Participle
make	*made*	*made*

Remember that *to do* and *to make* have similar meanings, but *do* is often used before complements that describe work and chores. *To make* is often used before complements that are derived from verbs.

DO an assignment	*MAKE an agreement*	*(to agree)*
the dishes	*an announcement*	*(to announce)*
a favor	*an attempt*	*(to attempt)*
homework	*a decision*	*(to decide)*
the laundry	*a discovery*	*(to discover)*
a paper	*an offer*	*(to offer)*
research	*a profit*	*(to profit)*
work	*a promise*	*(to promise)*

S	DO	C	M
We	do	our homework	before class every day
We	did	our homework	before class yesterday

S	MAKE	C	M
We	make	an agreement	with each other every semester
We	made	an agreement	with each other last semester

EXAMPLES

INCORRECT:	I really don't mind making the homework for this class.
CORRECT:	I really don't mind <u>doing</u> <u>the homework</u> for this class.
INCORRECT:	Did you do a mistake?
CORRECT:	Did you <u>make</u> <u>a mistake</u>?
INCORRECT:	Please make me a favor.
CORRECT:	Please <u>do</u> me <u>a favor</u>.
INCORRECT:	Are they doing progress on the new road?
CORRECT:	Are they <u>making</u> <u>progress</u> on the new road?
INCORRECT:	Have you done any interesting discoveries while you were doing your research?
CORRECT:	Have you <u>made</u> any interesting <u>discoveries</u> while you were <u>doing</u> your <u>research?</u>

EXERCISES

Part A: Choose the correct answer.

The president usually _____ unless his press secretary approves it.

    (A) doesn't do a statement
    (B) doesn't make a statement
    (C) doesn't statement
    (D) no statement

Part B: Choose the incorrect word or phrase and correct it.

A <u>one hundred-horsepower</u> tractor can make the work of
        (A)   (B) (C)
<u>a large number</u> of horses.
      (D)

19 **Prepositional Idioms**

Prefer these idioms	Avoid these errors
accede to	accede on, by
according to	according
approve of	approve for
ashamed of	ashamed with
bored with	bored of
capable of	capable to
compete with	compete together
composed of	composed from
concerned with	concerned of
conscious of	conscious for
depend on	depend in, to
effects on	effects in
equal to	equal as
except for	excepting for
from now on	after now on
from time to time	for, when time to time
frown on	frown to
glance at, through	glance
incapable of	incapable to
in conflict	on conflict
inferior to	inferior with
in the habit of	in the habit to
in the near future	at the near future
knowledge of	knowledge on
near; next to	near to
of the opinion	in opinion
on top of	on top
opposite	opposite over
prior to	prior
regard to	regard of
related to	related with
respect for	respect of
responsible for	responsible
similar to	similar as
since	ever since
until	up until
with regard to	with regard of

EXAMPLES

INCORRECT:	Excepting for the Gulf Coast region, most of the nation will have very pleasant weather tonight and tomorrow.
CORRECT:	<u>Except for</u> the Gulf Coast region, most of the nation will have very pleasant weather tonight and tomorrow.
INCORRECT:	In recent years, educators have become more concerned of bilingualism.
CORRECT:	In recent years, educators have become more <u>concerned with</u> bilingualism.
INCORRECT:	He always does what he pleases, without regard of the rules and regulations.
CORRECT:	He always does what he pleases, without <u>regard to</u> the rules and regulations.
INCORRECT:	The bank opposite over the university isn't open on Saturdays.
CORRECT:	The bank <u>opposite</u> the university isn't open on Saturdays.
INCORRECT:	The customs of other countries are not inferior with those of our own country.
CORRECT:	The customs of other countries are not <u>inferior to</u> those of our own country.

EXERCISES

Part A: Choose the correct answer.

_____ discovery of insulin, it was not possible to treat diabetes.

(A) Prior to the
(B) Prior
(C) The prior
(D) To prior

Part B: Choose the incorrect word or phrase and correct it.

The price of gold depends in several factors, including supply
  (A)   (B)   (C)

on

and demand in relation to the value of the dollar.
                (D)

Parts of Speech

Although it is usually very easy to identify the parts of speech, word families can be confusing. Word families are groups of words with similar meanings and spellings. Each word in the family is a different part of speech. For example, *agreement* is a noun; *agreeable* is an adjective; to *agree* is a verb.

The endings of words can help you identify the parts of speech.

Nouns Derived from Verbs

Verb	Ending	Noun
store	*-age*	*storage*
accept	*-ance*	*acceptance*
insist	*-ence*	*insistence*
agree	*-ment*	*agreement*
authorize	*-sion/-tion*	*authorization*

Nouns Derived from Adjectives

Adjective	Ending	Noun
convenient	*-ce*	*convenience*
redundant	*-cy*	*redundancy*
opposite	*-tion*	*opposition*
soft	*-ness*	*softness*
durable	*-ty*	*durability*

Adjectives Derived from Nouns

Noun	Ending	Adjective
possibility	-able/-ible	possible
intention	-al	intentional
distance	-ant	distant
frequency	-ent	frequent
juice	-y	juicy

juicy

Adverbs Derived from Adjectives

Adjective	Ending	Adverb
efficient	-ly	efficiently

efficiently

___
EXAMPLES

INCORRECT: The agreeing is not legal unless everyone signs his name.

CORRECT: The <u>agreement</u> is not legal unless everyone signs his name.

INCORRECT: Even young children begin to show able in mathematics.

CORRECT: Even young children begin to show <u>ability</u> in mathematics.

INCORRECT: Arranging have been made for the funeral.

CORRECT: <u>Arrangements</u> have been made for the funeral.

INCORRECT: A free educating is guaranteed to every citizen.

CORRECT: A free <u>education</u> is guaranteed to every citizen.

INCORRECT: The develop of hybrids has increased yields.

CORRECT: The <u>development</u> of hybrids has increased yields.

EXERCISES

Part A: Choose the correct answer.

Unless protected areas are established, the Bengal tiger, the blue whale, and the California condor face _____ of extinction.
(A) possible
(B) the possibility
(C) to be possible
(D) possibly

Part B: Choose the incorrect word or phrase and correct it.

Because blood from different individuals may different in the
(A)   (B)
type of antigen on the surface of the red cells and the type of
antibody in the plasma, a dangerous reaction can occur between
                                                        (C)
the donor and recipient in a blood transfusion.
        (D)

TYPES OF QUESTIONS

Multiple-Choice Questions

All of the questions on both the Paper-Based TOEFL and the Computer-Based TOEFL are multiple-choice. There are no computer-assisted questions with special directions.

Although the structure questions in this book are numbered, and the answer choices are lettered A, B, C, and D, the same questions on the CD-ROM that supplements the larger version of the book; *Barron's How to Prepare the TOEFL*, are not numbered and lettered. You need the numbers and letters in the book to refer to the Answer Key, the Explanatory Answers, and the Transcript for the Listening section. On the CD-ROM, you can refer to other chapters by clicking on the screen. The questions on the CD-ROM are like those on the Computer-Based TOEFL.

Paper-Based TOEFL

1. If water is heated to 121 degrees F, _____ as steam.
    (A)   it will boil and escape
    (B)   it is boiling and escaping
    (C)   it boil and escape
    (D)   it would boil and escape

2. If <u>water</u> freezes, <u>it</u> <u>has become</u> <u>a</u> solid.
       (A)   (B)   (C)   (D)

Answer Sheet

1. ● Ⓑ Ⓒ Ⓒ
2. Ⓐ Ⓑ ● Ⓓ

Computer-Based TOEFL

If water is heated to 121 degrees F, _____ as steam.

● it will boil and escape
○ it is boiling and escaping
○ it boil and escape
○ it would boil and escape

If <u>water</u> freezes, <u>it</u> has become

a solid.

Computer Tutorial for the Structure Section

In order to succeed on the Computer Based TOEFL, you must understand the computer vocabulary used for the test, and you must be familiar with the icons on the computer screens that you will see on the test. First, review the vocabulary that you learned in the Tutorial for Section 1 on pages 62–63. The same vocabulary is used for Section 2. Then study the computer screens in this Tutorial.

Testing Tools: Review of Vocabulary, Icons, and Keys

The following words are from the list of general vocabulary for the Computer-Based TOEFL introduced in the previous chapter. Using the word list, fill in the blanks in the ten sentences.

Arrow	**Mouse**
Click	**Mouse Pad**
Confirm Answer	**Next**
Dismiss Directions	**Oval**
Help (Question mark)	**Time (Clock)**
Icon	

1. A _____ is a small control with a button on it.

2. A _____ is a rectangular pad where you move the mouse.

3. An _____ is a marker on the screen that shows you where you are moving on the computer.

4. To _____ is to depress the button on the mouse. You _____ the mouse to make changes on the screen.

5. An _____ is a small picture or word or phrase in a box. Move the arrow to the _____ to tell the computer what to do.

6. Click on _____ to remove the directions from the screen.

7. Click on an _____ to choose an answer to one of the multiple-choice questions.

8. Click on _____, then click on _____ to see the next question.

9. Click on _____ to see a list of the icons and directions.

10. Click on _____ to hide or show the time you have left to finish the section of the test you are working on.

Computer Screens for Section 2

View the directions
with every question

10:15	Structure	1 of 20

When
finished
reading
directions
click on the
icon below

Dismiss
Directions

Directions: Click on the one word or phrase that best completes the sentence.

The Palo Verde tree _____ in spring.

● has beautiful yellow blossoms
○ beautiful yellow blossoms
○ having beautiful yellow blossoms
○ with beautiful yellow blossoms

Time

? Help   Answer Confirm   Next ➡

TIP: There are only two types of questions in Section 2. After you have read and understood the directions for both types of questions in this Tutorial, you will not need to read the top part of the screen every time.

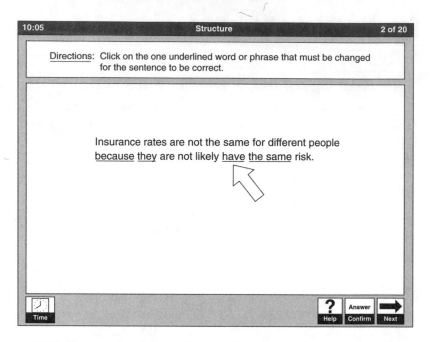

Directions: Click on the one underlined word or phrase that must be changed for the sentence to be correct.

Insurance rates are not the same for different people because they are not likely have the same risk.

Time   ?   Answer   ➡
            Help Confirm   Next

TIP: Be sure to click on **Next** before you click on **Answer Confirm.** If you do not click on these two icons in the correct order, the next question will not appear.

Simulations for Section 2

In order to prepare for the experience that you will have on the Computer-Based TOEFL, you can use the CD-ROM that supplements the larger version of this book, *Barron's How to Prepare for the TOEFL.* Locate the Structure section on the Model Tests. The computer will simulate the Structure section on the Computer-Based TOEFL. These Model Tests are computer-assisted.

As part of your study plan, be sure to review all of the questions in all of the Model Tests. Use the Explanatory Answers on the CD-ROM or on pages 377–420. Refer to the Review of Structure on the CD-ROM or on pages 75–194 of this book. Finally, if you have the CD-ROM, take the Cumulative Model Test. This test is computer-adaptive, which means that the computer will select questions for you at your level of language proficiency.

If you choose not to purchase the larger version of this book, or you do not have a computer, you can still simulate some of the features of the Computer-Based TOEFL. Section 2 in the Model Tests in Chapter 7 of this book presents both types of questions for the Structure section randomly. This is different from the Paper-Based TOEFL. You can become accustomed to making a quick decision about the kind of answer required—completion or correction.

Advice for the Structure Section: Computer-Based TOEFL

Become familiar with the directions. The two types of questions will appear at random. If you forget how to answer, look at the top of the screen. Directions will appear at the top of every screen for each question. To save time, learn to recognize the format for each question type, and be ready to respond without looking at the directions.

Move efficiently through the questions. In order to go to the next question, you must click on **Next** and then **Confirm Answer**. If you only click on **Next**, you will not be able to move to the next question. A screen will remind you to return to the previous question. You must enter an answer before you go to the next question. Click on **Return to Question** to move back to the question that you did not answer. Try to answer all questions without being referred to the **Return to Question** screen.

Change your answer before you confirm it. After you click on your answer and see the dark oval or dark box, you can still change your answer. Just click on a different choice. But remember that you cannot change your answer after you click on **Confirm Answer**. This means that you cannot go back to previous questions and change the answers. You must choose your answer, click on your choice, click on **Next**, click on **Confirm Answer**, and move to the next question.

Do your best. The computer will select the questions on this section of the test based on your responses. You will begin with questions that are considered of average difficulty. You will receive easier questions if you are not able to answer the average questions. You will receive more difficult questions if you are able to answer the average questions. You receive more points for the more difficult questions. Just do your best, and you will receive the most points for your level of structure ability.

Understand the **Help** *screen.* The **Help** screen has a question mark on it. It is mostly designed to repeat directions. Be careful. You can waste a lot of time on this screen. If you click on **Help** and you want to go back to the question you were answering, look at the box in the bottom right corner. Click on **Return to Where I Was.**

Get help from the test administrator. If you think that your computer is not performing correctly, notify one of the test administrators immediately. There should be several in the room. They cannot help you with the answers on the TOEFL, but they can help you use the computer. That is why they are there. Tell the administrator, "Excuse me. My computer won't _____." Show the administrator the problem on the computer.

Stay focused. There is only one test question on the screen at any time. Focus on it. If you need to rest your eyes or your neck muscles, don't look around at other people. Look down at your lap with your eyes closed. Then look up at the ceiling with your eyes closed. Then return to the question. Remember that you cannot return to previous questions, so give each question your full attention while it is on the screen. Then, get ready to focus on the next question.

REVIEW OF SECTION 3:
READING

Overview of the Reading Section

QUICK COMPARISON
PAPER-BASED TOEFL AND COMPUTER-BASED TOEFL
SECTION 3

Paper-Based TOEFL Reading Comprehension	Computer-Based TOEFL Reading
There are five reading passages with an average of ten questions after each passage.	There are three to six reading passages with an average of six to ten questions after each passage.
There are fifty questions.	There are between forty-four and fifty-five questions.
Everyone taking the TOEFL answers the same questions.	The computer does not select questions at your level of language proficiency. You will have the same questions as others who take the same form of the test.
There are no pictures or visual cues.	There may be pictures in the questions that refer to the content of the reading passage.
All of the questions are multiple-choice.	Most of the questions are multiple-choice, but some of the questions have special directions.
Every question has only one answer.	Some of the questions have two answers.

You answer on a paper answer sheet, filling in ovals marked (A), (B), (C), and (D).	You click on the screen in the oval that corresponds to the answer you have chosen, or you follow the directions on the screen.
You have fifty-five minutes to complete the section.	You have seventy to ninety minutes to complete the section.
You can return to previous passages and questions, erase, and change answers on your answer sheet.	You can return to previous passages and questions, change answers, and answer questions you have left blank.
You may not take notes.	You may not take notes.

Review of Problems and Questions for the Reading Section

This Review can be used to prepare for both the Supplemental Paper-Based TOEFL and the Computer-Based TOEFL. For the most part, the same types of problems are tested on both the Paper-Based TOEFL and the Computer-Based TOEFL. Most of the questions on both the Paper-Based TOEFL and the Computer-Based TOEFL are multiple-choice.

Some of the questions on the Computer-Based TOEFL are computer-assisted. Although the computer-assisted questions in this book are numbered, and the answer choices are lettered A, B, C, and D, the same questions on the CD-ROM that supplements the larger version of this book, *Barron's How to Prepare for the TOEFL*, are not numbered and lettered. You need the numbers and letters in the book to refer to the Answer Key, the Explanatory Answers, and the Transcript for the Listening section. On the CD-ROM, you can refer to other chapters by clicking on the screen. The CD-ROM and the following examples are like those on the Computer-Based TOEFL. The computer-assisted questions have special directions on the screen.

1 Previewing

Research shows that it is easier to understand what you are reading if you begin with a general idea of what the passage is about. Previewing helps you form a general idea of the topic in your mind.

To preview, read the first sentence of each paragraph and the last sentence of the passage. You should do this as quickly as possible. Remember, you are not reading for specific information, but for an impression of the *topic*.

EXERCISE

<u>DIRECTIONS:</u> Preview the following passage. Focus on the first sentence in each paragraph and the last sentence of the passage. Can you identify the topic? Check your answer using the key on page 363.

A black hole is a region of space created by the total gravitational collapse of matter. It is so intense that nothing, not even light or radiation, can escape. In other words, it is a one-way surface through which matter can fall inward but cannot emerge.

Some astronomers believe that a black hole may be formed when a large star collapses inward from its own weight. So long as they are emitting heat and light into space, stars support themselves against their own gravitational pull with the outward thermal pressure generated by heat from nuclear reactions deep in their interiors. But if a star eventually exhausts its nuclear fuel, then its unbalanced gravitational attraction could cause it to contract and collapse. Furthermore, it could begin to pull in surrounding matter, including nearby comets and planets, creating a black hole.

2   Reading for Main Ideas

By previewing, you can form a general idea of what a reading passage is about; that is, you identify the *topic*. By reading for main ideas, you identify the point of view of the author—that is, what the writer's *thesis* is. Specifically, what does the author propose to write about the topic? If you could reduce the reading to one sentence, what would it be?

Questions about the main idea can be worded in many ways. For example, the following questions are all asking for the same information: (1) What is the main idea? (2) What is the subject? (3) What is the topic? (4) What would be a good title?

EXERCISE

DIRECTIONS: The main idea usually occurs at the beginning of a reading passage. Look at the first two sentences in the following passage. Can you identify the main idea? What would be a good title for this passage? Check your answers using the key on pages 363–364.

For more than a century, despite attacks by a few opposing scientists, Charles Darwin's theory of evolution by natural selection has stood firm. Now, however, some respected biologists are beginning to question whether the theory accounts for major developments such as the shift from water to land habitation. Clearly, evolution has not proceeded steadily but has progressed by radical advances. Recent research in molecular biology, particularly in the study of DNA, provides us with a new possibility. Not only environmental change but also genetic codes in the underlying structure of DNA could govern evolution.

3   Using Contexts for Vocabulary

Before you can use a context, you must understand what a context is. In English, a context is the combination of vocabulary and grammar that surrounds a word. Context can be a sentence or a paragraph or a passage. Context helps you make a general *prediction* about meaning. If you know the general meaning of a sentence, you also know the general meaning of the words in the sentence.

Making predictions from contexts is very important when you are reading a foreign language. In this way, you can read and understand the meaning of a passage without stopping to look up every new word in a dictionary. On an examination like the TOEFL, dictionaries are not permitted in the room.

EXERCISE

DIRECTIONS: Read the following passage, paying close attention to the underlined words. Can you understand their meanings from the context without using a dictionary? Check your answers using the key on page 364.

At the age of sixty six, Harland Sanders had to <u>auction</u> off everything he owned in order to pay his debts. Once the successful <u>proprietor</u> of a large restaurant, Sanders saw his business suffer from the construction of a new freeway that bypassed his establishment and rerouted the traffic that had <u>formerly</u> passed.

With an income of only $105 a month in Social Security, he packed his car with a pressure cooker, some chickens, and sixty pounds of the seasoning that he had developed for frying chicken. He stopped at restaurants, where he cooked chicken for owners to <u>sample</u>. If they liked it, he offered to show them how to cook it. Then he sold them the seasoning and collected a <u>royalty</u> of four cents on each chicken they cooked. The rest is history. Eight years later, there were 638

Kentucky Fried Chicken franchises, and Colonel Sanders had sold his business again—this time for over two million dollars.

4 Scanning for Details

After reading a passage on the TOEFL, you will be expected to answer six to ten questions. Most of them are multiple-choice. First, read a question and find the important content words. Content words are usually nouns, verbs, or adjectives. They are called content words because they contain the content or meaning of a sentence.

Next, let your eyes travel quickly over the passage for the same content words or synonyms of the words. This is called *scanning*. By scanning, you can find a place in the reading passage where the answer to a question is found. Finally, read those specific sentences carefully and choose the answer that corresponds to the meaning of the sentences you have read.

EXERCISE

DIRECTIONS: First, read the following passage. Then, read the questions after the reading passage, and look for the content words. Finally, scan the passage for the same words or synonyms. Can you answer the questions? Check your answers using the key on pages 364–365.

To prepare for a career in engineering, a student must begin planning in high school. Mathematics and science should form the core curriculum. For example, in a school where sixteen credit hours are required for high school graduation, four should be in mathematics, one each in chemistry, biology, and physics. The remaining credits should include four in English and at least three in the humanities and social sciences. The average entering freshman in engineering should have achieved at least a 2.5 grade point average on a 4.0 scale in his or her high school. Although deficiencies can be corrected during the first year, the student who needs additional work should expect to spend five instead of four years to complete a degree.

1. What is the average grade point for an entering freshman in engineering?

2. When should a student begin planning for a career in engineering?

3. How can a student correct deficiencies in preparation?

4. How many credits should a student have in English?

5. How many credits are required for a high school diploma?

5 Making Inferences

Sometimes, in a reading passage, you will find a direct statement of fact. That is called evidence. But other times, you will not find a direct statement. Then you will need to use the evidence you have to make an inference. An *inference* is a logical conclusion based on evidence. It can be about the passage itself or about the author's viewpoint.

EXERCISE

DIRECTIONS: First, read the following passage. Then, read the questions after the passage, and make inferences. Can you find the evidence for your inference in the reading passage? Check your answers using the key on page 365.

When an acid is dissolved in water, the acid molecule divides into two parts, a hydrogen ion and another ion. An ion is an atom or a group of atoms that has an electrical charge. The charge can be either positive or negative. If hydrochloric acid is mixed with water, for example, it divides into hydrogen ions and chlorine ions.

A strong acid ionizes to a great extent, but a weak acid does not ionize so much. The strength of an acid, therefore, depends on how much it ionizes, not on how many hydrogen ions are produced. It is interesting that nitric acid and sulfuric acid become greatly ionized whereas boric acid and carbonic acid do not.

1. What kind of acid is sulfuric acid?

2. What kind of acid is boric acid?

6 Identifying Exceptions

After reading a passage on the TOEFL, you will be asked to select from four possible answers the one that is NOT mentioned in the reading.

Use your scanning skills to locate related words and phrases in the passage and the answer choices.

EXERCISE

DIRECTIONS: First, read the following passage. Then, read the question after the reading passage. Last, scan the passage again for related words and phrases. Try to eliminate three of the choices. Check your answer using the key on page 366.

All music consists of two elements—expression and design. Expression is inexact and subjective and may be enjoyed in a personal or instinctive way. Design, on the other hand, is exact and must be analyzed objectively in order to be understood and appreciated. The folk song, for example, has a definite musical design that relies on simple repetition with a definite beginning and ending. A folk song generally consists of one stanza of music repeated for each stanza of verse.

Because of their communal, and usually uncertain origin, folk songs are often popular verse set to music. They are not always recorded and tend to be passed on in a kind of musical version of oral history. Each singer revises and perfects the song. In part as a consequence of this continuous revision process, most folk songs are almost perfect in their construction and design. A particular singer's interpretation of the folk song may provide an interesting expression, but the simple design that underlies the song itself is stable and enduring.

1. All of the following are true of a folk song EXCEPT
   (A) there is a clear start and finish
   (B) the origin is often not known
   (C) the design may change in the interpretation
   (D) simple repetition is characteristic of its design

7 Locating References

After reading a passage on the TOEFL, you will be asked to find the antecedent of a pronoun. An antecedent is a word or phrase to which a pronoun refers. Usually, you will be given a pronoun such as "it," "its," "them," or "their," and you will be asked to locate the reference word or phrase in the passage.

First, find the pronoun in the passage. Then read the sentence using the four answer choices in place of the pronoun. The meaning of the sentence in the context of the passage will not change when you substitute the correct antecedent.

EXERCISE

DIRECTIONS: First, find the pronoun in the following passage. Next, start reading several sentences before the sentence in which the pronoun is found, and continue reading several sentences after it. Then, substitute the words or phrases in the answer choices. Which one does not change the meaning of the sentence? Check your answer using the key on pages 366–367.

The National Road, also known as the Cumberland Road, was constructed in the early 1800s to provide transportation between the established commercial areas of the East and Northwest Territory. By 1818, the road had reached Wheeling, West Virginia, 130 miles from its point of origin in Cumberland, Maryland. The cost was a monumental thirteen thousand dollars per mile.

Upon reaching the Ohio River, the National Road became one of the major trade routes to the western states and territories, providing Baltimore with a trade advantage over neighboring cities. In order to compete, New York state authorized the construction of the Erie Canal, and Philadelphia initiated a transportation plan to link it with Pittsburgh. Towns along the rivers, canals, and the new National Road became important trade centers.

1. The word its refers to
   (A) the Northwest Territory
   (B) 1818
   (C) the road
   (D) Wheeling, West Virginia

PROBLEM 8   Referring to the Passage

After reading the passage on the TOEFL, you will be asked to find certain information in the passage, and identify it by line number or paragraph.

First, read the question. Then refer to the line numbers and paragraph numbers in the answer choices to scan for the information in the question.

EXERCISE

DIRECTIONS: First, read the following passage. Then, refer back to the passage. Can you find the correct reference? Check your answer using the key on page 367.

In September of 1929, traders experienced a lack of confidence in the stock market's ability to continue its phenomenal rise. Prices fell. For many inexperienced investors, the drop produced a panic. They had all their money tied up in the market, and they were pressed to sell before the prices fell even lower. Sell orders were coming in so fast that the ticker tape at the New York Stock Exchange could not accommodate all the transactions.

To try to reestablish confidence in the market, a powerful group of New York bankers agreed to pool their funds and purchase stock above current market values. Although the buy orders were minimal, they were counting on their reputations to restore confidence on the part of the smaller investors, thereby affecting the number of sell orders. On Thursday, October 24, Richard Whitney, the Vice President of the New York Stock Exchange and a broker for the J.P. Morgan Company, made the effort on their behalf. Initially, it appeared to have been successful, then, on the following Tuesday, the crash began again and accelerated. By 1932, stocks were worth only twenty percent of their value at the 1929 high. The results of the crash had extended into every aspect of the economy, causing a long and painful depression, referred to in American history as the Great Depression.

1. Where in the passage does the author refer to the reason for the stock market crash?

2. Where in the passage does the author suggest that there was a temporary recovery in the stock market?

CUMULATIVE REVIEW EXERCISE FOR READING COMPREHENSION

Read the following passage, using the skills you have learned. Preview, read for main ideas, and use contexts for vocabulary. To read faster, read phrases instead of words. Then, answer the questions that follow the passage. Scan for details and evidence. Make inferences.

The computer-based version of this reading passage is best viewed on the CD-ROM that supplements the larger version of this book, *Barron's How to Prepare for the TOEFL*. Scroll through the passage, using the skills that you have learned. Check your answers on the screen. If you choose not to purchase the larger version or if you do not have a computer, then use the print version shown with the following computer-assisted questions.

Although each baby has an individual schedule of development, general patterns of growth have been observed. Three periods of development have been identified, including early infancy, which extends from the first to the sixth month; middle infancy, from the sixth to the ninth month; and late infancy, from the ninth to the fifteenth month. Whereas the newborn is
line
(9)
concerned with his or her inner world and responds primarily to hunger and pain, in early infancy the baby is already aware of the surrounding world. During the second month, many infants are awake more and can raise their heads to look at things. They also begin to smile at people. By four months, the baby is searching for things but not yet grasping them with its hands. It is also beginning to be wary of strangers and may scream when a visiting relative tries to pick it up. By five months, the baby is grabbing objects and putting them into its mouth. Some babies are trying to feed themselves with their hands.

In middle infancy, the baby concentrates on practicing a great many speech sounds. It loves to imitate actions and examine interesting objects. At about seven months, it begins to crawl, a skill that it masters at the end of middle infancy.

In late infancy, the baby takes an interest in games, songs, and even books. Progress toward walking moves through standing, balancing, bouncing in place, and walking with others. As soon as the baby walks well alone, it has passed from infancy into the active toddler stage.

TYPES OF QUESTIONS

Multiple-Choice Questions

Paper-Based TOEFL

1. What does this passage mainly discuss?
    (A) Growth in early infancy
    (B) The active toddler stage
    (C) How a baby learns to walk
    (D) The developmental stages of infancy

2. The word "primarily" in line 9 could best be replaced by
    (A) often
    (B) naturally
    (C) for the most part
    (D) in a loud way

3. According to this reading passage, what would a six-month-old baby like to do?
    (A) Smile at people
    (B) Crawl on the floor
    (C) Imitate actions
    (D) Play simple games

4. A baby in late infancy would be able to do all of the following EXCEPT
    (A) make many speech sounds
    (B) walk well alone
    (C) show interest in games
    (D) imitate actions

Answer Sheet

1. Ⓐ   Ⓑ   Ⓒ   ●
2. Ⓐ   Ⓑ   ●   Ⓓ
3. Ⓐ   Ⓑ   ●   Ⓓ
4. Ⓐ   ●   Ⓒ   Ⓓ

Computer-Based TOEFL

What does this passage mainly discuss?
- ○ Growth in early infancy
- ○ The active toddler stage
- ○ How a baby learns to walk
- ● The developmental stages of infancy

The word primarily could best be replaced by
- ○ often
- ○ naturally

- ● for the most part
- ○ in a loud way

According to this reading passage, what would a six-month-old baby like to do?
- ○ Smile at people
- ○ Crawl on the floor

- ● Imitate actions
- ○ Play simple games

A baby in late infancy would be able to do all of the following EXCEPT
- ○ make many speech sounds
- ● walk well alone
- ○ show interest in games
- ○ imitate actions

Computer-Assisted Questions

Location Questions

On some of the computer-assisted questions, you will be asked to locate information in the passage. These questions are like the multiple-choice questions on the Paper-Based TOEFL where you must locate information by identifying the line numbers in the passage. On the computer-assisted questions, you must click on the sentence or paragraph in the passage.

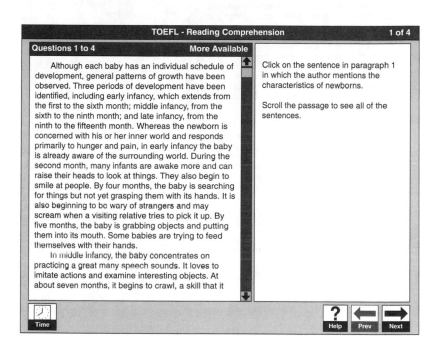

TOEFL - Reading Comprehension	1 of 4

Questions 1 to 4   **More Available**

Although each baby has an individual schedule of development, general patterns of growth have been observed. Three periods of development have been identified, including early infancy, which extends from the first to the sixth month; middle infancy, from the sixth to the ninth month; and late infancy, from the ninth to the fifteenth month. Whereas the newborn is concerned with his or her inner world and responds primarily to hunger and pain, in early infancy the baby is already aware of the surrounding world. During the second month, many infants are awake more and can raise their heads to look at things. They also begin to smile at people. By four months, the baby is searching for things but not yet grasping them with its hands. It is also beginning to be wary of strangers and may scream when a visiting relative tries to pick it up. By five months, the baby is grabbing objects and putting them into its mouth. Some babies are trying to feed themselves with their hands.

In middle infancy, the baby concentrates on practicing a great many speech sounds. It loves to imitate actions and examine interesting objects. At about seven months, it begins to crawl, a skill that it

Click on the sentence in paragraph 1 in which the author mentions the characteristics of newborns.

Scroll the passage to see all of the sentences.

Time   Help   Prev   Next

Synonyms

On some of the computer-assisted questions, you will be asked to locate synonyms in the reading passage. You must click on the word or phrase in the passage.

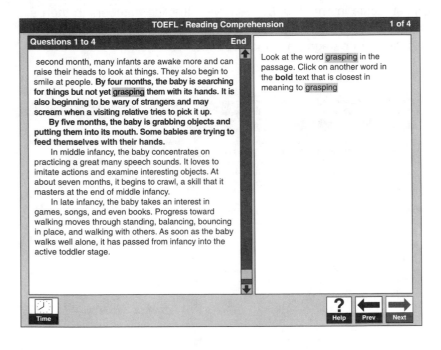

TOEFL - Reading Comprehension   1 of 4

Questions 1 to 4   **End**

second month, many infants are awake more and can raise their heads to look at things. They also begin to smile at people. **By four months, the baby is searching for things but not yet grasping them with its hands. It is also beginning to be wary of strangers and may scream when a visiting relative tries to pick it up.**

By five months, the baby is grabbing objects and putting them into its mouth. Some babies are trying to feed themselves with their hands.

In middle infancy, the baby concentrates on practicing a great many speech sounds. It loves to imitate actions and examine interesting objects. At about seven months, it begins to crawl, a skill that it masters at the end of middle infancy.

In late infancy, the baby takes an interest in games, songs, and even books. Progress toward walking moves through standing, balancing, bouncing in place, and walking with others. As soon as the baby walks well alone, it has passed from infancy into the active toddler stage.

Look at the word grasping in the passage. Click on another word in the **bold** text that is closest in meaning to grasping

Time

? Help   ← Prev   → Next

Paraphrased Sentences

On some of the computer-assisted questions, you will be asked to identify paraphrases of sentences in the passage.

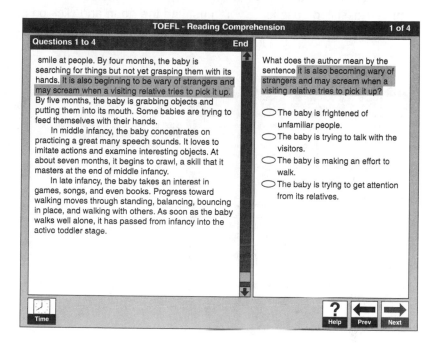

Reference Questions

On some of the computer-assisted questions, you will be asked to locate the nouns to which pronouns refer. These questions are like the multiple-choice questions on the Paper-Based TOEFL where you must choose the noun from four answer choices. On the computer-assisted questions, you must find the noun and click on it in the passage.

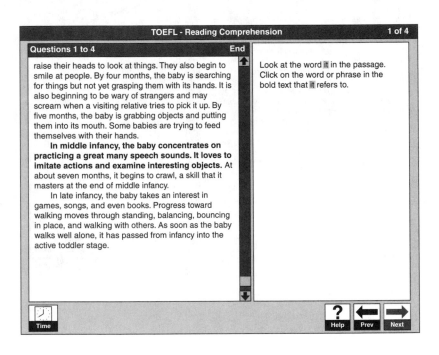

Sentence Insertion Questions

On some of the computer-assisted questions, you will be asked to locate the most logical place in the passage where a sentence could be inserted. You will have several options marked with a square (■) in the passage.

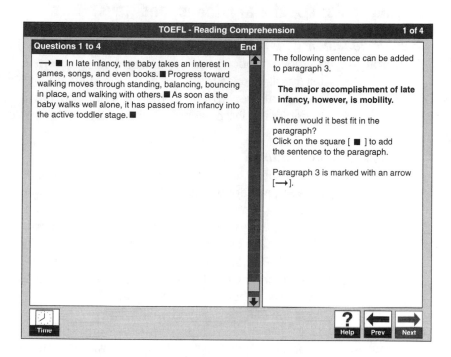

Computer Tutorial for the Reading Section

Testing Tools: Vocabulary, Icons, and Keys

Specific Vocabulary for Section 3

Scroll   To move through reading passages on a screen. If the reading passage is long, new sentences will appear at the top and sentences that you have already read will disappear at the bottom.

Specific Icons for Section 3

Scroll Bar   An *icon* used to move the reading passages on the screen so that you can see a long passage. First move the *arrow* to the top of the **scroll bar**; then hold the *mouse button* down to move the **scroll bar** from the beginning of the reading passage to the end. Remember, you can see the words *beginning*, *more available*, and *end* at the top of the **scroll bar**. These words show you the place in the passage that is displayed on the screen.

Proceed   An *icon* at the bottom of the screen with the reading passage. *Click* on **Proceed** after you have read the passage in order to see the first question. Remember, you cannot use **Proceed** until you have scrolled down to the end of the passage.

Previous   An *icon* at the bottom of the screen with the questions. *Click* on **Previous** to see the previous question.

Computer Screens for Section 3

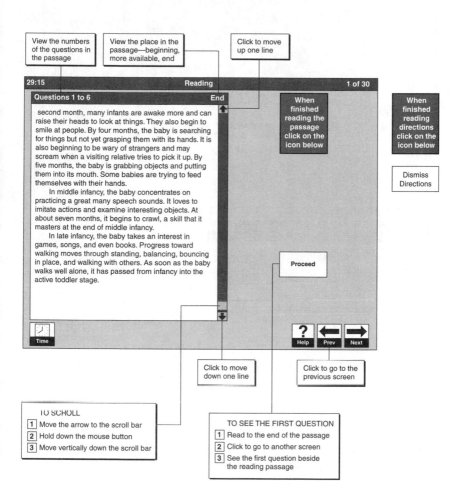

View the numbers of the questions in the passage

View the place in the passage—beginning, more available, end

Click to move up one line

| 29:15 | Reading | 1 of 30 |

Questions 1 to 6   End

second month, many infants are awake more and can raise their heads to look at things. They also begin to smile at people. By four months, the baby is searching for things but not yet grasping them with its hands. It is also beginning to be wary of strangers and may scream when a visiting relative tries to pick it up. By five months, the baby is grabbing objects and putting them into its mouth. Some babies are trying to feed themselves with their hands.

In middle infancy, the baby concentrates on practicing a great many speech sounds. It loves to imitate actions and examine interesting objects. At about seven months, it begins to crawl, a skill that it masters at the end of middle infancy.

In late infancy, the baby takes an interest in games, songs, and even books. Progress toward walking moves through standing, balancing, bouncing in place, and walking with others. As soon as the baby walks well alone, it has passed from infancy into the active toddler stage.

When finished reading the passage click on the icon below

When finished reading directions click on the icon below

Dismiss Directions

Proceed

Time

Help   Prev   Next

Click to move down one line

Click to go to the previous screen

TO SCROLL
1 Move the arrow to the scroll bar
2 Hold down the mouse button
3 Move vertically down the scroll bar

TO SEE THE FIRST QUESTION
1 Read to the end of the passage
2 Click to go to another screen
3 See the first question beside the reading passage

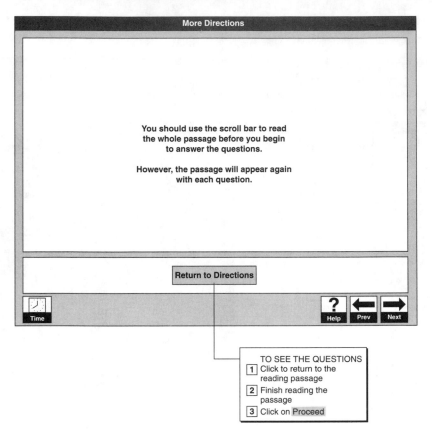

TIP: When you do not scroll to the end of the reading passage the first time you see it, this screen appears. You can spend a lot of time returning to the passage. Until you scroll to the bottom of the passage, you cannot see the questions.

TIP: The answer to the question on the right side of the screen is always found in the part of the passage visible on the left side of the screen. You usually do not have to scroll through the passage to find the answer.

Simulations for Section 3

In order to prepare for the experience that you will have on the Computer-Based TOEFL, you can use the CD-ROM that supplements the larger version of this book, *Barron's How to Prepare for the TOEFL*. Locate the Reading section on the Model Tests. The computer will simulate the Reading section on the Computer-Based TOEFL. These model tests are computer-assisted. The Reading section of the Computer-Based TOEFL is not computer-adaptive.

As part of your study plan, be sure to review all of the questions in all of the Model Tests. Use the Explanatory Answers on the CD-ROM or on pages 377–420.

If you choose not to purchase the larger version of this book, or if you do not have a computer, you can still simulate some of the features of the Computer-Based TOEFL. Section 3 of the Model Tests in Chapter 7 of this book is printed in two columns to give you the same kind of visual impression that you will have when you read from a computer screen. The on-screen directions for computer-assisted questions are also printed in the book.

Advice for the Reading Section: Computer-Based TOEFL

Practice reading on a computer screen. Reading on a computer screen is different from reading on a page. First, there is generally less text visible; second, you must scroll instead of turning pages; and finally, there may be quite a few icons or other distracting visuals surrounding the passage.

To become comfortable with reading on a computer screen, you should take advantage of every opportunity you have to practice. If you have a computer, spend time reading on the screen. Everything you read will help you improve this new skill.

Practice reading the kinds of topics you will find in the Reading section. An inexpensive encyclopedia on CD-ROM would be a good investment. The kinds of passages found on the Computer-Based TOEFL are very similar to those found in a basic English encyclopedia.

If you do not have a computer, you may be able to locate software for an English encyclopedia at a local library where a computer is available for public use.

Become familiar with the directions for each of the question types. The different types of questions will appear at random. Directions will appear with each question, but if you already recognize the type of question presented, and you are familiar with the directions, you will save time. The less time you have to spend reading directions, the more time you will have to read the passages.

REVIEW OF
WRITING ESSAYS

Overview of the Writing Section

QUICK COMPARISON
PAPER-BASED TOEFL AND COMPUTER-BASED TOEFL
ESSAY

Paper-Based TOEFL
Test of Written English

Computer-Based TOEFL
Writing

The essay, also called the Test of Written English (TWE), is offered five times each year. You must select a TOEFL test date when the TWE is scheduled if you need an essay score.

The essay is required as part of every TOEFL. You must write the essay as the last part of your TOEFL examination.

When you register for the TOEFL on one of the dates when the TWE is offered, you do not have to register separately for the TWE. It is offered at no additional cost.

When you register for the TOEFL, you are automatically registered for the Writing section. It is offered at no additional cost.

There is only one topic for each essay.

There is only one topic for each essay.

Everyone taking the TOEFL writes an essay on the same topic.

The computer selects a topic for you. It may not be the same topic that is selected for someone else taking the TOEFL that day.

You do not know any of the topics for the essay.

All of the topics for the essay are published in the *TOEFL Information Bulletin* for Computer-Based Testing free of charge from ETS. They are also listed on the ETS web site at *www.toefl.org*.

Most of the topics ask you to agree or disagree with a statement or to express an opinion.

There are three types of topics commonly used on the TWE:

1. *Argument.* Argue both sides of an issue, and take a position.

2. *Persuasion.* Agree or disagree with a statement, and support your opinion.

3. *Extension.* Based on several examples that support an argument, choose another example, and give reasons for the choice.

The topics are very general and do not require any specialized knowledge of the subject to answer them.

You have thirty minutes to complete the essay.

You handwrite your essay on paper provided in the test materials.

You have one page to organize your essay. This page is not graded. You may organize in any way that is helpful to you— notes, a list, an outline, or a

Most of the topics ask you to agree or disagree with a statement or to express an opinion.

There are three types of topics commonly used on the Writing Section:

1. *Argument.* Argue both sides of an issue, and take a position.

2. *Persuasion.* Agree or disagree with a statement, and support your opinion.

3. *Extension.* Based on several examples that support an argument, choose another example, and give reasons for the choice.

The topics are very general and do not require any specialized knowledge of the subject to answer them.

You have thirty minutes to complete the essay.

You can choose to handwrite your essay on paper or type it on the computer.

You have one page to organize your essay. This page is not graded. You may organize in any way that is helpful to you— notes, a list, an outline, or a drawing. You may use your first language on this page.

Your essay will not be scored for neatness, but the readers must be able to understand what you have written.

You should write about 300–500 words, or three to five short paragraphs.

A scale from 1 to 6 is used to grade the essay.

The scale is printed on page 234.

Your essay will be scored by two professional teachers, reading independently. When the two scores differ by more than one point, a third teacher will read and score your essay.

The score is reported separately from the TOEFL score. It will not be included in the computation of the total TOEFL score and will not affect your score on the multiple-choice TOEFL.

drawing. You may use your first language on this page.

Your essay will not be scored for neatness, but the readers must be able to understand what you have written.

You should write about 300–500 words, or three to five short paragraphs.

A scale from 1 to 6 is used to grade the essay.

The scale is printed on page 234.

Your essay will be scored by two professional teachers, reading independently. When the two scores differ by more than one point, a third teacher will read and score your essay.

The score is combined with the score on the Structure section. It will be factored in the section score at 50 percent.

Review of Strategies and Topics for the Writing Section

This Review can be used to prepare for both the Paper-Based TOEFL and the Computer-Based TOEFL. For the most part, the same types of topics are tested on both the Paper-Based TOEFL and the Computer-Based TOEFL. The essays on both the Paper-Based TOEFL and the Computer-Based TOEFL are scored using the same scale.

Three Steps for Writing Short Essays

There are three steps that most good writers follow in organizing their writing. You should use these steps when you write a short essay. First, tell your reader what you are going to write. Second, write it. Third, tell your reader what you wrote.

To look at these steps another way, your essay should have three parts:

1. A good beginning
2. Several good comments
3. A good ending

In this review of writing, we will discuss and give examples of the three parts of a short essay, using the types of topics that you will find on the TOEFL.

A Good Beginning

This is where you tell the reader what you are going to write. A good beginning has certain requirements.

A good beginning is short. Two or three sentences is enough to tell your reader how you plan to approach the topic.

A good beginning is direct. In the case of a comparison, state both sides of the argument in your first sentence. In a short composition, you don't have enough time for indirect approaches.

A good beginning is an outline. The second sentence usually outlines the organization. It gives the reader a general idea of your plan.

Good Comments

This is where you write.

Good comments include several points. A short essay may have between two and five points. Usually, the writer selects three. In the case of a comparison, three reasons is a standard argument.

Good comments are all related. All of the comments should relate to the general statement in the first sentence.

Good comments are logical. The points should be based on evidence. In the case of a comparison, the evidence should come from sources that can be cited, such as a television program that you have seen, an article that you have read in a magazine, a book that you have read, or a lecture that you have heard.

Good comments are not judgments. Opinions should be identified by phrases such as, "in my view," "in my opinion," or "it seems to me that." Furthermore, opinions should be based on evidence. Opinions that are not based on evidence are judgments. Judgments usually use words like "good" or "bad," "right" or "wrong." Judgments are not good comments.

A Good Ending

This is where you tell the reader what you wrote.

A good ending is a summary. The last sentence is similar to the first sentence. In a short essay, a good ending does not add new information. It does not introduce a new idea.

A good ending is not an apology. A good ending does not apologize for not having said enough, for not having had enough time, or for not using good English.

Scoring Scale for the Essay

The essay is scored on a scale of 1 to 6. A score between two points on the scale—5.5, 4.5, 3.5, 2.5, 1.5—can also be reported. The following guidelines are used by evaluators:

6 shows consistent proficiency	• Is well organized • Addresses the topic • Includes examples and details • Has few errors in grammar and vocabulary
5 shows inconsistent proficiency	• Is well organized • Addresses the topic • Includes fewer examples and details • Has more errors in grammar and vocabulary
4 shows minimal proficiency	• Is adequately organized • Addresses most of the topic • Includes some examples and details • Has errors in grammar and vocabulary that occasionally confuse meaning
3 shows developing proficiency	• Is inadequately organized • Addresses part of the topic • Includes few examples and details • Has many errors in grammar and vocabulary that confuse meaning
2 shows little proficiency	• Is disorganized • Does not address the topic • Does not include examples and details • Has many errors in grammar and vocabulary that consistently confuse meaning
1 shows no proficiency	• Is disorganized • Does not address the topic • Does not include examples and details • Has so many errors in grammar and vocabulary that meaning is not communicated
0 shows no comprehension	• Does not write an essay • Writes an essay on a different topic

Example Essay

The following example essay would receive a score of 6. It is well organized, it addresses the topic, it includes examples and details, and it has some but not many errors in grammar and vocabulary.

Read and study this example essay before you complete the Model Tests.

Some students in the United States work while they are earning their degrees in college; others receive support from their families. How should a student's education be supported? Argue both sides of the issue and defend your position.

Notes

Line
(5)

(10)

(15)

Some students in the United States work while they are earning their degrees; others receive support from their families. Both approaches have advantages and disadvantages. In this essay, I will name some of the advantages of each approach, and I will argue in favor family support.

In a society where independence and individual accomplishment are value, a student who earned his degree by working would be greatly admired. Friends would praise him for his initiation and perseverance. Future employers might be impressed by his work record. He might derive greater satisfaction from his personal investment in it.

(20) On the other hand, in a society where cooperation and family dependence are value, a student who received support would be better understood. Friends would praise him for his efforts on behalf of his family. Future employers would not expect a work record from a student. He might feel greater

(25) responsibility toward others in his family because the accomplishment was shared.

Thus, not one but every family member would assured some opportunity or benefit.

(30) For my part, I must argue in favor of family support. While I study at an American University, my older brother will send me money every month. When I finish my degree and find a good

(35) job, I will send my younger sister to a school or university. It may not be a better way, but it is the way that my society rewards.

Evaluator's Comments

This writing sample is well organized with a good topic sentence and good support statements. It addresses the question, and does not digress from the topic. There is a logical progression of ideas and excellent language proficiency, as evidenced by a variety of grammatical structures and appropriate vocabulary. There are only a few grammatical errors that have been corrected below:

Line 7	in favor of
Line 9	are valued
Lines 18–19	are valued
Line 28	would be assured

SCORE: 6

Computer Tutorial for the Writing Section

Testing Tools: Vocabulary, Icons, and Keys

Specific Vocabulary for the Essay

Text
All printed material on the screen. **Text** can refer to a word, a sentence, a paragraph, several paragraphs, or an essay.

Cursor
The line that shows you where you can begin typing. When you move the *mouse*, the **cursor** appears. You can move the **cursor** on your essay by moving the *mouse* on your *mouse pad*.

Blinking
Flashing on and off. The *cursor* is usually **blinking** to help you see it.

Highlight
To select *text* in your essay that you want to edit. To **highlight**, move the *cursor* to the beginning of the place in your essay that you want to change. Hold down the mouse button and move to the end of the place in your essay that you want to change. Release the mouse button. The **highlighted** *text* should be shaded.

Keys
The individual buttons on the keyboard used for typing and editing your essay.

Keys for the Essay

Arrow Keys
Keys that let you move around in your essay. There is an **up arrow**, **down arrow**, **left arrow**, and **right arrow**. They are found between the letters and the numbers on the keyboard. Use the **arrow keys** to move up, down, left, or right.

Page Up, Page Down   Keys that let you see your essay if it is longer than the screen. The **Page Up** and **Page Down** keys are above the *arrow keys* on the keyboard. Use **Page Up** to scroll to the beginning of your essay. Use **Page Down** to scroll to the end of your essay.

Backspace   A key that moves you back one space at a time. Use the **Backspace** key to erase *text* from right to left.

Space Bar   The long key at the bottom of the keyboard. Use the **Space Bar** two or three times to indent a paragraph. Remember, the *Tab* key does not function on your keyboard.

Icons for the Essay

Cut   An example of an *icon*. After you *highlight* the text you want to delete or move, click on **Cut**. The text will disappear. Use the **Cut** icon to delete text or as the first step in moving text.

Paste   An example of an *icon*. After you *cut* text, you can move the *cursor* to the place in the essay where you want to insert the text, and click on **Paste**. The text you *highlighted* will appear. Use the **Paste** icon as the second step in moving text.

Undo   An example of an *icon*. It lets you change your mind. For example, if you move a sentence, and then you want to move it back to the original place in your essay, click on **Undo**. **Undo** will return whatever you did last back to the way it looked before you made the change. Remember, **Undo** will only return your last change, not several changes.

Keyboard for the Essay

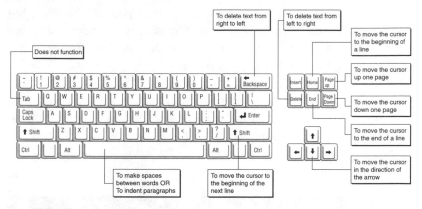

TIP: If you click the mouse, you can delete text. You may even delete your essay! If this happens, click on **Undo** immediately.

Computer Screen for the Essay

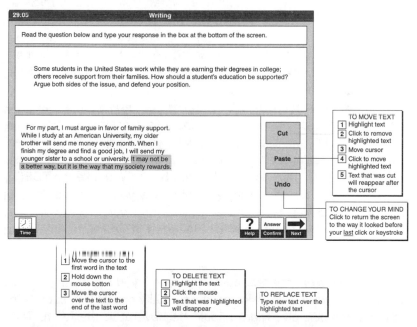

TIP: Be sure that you have completed the essay to your satisfaction before you click on **Answer Confirm**. After you click on **Answer Confirm**, you cannot continue writing or editing your essay.

Simulations for the Essay

In order to simulate the experience that you will have on the Computer-Based TOEFL, type the Model Test essays using the word processing program on the CD-ROM that supplements the larger version of this book, *Barron's How to Prepare for the TOEFL.* If you do not have a computer, handwrite the Model Test essays on paper. Be sure to complete your essay in thirty minutes.

As part of your study plan, it is a good idea to have an English teacher score your essays using the guidelines on page 234 of this book.

Advice for the Writing Section: Computer-Based TOEFL

Become familiar with the writing topics. All of the topics from the official TOEFL Writing section are listed in the *TOEFL Information Bulletin* for Computer-Based Testing, available free from Educational Testing Service. Read through the questions and think about how you would respond to each of the topics. Since most of them require you to state an opinion, it is helpful to form a general opinion on each topic.

Decide whether you will handwrite or type your essay. The word processing program for the computer is very simple. If you know how to use Windows, it should be easy for you to adjust. But if you feel uncomfortable using the computer to write the essay, you may choose to handwrite it. By making your decision before you take the TOEFL, you will not waste time thinking about the way you will complete your test. You can use every minute to organize and write the essay.

Write on the topic you are assigned. If you write on a topic other than the one you have been assigned, your test will not be scored.

Get help from the test administrator. If you are having a problem with the word processing program, notify one of the test administrators immediately. There should be several in the room. They cannot help you with the answers on the TOEFL, but they can help you use the computer. That is why they are there. Tell the administrator, "Excuse me. I am trying to _____. What should I do?"

TOEFL
MODEL TESTS

There are two types of Model Tests to help you prepare for the TOEFL. The questions on Model Tests 1–4 are like those that frequently appear on the Computer-Based TOEFL. The questions on the Cumulative Model Test are also like those that frequently appear on the Computer-Based TOEFL.

The difference between Model Tests 1–4 and the Cumulative Model Test is that Model Tests 1–4 are simulations of a Computer-Based TOEFL. A simulation is an experience that is similar, but not exactly the same. On these Model Tests, you will see the same types of questions, and you will answer them in the same way that you will on the actual Computer-Based TOEFL that you take, but the computer will not be selecting questions for you at your level of language proficiency. These Model Tests are computer-assisted, but not computer-adaptive. On the Cumulative Model Test, you will see the same types of questions, and you will answer them in the same way that you will on the actual Computer-Based TOEFL. In addition, the computer will be selecting questions for you at your level of language proficiency. This Model Test is computer-adaptive. Both types of Model Tests are found on the CD-ROM that supplements the larger version of this book, *Barron's How to Prepare for the TOEFL*.

First, take Model Tests 1–4 and study the Explanatory Answers. If you have the CD-ROM, take the Cumulative Model Test (computer-adaptive) and repeat it until you are answering correctly at least 80 percent of the time.

How to Answer Questions for Model Tests 1–4

If you use the CD-ROM to take the Model Tests, you will not need to write in your book. If you do not have access to a computer, mark your responses to Model Tests 1–4 directly on the tests in the book.

For multiple-choice questions that require you to choose one answer, fill in the oval of the letter that corresponds to the answer you have chosen.

The Palo Verde tree _____ in spring.

● has beautiful yellow blossoms
Ⓑ beautiful yellow blossoms
Ⓒ having beautiful yellow blossoms
Ⓓ with beautiful yellow blossoms

For questions that require you to choose two answers, mark an X in the squares that correspond to the answers you have chosen.

According to the professor, what was the Hemingway style?

Click on two answers.

☒ Powerful descriptions
☐ B Imaginative details
☒ Short sentences
☐ D Difficult symbolism

For questions that require you to click on sentences to move them into categories on charts, write letters on the charts that correspond to the sentences you have chosen.

How did Hemingway use his experience in different novels?

Click on the sentence.
Then click on the space where
it belongs. Use each sentence
only once.

[A] He was fishing in the Gulf of Mexico.
[B] He was driving an ambulance in Italy.
[C] He was working as a newspaper reporter in Paris.

The Sun Also Rises	C
A Farewell to Arms	B
The Old Man and the Sea	A

For questions that require you to put events in order, write letters in the numbered boxes that correspond to the sequence you have chosen.

The professor briefly describes Hemingway's life as an author. Summarize the biographical data by putting the events in order.

Click on the sentence.
Then click on the space where
it belongs. Use each sentence
only once.

A Hemingway wrote about his experiences as an ambulance driver during the war.

B Hemingway received the Nobel Prize for literature.

C Hemingway published *The Old Man and the Sea*.

D Hemingway was a newspaper reporter in Paris.

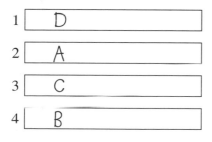

1   D

2   A

3   C

4   B

For questions that require you to click on a word or phrase, circle the word or phrase in the passage.

Look at the word one in the passage.
Click on the word or phrase in the bold
text that one refers to.

Solar astronomers do know that the sun is divided into five general layers or zones. Starting at the outside and going down into the sun, the zones are the corona, chromosphere, photosphere, convection zone, and finally the core. The first three zones are regarded as the sun's atmosphere. But since the sun has no solid surface, it is hard to tell where the atmosphere ends and the main body of the sun begins.

The sun's outermost layer begins about 10,000 miles above the visible surface and goes outward for millions of miles.This is the only part of the sun that can be seen during an eclipse such as the one in February 1979. At any other time, the corona can be seen only when special instruments are used on cameras and telescopes to block the light from the photosphere.

The corona is a brilliant, pearly white, filmy light, about as bright as the full moon. Its beautiful rays are a sensational sight during an eclipse. The corona's rays flash out in a brilliant fan that has wispy spikelike rays near the sun's north and south poles. The corona is generally thickest at the sun's equator.

The corona is made up of gases streaming

For questions that require you to click on a sentence, circle the sentence in the passage.

Click on the sentence in paragraph 4 or 5 in which the author compares the light of the sun's outermost layer to that of another astronomical body.

Paragraphs 4 and 5 are marked with arrows [→]

cameras and telescopes to block the light from the photosphere.

→ The corona is a brilliant, pearly white, filmy light, about as bright as the full moon. Its beautiful rays are a sensational sight during an eclipse. The corona's rays flash out in a brilliant fan that has wispy spikelike rays near the sun's north and south poles. The corona is generally thickest at the sun's equator.

→ The corona is made up of gases streaming outward at tremendous speeds that reach a temperature of more than 2 million degrees Fahrenheit. The gas thins out as it reaches the space around the planets. By the time the gas of the corona reaches the Earth it has a relatively low density.

For questions that require you to add a sentence, circle the square [■] where the sentence is to be inserted.

The following sentence can be added to paragraph 1.

At the center of the Earth's solar system lies the sun.

Where would it best fit in paragraph 1? Click on the square [■] to add the sentence to the paragraph.

Paragraph 1 is marked with an arrow [→].

→(■)The temperature of the sun is over 10,000 degrees Fahrenheit at the surface, but it rises to perhaps more than 27,000,000° at the center. ■The sun is so much hotter than the Earth that matter can exist only as a gas, except perhaps at the core. In the core of the sun, the pressures are so great that, despite the high temperature, there may be a small solid core. ■However, no one really knows, since the center of the sun can never be directly observed. ■

Solar astronomers do know that the sun is divided into five general layers or zones. Starting at the outside and going down into the sun, the zones are the corona, chromosphere, photosphere, convection zone, and finally the core. The first three zones are regarded as the sun's atmosphere. But since the sun has no solid surface, it is hard to tell where the atmosphere ends and the main body of the sun begins.

The sun's outermost layer begins about 10,000 miles above the visible surface and goes outward for millions of miles. This is the only part of the sun that can be seen during an eclipse such as the one in

Model Test 1
Computer-Assisted TOEFL

Section 1:
Listening

The Listening section of the test measures the ability to understand conversations and talks in English. You will use headphones to listen to the conversations and talks. While you are listening, pictures of the speakers or other information will be presented on your computer screen. There are two parts to the Listening section, with special directions for each part.

On the day of the test, the amount of time you will have to answer all of the questions will appear on the computer screen. The time you spend listening to the test material will not be counted. The listening material and questions about it will be presented only one time. You will not be allowed to take notes or have any paper at your computer. You will both see and hear the questions before the answer choices appear. You can take as much time as you need to select an answer; however, it will be to your advantage to answer the questions as quickly as possible. You may change your answer as many times as you want before you confirm it. After you have confirmed an answer, you will not be able to return to the question.

Before you begin working on the Listening section, you will have an opportunity to adjust the volume of the sound. You will not be able to change the volume after you have started the test.

QUESTION DIRECTIONS—Part A

In Part A of the Listening section, you will hear short conversations between two people. In some of the conversations, each person speaks only once. In other conversations, one or both of the people speak more than once. Each conversation is followed by one question about it.

Each question in this part has four answer choices. You should click on the best answer to each question. Answer the questions on the basis of what is stated or implied by the speakers.

1. What is the man's problem?

   Ⓐ He doesn't mind the traffic.
   Ⓑ He takes the bus to school.
   Ⓒ He has to stand on the bus if he takes it to school.
   Ⓓ He wants to ride to school with the woman.

2. What does the man mean?

   Ⓐ The woman should not consider her advisor in the decision.
   Ⓑ The woman should not take Dr. Sullivan's section.
   Ⓒ The woman's advisor will not be offended.
   Ⓓ The woman should not take a physics course.

3. What does the woman imply?

   Ⓐ She is not interested in the man.
   Ⓑ She does not like lectures.
   Ⓒ She would go out with the man on another occasion.
   Ⓓ She would rather stay at home.

4. What does the woman mean?

   Ⓐ The bike is in good condition.
   Ⓑ The man needs to replace the bike.
   Ⓒ The bike is missing.
   Ⓓ It is a new bike.

5. What does the man want to drink?

   Ⓐ Something cold.
   Ⓑ Coffee.
   Ⓒ Tea.
   Ⓓ Both coffee and tea.

6. What does the man suggest the woman do?

   Ⓐ Ask directions.
   Ⓑ Walk to the shopping center.
   Ⓒ Take a taxi.
   Ⓓ Wait for the bus.

7. What can be inferred about the man?

   Ⓐ He does not plan to study.
   Ⓑ He has a very busy schedule.
   Ⓒ He is lost.
   Ⓓ He has not registered yet.

8. What does the man mean?

   Ⓐ He does not want to listen to the radio.
   Ⓑ He has changed his opinion about turning on the radio.
   Ⓒ The radio will not bother him.
   Ⓓ The radio is not working very well.

9. What does the woman suggest Anna do?

   Ⓐ Stop worrying.
   Ⓑ Go out more.
   Ⓒ Talk to a friend.
   Ⓓ Get counseling.

10. What does the man mean?

    Ⓐ He prefers to talk another time.
    Ⓑ He wants the woman to go away.
    Ⓒ He would like the woman to continue.
    Ⓓ He doesn't know what to think.

11. What will the man probably do?

    Ⓐ Accept the woman's apology.
    Ⓑ Allow the woman to go ahead of him.
    Ⓒ Apologize to the woman.
    Ⓓ Go to the front of the line.

12. What does the woman imply?

    Ⓐ The neighbors have parties often.
    Ⓑ She does not like her neighbors.
    Ⓒ The neighbors' party is disturbing her.
    Ⓓ She will not be invited to the neighbors' party.

13. What had the man assumed?

    Ⓐ Dr. Franklin is not very understanding.
    Ⓑ The extension was a very bad idea.
    Ⓒ He is surprised that the woman was denied her request.
    Ⓓ The professor's answer is not surprising.

14. What problem do the man and woman have?

    Ⓐ They do not have a telephone.
    Ⓑ They are late.
    Ⓒ They have been left.
    Ⓓ They got lost.

15. What is the woman probably going to do?

    Ⓐ Pay the rent for half a month.
    Ⓑ Help the man move.
    Ⓒ Stay where she is living until the 15th.
    Ⓓ Move out of the apartment.

16. What had the man assumed about MaryAnne?

    Ⓐ She had already taken the test.
    Ⓑ She did not want to take classes.
    Ⓒ She had not taken the placement test.
    Ⓓ She would take the math classes later.

17. What does the man mean?

    Ⓐ The plan is to remain in the class.
    Ⓑ It is not comfortable in the classroom.
    Ⓒ He has been absent because he was sick.
    Ⓓ The weather has been very bad.

QUESTION DIRECTIONS—Part B

In Part B of the Listening section, you will hear several longer conversations and talks. Each conversation or talk is followed by several questions. The conversations, talks, and questions will not be repeated.

The conversations and talks are about a variety of topics. You do not need special knowledge of the topics to answer the questions correctly. Rather, you should answer each question on the basis of what is stated or implied by the speakers in the conversations or talks.

For most of the questions, you will need to click on the best of four possible answers. Some questions will have special directions. The special directions will appear in a box on the computer screen.

18. What is Mike's problem?

    Ⓐ He was late arriving at registration.
    Ⓑ He needs an advisor's signature on a course request form.
    Ⓒ He is not doing well in the class because it is so large.
    Ⓓ He must have the permission of the instructor to enroll in a class.

19. What does Mike want Professor Day to do?

    Ⓐ Help him with the class.
    Ⓑ Explain some technical vocabulary.
    Ⓒ Give him special permission to take the class.
    Ⓓ Take a form to the registration area.

20. What does Mike say about graduation?

    Ⓐ He has planned to graduate in the fall.
    Ⓑ He has to take Professor Day's class in order to graduate.
    Ⓒ He needs the professor to sign his application for graduation.
    Ⓓ He does not have enough credits for graduation.

21. What does Professor Day decide to do?

    Ⓐ Enroll Mike in the class next year.
    Ⓑ Allow Mike to take the class this term.
    Ⓒ Give Mike permission to graduate without the class.
    Ⓓ Register Mike for another class.

22. What is MUZAK?

    Ⓐ A slow, soft song.
    Ⓑ Music in restaurants.
    Ⓒ Background music.
    Ⓓ A pleasant addition to the environment.

23. What is the average increase in productivity when MUZAK is introduced?

    Ⓐ Thirteen percent.
    Ⓑ Five to ten percent.
    Ⓒ One hundred percent.
    Ⓓ Thirty percent.

24. What is stimulus progression?

    Ⓐ Background music that is low in stimulus value.
    Ⓑ Upbeat music that stimulates sales.
    Ⓒ Music engineered to reduce stress.
    Ⓓ Music that starts slow and gets faster at times of the day when people get tired.

25. How does MUZAK influence sales in supermarkets?

   Ⓐ It can cause shoppers to go through the line faster.
   Ⓑ It can cause shoppers to buy thirty percent more or less.
   Ⓒ It can cause shoppers to walk slower and buy more.
   Ⓓ It does not influence sales.

26. What is this announcement mainly about?

   Ⓐ The "Sun-Up Semester" program.
   Ⓑ The Community College campus.
   Ⓒ Video telecourses.
   Ⓓ Technology for distance learning.

27. Why does the speaker mention the "Sun-Up Semester"?

   Ⓐ To clarify how to register.
   Ⓑ To advertise the college.
   Ⓒ To provide a listing of courses.
   Ⓓ To give students an alternative to video tapes.

28. How can students register for a course?

   Ⓐ They should come to campus.
   Ⓑ They can call the Community College.
   Ⓒ They must contact the instructor.
   Ⓓ They can use computers.

29. How can students contact the instructor?

   Ⓐ By using e-mail.
   Ⓑ By calling KCC-TV.
   Ⓒ By writing letters.
   Ⓓ By making video tapes.

30. What is the main topic of this conversation?

   Ⓐ The woman's health.
   Ⓑ The woman's grades.
   Ⓒ The man's joke.
   Ⓓ The man's stress.

31. What was the woman's problem?

   Ⓐ She was taking too many classes.
   Ⓑ She was very tired because she studied too late.
   Ⓒ She had been ill last semester.
   Ⓓ She may have to withdraw from school this semester.

32. Why is mono called the "college disease"?

   Ⓐ Many students get mono while they are in college.
   Ⓑ If one student gets mono, the whole college becomes infected.
   Ⓒ It is a joke about college students that the woman tells.
   Ⓓ The disease was first identified on a college campus.

33. What advice does the woman give the man?

   Ⓐ Drop out of school for a semester and return later.
   Ⓑ Study harder to learn all the lessons this semester.
   Ⓒ Take fewer hours each semester and add one semester to the program.
   Ⓓ Add extra classes to the program even if it requires another semester.

34. What central theme does the lecture examine?

    Ⓐ The relationship between language and culture.
    Ⓑ The culture of Hopi society.
    Ⓒ Native American cultures.
    Ⓓ The life of Benjamin Lee Whorf.

35. Which languages did Whorf use in his research?

    Ⓐ European languages.
    Ⓑ South American languages.
    Ⓒ Native American languages.
    Ⓓ Computer languages.

36. According to the lecturer, what is linguistic relativity?

    Ⓐ All languages are related.
    Ⓑ All Native American languages are related.
    Ⓒ Language influences the manner in which an individual understands reality.
    Ⓓ Language and culture are not related.

37. What is another name for linguistic relativity?

    Ⓐ The Sapir Hypothesis.
    Ⓑ The Sapir-Whorf Hypothesis.
    Ⓒ The Sapir-Whorf-Boas Hypothesis.
    Ⓓ The American Indian Model of the Universe.

38. What is the topic of this discussion?

    Ⓐ Air pollution.
    Ⓑ Acid rain.
    Ⓒ Fossil fuels.
    Ⓓ The Great Lakes.

39. What is acid rain?

    Ⓐ Precipitation that is polluted by sulfuric acid and nitric acid.
    Ⓑ Rain that falls after a long period of severe drought.
    Ⓒ Large concentrations of acid in the soil around the Great Lakes.
    Ⓓ Water vapor that is mixed with a high concentration of sulfur.

40. In which two ways has the environment been damaged along the Great Lakes?

    Click on 2 answers.

    Ⓐ The air now contains dangerous levels of carbon monoxide.
    Ⓑ Weather patterns have been disturbed.
    Ⓒ Water resources have been polluted.
    Ⓓ The soil has been depleted of nutrients.

41. What are the conditions of the Air Quality Accord?

    Ⓐ Companies in the United States must control pollution that could affect Canadian resources.
    Ⓑ There are limits placed on the quantity of acidic deposits that can cross the border.
    Ⓒ Governments and agencies will regulate automobile emissions.
    Ⓓ Fuels cannot contain any sulfur near the border.

42. What is the topic of this lecture?

     Ⓐ Three major types of bacteria.
     Ⓑ How microscopic organisms are measured.
     Ⓒ How bacteria is used for research in genetics.
     Ⓓ Diseases caused by bacteria.

43. Which two characteristics are common in bacteria?

     Click on 2 answers.

     Ⓐ They have one cell.
     Ⓑ They are harmful to humans.
     Ⓒ They reproduce quickly.
     Ⓓ They die when exposed to air.

44. Which of the following slides contain cocci bacteria?

A   B   C

45. Why are bacteria being used in the research study at the University?

     Ⓐ Bacteria have unusual cell formations.
     Ⓑ Bacteria live harmlessly on the skin, mouth, and intestines.
     Ⓒ Bacteria are similar to other life forms.
     Ⓓ Bacteria cause many diseases in humans.

46. What is the purpose of this conversation?

     Ⓐ The man needs help changing his schedule.
     Ⓑ The man is looking for a job in the morning.
     Ⓒ The man is trying to get a student loan.
     Ⓓ The man is changing his major to sociology.

47. Why does the man need to take at least twelve hours?

     Ⓐ He wants to graduate as soon as possible.
     Ⓑ He must be a full-time student to qualify for his loan.
     Ⓒ His advisor insists that he study full time.
     Ⓓ All the courses are required.

48. Why does the man prefer Sociology 560?

     Ⓐ It is a required course.
     Ⓑ It is offered in the afternoon.
     Ⓒ It is taught by Dr. Brown.
     Ⓓ It is a sociology class.

49. What will Dr. Kelly do?

     Ⓐ Help the man withdraw from school.
     Ⓑ Change the man's class schedule.
     Ⓒ Give the man a student loan.
     Ⓓ Change the man's major.

50. What will the man probably do after the conversation?

     Ⓐ Go to Dr. Brown's office.
     Ⓑ See Dr. Brown in class.
     Ⓒ Call Dr. Brown.
     Ⓓ Send the form to Dr. Brown.

Section 2: Structure

This section measures the ability to recognize language that is appropriate for standard written English. There are two types of questions in this section.

In the first type of question, there are incomplete sentences. Beneath each sentence, there are four words or phrases. You will choose the one word or phrase that best completes the sentence.

Clicking on a choice darkens the oval. After you click on **Next** and **Confirm Answer**, the next question will be presented.

The second type of question has four underlined words or phrases. You will choose the one underlined word or phrase that must be changed for the sentence to be correct.

Clicking on an underlined word or phrase will darken it. After you click on **Next** and **Confirm Answer**, the next question will be presented.

1. Justice Sandra Day O'Connor was _____ to serve on the U.S. Supreme Court.

   Ⓐ the woman who first
   Ⓑ the first woman
   Ⓒ who the first woman
   Ⓓ the first and a woman

2. North Carolina is well known not only for the Great Smoky Mountains National Park _____ for the Cherokee settlements.

   Ⓐ also
   Ⓑ and
   Ⓒ but also
   Ⓓ because of

3. If biennials were planted this year, they <u>will be</u> <u>likely</u>
                 Ⓐ   Ⓑ
   <u>to bloom</u> <u>next year</u>.
     Ⓒ   Ⓓ

4. The value <u>of the dollar</u> <u>declines</u>
             Ⓐ   Ⓑ
   <u>as</u> the rate of inflation <u>raises</u>.
    Ⓒ   Ⓓ

5. General Grant had General Lee _____ him at Appomattox to sign the official surrender of the Confederate forces.

   Ⓐ to meet
   Ⓑ met
   Ⓒ meet
   Ⓓ meeting

6. Anthropologists assert that many of the early Native Americans who lived on the Plains did not engage in planting crops <u>but</u>
                           Ⓐ
   to hunt, <u>living</u> <u>primarily</u> on
          Ⓑ   Ⓒ   Ⓓ
   buffalo meat.

7. The differential attractions of the sun and the moon <u>have</u> a direct
                   Ⓐ
   effect <u>in</u> the <u>rising</u> and falling <u>of</u>
        Ⓑ   Ⓒ   Ⓓ
   the tides.

8. _____ both men and women have often achieved their career ambitions by midlife, many people are afflicted by at least a temporary period of dissatisfaction and depression.

   Ⓐ Because
   Ⓑ So
   Ⓒ A
   Ⓓ Who

9. With special enzymes that are
   call restriction enzymes, it is
   Ⓐ
   possible to split off segments of
           Ⓑ
   DNA from the donor organism.
       Ⓒ   Ⓓ

10. Because of the movement of a
    Ⓐ
    glacier, the form of the Great
            Ⓑ   Ⓒ
    Lakes was very slow.
                    Ⓓ

11. _____ small specimen of the embryonic fluid is removed from a fetus, it will be possible to determine whether the baby will be born with birth defects.

    Ⓐ A
    Ⓑ That a
    Ⓒ If a
    Ⓓ When it is a

12. To generate income, magazine publishers must decide whether to increase the subscription price or _____.

    Ⓐ to sell advertising
    Ⓑ if they should sell advertising
    Ⓒ selling advertising
    Ⓓ sold advertising

13. If it receives enough rain at the
    Ⓐ   Ⓑ
    proper time, hay will grow
                    Ⓒ
    quickly, as grass.
             Ⓓ

14. Psychology Today is interesting,
                    Ⓐ   Ⓑ
    informative, and it is easy
                    Ⓒ
    to read.
    Ⓓ

15. Before she died, Andrew
    Ⓐ
    Jackson's daughter, who lives in
                    Ⓑ   Ⓒ
    the family mansion, used to take
                        Ⓓ
    tourists through her home.

16. If it _____ more humid in the desert of the Southwest, the hot temperatures would be unbearable.

    Ⓐ be
    Ⓑ is
    Ⓒ was
    Ⓓ were

17. _____ Java Man, who lived before the first Ice Age, is the first manlike animal.

    Ⓐ It is generally believed that
    Ⓑ Generally believed it is
    Ⓒ Believed generally is
    Ⓓ That is generally believed

18. It is essential that the
    temperature is not elevated
                Ⓐ
    to a point where the substance
    Ⓑ
    formed may become unstable
            Ⓒ
    and decompose into its
                        Ⓓ
    constituent elements.

19. John Philip Sousa, who many
    _____(A)__(B)___
    people consider the greatest
    _____(C)___
    composer of marches, wrote his
    music during the era known as
    _____(D)___
    the Gay 90s.

20. For the investor who
    _____ money, silver or
    bonds are good options.

    (A) has so little a
    (B) has very little
    (C) has so few
    (D) has very few

21. Although it can be derived from
    _____(A)_____(B)____
    oil, coal, and tar, kerosene is
    usually produced by refine it
    _____(C)_____(D)____
    from petroleum.

22. Aeronomy is the study of
    _____(A)__(B)____
    the earth's upper atmosphere,
    ___(C)___
    which includes their
    _____(D)__
    composition, temperature,
    density, and chemical reactions.

23. The purpose of the United
    _____(A)_____
    Nations, broad speaking, is to
    _____(B)_____(C)__
    maintain peace and security and
    to encourage respect for human
    ___(D)___
    rights.

24. Of all the cereals, rice is the one
    _____ food for more
    people than any of the other
    grain crops.

    (A) it provides
    (B) that providing
    (C) provides
    (D) that provides

25. Although Congressional
    representatives and senators may
    serve an unlimited number of
    term, the president is limited to
    (A)_____(B)____
    two, for a total of eight years.
    ___(C)_____(D)_____

Section 3:
Reading

This section measures the ability to read and understand short passages similar in topic and style to those that students are likely to encounter in North American universities and colleges. This section contains reading passages and questions about the passages. There are several different types of questions in this section.

In the Reading section, you will first have the opportunity to read the passage.

You will use the scroll bar to view the rest of the passage.

When you have finished reading the passage, you will use the mouse to click on **Proceed**. Then the questions about the passage will be presented. You are to choose the one best answer to each question. Answer all questions about the information in a passage on the basis of what is stated or implied in that passage.

Most of the questions will be multiple-choice questions. To answer these questions you will click on a choice below the question.

To answer some questions, you will click on a word or phrase.

To answer some questions, you will click on a sentence in the passage.

To answer some questions, you will click on a square to add a sentence to the passage.

The computer screens for selected questions in the Reading section have been printed in this book to provide you with orientation to the format of the Computer-Based TOEFL. Use the screen to find the place in the original reading passage that corresponds to the question you are answering.

It has long been known that when the green parts of plants are exposed to light under suitable conditions of temperature and moisture, carbon dioxide is absorbed by the plant from the atmospheric CO_2, and oxygen is released into the air. This exchange of gases in plants is the opposite of the process that occurs in respiration. In this plant process, which is called photosynthesis, carbohydrates are synthesized in the presence of light from carbon dioxide and water by specialized structures in the cytoplasm of plant cells called chloroplasts. These chloroplasts contain not only two types of light-trapping green chlorophyll but also a vast array of protein substances called enzymes. In most plants, the water required by the photosynthesis process is absorbed from the soil by the roots and translocated through the xylem of the root and stem to the chlorophyll-laden leaves. Except for the usually small percentage used in respiration, the oxygen released in the process diffuses out of the leaf into the atmosphere through stomates. In simple terms, carbon dioxide is the fuel, and oxygen is the product of the chemical reaction. For each molecule of carbon dioxide used, one molecule of oxygen is released. Here is a summary chemical equation for photosynthesis:

$$6CO_2 + 6H_2O \rightarrow C_6H_{12}O_6 + 6O_2$$

As a result of this process, radiant energy from the sun is stored as chemical energy. In turn, the chemical energy is used to decompose carbon dioxide and water. The products of their decomposition are recombined into a new compound, which successively builds up into the more and more complex substances that comprise the plant. These organic substances, that is, the sugars, starches, and cellulose, all belong to the class of organic molecules. In other words, the process of photosynthesis can be

understood as an enzyme-induced chemical
change from carbon dioxide and water into the
simple sugar glucose. This carbohydrate, in turn,
is utilized by the plant to generate other forms
of energy, such as the long chains of plant cells or
polymers that comprise the cellular structures of
starches or cellulose. Many intermediate steps are
involved in the production of a simple sugar
or starch. At the same time, a balance of gases is
preserved in the atmosphere by the process of
photosynthesis.

1. Which title best expresses the
   ideas in this passage?

   (A) A Chemical Equation
   (B) The Process of
       Photosynthesis
   (C) The Parts of Vascular Plants
   (D) The Production of Sugar

2. The combination of carbon
   dioxide and water to form sugar
   results in an excess of

   (A) water
   (B) oxygen
   (C) carbon
   (D) chlorophyll

3. Which process is the opposite of
   photosynthesis?

   (A) Decomposition
   (B) Synthesization
   (C) Diffusion
   (D) Respiration

4. In photosynthesis, energy from
   the sun is

   (A) changed to chemical energy
   (B) conducted from the xylem
       to the leaves of green plants
   (C) not necessary to the process
   (D) released one to one for each
       molecule of carbon dioxide
       used

5. Click on the sentence in
   paragraph 1 that describes how
   oxygen is released into the
   atmosphere.

   Paragraph 1 is marked with an
   arrow (→).

Beginning

→ It has long been known that when the green
parts of plants are exposed to light under suitable
conditions of temperature and moisture, carbon
dioxide is absorbed by the plant from the
atmospheric CO_2, and oxygen is released into the
air. This exchange of gases in plants is the
opposite of the process that occurs in respiration.
In this plant process, which is called photosynthesis,
carbohydrates are synthesized in the presence of
light from carbon dioxide and water by specialized
structures in the cytoplasm of plant cells called
chloroplasts. These chloroplasts contain not only
two types of light-trapping green chlorophyll but
also a vast array of protein substances called
enzymes. In most plants, the water required by
the photosynthesis process is absorbed from the
soil by the roots and translocated through the
xylem of the root and stem to the chlorophyll-laden
leaves. Except for the usually small percentage
used in respiration, the oxygen released in the
process diffuses out of the leaf into the atmosphere
through stomates. In simple terms, carbon dioxide
is the fuel, and oxygen is the product of the chemical
reaction. For each molecule of carbon dioxide

6. The word stored in paragraph 2 is closest in meaning to

(A) retained
(B) converted
(C) discovered
(D) specified

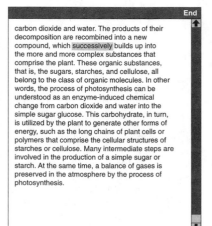

More Available

leaves. Except for the usually small percentage used in respiration, the oxygen released in the process diffuses out of the leaf into the atmosphere through stomates. In simple terms, carbon dioxide is the fuel, and oxygen is the product of the chemical reaction. For each molecule of carbon dioxide used, one molecule of oxygen is released. Here is a summary chemical equation for photosynthesis:

$$6CO_2 + 6H_2O \rightarrow C_6H_{12}O_6 + 6O_2$$

As a result of this process, radiant energy from the sun is stored as chemical energy. In turn, the chemical energy is used to decompose carbon dioxide and water. The products of their decomposition are recombined into a new compound, which successively builds up into the more and more complex substances that comprise the plant. These organic substances, that is, the sugars, starches, and cellulose, all belong to the class of organic molecules. In other words, the process of photosynthesis can be understood as an enzyme-induced chemical change from carbon dioxide and water into the simple sugar glucose. This carbohydrate, in turn, is utilized by the plant to generate other forms of

7. The word their in paragraph 2 refers to

(A) radiant energy and chemical energy
(B) carbon dioxide and water
(C) products
(D) complex substances

End

As a result of this process, radiant energy from the sun is stored as chemical energy. In turn, the chemical energy is used to decompose carbon dioxide and water. The products of their decomposition are recombined into a new compound, which successively builds up into the more and more complex substances that comprise the plant. These organic substances, that is, the sugars, starches, and cellulose, all belong to the class of organic molecules. In other words, the process of photosynthesis can be understood as an enzyme-induced chemical change from carbon dioxide and water into the simple sugar glucose. This carbohydrate, in turn, is utilized by the plant to generate other forms of energy, such as the long chains of plant cells or polymers that comprise the cellular structures of starches or cellulose. Many intermediate steps are involved in the production of a simple sugar or starch. At the same time, a balance of gases is preserved in the atmosphere by the process of photosynthesis.

8. The word successively in paragraph 2 is closest in meaning to

(A) with effort
(B) in a sequence
(C) slowly
(D) carefully

End

carbon dioxide and water. The products of their decomposition are recombined into a new compound, which successively builds up into the more and more complex substances that comprise the plant. These organic substances, that is, the sugars, starches, and cellulose, all belong to the class of organic molecules. In other words, the process of photosynthesis can be understood as an enzyme-induced chemical change from carbon dioxide and water into the simple sugar glucose. This carbohydrate, in turn, is utilized by the plant to generate other forms of energy, such as the long chains of plant cells or polymers that comprise the cellular structures of starches or cellulose. Many intermediate steps are involved in the production of a simple sugar or starch. At the same time, a balance of gases is preserved in the atmosphere by the process of photosynthesis.

9. Besides the manufacture of food for plants, what is another benefit of photosynthesis?

(A) It produces solar energy.
(B) It diffuses additional carbon dioxide into the air.
(C) It maintains a balance of gases in the atmosphere.
(D) It removes harmful gases from the air.

10. Which of the following is NOT true of the oxygen used in photosynthesis?

(A) Oxygen is absorbed by the roots.
(B) Oxygen is the product of photosynthesis.
(C) Oxygen is used in respiration.
(D) Oxygen is released into the atmosphere through the leaves.

Alfred Bernhard Nobel, a Swedish inventor and philanthropist, bequeathed most of his vast fortune to a trust that he designated as a fund from which annual prizes could be awarded to the individuals and organizations that had achieved through invention or discovery that which would have the greatest benefit to humanity in a particular year. According to the legend, Nobel's death had been erroneously reported in a newspaper, and the focus of the obituary was the fact that Nobel had invented dynamite. He rewrote his will in 1895, thereby establishing, with the original amount of nine million dollars, the Nobel Foundation as the legal owner and administering agent of the funds, and instituting the prizes that are named after him. Statutes to govern the awarding of the prizes were written, along with guidelines for operating procedures. Five years after Nobel's death, the first five prizes, worth about forty thousand dollars each, were to be awarded.

Originally the five classifications for outstanding contributions designated in Nobel's will included chemistry, physics, physiology or medicine, literature, and international peace. These prizes have been administered continually by the Nobel Foundation in Stockholm since they were first awarded in 1901. In 1969, a sixth prize, for accomplishments in the field of economics and endowed by the Central Bank of Sweden, was added. Candidates for the prizes must be nominated in writing by February 1 of each year by a qualified and recognized authority in each of the fields of competition. Recipients in physics, chemistry, and economics are selected by the Royal Swedish Academy, whereas recipients in peace are chosen by the Norwegian Nobel Committee appointed by Norway's parliament. With the King of Sweden officiating, the prizes are usually presented in Stockholm on December 10, the anniversary of Nobel's death. The value, fame, and prestige of the Nobel Prizes have continued to grow. Today the prize includes a medal, a diploma, and a cash award of about one million dollars.

11. What does this passage mainly discuss?

Ⓐ Alfred Bernhard Nobel
Ⓑ The Nobel Prizes
Ⓒ Great contributions to mankind
Ⓓ Swedish philanthropy

12. Why were the prizes named for Alfred Bernhard Nobel?

Ⓐ He left money in his will to establish a fund for the prizes.
Ⓑ He won the first Nobel Prize for his work in philanthropy.
Ⓒ He is now living in Sweden.
Ⓓ He serves as chairman of the committee to choose the recipients of the prizes.

13. The word will in paragraph 1 refers to

Ⓐ Nobel's wishes
Ⓑ a legal document
Ⓒ a future intention
Ⓓ a free choice

More Available

particular year. According to the legend, Nobel's death had been erroneously reported in a newspaper, and the focus of the obituary was the fact that Nobel had invented dynamite. He rewrote his will in 1895, thereby establishing, with the original amount of nine million dollars, the Nobel Foundation as the legal owner and administering agent of the funds, and instituting the prizes that are named after him. Statutes to govern the awarding of the prizes were written, along with guidelines for operating procedures. Five years after Nobel's death, the first five prizes, worth about forty thousand dollars each, were to be awarded.

Originally the five classifications for outstanding contributions designated in Nobel's will included chemistry, physics, physiology or medicine, literature, and international peace. These prizes have been administered continually by the Nobel Foundation in Stockholm since they were first awarded in 1901. In 1969, a sixth prize, for accomplishments in the field of economics and endowed by the Central Bank of Sweden, was added. Candidates for the prizes must be

14. How often are the Nobel Prizes awarded?

Ⓐ Five times a year
Ⓑ Once a year
Ⓒ Twice a year
Ⓓ Once every two years

15. The following sentence can be added to the passage.

> **When he read this objective summary of his life, the great chemist, it is said, decided that he wanted his name to be remembered for something more positive and humanitarian than inventing an explosive that was a potential weapon.**

Where would it best fit in the passage?

Click on the square (■) to add the sentence to the passage.

Scroll the passage to see all of the choices.

More Available

particular year. According to the legend, Nobel's death had been erroneously reported in a newspaper, and the focus of the obituary was the fact that Nobel had invented dynamite. ■ He rewrote his will in 1895, thereby establishing, with the original amount of nine million dollars, the Nobel Foundation as the legal owner and administering agent of the funds, and instituting the prizes that are named after him. ■ Statutes to govern the awarding of the prizes were written, along with guidelines for operating procedures. ■ Five years after Nobel's death, the first five prizes, worth about forty thousand dollars each, were to be awarded. ■

Originally the five classifications for outstanding contributions designated in Nobel's will included chemistry, physics, physiology or medicine, literature, and international peace. These prizes have been administered continually by the Nobel Foundation in Stockholm since they were first awarded in 1901. In 1969, a sixth prize, for accomplishments in the field of economics and endowed by the Central Bank of Sweden, was added. Candidates for the prizes must be

---

16. The word outstanding in paragraph 2 could best be replaced by

- Ⓐ recent
- Ⓑ unusual
- Ⓒ established
- Ⓓ exceptional

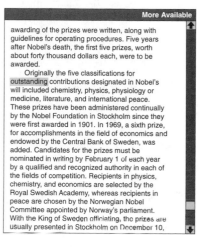

More Available

awarding of the prizes were written, along with guidelines for operating procedures. Five years after Nobel's death, the first five prizes, worth about forty thousand dollars each, were to be awarded.

Originally the five classifications for outstanding contributions designated in Nobel's will included chemistry, physics, physiology or medicine, literature, and international peace. These prizes have been administered continually by the Nobel Foundation in Stockholm since they were first awarded in 1901. In 1969, a sixth prize, for accomplishments in the field of economics and endowed by the Central Bank of Sweden, was added. Candidates for the prizes must be nominated in writing by February 1 of each year by a qualified and recognized authority in each of the fields of competition. Recipients in physics, chemistry, and economics are selected by the Royal Swedish Academy, whereas recipients in peace are chosen by the Norwegian Nobel Committee appointed by Norway's parliament. With the King of Sweden officiating, the prizes are usually presented in Stockholm on December 10,

---

17. A Nobel Prize would NOT be given to

- Ⓐ an author who wrote a novel
- Ⓑ a doctor who discovered a vaccine
- Ⓒ a composer who wrote a symphony
- Ⓓ a diplomat who negotiated a peace settlement

18. What does the author mean by the statement These prizes have been administered continually by the Nobel Foundation in Stockholm since they were first awarded in 1901?

  Ⓐ The Nobel Foundation oversees the management of the money and the distribution of the prizes.
  Ⓑ The Nobel Foundation selects the recipients of the prizes.
  Ⓒ The Nobel Foundation solicits applications and recommendations for the prizes.
  Ⓓ The Nobel Foundation recommends new prize classifications.

> **End**
>
> Originally the five classifications for outstanding contributions designated in Nobel's will included chemistry, physics, physiology or medicine, literature, and international peace. These prizes have been administered continually by the Nobel Foundation in Stockholm since they were first awarded in 1901. In 1969, a sixth prize, for accomplishments in the field of economics and endowed by the Central Bank of Sweden, was added. Candidates for the prizes must be nominated in writing by February 1 of each year by a qualified and recognized authority in each of the fields of competition. Recipients in physics, chemistry, and economics are selected by the Royal Swedish Academy, whereas recipients in peace are chosen by the Norwegian Nobel Committee appointed by Norway's parliament. With the King of Sweden officiating, the prizes are usually presented in Stockholm on December 10, the anniversary of Nobel's death. The value, fame, and prestige of the Nobel Prizes have continued to grow. Today the prize includes a medal, a diploma, and a cash award of about one million dollars.

19. Why are the awards presented on December 10?

  Ⓐ It is a tribute to the King of Sweden.
  Ⓑ Alfred Bernhard Nobel died on that day.
  Ⓒ That date was established in Alfred Nobel's will.
  Ⓓ The Central Bank of Sweden administers the trust.

20. Look at the word prize in the passage. Click on the word or phrase in the **bold** text that is closest in meaning to prize.

> **End**
>
> by a qualified and recognized authority in each of the fields of competition. Recipients in physics, chemistry, and economics are selected by the Royal Swedish Academy, whereas recipients in peace are chosen by the Norwegian Nobel Committee appointed by Norway's parliament. **With the King of Sweden officiating, the prizes are usually presented in Stockholm on December 10, the anniversary of Nobel's death. The value, fame, and prestige of the Nobel Prizes have continued to grow. Today the prize includes a medal, a diploma, and a cash award of about one million dollars.**

Although stage plays have been set to music since the era of the ancient Greeks, when the dramas of Sophocles and Aeschylus were accompanied by lyres and flutes, the usually accepted date for the beginning of opera as we know it is 1600. As a part of the celebration of the marriage of King Henry IV of France to the Italian aristocrat Maria de Medici, the Florentine composer Jacopo Perí produced his famous *Euridice*, generally considered to be the first opera. Following his example, a group of Italian musicians, poets, and noblemen called the Camerata began to revive the style of musical story that had been used in Greek tragedy. The Camerata took most of the plots for their operas from Greek and Roman history and mythology, beginning the process of creating an opera by writing a libretto or drama that could be used to establish the framework for the music. They called their compositions *opera in musica* or musical works. It is from this phrase that the word "opera" was borrowed and abbreviated.

For several years, the center of opera was Florence in northern Italy, but gradually, during the baroque period, it spread throughout Italy. By the late 1600s, operas were being written and performed in many places throughout Europe, especially in England, France, and Germany. However, for many years, the Italian opera was considered the ideal, and many non-Italian composers continued to use Italian librettos. The European form deemphasized the dramatic aspect of the Italian model. Now orchestral interludes and even ballet were introduced under the guise of opera. Composers gave in to the demands of singers, writing many operas that were little more than a succession of brilliant tricks for the voice, designed to showcase the splendid voices of the singers who had requested them. It was thus that complicated arias, recitatives, and duets evolved. The aria, which is a long solo, may be compared to a song in which the characters express their thoughts and feelings. The recitative, which is also a solo of sorts, is a recitation set to music, the purpose of which is to continue the story line. The duet is a musical piece written for two voices, a musical device that may serve the function of either an aria or a recitative within the opera.

21. This passage is a summary of

Ⓐ opera in Italy
Ⓑ the Camerata
Ⓒ the development of opera
Ⓓ *Euridice*

22. Look at the word usually in the passage. Click on the word or phrase in the **bold** text that is closest in meaning to usually.

   Although stage plays have been set to music since the era of the ancient Greeks, when the dramas of Sophocles and Aeschylus were accompanied by lyres and flutes, the usually accepted date for the beginning of opera as we know it is 1600. As a part of the celebration of the marriage of King Henry IV of France to the Italian aristocrat Maria de Medici, the Florentine composer Jacopo Perí produced his famous *Euridice*, generally considered to be the first opera. Following his example, a group of Italian musicians, poets, and noblemen called the Camerata began to revive the style of musical story that had been used in Greek tragedy. The Camerata took most of the plots for their operas from Greek and Roman history and mythology, beginning the process of creating an opera by writing a libretto or drama that could be used to establish the framework for the music. They called their compositions *opera in musica* or musical works. It is from this phrase that the word "opera" was borrowed and abbreviated.

   For several years, the center of opera was Florence in northern Italy, but gradually, during the

23. According to this passage, when did modern opera begin?

Ⓐ In the time of the ancient Greeks
Ⓑ In the fifteenth century
Ⓒ At the beginning of the sixteenth century
Ⓓ At the beginning of the seventeenth century

24. The word it in paragraph 1 refers to

Ⓐ opera
Ⓑ date
Ⓒ era
Ⓓ music

Beginning

   Although stage plays have been set to music since the era of the ancient Greeks, when the dramas of Sophocles and Aeschylus were accompanied by lyres and flutes, the usually accepted date for the beginning of opera as we know it is 1600. As a part of the celebration of the marriage of King Henry IV of France to the Italian aristocrat Maria de Medici, the Florentine composer Jacopo Perí produced his famous *Euridice*, generally considered to be the first opera. Following his example, a group of Italian musicians, poets, and noblemen called the Camerata began to revive the style of musical story that had been used in Greek tragedy. The Camerata took most of the plots for their operas from Greek and Roman history and mythology, beginning the process of creating an opera by writing a libretto or drama that could be used to establish the framework for the music. They called their compositions *opera in musica* or musical works. It is from this phrase that the word "opera" was borrowed and abbreviated.

   For several years, the center of opera was Florence in northern Italy, but gradually, during the

25. According to the author, what did Jacopo Perí write?

Ⓐ Greek tragedy
Ⓑ The first opera
Ⓒ The opera *Maria de Medici*
Ⓓ The opera *The Camerata*

26. The author suggests that *Euridice* was produced

Ⓐ in France
Ⓑ originally by Sophocles and Aeschylus
Ⓒ without much success
Ⓓ for the wedding of King Henry IV

27. What was the Camerata?

Ⓐ A group of Greek musicians
Ⓑ Musicians who developed a new musical drama based upon Greek drama
Ⓒ A style of music not known in Italy
Ⓓ The name given to the court of King Henry IV

28. The word revive in paragraph 1 could best be replaced by

Ⓐ appreciate
Ⓑ resume
Ⓒ modify
Ⓓ investigate

29. The word plots in paragraph 1 is closest in meaning to

Ⓐ locations
Ⓑ instruments
Ⓒ stories
Ⓓ inspiration

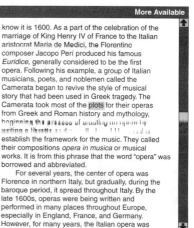

30. From what did the term "opera" derive?

    Ⓐ Greek and Roman history and mythology

    Ⓑ Non-Italian composers

    Ⓒ The Italian phrase that means "musical works"

    Ⓓ The ideas of composer Jacopo Perí

31. Look at the word them in the passage. Click on the word or phrase in the **bold** text that them refers to.

> **End** ↑
>
> However, for many years, the Italian opera was considered the ideal, and many non-Italian composers continued to use Italian librettos. The European form deemphasized the dramatic aspect of the Italian model. **New orchestral effects and even ballet were introduced under the guise of opera. Composers gave in to the demands of singers, writing many operas that were little more than a succession of brilliant tricks for the voice, designed to showcase the splendid voices of the singers who had requested them. It was thus that complicated arias, recitatives, and duets evolved.** The aria, which is a long solo, may be compared to a song in which the characters express their thoughts and feelings. The recitative, which is also a solo of sorts, is a recitation set to music, the purpose of which is to continue the story line. The duet is a musical piece written for two voices, a musical device that may serve the function of either an aria or a recitative within the opera.
>
> ▓ ↓

32. Look at the word function in the passage. Click on the word or phrase in the **bold** text that is closest in meaning to function.

> **End** ↑
>
> aspect of the Italian model. New orchestral effects and even ballet were introduced under the guise of opera. Composers gave in to the demands of singers, writing many operas that were little more than a succession of brilliant tricks for the voice, designed to showcase the splendid voices of the singers who had requested them. **It was thus that complicated arias, recitatives, and duets evolved. The aria, which is a long solo, may be compared to a song in which the characters express their thoughts and feelings. The recitative, which is also a solo of sorts, is a recitation set to music, the purpose of which is to continue the story line. The duet is a musical piece written for two voices, a musical device that may serve the function of either an aria or a recitative within the opera.**
>
> ▓ ↓

According to the controversial sunspot theory, great storms or eruptions on the surface of the sun hurl streams of solar particles into space and eventually into the atmosphere of our planet, causing shifts in the weather on the Earth and interference with radio and television communications.

A typical sunspot consists of a dark central umbra, a word derived from the Latin word for shadow, which is surrounded by a lighter penumbra of light and dark threads extending out from the center like the spokes of a wheel. Actually, the sunspots are cooler than the rest of the photosphere, which may account for their apparently darker color. Typically, the temperature in a sunspot umbra is about 4000 K, whereas the temperature in a penumbra registers 5500 K, and the granules outside the spot are 6000 K.

Sunspots range in size from tiny granules to complex structures with areas stretching for billions of square miles. About 5 percent of all sunspots are large enough so that they can be seen from Earth without instruments; consequently, observations of sunspots have been recorded for thousands of years.

Sunspots have been observed in arrangements of one to more than one hundred spots, but they tend to occur in pairs. There is also a marked tendency for the two spots of a pair to have opposite magnetic polarities. Furthermore, the strength of the magnetic field associated with any given sunspot is closely related to the spot's size. Sunspots have also been observed to occur in cycles, over a period of eleven years. At the beginning of a cycle, the storms occur between 20 and 40 degrees north and south of the equator on the sun. As the cycle continues, some of the storms move closer to the equator. As the cycle diminishes, the number of sunspots decreases to a minimum and they cluster between 5 and 15 degrees north and south latitude.

Although there is no theory that completely explains the nature and function of sunspots, several models show scientists' attempts to relate the phenomenon to magnetic field lines along the lines of longitude from the north and south poles of the sun.

33. What is the author's main purpose in the passage?

Ⓐ To propose a theory to explain sunspots
Ⓑ To describe the nature of sunspots
Ⓒ To compare the umbra and the penumbra in sunspots
Ⓓ To argue for the existence of magnetic fields in sunspots

34. The word controversial in paragraph 1 is closest in meaning to

Ⓐ widely accepted
Ⓑ open to debate
Ⓒ just introduced
Ⓓ very complicated

35. Solar particles are hurled into space by

Ⓐ undetermined causes
Ⓑ disturbances of wind
Ⓒ small rivers on the surface of the sun
Ⓓ changes in the Earth's atmosphere

36. The word particles in paragraph 1 refers to

Ⓐ gas explosions in the atmosphere
Ⓑ light rays from the sun
Ⓒ liquid streams on the sun
Ⓓ small pieces of matter from the sun

Beginning

According to the controversial sunspot theory, great storms or eruptions on the surface of the sun hurl streams of solar particles into space and eventually into the atmosphere of our planet, causing shifts in the weather on the Earth and interference with radio and television communications.

A typical sunspot consists of a dark central umbra, a word derived from the Latin word for shadow, which is surrounded by a lighter penumbra of light and dark threads extending out from the center like the spokes of a wheel. Actually, the sunspots are cooler than the rest of the photosphere, which may account for their apparently darker color. Typically, the temperature in a sunspot umbra is about 4000 K, whereas the temperature in a penumbra registers 5500 K, and the granules outside the spot are 6000 K.

Sunspots range in size from tiny granules to complex structures with areas stretching for billions of square miles. About 5 percent of all sunspots are large enough so that they can be seen from Earth without instruments; consequently, observations of sunspots have been recorded for thousands of years.

Beginning

According to the controversial sunspot theory, great storms or eruptions on the surface of the sun hurl streams of solar particles into space and eventually into the atmosphere of our planet, causing shifts in the weather on the Earth and interference with radio and television communications.

A typical sunspot consists of a dark central umbra, a word derived from the Latin word for shadow, which is surrounded by a lighter penumbra of light and dark threads extending out from the center like the spokes of a wheel. Actually, the sunspots are cooler than the rest of the photosphere, which may account for their apparently darker color. Typically, the temperature in a sunspot umbra is about 4000 K, whereas the temperature in a penumbra registers 5500 K, and the granules outside the spot are 6000 K.

Sunspots range in size from tiny granules to complex structures with areas stretching for billions of square miles. About 5 percent of all sunspots are large enough so that they can be seen from Earth without instruments; consequently, observations of sunspots have been recorded for thousands of years.

37. How can we describe matter from the sun that enters the Earth's atmosphere?

   Ⓐ Very small
   Ⓑ Very hot
   Ⓒ Very bright
   Ⓓ Very hard

38. What does the author mean by the statement Actually, the sunspots are cooler than the rest of the photosphere, which may account for their apparently darker color?

   Ⓐ Neither sunspots nor the photosphere is hot.
   Ⓑ Sunspots in the photosphere do not have any color.
   Ⓒ The color of sunspots could be affected by their temperature.
   Ⓓ The size of a sunspot affects its temperature.

More Available

of light and dark threads extending out from the center like the spokes of a wheel. Actually, the sunspots are cooler than the rest of the photosphere, which may account for their apparently darker color. Typically, the temperature in a sunspot umbra is about 4000 K, whereas the temperature in a penumbra registers 5500 K, and the granules outside the spot are 6000 K.

Sunspots range in size from tiny granules to complex structures with areas stretching for billions of square miles. About 5 percent of all sunspots are large enough so that they can be seen from Earth without instruments; consequently, observations of sunspots have been recorded for thousands of years.

Sunspots have been observed in arrangements of one to more than one hundred spots, but they tend to occur in pairs. There is also a marked tendency for the two spots of a pair to have opposite magnetic polarities. Furthermore, the strength of the magnetic field associated with any given sunspot is closely related to the spot's size. Sunspots have also been observed to occur in cycles, over a period of eleven years. At the

39. Look at the word tiny in the passage. Click on the word or phrase in the **bold** text that is opposite in meaning to tiny.

More Available

color. Typically, the temperature in a sunspot umbra is about 4000 K, whereas the temperature in a penumbra registers 5500 K, and the granules outside the spot are 6000 K.

Sunspots range in size from tiny granules to complex structures with areas stretching for billions of square miles. About 5 percent of all sunspots are large enough so that they can be seen from Earth without instruments; consequently, observations of sunspots have been recorded for thousands of years.

Sunspots have been observed in arrangements of one to more than one hundred spots, but they tend to occur in pairs. There is also a marked tendency for the two spots of a pair to have opposite magnetic polarities. Furthermore, the strength of the magnetic field associated with any given sunspot is closely related to the spot's size. Sunspots have also been observed to occur in cycles, over a period of eleven years. At the beginning of a cycle, the storms occur between 20 and 40 degrees north and south of the equator on the sun. As the cycle continues, some of the storms move closer to the equator. As the cycle

40. The word they in paragraph 2 refers to

   Ⓐ structures
   Ⓑ spots
   Ⓒ miles
   Ⓓ granules

More Available

color. Typically, the temperature in a sunspot umbra is about 4000 K, whereas the temperature in a penumbra registers 5500 K, and the granules outside the spot are 6000 K.

Sunspots range in size from tiny granules to complex structures with areas stretching for billions of square miles. About 5 percent of all sunspots are large enough so that they can be seen from Earth without instruments; consequently, observations of sunspots have been recorded for thousands of years.

Sunspots have been observed in arrangements of one to more than one hundred spots, but they tend to occur in pairs. There is also a marked tendency for the two spots of a pair to have opposite magnetic polarities. Furthermore, the strength of the magnetic field associated with

in cycles, over a period of eleven years. At the beginning of a cycle, the storms occur between 20 and 40 degrees north and south of the equator on the sun. As the cycle continues, some of the storms move closer to the equator. As the cycle

41. The word consequently in paragraph 2 could best be replaced by

    Ⓐ as a result
    Ⓑ nevertheless
    Ⓒ without doubt
    Ⓓ in this way

More Available

color. Typically, the temperature in a sunspot umbra is about 4000 K, whereas the temperature in a penumbra registers 5500 K, and the granules outside the spot are 6000 K.

Sunspots range in size from tiny granules to complex structures with areas stretching for billions of square miles. About 5 percent of all sunspots are large enough so that they can be seen from Earth without instruments; consequently, observations of sunspots have been recorded for thousands of years.

Sunspots have been observed in arrangements of one to more than one hundred spots, but they tend to occur in pairs. There is also a marked tendency for the two spots of a pair to have opposite magnetic polarities. Furthermore, the strength of the magnetic field associated with any given sunspot is closely related to the spot's size. Sunspots have also been observed to occur in cycles, over a period of eleven years. At the beginning of a cycle, the storms occur between 20 and 40 degrees north and south of the equator on the sun. As the cycle continues, some of the storms move closer to the equator. As the cycle

---

42. In which configuration do sunspots usually occur?

    Ⓐ In one spot of varying size
    Ⓑ In a configuration of two spots
    Ⓒ In arrangements of one hundred or more spots
    Ⓓ In groups of several thousand spots

43. How are sunspots explained?

    Ⓐ Sunspots appear to be related to magnetic fields on the Earth.
    Ⓑ Sunspots may be related to magnetic fields that follow longitudinal lines on the sun.
    Ⓒ Sunspots are explained by storms that occur on the Earth.
    Ⓓ Sunspots have no theory or model to explain them.

44. Click on the paragraph that discusses the visibility of sunspots.

    Scroll the passage to see all of the paragraphs.

45. The sunspot theory is

    Ⓐ not considered very important
    Ⓑ widely accepted
    Ⓒ subject to disagreement
    Ⓓ relatively new

To check your answers for Model Test 1, refer to the Answer Key on pages 368–369. For an explanation of the answers, refer to the Explanatory Answers for Model Test 1 on pages 377–388.

Writing Section Model Test 1

When you take a Model Test, you should use one sheet of paper, both sides. Time each Model Test carefully. After you have read the topic, you should spend 30 minutes writing. For results that would be closest to the actual testing situation, it is recommended that an English teacher score your test, using the guidelines on page 234 of this book.

Many people enjoy participating in sports for recreation; others enjoy participating in the arts. Give the benefits of each, take a position, and defend it.

Notes

Model Test 2
Computer-Assisted TOEFL

Section 1: Listening

The Listening section of the test measures the ability to understand conversations and talks in English. You will use headphones to listen to the conversations and talks. While you are listening, pictures of the speakers or other information will be presented on your computer screen. There are two parts to the Listening section, with special directions for each part.

On the day of the test, the amount of time you will have to answer all of the questions will appear on the computer screen. The time you spend listening to the test material will not be counted. The listening material and questions about it will be presented only one time. You will not be allowed to take notes or have any paper at your computer. You will both see and hear the questions before the answer choices appear. You can take as much time as you need to select an answer; however, it will be to your advantage to answer the questions as quickly as possible. You may change your answer as many times as you want before you confirm it. After you have confirmed an answer, you will not be able to return to the question.

Before you begin working on the Listening section, you will have an opportunity to adjust the volume of the sound. You will not be able to change the volume after you have started the test.

QUESTION DIRECTIONS—Part A

In Part A of the Listening section, you will hear short conversations between two people. In some of the conversations, each person speaks only once. In other conversations, one or both of the people speak more than once. Each conversation is followed by one question about it.

Each question in this part has four answer choices. You should click on the best answer to each question. Answer the questions on the basis of what is stated or implied by the speakers.

1. What had the man assumed?

   Ⓐ The woman was not truthful.
   Ⓑ Fewer students would attend.
   Ⓒ There would be a large group.
   Ⓓ Only foreign students would come.

2. What does the woman imply that the man should do?

   Ⓐ Knock on the door.
   Ⓑ Come back later.
   Ⓒ See Dr. Smith.
   Ⓓ Look at the sign.

3. What is the woman probably going to do?

   Ⓐ Take a class from Professor Wilson.
   Ⓑ Help the man with his class.
   Ⓒ Take an extra class.
   Ⓓ Do a project for her class.

4. What does the woman say about Paul?

   Ⓐ That he wants something to eat.
   Ⓑ That he will tell them if there is a problem.
   Ⓒ That he is not hungry.
   Ⓓ That he is angry.

5. What does the woman mean?

   Ⓐ Good grades are not that important to her.
   Ⓑ She did not get an A on the exam either.
   Ⓒ Two students got higher grades than she did.
   Ⓓ Besides hers, there were several other A grades.

6. What problem does the woman have?

   Ⓐ There is no time to finish.
   Ⓑ She cannot do it quickly.
   Ⓒ She needs to study.
   Ⓓ She doesn't know what time it is.

7. What does the woman mean?

   Ⓐ She does not agree with the man.
   Ⓑ She thinks that it is better to wait.
   Ⓒ She thinks that it is better to drive at night.
   Ⓓ She does not think that the man made a wise decision.

8. What is the man going to do?

   Ⓐ Go to class.
   Ⓑ See a movie.
   Ⓒ Study at the library.
   Ⓓ Make an appointment.

9. What does the man mean?

   Ⓐ The message was not clear.
   Ⓑ There was no message on the machine.
   Ⓒ It was his intention to return the woman's call.
   Ⓓ He did not hear the woman's message.

10. What does the woman mean?

   Ⓐ They do not have as many people working as usual.
   Ⓑ The machine is broken.
   Ⓒ The man is next to be served.
   Ⓓ There is usually a long line.

11. What does the woman suggest that the man do?

  Ⓐ Get directions to the Math Department.
  Ⓑ Speak with the secretary.
  Ⓒ Go into Dr. Davis's office.
  Ⓓ Take the elevator to the fourth floor.

12. What can be inferred about Tom?

  Ⓐ He has finished the class.
  Ⓑ He has been sick.
  Ⓒ He does not have to take the final exam.
  Ⓓ He is not very responsible.

13. What does the man mean?

  Ⓐ He cannot find the woman's house.
  Ⓑ He has to change their plans.
  Ⓒ He will be happy to see the woman.
  Ⓓ He wants to know whether they have a date.

14. What will the woman probably do?

  Ⓐ Register for Dr. Collin's class.
  Ⓑ Graduate at a later date.
  Ⓒ Enroll in the section marked "staff."
  Ⓓ Find out who is teaching the other section of the class.

15. What does the woman think that the man should do?

  Ⓐ Wait for the results to be mailed.
  Ⓑ Call about the score.
  Ⓒ Take the test.
  Ⓓ Show more concern.

16. What does the woman mean?

  Ⓐ They have more time to travel.
  Ⓑ They are taking advantage of travel opportunities.
  Ⓒ They travel more than the man does.
  Ⓓ They spend most of their time traveling.

17. What does the man mean?

  Ⓐ The tickets are lost.
  Ⓑ Judy was responsible for getting the tickets.
  Ⓒ There were no tickets available.
  Ⓓ He does not have the tickets yet.

QUESTION DIRECTIONS—Part B

In Part B of the Listening section, you will hear several longer conversations and talks. Each conversation or talk is followed by several questions. The conversations, talks, and questions will not be repeated.

The conversations and talks are about a variety of topics. You do not need special knowledge of the topics to answer the questions correctly. Rather, you should answer each question on the basis of what is stated or implied by the speakers in the conversations or talks.

For most of the questions, you will need to click on the best of four possible answers. Some questions will have special directions. The special directions will appear in a box on the computer screen.

18. What are the man and woman talking about?

   Ⓐ A chapter in their textbook.
   Ⓑ An experiment referred to in a group presentation.
   Ⓒ A lecture in class.
   Ⓓ A program on television.

19. Why is the moon an ideal environment for the experiment?

   Ⓐ There is no air resistance on the moon.
   Ⓑ There is no gravitational acceleration on the moon.
   Ⓒ The gravity on the moon affects vertical motion.
   Ⓓ There is no horizontal resistance for motions like pushing.

20. Why was it easier to lift the hammer on the moon?

   Ⓐ The moon's gravitational acceleration was lower.
   Ⓑ The hammer fell when it was released.
   Ⓒ The surface of the moon encouraged motion.
   Ⓓ The hammer was created for that environment.

21. How did the woman feel about the presentation?

   Ⓐ She was surprised by it.
   Ⓑ She was not interested in it.
   Ⓒ She was impressed by it.
   Ⓓ She was confused about it.

22. What was the video about?

   Ⓐ The national health.
   Ⓑ Stress.
   Ⓒ Heart attacks.
   Ⓓ Health care for women.

23. What did the students learn about women?

   Ⓐ They are under more stress than men.
   Ⓑ They have more heart attacks than men.
   Ⓒ They do not get the same level of care as men.
   Ⓓ They have less serious heart attacks than men.

24. How did the man feel about the video?

   Ⓐ He did not see it.
   Ⓑ He thought it was interesting.
   Ⓒ He would not recommend it.
   Ⓓ He was not surprised by it.

25. What will the woman probably do?

   Ⓐ Discuss the video with the man.
   Ⓑ Go to the library to see the video.
   Ⓒ Check the video out of the library.
   Ⓓ Get ready for class.

26. What is the main topic of this lecture?

    Ⓐ Poet laureates.
    Ⓑ The Victorian period.
    Ⓒ Love poems in the English language.
    Ⓓ Elizabeth Barrett Browning.

27. According to the lecturer, what was one reason that Elizabeth Barrett was considered for the title of Poet Laureate?

    Ⓐ Because her husband was a famous poet.
    Ⓑ Because of her publication, *Sonnets from the Portuguese*.
    Ⓒ Because the monarch was a woman.
    Ⓓ Because of her friendship with William Wordsworth.

28. Where did Elizabeth and Robert Browning live after their elopement?

    Ⓐ In Spain.
    Ⓑ In Italy.
    Ⓒ In Portugal.
    Ⓓ In England.

29. When did Elizabeth Barrett Browning die?

    Ⓐ In 1843.
    Ⓑ In 1849.
    Ⓒ In 1856.
    Ⓓ In 1861.

30. What is the main topic of this lecture?

    Ⓐ The history of medicine in Greece.
    Ⓑ The contributions of biology to medicine.
    Ⓒ The scientific method.
    Ⓓ Medical advances in the twentieth century.

31. What was Hippocrates' greatest contribution to medicine?

    Ⓐ The classification of plants on the basis of body structure.
    Ⓑ The sterilization of surgical instruments.
    Ⓒ The scientific recording of symptoms and treatments.
    Ⓓ The theory that disease was caused by the gods.

32. Who is known as the father of biology?

    Ⓐ Hippocrates.
    Ⓑ Aristotle.
    Ⓒ Dioscorides.
    Ⓓ Edward Jenner.

33. What was the contribution made to medicine by William Harvey?

    Ⓐ The theory of germs and bacteria.
    Ⓑ The discovery of a vaccine against smallpox.
    Ⓒ The discovery of a mechanism for the circulation of the blood.
    Ⓓ The *Materia Medica*.

34. What was surprising about Thrasher's study?

    Ⓐ The size of the study, which included 1300 gangs.
    Ⓑ The excellent summary by the student who located the research.
    Ⓒ The changes that were reported in the history of gangs in the United States.
    Ⓓ The fact that gang activity has been prevalent for many years.

35. According to the study by Moore, what causes gang activity?

    Ⓐ Cliques that form in high school.
    Ⓑ Normal feelings of insecurity that teenagers experience.
    Ⓒ Dangerous neighborhoods and schools.
    Ⓓ Loyalty to friends and family.

36. In which two ways are gang members identified by law enforcement authorities?

    Click on 2 answers.

    Ⓐ By their tattoos.
    Ⓑ By their clothing.
    Ⓒ By maps of their territories.
    Ⓓ By research studies.

37. What is the role of women in gangs?

    Ⓐ Women are full members of the gangs.
    Ⓑ Women are protected by the gangs.
    Ⓒ Women are a support system for the gangs.
    Ⓓ Women do not have any contact with the gangs.

38. What is Mary's problem?

    Ⓐ She does not want to work for Dr. Brown.
    Ⓑ She has a schedule conflict.
    Ⓒ She has been late to work too often.
    Ⓓ She needs to obtain a work-study position.

39. When is Mary's class next semester?

    Ⓐ Every day in the afternoon.
    Ⓑ Three hours a day, three times a week.
    Ⓒ Ten-thirty on Monday.
    Ⓓ Nine o'clock, three times a week.

40. How does Dr. Brown resolve the problem?

    Ⓐ He changes her work hours.
    Ⓑ He assigns her fewer hours.
    Ⓒ He finds a different job for her.
    Ⓓ He gives her permission to arrive late.

41. What is a work-study employee?

    Ⓐ A person who works on campus.
    Ⓑ A new employee who is being trained.
    Ⓒ A student who can study at work after the job is complete.
    Ⓓ A part-time student with a full-time job.

42. What is the topic of this lecture?

    Ⓐ Reinforced concrete in buildings.
    Ⓑ Shear walls in earthquakes.
    Ⓒ Earthquake-resistant buildings.
    Ⓓ Understanding construction sites.

43. Which technique is used to reinforce walls?

    Ⓐ Cross-bracing.
    Ⓑ Shear cores.
    Ⓒ Bolts.
    Ⓓ Base isolators.

44. Which two materials are used in base isolators?

    Click on 2 answers.

    A Rubber.
    B Steel.
    C Concrete.
    D Soil.

45. What happens to fill dirt during an earthquake?

    Ⓐ It allows the building to sway.
    Ⓑ It reduces earthquake damage.
    Ⓒ It collapses.
    Ⓓ It creates shock waves.

46. Which two types represent the most common vein patterns in leaves?

    Click on 2 answers.

    A Needle leaves.
    B Parallel leaves.
    C Palmate leaves.
    D Pinnate leaves.

47. According to the lecturer, what is a midrib?

    Ⓐ One of the major classifications of veins in plants.
    Ⓑ The large vein that extends down the middle of a pinnate leaf.
    Ⓒ The central vein in a parallel leaf.
    Ⓓ The stem of a plant.

48. How does the lab assistant help students remember the palmate classification?

    Ⓐ She shows them a visual.
    Ⓑ She explains it carefully.
    Ⓒ She compares it to her hand.
    Ⓓ She refers them to their lab manual.

49. Match the leaves with their vein patterns.

    Click on the leaf. Then click on the empty box in the correct row. Use each leaf only once.

    | A | B | C |

	Pinnate
	Palmate
	Parallel

50. What will the students probably do after the short lecture?

    Ⓐ Classify leaves.
    Ⓑ Take a lab quiz.
    Ⓒ Read fifty-two pages in their manuals.
    Ⓓ Discuss the lecture.

Section 2: Structure

This section measures the ability to recognize language that is appropriate for standard written English. There are two types of questions in this section.

In the first type of question, there are incomplete sentences. Beneath each sentence, there are four words or phrases. You will choose the one word or phrase that best completes the sentence.

Clicking on a choice darkens the oval. After you click on **Next** and **Confirm Answer**, the next question will be presented.

The second type of question has four underlined words or phrases. You will choose the one underlined word or phrase that must be changed for the sentence to be correct.

Clicking on an underlined word or phrase will darken it. After you click on **Next** and **Confirm Answer**, the next question will be presented.

1. One of the most effective vegetable protein substitutes is the soybean _____ used to manufacture imitation meat products.

   (A) which can be
   (B) it can be
   (C) who can be
   (D) can be

2. _____ 1000 species of finch have been identified.

   (A) As many as
   (B) As many
   (C) As much as
   (D) Much as

3. The first electric lamp had two
      (A)
   carbon rods from which vapor
             (B)
   serves to conduct the current
    (C)   (D)
   across the gap.

4. A thunderhead, dense clouds that
   (A)
   rise high into the sky in huge
   (B) (C)
   columns, produce hail, rain, or
         (D)
   snow.

5. According to the economic laws, the greater the demand, _____ the price.

   (A) higher
   (B) high
   (C) the higher
   (D) the high

6. Although no country has exactly
         (A)
   the same folk music like that of
             (B) (C)
   any other, it is significant that similar songs exist among
   widely separated people.
   (D)

7. Despite of the Taft-Hartley Act
     (A)
   which forbids unfair union
        (B)
   practices, some unions such as
             (C)
   the air traffic controllers have
   voted to strike even though this
       (D)
   action might endanger the national security.

8. The Continental United States is _____ that there are four time zones.

   Ⓐ much big
   Ⓑ too big
   Ⓒ so big
   Ⓓ very big

9. Benjamin West contributed a great deal to American art: _____.

   Ⓐ painting, teaching, and lecturing
   Ⓑ painting, as a teacher and lecturer
   Ⓒ painting, teaching, and as a lecturer
   Ⓓ painting, a teacher, and a lecturer

10. Operant conditioning involves rewarding or punishing certain behave to reinforce or extinguish
    Ⓐ   Ⓑ   Ⓒ
    its occurrence.
    Ⓓ

11. There is an unresolved
    Ⓐ
    controversy as to whom is the
                    Ⓑ Ⓒ
    real author of the Elizabethan plays commonly credited to
                      Ⓓ
    William Shakespeare.

12. A catalytic agent such platinum
                      Ⓐ
    may be used so that the chemical
                Ⓑ
    reaction advances more rapidly.
             Ⓒ   Ⓓ

13. Upon hatching, _____ .

    Ⓐ young ducks know how to swim
    Ⓑ swimming is known by young ducks
    Ⓒ the knowledge of swimming is in young ducks
    Ⓓ how to swim is known in young ducks

14. The observation deck at the World Trade Center _____ in New York.

    Ⓐ is highest than any other one
    Ⓑ is higher than any other one
    Ⓒ is highest that any other one
    Ⓓ is higher that any other one

15. When a patient's blood pressure is much higher than it should be,
              Ⓐ   Ⓑ   Ⓒ
    a doctor usually insists that he will not smoke.
                    Ⓓ

16. It was the invent of the hand-
    ⒶⒷ   Ⓒ
    held electronic calculator that provided the original technology for the present generation of
            Ⓓ
    small but powerful computers.

17. _____ is necessary for the development of strong bones and teeth.

    Ⓐ It is calcium
    Ⓑ That calcium
    Ⓒ Calcium
    Ⓓ Although calcium

18. Located <u>in</u> the cranial cavity in
Ⓐ
the skull, <u>the brain</u> is the <u>larger</u>
Ⓑ   Ⓒ
mass of nerve tissue in the
<u>human body</u>.
Ⓓ

19. <u>Alike</u> other forms of energy,
Ⓐ
natural gas <u>may be used</u> <u>to heat</u>
Ⓑ   Ⓒ
homes, cook food, and even <u>run</u>
Ⓓ
automobiles.

20. An organ <u>is</u> a group <u>of tissues</u>
Ⓐ   Ⓑ
capable <u>to perform</u> some special
Ⓒ
function, as, <u>for example</u>, the
Ⓓ
heart, the liver, or the lungs.

21. -------------- withstands testing,
we may not conclude that it is
true, but we may retain it.

Ⓐ If a hypothesis
Ⓑ That a hypothesis
Ⓒ A hypothesis
Ⓓ Hypothesis

22. <u>Insulin, it is</u> used <u>to treat</u>
Ⓐ   Ⓑ
diabetes and <u>is</u> secured <u>chiefly</u>
Ⓒ   Ⓓ
from the pancreas of cattle and
hogs.

23. Not until a monkey is several
years old -------------- to exhibit
signs of independence from its
mother.

Ⓐ it begins
Ⓑ does it begin
Ⓒ and begin
Ⓓ beginning

24. Since Elizabeth Barrett
Browning's father never
approved of -------------- Robert
Browning, the couple eloped to
Italy, where they lived and
wrote.

Ⓐ her to marry
Ⓑ her marrying
Ⓒ she marrying
Ⓓ she to marry

25. <u>In autumn</u>, brilliant yellow,
Ⓐ
orange, and red leaves are
<u>commonly</u> <u>to</u> both the Sweet
Ⓑ   Ⓒ
Gum tree <u>and</u> the Maple.
Ⓓ

Section 3:
Reading

This section measures the ability to read and understand short passages similar in topic and style to those that students are likely to encounter in North American universities and colleges. This section contains reading passages and questions about the passages. There are several different types of questions in this section.

In the Reading section, you will first have the opportunity to read the passage.

You will use the scroll bar to view the rest of the passage.

When you have finished reading the passage, you will use the mouse to click on **Proceed**. Then the questions about the passage will be presented. You are to choose the one best answer to each question. Answer all questions about the information in a passage on the basis of what is stated or implied in that passage.

Most of the questions will be multiple-choice questions. To answer these questions you will click on a choice below the question.

To answer some questions, you will click on a word or phrase.

To answer some questions, you will click on a sentence in the passage.

To answer some questions, you will click on a square to add a sentence to the passage.

   The computer screens for selected questions in the Reading section have been printed in this book to provide you with orientation to the format of the Computer-Based TOEFL. Use the screen to find the place in the original reading passage that corresponds to the question you are answering.

Recent technological advances in manned and unmanned undersea vehicles, along with breakthroughs in satellite technology and computer equipment, have overcome some of the limitations of divers and diving equipment for scientists doing research on the great oceans of the world. Without a vehicle, divers often became sluggish, and their mental concentration was severely limited. Because undersea pressure affects their speech organs, communication among divers has always been difficult or impossible. But today, most oceanographers avoid the use of vulnerable human divers, preferring to reduce the risk to human life and make direct observations by means of instruments that are lowered into the ocean, from samples taken from the water, or from photographs made by orbiting satellites. Direct observations of the ocean floor can be made not only by divers but also by deep-diving submarines in the water and even by the technology of sophisticated aerial photography from vantage points above the surface of the water. Some submarines can dive to depths of more than seven miles and cruise at depths of fifteen thousand feet. In addition, radio-equipped buoys can be operated by remote control in order to transmit information back to land-based laboratories via satellite. Particularly important for ocean study are data about water temperature, currents, and weather. Satellite photographs can show the distribution of sea ice, oil slicks, and cloud formations over the ocean. Maps created from satellite pictures can represent the temperature and the color of the ocean's surface, enabling researchers to study the ocean currents from laboratories on dry land. Furthermore, computers help oceanographers to collect, organize, and analyze data from submarines and satellites. By creating a model of the ocean's movement and characteristics, scientists can predict the patterns and possible effects of the ocean on the environment.

Recently, many oceanographers have been relying more on satellites and computers than on research ships or even submarine vehicles because they can supply a greater range of information more quickly and more effectively. Some of humankind's most serious problems, especially those concerning energy and food, may be solved with the help of observations made possible by this new technology.

1. With what topic is the passage primarily concerned?

   Ⓐ Technological advances in oceanography
   Ⓑ Communication among divers
   Ⓒ Direct observation of the ocean floor
   Ⓓ Undersea vehicles

2. The word sluggish in paragraph 1 is closest in meaning to

   Ⓐ nervous
   Ⓑ confused
   Ⓒ slow moving
   Ⓓ very weak

3. Divers have had problems in communicating underwater because

   Ⓐ the pressure affected their speech organs
   Ⓑ the vehicles they used have not been perfected
   Ⓒ they did not pronounce clearly
   Ⓓ the water destroyed their speech organs

4. This passage suggests that the successful exploration of the ocean depends upon

   Ⓐ vehicles as well as divers
   Ⓑ radios that divers use to communicate
   Ⓒ controlling currents and the weather
   Ⓓ the limitations of diving equipment

5. Undersea vehicles

   Ⓐ are too small for a man to fit inside
   Ⓑ are very slow to respond
   Ⓒ have the same limitations that divers have
   Ⓓ make direct observations of the ocean floor

Beginning

Recent technological advances in manned and unmanned undersea vehicles, along with breakthroughs in satellite technology and computer equipment, have overcome some of the limitations of divers and diving equipment for scientists doing research on the great oceans of the world. Without a vehicle, divers often became sluggish, and their mental concentration was severely limited. Because undersea pressure affects their speech organs, communication among divers has always been difficult or impossible. But today, most oceanographers avoid the use of vulnerable human divers, preferring to reduce the risk to human life and make direct observations by means of instruments that are lowered into the ocean, from samples taken from the water, or from photographs made by orbiting satellites. Direct observations of the ocean floor can be made not only by divers but also by deep-diving submarines in the water and even by the technology of sophisticated aerial photography from vantage points above the surface of the water. Some submarines can dive to depths of more than seven miles and cruise at

6. The word cruise in paragraph 1 could best be replaced by

   Ⓐ travel at a constant speed
   Ⓑ function without problems
   Ⓒ stay in communication
   Ⓓ remain still

More Available

affects their speech organs, communication among divers has always been difficult or impossible. But today, most oceanographers avoid the use of vulnerable human divers, preferring to reduce the risk to human life and make direct observations by means of instruments that are lowered into the ocean, from samples taken from the water, or from photographs made by orbiting satellites. Direct observations of the ocean floor can be made not only by divers but also by deep-diving submarines in the water and even by the technology of sophisticated aerial photography from vantage points above the surface of the water. Some submarines can dive to depths of more than seven miles and cruise at depths of fifteen thousand feet. In addition, radio-equipped buoys can be operated by remote control in order to transmit information back to land-based laboratories via satellite. Particularly important for ocean study are data about water temperature, currents, and weather. Satellite photographs can show the distribution of sea ice, oil slicks, and cloud formations over the ocean. Maps created from satellite pictures can represent

---

7. How is a radio equipped buoy operated?

   Ⓐ By operators inside the vehicle in the part underwater
   Ⓑ By operators outside the vehicle on a ship
   Ⓒ By operators outside the vehicle on a diving platform
   Ⓓ By operators outside the vehicle in a laboratory on shore

8. Look at the word information in the passage. Click on the word or phrase in the **bold** text that is closest in meaning to information.

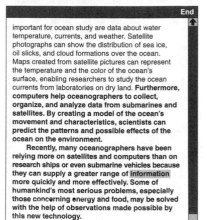

End

important for ocean study are data about water temperature, currents, and weather. Satellite photographs can show the distribution of sea ice, oil slicks, and cloud formations over the ocean. Maps created from satellite pictures can represent the temperature and the color of the ocean's surface, enabling researchers to study the ocean currents from laboratories on dry land. **Furthermore, computers help oceanographers to collect, organize, and analyze data from submarines and satellites. By creating a model of the ocean's movement and characteristics, scientists can predict the patterns and possible effects of the ocean on the environment.**

Recently, many oceanographers have been relying more on satellites and computers than on research ships or even submarine vehicles because they can supply a greater range of information more quickly and more effectively. Some of humankind's most serious problems, especially those concerning energy and food, may be solved with the help of observations made possible by this new technology.

9. Which of the following are NOT shown in satellite photographs?

   Ⓐ The temperature of the ocean's surface
   Ⓑ Cloud formations over the ocean
   Ⓒ A model of the ocean's movements
   Ⓓ The location of sea ice

10. Look at the word those in the passage. Click on the word or phrase in the **bold** text that those refers to.

End

important for ocean study are data about water temperature, currents, and weather. Satellite photographs can show the distribution of sea ice, oil slicks, and cloud formations over the ocean. Maps created from satellite pictures can represent the temperature and the color of the ocean's surface, enabling researchers to study the ocean currents from laboratories on dry land. Furthermore, computers help oceanographers to collect, organize, and analyze data from submarines and satellites. By creating a model of the ocean's movement and characteristics, scientists can predict the patterns and possible effects of the ocean on the environment.

Recently, many oceanographers have been relying more on satellites and computers than on research ships or even submarine vehicles because they can supply a greater range of information more quickly and more effectively. Some of humankind's most serious problems, especially those concerning energy and food, may be solved with the help of observations made possible by this new technology.

---

11. Click on the paragraph in the passage that discusses problems that new technology might help eliminate.

Scroll the passage to see all of the paragraphs.

Although speech is generally accepted as the most advanced form of communication, there are many ways of communicating without using words. In every known culture, signals, signs, symbols, and gestures are commonly utilized as instruments of communication. There is a great deal of agreement among communication scientists as to what each of these methods is and how each differs from the others. For instance, the basic function of any signal is to impinge upon the environment in such a way that it attracts attention, as, for example, the dots and dashes that can be applied in a telegraph circuit. Coded to refer to speech, the potential for communication through these dots and dashes—short and long intervals as the circuit is broken—is very great. Less adaptable to the codification of words, signs also contain agreed upon meaning; that is, they convey information in and of themselves. Two examples are the hexagonal red sign that conveys the meaning of *stop*, and the red and white swirled pole outside a shop that communicates the meaning of *barber*.

Symbols are more difficult to describe than either signals or signs because of their intricate relationship with the receiver's cultural perceptions. In some cultures, applauding in a theater provides performers with an auditory symbol of approval. In other cultures, if done in unison, applauding can be a symbol of the audience's discontent with the performance. Gestures such as waving and handshaking also communicate certain cultural messages.

Although signals, signs, symbols, and gestures are very useful, they also have a major disadvantage in communication. They usually do not allow ideas to be shared without the sender being directly adjacent to the receiver. Without an exchange of ideas, interaction comes to a halt. As a result, means of communication intended to be used across long distances and extended periods

> must be based upon speech. To radio, television, and the telephone, one must add fax, paging systems, electronic mail, and the Internet, and no one doubts but that there are more means of communication on the horizon.

12. Which of the following would be the best title for the passage?

    Ⓐ Signs and Signals
    Ⓑ Gestures
    Ⓒ Communication
    Ⓓ Speech

13. What does the author say about speech?

    Ⓐ It is the only true form of communication.
    Ⓑ It is dependent upon the advances made by inventors.
    Ⓒ It is necessary for communication to occur.
    Ⓓ It is the most advanced form of communication.

14. Click on the sentence in paragraph 1 that defines the function of a signal.

    Paragraph 1 is marked with an arrow (→).

15. The phrase impinge upon in paragraph 1 is closest in meaning to

    Ⓐ intrude
    Ⓑ improve
    Ⓒ vary
    Ⓓ prohibit

Beginning

Although speech is generally accepted as the most advanced form of communication, there are many ways of communicating without using words. In every known culture, signals, signs, symbols, and gestures are commonly utilized as instruments of communication. There is a great deal of agreement among communication scientists as to what each of these methods is and how each differs from the others. For instance, the basic function of any signal is to impinge upon the environment in such a way that it attracts attention, as, for example, the dots and dashes that can be applied in a telegraph circuit. Coded to refer to speech, the potential for communication through these dots and dashes—short and long intervals as the circuit is broken—is very great. Less adaptable to the codification of words, signs also contain agreed upon meaning; that is, they convey information in and of themselves. Two examples are the hexagonal red sign that conveys the meaning of *stop*, and the red and white swirled pole outside a shop that communicates the meaning of *barber*.

Symbols are more difficult to describe than

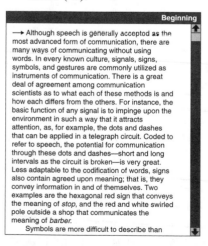

Beginning

→ Although speech is generally accepted as the most advanced form of communication, there are many ways of communicating without using words. In every known culture, signals, signs, symbols, and gestures are commonly utilized as instruments of communication. There is a great deal of agreement among communication scientists as to what each of these methods is and how each differs from the others. For instance, the basic function of any signal is to impinge upon the environment in such a way that it attracts attention, as, for example, the dots and dashes that can be applied in a telegraph circuit. Coded to refer to speech, the potential for communication through these dots and dashes—short and long intervals as the circuit is broken—is very great. Less adaptable to the codification of words, signs also contain agreed upon meaning; that is, they convey information in and of themselves. Two examples are the hexagonal red sign that conveys the meaning of *stop*, and the red and white swirled pole outside a shop that communicates the meaning of *barber*.

Symbols are more difficult to describe than

16. The word **it** in paragraph 1 refers to

    Ⓐ function
    Ⓑ signal
    Ⓒ environment
    Ⓓ way

> **Beginning**
>
>   Although speech is generally accepted as the most advanced form of communication, there are many ways of communicating without using words. In every known culture, signals, signs, symbols, and gestures are commonly utilized as instruments of communication. There is a great deal of agreement among communication scientists as to what each of these methods is and how each differs from the others. For instance, the basic function of any signal is to impinge upon the environment in such a way that **it** attracts attention, as, for example, the dots and dashes that can be applied in a telegraph circuit. Coded to refer to speech, the potential for communication through these dots and dashes—short and long intervals as the circuit is broken—is very great. Less adaptable to the codification of words, signs also contain agreed upon meaning; that is, they convey information in and of themselves. Two examples are the hexagonal red sign that conveys the meaning of *stop*, and the red and white swirled pole outside a shop that communicates the meaning of *barber*.
>   Symbols are more difficult to describe than

17. The word **potential** in paragraph 1 could best be replaced by

    Ⓐ range
    Ⓑ advantage
    Ⓒ organization
    Ⓓ possibility

> **Beginning**
>
>   Although speech is generally accepted as the most advanced form of communication, there are many ways of communicating without using words. In every known culture, signals, signs, symbols, and gestures are commonly utilized as instruments of communication. There is a great deal of agreement among communication scientists as to what each of these methods is and how each differs from the others. For instance, the basic function of any signal is to impinge upon the environment in such a way that it attracts attention, as, for example, the dots and dashes that can be applied in a telegraph circuit. Coded to refer to speech, the **potential** for communication through these dots and dashes ... short and ... ... group. Less adaptable to the codification of words, signs also contain agreed upon meaning; that is, they convey information in and of themselves. Two examples are the hexagonal red sign that conveys the meaning of *stop*, and the red and white swirled pole outside a shop that communicates the meaning of *barber*.
>   Symbols are more difficult to describe than

18. Look at the word **themselves** in the passage. Click on the word or phrase in the **bold** text that **themselves** refers to.

> **More Available**
>
> scientists as to what each of these methods is and how each differs from the others. For instance, the basic function of any signal is to impinge upon the environment in such a way that it attracts attention, as, for example, the dots and dashes that can be applied in a telegraph circuit. **Coded to refer to speech, the potential for communication through these dots and dashes—short and long intervals as the circuit is broken—is very great. Less adaptable to the codification of words, signs also contain agreed upon meaning; that is, they convey information in and of themselves. Two examples are the hexagonal red sign that conveys the meaning of *stop*, and the red and white swirled pole outside a shop that communicates the meaning of *barber*.**
>   Symbols are more difficult to describe than either signals or signs because of their intricate relationship with the receiver's cultural perceptions. In some cultures, applauding in a theater provides performers with an auditory symbol of approval. In other cultures, if done in unison, applauding can be a symbol of the audience's discontent with the performance. Gestures such as waving and

19. The word **intricate** in paragraph 2 could best be replaced by which of the following?

    Ⓐ inefficient
    Ⓑ complicated
    Ⓒ historical
    Ⓓ uncertain

> **More Available**
>
> also contain agreed upon meaning; that is, they convey information in and of themselves. Two examples are the hexagonal red sign that conveys the meaning of *stop*, and the red and white swirled pole outside a shop that communicates the meaning of *barber*.
>   Symbols are more difficult to describe than either signals or signs because of their **intricate** relationship with the receiver's cultural perceptions. In some cultures, applauding in a theater provides performers with an auditory symbol of approval. In other cultures, if done in unison, applauding can be a symbol of the audience's discontent with the performance. Gestures such as waving and handshaking also communicate certain cultural messages.
>   ... ... they also have a major disadvantage in communication. They usually do not allow ideas to be shared without the sender being directly adjacent to the receiver. Without an exchange of ideas, interaction comes to a halt. As a result, means of communication intended to be used across long distances and extended periods

20. Applauding was cited as an example of

    Ⓐ a signal
    Ⓑ a sign
    Ⓒ a symbol
    Ⓓ a gesture

21. The following sentence can be added to the passage.

    A loud smacking of the lips after a meal can be either a kinesthetic and auditory symbol of approval and appreciation, or simply a rude noise.

    Where would it best fit in the passage?

    Click on the square (■) to add the sentence to the passage.

    Scroll the passage to see all of the choices.

    More Available

    also contain agreed upon meaning; that is, they convey information in and of themselves. ■ Two examples are the hexagonal red sign that conveys the meaning of *stop*, and the red and white swirled pole outside a shop that communicates the meaning of *barber*.

    ■ Symbols are more difficult to describe than either signals or signs because of their intricate relationship with the receiver's cultural perceptions. In some cultures, applauding in a theater provides performers with an auditory symbol of approval. In other cultures, if done in unison, applauding can be a symbol of the audience's discontent with the performance. ■ Gestures such as waving and handshaking also communicate certain cultural messages.

    Although signals, signs, symbols, and gestures are very useful, they also have a major disadvantage in communication. ■ They usually do not allow ideas to be shared without the sender being directly adjacent to the receiver. Without an exchange of ideas, interaction comes to a halt. As a result, means of communication intended to be used across long distances and extended periods

22. Why were the telephone, radio, and TV invented?

    Ⓐ People were unable to understand signs, symbols, and signals.
    Ⓑ People wanted to communicate across long distances.
    Ⓒ People believed that signs, signals, and symbols were obsolete.
    Ⓓ People wanted new forms of entertainment.

23. Look at the word communication in the passage. Click on the word or phrase in the **bold** text that is closest in meaning to communication.

    End

    In some cultures, applauding in a theater provides performers with an auditory symbol of approval. In other cultures, if done in unison, applauding can be a symbol of the audience's discontent with the performance. Gestures such as waving and handshaking also communicate certain cultural messages.

    Although signals, signs, symbols, and gestures are very useful, they also have a major disadvantage in communication. They usually do not allow ideas to be shared without the sender being directly adjacent to the receiver. Without an exchange of ideas, interaction comes to a halt. As a result, means of communication intended to be used across long distances and extended periods must be based upon speech. To radio, television, and the telephone, one must add fax, paging systems, electronic mail, and the Internet, and no one doubts but that there are more means of communication on the horizon.

Fertilizer is any substance that can be added to the soil to provide chemical elements essential for plant nutrition so that the yield can be increased. Natural substances such as animal droppings, ashes from wood fires, and straw have been used as fertilizers in fields for thousands of years, and lime has been used since the Romans introduced it during the Empire. It was not until the nineteenth century, however, that chemical fertilizers became widely accepted as normal agricultural practice. Today, both natural and synthetic fertilizers are available in a variety of forms.

A complete fertilizer is usually marked with a formula consisting of three numbers, such as 4-8-2 or 6-6-4, which designate the percentage of content of nitrogen, phosphoric acid, and potash in the order stated. Synthetic fertilizers, produced by factories, are available in either solid or liquid form. Solids, in the shape of chemical granules, are in demand because they are not only easy to store but also easy to apply. Recently, liquids have shown an increase in popularity, accounting for about 20 percent of the nitrogen fertilizer used throughout the world. Formerly, powders were also used, but they were found to be less convenient than either solids or liquids.

Fertilizers have no harmful effects on the soil, the crop, or the consumer as long as they are used according to recommendations based on the results of local research. Occasionally, however, farmers may use more fertilizer than necessary, in which case the plants do not need, and therefore do not absorb, the total amount of fertilizer applied to the soil. The surplus of fertilizer thus can damage not only the crop but also the animals or human beings that eat the crop. Furthermore, fertilizer that is not used in the production of a healthy plant is leached into the water table. Accumulations of chemical fertilizer in the water supply accelerate the growth of algae and, consequently, may disturb the natural cycle of life, contributing to the death of fish. Too much fertilizer on grass can cause digestive disorders in cattle and in infants who drink cow's milk. Fertilizer must be used with great attention to responsible use or it can harm the environment.

24. With which of the following topics is the passage primarily concerned?

Ⓐ Local research and harmful effects of fertilizer
Ⓑ Advantages and disadvantages of liquid fertilizer
Ⓒ A formula for the production of fertilizer
Ⓓ Content, form, and effects of fertilizer

25. The word essential in paragraph 1 could best be replaced by which of the following?

Ⓐ limited
Ⓑ preferred
Ⓒ anticipated
Ⓓ required

26. Which of the following has the smallest percentage content in the formula 4-8-2?

Ⓐ Nitrogen
Ⓑ Phosphorus
Ⓒ Acid
Ⓓ Potash

27. What is the percentage of nitrogen in a 5-8-7 formula fertilizer?

Ⓐ 3 percent
Ⓑ 5 percent
Ⓒ 7 percent
Ⓓ 8 percent

28. The word designate in paragraph 2 could be replaced by

Ⓐ modify
Ⓑ specify
Ⓒ limit
Ⓓ increase

Beginning

Fertilizer is any substance that can be added to the soil to provide chemical elements essential for plant nutrition so that the yield can be increased. Natural substances such as animal droppings, ashes from wood fires, and straw have been used as fertilizers in fields for thousands of years, and lime has been used since the Romans introduced it during the Empire. It was not until the nineteenth century, however, that chemical fertilizers became widely accepted as normal agricultural practice. Today, both natural and synthetic fertilizers are available in a variety of forms.

A complete fertilizer is usually marked with a formula consisting of three numbers, such as 4-8-2 or 6-6-4, which designate the percentage of content of nitrogen, phosphoric acid, and potash in the order stated. Synthetic fertilizers, produced by factories, are available in either solid or liquid form. Solids, in the shape of chemical granules, are in demand because they are not only easy to store but also easy to apply. Recently, liquids have shown an increase in popularity, accounting for about 20 percent of the nitrogen fertilizer used throughout the world. Formerly, powders were

Beginning

Fertilizer is any substance that can be added to the soil to provide chemical elements essential for plant nutrition so that the yield can be increased. Natural substances such as animal droppings, ashes from wood fires, and straw have been used as fertilizers in fields for thousands of years, and lime has been used since the Romans introduced it during the Empire. It was not until the nineteenth century, however, that chemical fertilizers became widely accepted as normal agricultural practice. Today, both natural and synthetic fertilizers are available in a variety of forms.

A complete fertilizer is usually marked with a formula consisting of three numbers, such as 4-8-2 or 6-6-4, which designate the percentage of content of nitrogen, phosphoric acid, and potash in the order stated. Synthetic fertilizers, produced by factories, are available in either solid or liquid form. Solids, in the shape of chemical granules, are in demand because they are not only easy to store but also easy to apply. Recently, liquids have shown an increase in popularity, accounting for about 20 percent of the nitrogen fertilizer used throughout the world. Formerly, powders were

29. Which of the following statements about fertilizer is true?

    Ⓐ Powders are more popular than ever.
    Ⓑ Solids are difficult to store.
    Ⓒ Liquids are increasing in popularity.
    Ⓓ Chemical granules are difficult to apply.

30. The word they in paragraph 2 refers to

    Ⓐ powders
    Ⓑ solids
    Ⓒ liquids
    Ⓓ fertilizer

More Available

content of nitrogen, phosphoric acid, and potash in the order stated. Synthetic fertilizers, produced by factories, are available in either solid or liquid form. Solids, in the shape of chemical granules, are in demand because they are not only easy to store but also easy to apply. Recently, liquids have shown an increase in popularity, accounting for about 20 percent of the nitrogen fertilizer used throughout the world. Formerly, powders were also used, but they were found to be less convenient than either solids or liquids.

Fertilizers have no harmful effects on the soil, the crop, or the consumer as long as they are used according to recommendations based on the results of local research. Occasionally, however, farmers may use more fertilizer than necessary, in which case the plants do not need, and therefore do not absorb, the total amount of fertilizer applied to the soil. The surplus of fertilizer thus can damage not only the crop but also the animals or human beings that eat the crop. Furthermore, fertilizer that is not used in the production of a healthy plant is leached into the water table. Accumulations of chemical fertilizer in the water

31. The word convenient in paragraph 2 is closest in meaning to

    Ⓐ effective
    Ⓑ plentiful
    Ⓒ easy to use
    Ⓓ cheap to produce

More Available

content of nitrogen, phosphoric acid, and potash in the order stated. Synthetic fertilizers, produced by factories, are available in either solid or liquid form. Solids, in the shape of chemical granules, are in demand because they are not only easy to store but also easy to apply. Recently, liquids have shown an increase in popularity, accounting for about 20 percent of the nitrogen fertilizer used throughout the world. Formerly, powders were also used, but they were found to be less convenient than either solids or liquids.

Fertilizers have no harmful effects on the soil, the crop, or the consumer as long as they are used according to recommendations based on the results of local research. Occasionally, however, farmers may use more fertilizer than necessary, in which case the plants do not need, and therefore do not absorb, the total amount of fertilizer applied to the soil. The surplus of fertilizer thus can damage not only the crop but also the animals or human beings that eat the crop. Furthermore, fertilizer that is not used in the production of a healthy plant is leached into the water table. Accumulations of chemical fertilizer in the water

32. Click on the sentence in paragraph 3 that describes the effect of an accumulation of fertilizer in the water supply.

Paragraph 3 is marked with an arrow (→).

End

→ Fertilizers have no harmful effects on the soil, the crop, or the consumer as long as they are used according to recommendations based on the results of local research. Occasionally, however, farmers may use more fertilizer than necessary, in which case the plants do not need, and therefore do not absorb, the total amount of fertilizer applied to the soil. The surplus of fertilizer thus can damage not only the crop but also the animals or human beings that eat the crop. Furthermore, fertilizer that is not used in the production of a healthy plant is leached into the water table. Accumulations of chemical fertilizer in the water supply accelerate the growth of algae and, consequently, may disturb the natural cycle of life, contributing to the death of fish. Too much fertilizer on grass can cause digestive disorders in cattle and in infants who drink cow's milk. Fertilizer must be used with great attention to responsible use or it can harm the environment.

33. Look at the word harm in the passage. Click on the word or phrase in the **bold** text that is closest in meaning to harm.

> End
>
> Fertilizers have no harmful effects on the soil, the crop, or the consumer as long as they are used according to recommendations based on the results of local research. Occasionally, however, farmers may use more fertilizer than necessary, in which case the plants do not need, and therefore do not absorb, the total amount of fertilizer applied to the soil. **The surplus of fertilizer thus can damage not only the crop but also the animals or human beings that eat the crop. Furthermore, fertilizer that is not used in the production of a healthy plant is leached into the water table. Accumulations of chemical fertilizer in the water supply accelerate the growth of algae and, consequently, may disturb the natural cycle of life, contributing to the death of fish. Too much fertilizer on grass can cause digestive disorders in cattle and in infants who drink cow's milk. Fertilizer must be used with great attention to responsible use or it can harm the environment.**

34. The following sentence can be added to the passage.

One objection to powders was their propensity to become solid chunks if the bags got damp.

Where would it best fit in the passage?

Click on the square (■) to add the sentence to the passage.

Scroll the passage to see all of the choices.

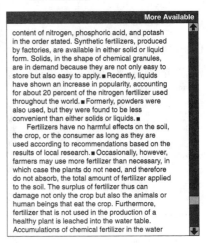

> More Available
>
> content of nitrogen, phosphoric acid, and potash in the order stated. Synthetic fertilizers, produced by factories, are available in either solid or liquid form. Solids, in the shape of chemical granules, are in demand because they are not only easy to store but also easy to apply. ■ Recently, liquids have shown an increase in popularity, accounting for about 20 percent of the nitrogen fertilizer used throughout the world. ■ Formerly, powders were also used, but they were found to be less convenient than either solids or liquids. ■
>
> Fertilizers have no harmful effects on the soil, the crop, or the consumer as long as they are used according to recommendations based on the results of local research. ■ Occasionally, however, farmers may use more fertilizer than necessary, in which case the plants do not need, and therefore do not absorb, the total amount of fertilizer applied to the soil. The surplus of fertilizer thus can damage not only the crop but also the animals or human beings that eat the crop. Furthermore, fertilizer that is not used in the production of a healthy plant is leached into the water table. Accumulations of chemical fertilizer in the water

The development of the horse has been recorded from the beginning through all of its evolutionary stages to the modern form. It is, in fact, one of the most complete and well-documented chapters of paleontological history. Fossil finds provide us not only with detailed information about the horse itself but also with valuable insights into the migration of herds, and even evidence for speculation about the climatic conditions that could have instigated such migratory behavior.

Geologists believe that the first horses appeared on Earth about sixty million years ago as compared with two million years ago for the appearance of human beings. There is evidence of early horses on both the American and European continents, but it has been documented that, almost twelve million years ago at the beginning of the Pliocene Age, a horse about midway through its evolutionary development crossed a land bridge where the Bering Strait is now located, from Alaska into the grasslands of Asia, and traveled all the way to Europe. This early horse was a hipparion, about the size of a modern-day pony with three toes and specialized cheek teeth for grazing. In Europe, the hipparion encountered another less advanced horse called the anchitheres, which had previously invaded Europe by the same route, probably during the Miocene Period. Less developed and smaller than the hipparion, the anchitheres was eventually completely replaced by it.

By the end of the Pleistocene Age both the anchitheres and the hipparion had become extinct in North America, where they had originated, as fossil evidence clearly indicates. In Europe, they evolved into the larger and stronger animal that is very similar to the horse as we know it today. For many years, the horse was probably hunted for food by early tribes of human beings. Then the qualities of the horse that would have made it a good servant were noted—mainly its strength and speed. It was time for the horse to be tamed, used as a draft animal at the dawning of agriculture, and then ridden as the need for transportation increased. It was the descendant of this domesticated horse that was brought back to the Americas by European colonists.

35. What is this passage mainly about?

    Ⓐ The evolution of the horse
    Ⓑ The migration of horses
    Ⓒ The modern-day pony
    Ⓓ The replacement of the anchitheres by the hipparion

36. According to the author, fossils are considered valuable for all of the following reasons EXCEPT

    Ⓐ they suggest how the climate may have been
    Ⓑ they provide information about migration
    Ⓒ they document the evolution of the horse
    Ⓓ they maintain a record of life prior to the Miocene Age

37. The word instigated in paragraph 1 could best be replaced by

    Ⓐ explained
    Ⓑ caused
    Ⓒ improved
    Ⓓ influenced

Beginning

The development of the horse has been recorded from the beginning through all of its evolutionary stages to the modern form. It is, in fact, one of the most complete and well-documented chapters of paleontological history. Fossil finds provide us not only with detailed information about the horse itself but also with valuable insights into the migration of herds, and even evidence for speculation about the climatic conditions that could have instigated such migratory behavior.

Geologists believe that the first horses appeared on Earth about sixty million years ago as compared with two million years ago for the appearance of human beings. There is evidence of early horses on both the American and European continents, but it has been documented that, almost twelve million years ago at the beginning of the Pliocene Age, a horse about midway through its evolutionary development crossed a land bridge where the Bering Strait is now located, from Alaska into the grasslands of Asia, and traveled all the way to Europe. This early horse was a hipparion, about the size of a modern-day pony with three toes and specialized

38. What does the author mean by the statement Geologists believe that the first horses appeared on Earth about sixty million years ago as compared with two million years ago for the appearance of human beings?

(A) Horses appeared long before human beings according to the theories of geologists.

(B) Both horses and human beings appeared several million years ago, if we believe geologists.

(C) The geological records for the appearance of horses and human beings are not very accurate.

(D) Horses and human beings cannot be compared by geologists because they appeared too long ago.

Beginning

The development of the horse has been recorded from the beginning through all of its evolutionary stages to the modern form. It is, in fact, one of the most complete and well-documented chapters of paleontological history. Fossil finds provide us not only with detailed information about the horse itself but also with valuable insights into the migration of herds, and even evidence for speculation about the climatic conditions that could have instigated such migratory behavior. Geologists believe that the first horses appeared on Earth about sixty million years ago as compared with two million years ago for the appearance of human beings. There is evidence of early horses on both the American and European continents, but it has been documented that, almost twelve million years ago at the beginning of the Pliocene Age, a horse about midway through its evolutionary development crossed a land bridge where the Bering Strait is now located, from Alaska into the grasslands of Asia, and traveled all the way to Europe. This early horse was a hipparion, about the size of a modern-day pony with three toes and specialized

---

39. Which of the following conclusions may be made on the basis of information in the passage?

(A) The hipparions migrated to Europe to feed in developing grasslands.

(B) There are no fossil remains of either the anchitheres or the hipparion.

(C) There were horses in North America when the first European colonists arrived.

(D) Very little is known about the evolution of the horse.

40. According to this passage, the hipparions were

(A) five-toed animals

(B) not as highly developed as the anchitheres

(C) larger than the anchitheres

(D) about the size of a small dog

41. The word it in paragraph 2 refers to

(A) anchitheres

(B) hipparion

(C) Miocene Period

(D) route

More Available

appearance of human beings. There is evidence of early horses on both the American and European continents, but it has been documented that, almost twelve million years ago at the beginning of the Pliocene Age, a horse about midway through its evolutionary development crossed a land bridge where the Bering Strait is now located, from Alaska into the grasslands of Asia, and traveled all the way to Europe. This early horse was a hipparion, about the size of a [modern-day pony with three toes and specialized] cheek teeth for grazing. In Europe, the hipparion encountered another less advanced horse called the anchitheres, which had previously invaded Europe by the same route, probably during the Miocene Period. Less developed and smaller than the hipparion, the anchitheres was eventually completely replaced by it.

By the end of the Pleistocene Age both the anchitheres and the hipparion had become extinct in North America, where they had originated, as fossil evidence clearly indicates. In Europe, they evolved into the larger and stronger animal that is very similar to the horse as we know it today. For

42. The word extinct in paragraph 3 is closest in meaning to

    Ⓐ familiar
    Ⓑ widespread
    Ⓒ nonexistent
    Ⓓ tame

    End

    cheek teeth for grazing. In Europe, the hipparion encountered another less advanced horse called the anchitheres, which had previously invaded Europe by the same route, probably during the Miocene Period. Less developed and smaller than the hipparion, the anchitheres was eventually completely replaced by it.
    By the end of the Pleistocene Age both the anchitheres and the hipparion had become extinct in North America, where they had originated, as fossil evidence clearly indicates. In Europe, they evolved into the larger and stronger animal that is very similar to the horse as we know it today. For many years, the horse was probably hunted for food by early tribes of human beings. Then the qualities of the horse that would have made it a good servant were noted—mainly its strength and speed. It was time for the horse to be tamed, used as a draft animal at the dawning of agriculture, and then ridden as the need for transportation increased. It was the descendant of this domesticated horse that was brought back to the Americas by European colonists.

43. Click on the paragraph that refers to the potential for conclusions from the evidence supplied by fossil remains.

    Scroll the passage to see all of the paragraphs.

44. Look at the word domesticated in the passage. Click on the word or phrase in the **bold** text that is closest in meaning to domesticated.

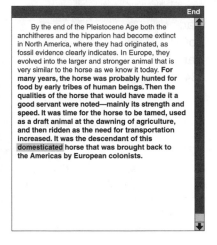

    End

    By the end of the Pleistocene Age both the anchitheres and the hipparion had become extinct in North America, where they had originated, as fossil evidence clearly indicates. In Europe, they evolved into the larger and stronger animal that is very similar to the horse as we know it today. **For many years, the horse was probably hunted for food by early tribes of human beings. Then the qualities of the horse that would have made it a good servant were noted—mainly its strength and speed. It was time for the horse to be tamed, used as a draft animal at the dawning of agriculture, and then ridden as the need for transportation increased. It was the descendant of this domesticated horse that was brought back to the Americas by European colonists.**

45. It can be concluded from this passage that the

    Ⓐ Miocene Period was prior to the Pliocene
    Ⓑ Pleistocene Period was prior to the Miocene
    Ⓒ Pleistocene Period was prior to the Pliocene
    Ⓓ Pliocene Period was prior to the Miocene

To check your answers for Model Test 2, refer to the Answer Key on pages 369–370. For an explanation of the answers, refer to the Explanatory Answers for Model Test 2 on pages 388–398.

Writing Section Model Test 2

When you take a Model Test, you should use one sheet of paper, both sides. Time each Model Test carefully. After you have read the topic, you should spend 30 minutes writing. For results that would be closest to the actual testing situation, it is recommended that an English teacher score your test, using the guidelines on page 234 of this book.

Read and think about the following statement:

Pets should be treated like family members.

Do you agree or disagree with the statement? Give reasons to support your opinion.

Notes

Model Test 3
Computer-Assisted TOEFL

Section 1:
Listening

The Listening section of the test measures the ability to understand conversations and talks in English. You will use headphones to listen to the conversations and talks. While you are listening, pictures of the speakers or other information will be presented on your computer screen. There are two parts to the Listening section, with special directions for each part.

On the day of the test, the amount of time you will have to answer all of the questions will appear on the computer screen. The time you spend listening to the test material will not be counted. The listening material and questions about it will be presented only one time. You will not be allowed to take notes or have any paper at your computer. You will both see and hear the questions before the answer choices appear. You can take as much time as you need to select an answer; however, it will be to your advantage to answer the questions as quickly as possible. You may change your answer as many times as you want before you confirm it. After you have confirmed an answer, you will not be able to return to the question.

Before you begin working on the Listening section, you will have an opportunity to adjust the volume of the sound. You will not be able to change the volume after you have started the test.

QUESTION DIRECTIONS—Part A

In Part A of the Listening section, you will hear short conversations between two people. In some of the conversations, each person speaks only once. In other conversations, one or both of the people speak more than once. Each conversation is followed by one question about it.

Each question in this part has four answer choices. You should click on the best answer to each question. Answer the questions on the basis of what is stated or implied by the speakers.

1. What does the woman mean?

   (A) She will not go home for spring vacation.
   (B) She has not taken a vacation for a long time.
   (C) She does not plan to graduate.
   (D) She does not want to go home after graduation in May.

2. What are the speakers talking about?

   (A) The class.
   (B) The weekend.
   (C) Homework.
   (D) Books.

3. What does the man mean?

   (A) He should have prepared more.
   (B) He is very worried.
   (C) He has been studying a lot.
   (D) He needs a few more days.

4. What will the man probably do?

   (A) Buy a textbook.
   (B) Come back later.
   (C) Go to the bookstore.
   (D) Drop his English class.

5. What does the woman mean?

   (A) She does not like the class.
   (B) Her classmates are really great.
   (C) The professor is not very nice.
   (D) The class is interesting.

6. What will the woman probably do?

   (A) Make an appointment with Dr. Peterson's T.A.
   (B) Cancel her appointment with the T.A.
   (C) Postpone her appointment with Dr. Peterson's T.A.
   (D) See the T.A. more often.

7. What does the man mean?

   (A) He would rather have American food.
   (B) He has always liked American food.
   (C) He is accustomed to eating American food.
   (D) He ate American food more in the past.

8. What does the man mean?

   (A) He should go to bed.
   (B) He did not know the time.
   (C) He is trying to bring his work up to date.
   (D) He is not sleepy yet.

9. What is the woman going to do?

   (A) Spend some time with the man.
   (B) Make a list of the names.
   (C) Pass out the names.
   (D) Let someone else call the names.

10. What does the man mean?

   (A) The woman has missed the deadline.
   (B) He will investigate the situation.
   (C) The deadline has been canceled.
   (D) An exception might be possible.

11. What does the man mean?

    Ⓐ The book is confusing.
    Ⓑ He is doing well in the class.
    Ⓒ The teacher is not very clear.
    Ⓓ The lectures are from the book.

12. What does the woman mean?

    Ⓐ She wants to submit her paper early.
    Ⓑ The answers on the paper are all correct.
    Ⓒ The deadline has passed for the paper.
    Ⓓ The paper is not quite finished.

13. What does the woman say about the class?

    Ⓐ She does not like the class.
    Ⓑ It is not a required class.
    Ⓒ She has already taken the class.
    Ⓓ The man will have to take the class.

14. What did the T.A. suggest the students do?

    Ⓐ Study together.
    Ⓑ Prepare for an oral final.
    Ⓒ Review the quizzes.
    Ⓓ Take the professor's advice.

15. What is the woman going to do?

    Ⓐ Make an appointment.
    Ⓑ Give the man a pen.
    Ⓒ Sign the form for the man.
    Ⓓ Wait for the man.

16. What is the woman going to do?

    Ⓐ Revise her work.
    Ⓑ Close the window.
    Ⓒ Copy from the man.
    Ⓓ Hand in the work.

17. What had the man assumed about the loan payment?

    Ⓐ The computer made an error.
    Ⓑ The payment is due on the fifth of every month.
    Ⓒ The loan must be paid by the first of the month.
    Ⓓ The loan had already been paid in full.

QUESTION DIRECTIONS—Part B

In Part B of the Listening section, you will hear several longer conversations and talks. Each conversation or talk is followed by several questions. The conversations, talks, and questions will not be repeated.

    The conversations and talks are about a variety of topics. You do not need special knowledge of the topics to answer the questions correctly. Rather, you should answer each question on the basis of what is stated or implied by the speakers in the conversations or talks.

    For most of the questions, you will need to click on the best of four possible answers. Some questions will have special directions. The special directions will appear in a box on the computer screen.

18. Why did Betty call Professor Hayes?

    (A) To enroll in a class.
    (B) To ask his opinion about a university.
    (C) To find out who is chair of the selection committee.
    (D) To get a letter for graduate school.

19. What does Professor Hayes think about Betty?

    (A) She might need to take his seminar.
    (B) She should do well in graduate school.
    (C) She had better go to another university.
    (D) She needs to apply before the end of April.

20. Who will decide whether Betty is accepted to the program?

    (A) The chair of the selection committee.
    (B) The entire selection committee.
    (C) Professor Hayes.
    (D) Dr. Warren.

21. When does Betty need to submit all her materials?

    (A) On May 1.
    (B) In three days.
    (C) Before the April 30th deadline.
    (D) Today.

22. Who is the speaker?

    (A) A professor of religion.
    (B) A professor of history.
    (C) A guest lecturer in a drama class.
    (D) A guest lecturer in a writing class.

23. According to the speaker, how did England control trade in the eighteenth century?

    (A) By threatening to go to war.
    (B) By competing with farmers.
    (C) By keeping manufacturing processes secret.
    (D) By stealing plans from the colonies.

24. What did Samuel Slater do?

    (A) He kept designs for English machinery from being used in the colonies.
    (B) He prevented Moses Brown from opening a mill.
    (C) He committed designs for English machinery to memory.
    (D) He smuggled drawings for English machines into the United States.

25. What happened as a result of the Slater-Brown partnership?

    (A) A change from agriculture to industry began to occur in the United States.
    (B) A rise in prices for English goods was evidenced.
    (C) Many small farmers began to send their products to England.
    (D) Americans had to keep their manufacturing processes secret.

26. What is the purpose of this conversation?

  (A) The man wants to reserve textbooks for the following semester.
  (B) The man is complaining about not having his books this semester.
  (C) The woman needs to order enough books for the class.
  (D) The woman is helping the man register for his courses.

27. What was the man's problem last semester?

  (A) The bookstore was closed for three weeks.
  (B) His books did not arrive before the semester began.
  (C) He did not have any books this semester.
  (D) He did not understand how to order his books.

28. How can the man order books?

  (A) The teacher will order books for the class.
  (B) He could fill out a form and pay for the books now.
  (C) He must wait until the semester begins.
  (D) He has to register for the classes, and the books will be ordered for him.

29. How will the man know that the books have arrived?

  (A) He will receive a form in the mail.
  (B) He will get a phone call.
  (C) He will stop by the bookstore at the beginning of the semester.
  (D) He will receive the books from his teacher in class.

30. What is the instructor defining?

  (A) The term "essay."
  (B) Prose writing.
  (C) Personal viewpoint.
  (D) Brainstorming.

31. What is the main point of the talk?

  (A) The work of Alexander Pope.
  (B) The difference between prose and poetry.
  (C) The general characteristics of essays.
  (D) The reason that the phrase "personal essay" is redundant.

32. According to the talk, which of the characteristics are NOT true of an essay?

  (A) It is usually short.
  (B) It can be either prose or poetry.
  (C) It expresses a personal point of view.
  (D) It discusses one topic.

33. What will the students probably do as an assignment?

  (A) They will prepare for a quiz.
  (B) They will write their first essay.
  (C) They will read works by Pope.
  (D) They will review their notes.

34. What is the main purpose of this talk?

Ⓐ To provide an overview of U.S. history from 1743 to 1826.
Ⓑ To discuss Jefferson's contribution to the American Revolution.
Ⓒ To analyze Jefferson's presidency.
Ⓓ To summarize Jefferson's life.

35. Jefferson was a member of which political group?

Ⓐ Monarchist.
Ⓑ Federalist.
Ⓒ Republican.
Ⓓ Democrat.

36. How did Jefferson become president?

Ⓐ He received the most votes.
Ⓑ Congress approved him.
Ⓒ Aaron Burr withdrew from the race.
Ⓓ As vice president, he automatically became president.

37. According to the lecturer, what was it that Jefferson was NOT?

Ⓐ An effective public speaker.
Ⓑ An architect.
Ⓒ A literary draftsman.
Ⓓ A diplomat.

38. What are the two most common places where fossils may be found?

Click on 2 answers.

[A] Ice.
[B] Mud.
[C] Sand.
[D] Water.

39. The professor briefly explains a process. Summarize the process by putting the events in order.

Click on a sentence. Then click on the space where it belongs. Use each sentence only once.

[A] A mold of the organism preserves the shape of the organism.
[B] Water soaks into the organism.
[C] Organisms are buried in mud or sand.
[D] Minerals in the water dissolve the original organism.

1 | |
2 | |
3 | |
4 | |

40. What is lost in the process of replacement?

Ⓐ The fine shapes of fragile structures.
Ⓑ The internal features of the plant or animal.
Ⓒ The minerals in the deposit.
Ⓓ The original fossil mold.

41. Why are the layers of sedimentary rock important to the fossil record?

Ⓐ The ages of the fossils may be determined by their location in the layers of rock.
Ⓑ The shapes of the fossils may be preserved in the layers of rock.
Ⓒ The rock protects the fossils from the mineral water that dissolves them.
Ⓓ Plants and animals that are formed at the same time are buried in different layers of rock.

42. Why didn't the man apply for graduation?

Ⓐ He wasn't sure that he had completed the requirements.
Ⓑ He did not have enough credit hours.
Ⓒ He did not have a program of study.
Ⓓ He did not understand that it was necessary.

43. How did the man select his courses?

Ⓐ By reading the catalog.
Ⓑ By consulting with the woman.
Ⓒ By referring to his signed program of study.
Ⓓ By making an appointment with his advisor.

44. What does the woman suggest?

Ⓐ The man should take the required courses for graduation.
Ⓑ The man should see an academic advisor to help him.
Ⓒ The man should read the requirements in the college catalog.
Ⓓ The man should bring her a copy of his transcript.

45. What is the man's problem?

Ⓐ He may not have enough credit hours to graduate.
Ⓑ He may not have taken the correct classes to graduate.
Ⓒ He may not be able to see an academic advisor before graduation.
Ⓓ He may not have time to take the rest of the required courses.

46. In which class would this discussion probably take place?

Ⓐ Sociology.
Ⓑ Education.
Ⓒ Linguistics.
Ⓓ Geography.

47. According to the discussion, what is the definition of a standard dialect?

Ⓐ The dialect that is selected by the government.
Ⓑ The dialect that is of a higher value than the others.
Ⓒ The dialect that is able to express everything necessary.
Ⓓ The dialect that is the model taught in schools.

48. What is the linguistic perspective put forward in the articles that were assigned?

   Ⓐ Some accents are not permitted in schools.
   Ⓑ There is only one standard accent in the United States.
   Ⓒ There is one major dialect in the United States.
   Ⓓ All dialects are of equal value.

49. Which two linguistic components are included in a dialect?

   Click on 2 answers.

   Ⓐ Grammar.
   Ⓑ Pronunciation.
   Ⓒ Vocabulary.
   Ⓓ Spelling.

50. What do sociologists tell us about accents?

   Ⓐ Some accents are more prestigious because they are spoken by the upper classes.
   Ⓑ Because they are more comprehensible, some accents are inherently better than others.
   Ⓒ One of the purposes of schools is to teach the accents that are considered most important.
   Ⓓ In general, accents are not as important as dialects because there is no standard for them.

Section 2: Structure

This section measures the ability to recognize language that is appropriate for standard written English. There are two types of questions in this section.

In the first type of question, there are incomplete sentences. Beneath each sentence, there are four words or phrases. You will choose the one word or phrase that best completes the sentence.

Clicking on a choice darkens the oval. After you click on **Next** and **Confirm Answer**, the next question will be presented.

The second type of question has four underlined words or phrases. You will choose the one underlined word or phrase that must be changed for the sentence to be correct.

Clicking on an underlined word or phrase will darken it. After you click on **Next** and **Confirm Answer**, the next question will be presented.

1. In simple animals,--------------
reflex movement or involuntary
response to stimuli.

   Ⓐ behavior mostly
   Ⓑ most is behavior
   Ⓒ most behavior is
   Ⓓ the most behavior

2. Although the weather in
Martha's Vineyard isn't
-------------- to have a year-
round tourist season, it has
become a favorite summer
resort.

   Ⓐ goodly enough
   Ⓑ good enough
   Ⓒ good as enough
   Ⓓ enough good

3. A swarm of locusts
is responsible the consumption
   Ⓐ
of enough plant material to feed
        Ⓑ   Ⓒ
a million and a half people.
          Ⓓ

4. Oyster farming has been practice
          Ⓐ   Ⓑ
in most parts of the world for
   Ⓒ   Ⓓ
many years.

5. It was Shirley Temple Black
   Ⓐ
which represented her country in
   Ⓑ   Ⓒ
the United Nations and later
                        Ⓓ
became an ambassador.

6. According to the wave theory, --
------------- population of the
Americas may have been the
result of a number of separate
migrations.

   Ⓐ the
   Ⓑ their
   Ⓒ that
   Ⓓ whose

7. It is presumed that rules
governing the sharing of food
influenced -------------- that the
earliest cultures evolved.

   Ⓐ that the way
   Ⓑ is the way
   Ⓒ the way
   Ⓓ which way

8. The prices at chain stores are as
             Ⓐ   Ⓑ
reasonable, if not more
             Ⓒ
reasonable, as those at discount
             Ⓓ
stores.

9. Historically there has been only
   Ⓐ   Ⓑ   Ⓒ   Ⓓ
two major factions in the
Republican Party—the liberals
and the conservatives.

10. Whitman wrote *Leaves of Grass*
as a tribute to the Civil War
soldiers who had laid on the
                  Ⓐ
battlefields and whom he
                  Ⓑ
had seen while serving as an
   Ⓒ   Ⓓ
army nurse.

11. Calculus, _____ elegant and economical symbolic system, can reduce complex problems to simple terms.

    (A) it is an
    (B) that an
    (C) an
    (D) is an

12. Canada does not require that U.S. citizens obtain passports to enter the country, and

    _____ .

    (A) Mexico does neither
    (B) Mexico doesn't either
    (C) neither Mexico does
    (D) either does Mexico

13. The Chinese were the first and
    ___(A)___
    large ethnic group to work on
    ___(B)___   ___(C)___
    the construction of the
                      ___(D)___
    transcontinental railroad system.

14. The range of plant life on a mountainside is a results of
                      ___(A)__ __(B)___
    differences in temperature and
    ___(C)___
    precipitation at varying altitudes.
                      ___(D)___

15. The poet _____ just beginning to be recognized as an important influence at the time of his death.

    (A) being Walt Whitman
    (B) who was Walt Whitman
    (C) Walt Whitman
    (D) Walt Whitman was

16. _____ the formation of the sun, the planets, and other stars began with the condensation of an interstellar cloud.

    (A) It accepted that
    (B) Accepted that
    (C) It is accepted that
    (D) That is accepted

17. The more the relative humidity reading rises, the worst the heat
                      ___(A)___   ___(B)___
    affects us.
    ___(C)___ ___(D)___

18. Because correlations are not causes, statistical data which are
    ___(A)___   ___(B)___
    extremely easy to misuse.
    ___(C)___   ___(D)___

19. As a general rule, the standard of living _____ by the average output of each person in society.

    (A) is fixed
    (B) fixed
    (C) has fixed
    (D) fixes

20. Despite of many attempts
    ___(A)___ __(B)___
    to introduce a universal
    ___(C)___
    language, notably Esperanto and Idiom Neutral, the effort has met with very little success.
                      ___(D)___

21. The Consumer Price Index lists

    _____ .

    (A) how much costs every car
    (B) how much does every car cost
    (C) how much every car costs
    (D) how much are every car cost

22. As every other nation, the
    Ⓐ   Ⓑ
    United States used to define its
                    Ⓒ   Ⓓ
    unit of currency, the dollar, in
    terms of the gold standard.

23. The Ford Theater where Lincoln
    was shot _____ .

    Ⓐ must restore
    Ⓑ must be restoring
    Ⓒ must have been restored
    Ⓓ must restored

24. John Dewey thought that
    children will learn better through
                Ⓐ   Ⓑ
    participating in experiences
    rather than through listening to
    Ⓒ   Ⓓ
    lectures.

25. Some methods to prevent soil
    Ⓐ   Ⓑ
    erosion are plowing parallel with
            Ⓒ
    the slopes of hills, to plant trees
                        Ⓓ
    on unproductive land, and
    rotating crops.

Section 3:
Reading

This section measures the ability to read and understand short passages similar in topic and style to those that students are likely to encounter in North American universities and colleges. This section contains reading passages and questions about the passages. There are several different types of questions in this section.

In the Reading section, you will first have the opportunity to read the passage.

You will use the scroll bar to view the rest of the passage.

When you have finished reading the passage, you will use the mouse to click on **Proceed**. Then the questions about the passage will be presented. You are to choose the one best answer to each question. Answer all questions about the information in a passage on the basis of what is stated or implied in that passage.

Most of the questions will be multiple-choice questions. To answer these questions you will click on a choice below the question.

To answer some questions, you will click on a word or phrase.

To answer some questions, you will click on a sentence in the passage.

To answer some questions, you will click on a square to add a sentence to the passage.

   The computer screens for selected questions in the Reading section have been printed in this book to provide you with orientation to the format of the Computer-Based TOEFL. Use the screen to find the place in the original reading passage that corresponds to the question you are answering.

Few men have influenced the development of American English to the extent that Noah Webster did. Born in West Hartford, Connecticut, in 1758, Webster graduated from Yale in 1778. He was admitted to the bar in 1781 and thereafter began to practice law in Hartford. Later, when he turned to teaching, he discovered how inadequate the available schoolbooks were for the children of a new and independent nation. In response to the need for truly American textbooks, Webster published *A Grammatical Institute of the English Language*, a three-volume work that consisted of a speller, a grammar, and a reader. The first volume, which was generally known as *The American Spelling Book*, was so popular that eventually it sold more than 80 million copies and provided him with a considerable income for the rest of his life. While teaching, Webster began work on the *Compendious Dictionary of the English Language*, which was published in 1806, and was also very successful.

In 1807, Noah Webster began his greatest work, *An American Dictionary of the English Language*. In preparing the manuscript, he devoted ten years to the study of English and its relationship to other languages, and seven more years to the writing itself. Published in two volumes in 1828, *An American Dictionary of the English Language* has become the recognized authority for usage in the United States. Webster's purpose in writing it was to demonstrate that the American language was developing distinct meanings, pronunciations, and spellings from those of British English. He is responsible for advancing simplified spelling forms: *develop* instead of *develope*; *plow* instead of *plough*; *jail* instead of *gaol*; *theater* and *center* instead of *theatre* and *centre*; *color* and *honor* instead of *colour* and *honour*.

Webster was the first author to gain copyright protection in the United States by being awarded a copyright for his *American Speller*. He continued, for the next fifty years, to lobby for improvements in the protection of intellectual properties, that is, authors' rights. In 1840 Webster brought out a second edition of his dictionary, which included 70,000 entries instead of the original 38,000. The name Webster has become synonymous with American dictionaries. This edition served as the basis for the many revisions that have been produced by others, ironically, under the uncopyrighted Webster name.

1. Which of the following would be the best title for the passage?

   (A) Webster's Work
   (B) Webster's Dictionaries
   (C) Webster's School
   (D) Webster's Life

2. The word inadequate in paragraph 1 could best be replaced by

   (A) unavailable
   (B) expensive
   (C) difficult
   (D) unsatisfactory

3. Why did Webster write *A Grammatical Institute of the English Language*?

   (A) He wanted to supplement his income.
   (B) There were no books available after the Revolutionary War.
   (C) He felt that British books were not appropriate for American children.
   (D) The children did not know how to spell.

4. From which publication did Webster earn a lifetime income?

   (A) *Compendious Dictionary of the English Language*
   (B) *An American Dictionary of the English Language*
   (C) *An American Dictionary of the English Language: Second Edition*
   (D) *The American Spelling Book*

Beginning

Few men have influenced the development of American English to the extent that Noah Webster did. Born in West Hartford, Connecticut, in 1758, Webster graduated from Yale in 1778. He was admitted to the bar in 1781 and thereafter began to practice law in Hartford. Later, when he turned to teaching, he discovered how inadequate the available schoolbooks were for the children of a new and independent nation. In response to the need for truly American textbooks, Webster published *A Grammatical Institute of the English Language*, a three-volume work that consisted of a speller, a grammar, and a reader. The first volume, which was generally know as *The American Spelling Book*, was so popular that eventually it sold more than 80 million copies and provided him with a considerable income for the rest of his life. While teaching, Webster began work on the *Compendious Dictionary of the English Language*, which was published in 1806, and was also very successful.

In 1807, Noah Webster began his greatest work, *An American Dictionary of the English Language*. In preparing the manuscript, he devoted

5. Look at the word popular in the passage. Click on the word or phrase in the **bold** text that is closest in meaning to popular.

Few men have influenced the development of American English to the extent that Noah Webster did. Born in West Hartford, Connecticut, in 1758, Webster graduated from Yale in 1778. He was admitted to the bar in 1781 and thereafter began to practice law in Hartford. Later, when he turned to teaching, he discovered how inadequate the available schoolbooks were for the children of a new and independent nation. **In response to the need for truly American textbooks, Webster published *A Grammatical Institute of the English Language*, a three-volume work that consisted of a speller, a grammar, and a reader. The first volume, which was generally know as *The American Spelling Book*, was so popular that eventually it sold more than 80 million copies and provided him with a considerable income for the rest of his life. While teaching, Webster began work on the *Compendious Dictionary of the English Language*, which was published in 1806, and was also very successful.**

In 1807, Noah Webster began his greatest work, *An American Dictionary of the English Language*. In preparing the manuscript, he devoted

6. The word considerable in paragraph 1 most nearly means

- (A) large
- (B) prestigious
- (C) steady
- (D) unexpected

Few men have influenced the development of American English to the extent that Noah Webster did. Born in West Hartford, Connecticut, in 1758, Webster graduated from Yale in 1778. He was admitted to the bar in 1781 and thereafter began to practice law in Hartford. Later, when he turned to teaching, he discovered how inadequate the available schoolbooks were for the children of a new and independent nation. In response to the need for truly American textbooks, Webster published *A Grammatical Institute of the English Language*, a three-volume work that consisted of a speller, a grammar, and a reader. The first volume, which was generally know as *The American Spelling Book*, was so popular that eventually it sold more than 80 million copies and provided him with a considerable income for the rest of his life. While teaching, Webster began work on the *Compendious Dictionary of the English Language*, which was published in 1806, and was also very successful.

In 1807, Noah Webster began his greatest work, *An American Dictionary of the English Language*. In preparing the manuscript, he devoted

7. When was *An American Dictionary of the English Language* published?

- (A) 1817
- (B) 1807
- (C) 1828
- (D) 1824

8. The word it in paragraph 2 refers to

- (A) language
- (B) usage
- (C) authority
- (D) dictionary

American Spelling Book, was so popular that eventually it sold more than 80 million copies and provided him with a considerable income for the rest of his life. While teaching, Webster began work on the *Compendious Dictionary of the English Language*, which was published in 1806, and was also very successful.

In 1807, Noah Webster began his greatest work, *An American Dictionary of the English Language*. In preparing the manuscript, he devoted ten years to the study of English and its relationship to other languages, and seven more years to the writing itself. Published in two volumes in 1828, *An American Dictionary of the English Language* has become the recognized authority for usage in the United States. Webster's purpose in writing it was to demonstrate that the American language was developing distinct meanings, pronunciations, and spellings from those of British English. He is responsible for advancing simplified spelling forms: *develop* instead of *develope; plow* instead of *plough; jail* instead of *gaol; theater* and *center* instead of *theatre* and *centre; color* and *honor* instead of *colour* and *honour*.

9. Click on the sentence in paragraph 2 that explains Webster's purpose for writing an American dictionary.

   Paragraph 2 is marked with an arrow (→).

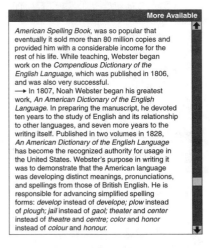

> **More Available**
>
> *American Spelling Book,* was so popular that eventually it sold more than 80 million copies and provided him with a considerable income for the rest of his life. While teaching, Webster began work on the *Compendious Dictionary of the English Language,* which was published in 1806, and was also very successful.
> → In 1807, Noah Webster began his greatest work, *An American Dictionary of the English Language.* In preparing the manuscript, he devoted ten years to the study of English and its relationship to other languages, and seven more years to the writing itself. Published in two volumes in 1828, *An American Dictionary of the English Language* has become the recognized authority for usage in the United States. Webster's purpose in writing it was to demonstrate that the American language was developing distinct meanings, pronunciations, and spellings from those of British English. He is responsible for advancing simplified spelling forms: *develop* instead of *develope; plow* instead of *plough; jail* instead of *gaol; theater* and *center* instead of *theatre* and *centre; color* and *honor* instead of *colour* and *honour.*

10. The word distinct in paragraph 2 is closest in meaning to

    (A) new
    (B) simple
    (C) different
    (D) exact

> **More Available**
>
> *American Spelling Book,* was so popular that eventually it sold more than 80 million copies and provided him with a considerable income for the rest of his life. While teaching, Webster began work on the *Compendious Dictionary of the English Language,* which was published in 1806, and was also very successful.
> In 1807, Noah Webster began his greatest work, *An American Dictionary of the English Language.* In preparing the manuscript, he devoted ten years to the study of English and its relationship to other languages, and seven more years to the writing itself. Published in two volumes in 1828, *An American Dictionary of the English Language* has become the recognized authority for usage in the United States. Webster's purpose in writing it was to demonstrate that the American language was developing distinct meanings, pronunciations, and spellings from those of British English. He is responsible for advancing simplified spelling forms: *develop* instead of *develope; plow* instead of *plough; jail* instead of *gaol; theater* and *center* instead of *theatre* and *centre; color* and *honor* instead of *colour* and *honour.*

11. According to this passage, which one of the following spellings would Webster have approved in his dictionaries?

    (A) *Develope*
    (B) *Theatre*
    (C) *Color*
    (D) *Honour*

The San Andreas Fault line is a fracture at the congruence of two major plates of the Earth's crust, one of which supports most of the North American continent, and the other of which underlies the coast of California and part of the ocean floor of the Pacific Ocean. The fault originates about six hundred miles south of the Gulf of California, runs north in an irregular line along the western coast to San Francisco, and continues north for about two hundred more miles before angling off into the ocean. In places, the trace of the fault is marked by a trench, or, in geological terms, a rift, and small ponds called sag ponds dot the landscape. Its western side always moves north in relation to its eastern side. The total net slip along the San Andreas Fault and the length of time it has been active are matters of conjecture, but it has been estimated that, during the past fifteen million years, coastal California along the San Andreas Fault has moved about 190 miles in a northwesterly direction with respect to the North American plate. Although the movement along the fault averages only a few inches a year, it is intermittent and variable. Some segments of the fault do not move at all for long periods of time, building up tremendous pressure that must be released. For this reason, tremors are not unusual along the San Andreas Fault, some of which are classified as major earthquakes. Also for this reason, small tremors are interpreted as safe, since they are understood to be pressure that releases without causing much damage.

It is worth noting that the San Andreas Fault passes uncomfortably close to several major metropolitan areas, including Los Angeles and San Francisco. In addition, the San Andreas Fault has created smaller fault systems, many of which underlie the smaller towns and cities along the California coast. For this reason, Californians have long anticipated the recurrence of what they refer to as the "Big One," a chain reaction of destructive earthquakes that would measure near 8 on the Richter scale, similar in intensity to those that occurred in 1857 and 1906. Such a quake would wreak devastating effects on the life and property in the region. Unfortunately, as pressure continues to build along the fault, the likelihood of such an earthquake increases substantially.

12. What is the author's main purpose in the passage?

    (A) To describe the San Andreas Fault
    (B) To give a definition of a fault
    (C) To explain the reason for tremors and earthquakes
    (D) To classify different kinds of faults

13. How does the author define the San Andreas Fault?

    (A) A plate that underlies the North American continent
    (B) A crack in the Earth's crust between two plates
    (C) Occasional tremors and earthquakes
    (D) Intense pressure that builds up

14. The word originates in paragraph 1 could best be replaced by

    (A) gets wider
    (B) changes direction
    (C) begins
    (D) disappears

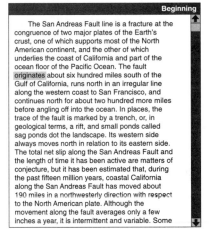

Beginning

The San Andreas Fault line is a fracture at the congruence of two major plates of the Earth's crust, one of which supports most of the North American continent, and the other of which underlies the coast of California and part of the ocean floor of the Pacific Ocean. The fault originates about six hundred miles south of the Gulf of California, runs north in an irregular line along the western coast to San Francisco, and continues north for about two hundred more miles before angling off into the ocean. In places, the trace of the fault is marked by a trench, or, in geological terms, a rift, and small ponds called sag ponds dot the landscape. Its western side always moves north in relation to its eastern side. The total net slip along the San Andreas Fault and the length of time it has been active are matters of conjecture, but it has been estimated that, during the past fifteen million years, coastal California along the San Andreas Fault has moved about 190 miles in a northwesterly direction with respect to the North American plate. Although the movement along the fault averages only a few inches a year, it is intermittent and variable. Some

15. In which direction does the western side of the fault move?

    (A) West
    (B) East
    (C) North
    (D) South

16. The word it in paragraph 1 refers to

    (A) San Francisco
    (B) ocean
    (C) coast
    (D) fault

Beginning

The San Andreas Fault line is a fracture at the congruence of two major plates of the Earth's crust, one of which supports most of the North American continent, and the other of which underlies the coast of California and part of the ocean floor of the Pacific Ocean. The fault originates about six hundred miles south of the Gulf of California, runs north in an irregular line along the western coast to San Francisco, and continues north for about two hundred more miles before angling off into the ocean. In places, the trace of the fault is marked by a trench, or, in geological terms, a rift, and small ponds called sag ponds dot the landscape. Its western side always moves north in relation to its eastern side. The total net slip along the San Andreas Fault and the length of time it has been active are matters of conjecture, but it has been estimated that, during the past fifteen million years, coastal California along the San Andreas Fault has moved about 190 miles in a northwesterly direction with respect to the North American plate. Although the movement along the fault averages only a few inches a year, it is intermittent and variable. Some

---

17. The word intermittent in paragraph 1 could best be replaced by which of the following?

    (A) dangerous
    (B) predictable
    (C) uncommon
    (D) occasional

Beginning

The San Andreas Fault line is a fracture at the congruence of two major plates of the Earth's crust, one of which supports most of the North American continent, and the other of which underlies the coast of California and part of the ocean floor of the Pacific Ocean. The fault originates about six hundred miles south of the Gulf of California, runs north in an irregular line along the western coast to San Francisco, and continues north for about two hundred more miles before angling off into the ocean. In places, the trace of the fault is marked by a trench, or, in geological terms, a rift, and small ponds called sag ponds dot the landscape. Its western side always moves north in relation to its eastern side. The total net slip along the San Andreas Fault and the length of time it has been active are matters of conjecture, but it has been estimated that, during the past fifteen million years, coastal California along the San Andreas Fault has moved about 190 miles in a northwesterly direction with respect to the North American plate. Although the movement along the fault averages only a few inches a year, it is intermittent and variable. Some

---

18. Along the San Andreas Fault, tremors are

    (A) small and insignificant
    (B) rare, but disastrous
    (C) frequent events
    (D) very unpredictable

19. The phrase "the Big One" refers to which of the following?

    (A) A serious earthquake
    (B) The San Andreas Fault
    (C) The Richter scale
    (D) California

20. Look at the word destructive in the passage. Click on the word or phrase in the **bold** text that is closest in meaning to destructive.

End

It is worth noting that the San Andreas Fault passes uncomfortably close to several major metropolitan areas, including Los Angeles and San Francisco. In addition, the San Andreas Fault has created smaller fault systems, many of which underlie the smaller towns and cities along the California coast. **For this reason, Californians have long anticipated the recurrence of what they refer to as the "Big One," a chain reaction of destructive earthquakes that would measure near 8 on the Richter scale, similar in intensity to those that occurred in 1857 and 1906. Such a quake would wreak devastating effects on the life and property in the region. Unfortunately, as pressure continues to build along the fault, the likelihood of such an earthquake increases substantially.**

21. Look at the word those in the passage. Click on the word or phrase in the **bold** text that those refers to.

End

It is worth noting that the San Andreas Fault passes uncomfortably close to several major metropolitan areas, including Los Angeles and San Francisco. In addition, the San Andreas Fault has created smaller fault systems, many of which underlie the smaller towns and cities along the California coast. For this reason, Californians have long anticipated the recurrence of what they refer to as the "Big One," a chain reaction of destructive earthquakes that would measure near 8 on the Richter scale, similar in intensity to those that occurred in 1857 and 1906. Such a quake would wreak devastating effects on the life and property in the region. Unfortunately, as pressure continues to build along the fault, the likelihood of such an earthquake increases substantially.

22. Which of the following words best describes the San Andreas Fault?

Ⓐ Straight
Ⓑ Deep
Ⓒ Wide
Ⓓ Rough

The body of an adult insect is subdivided into three sections, including a head, a three-segment thorax, and segmented abdomen. Ordinarily, the thorax bears three pairs of legs and a single or double pair of wings. The vision of most adult insects is specialized through two large compound eyes and multiple simple eyes.

Features of an insect's mouth parts are used in classifying insects into types. Biting mouth parts, called mandibles, such as the mouth parts found in grasshoppers and beetles, are common among insects. Behind the mandibles are located the maxillae, or lower jaw parts, which serve to direct food into the mouth between the jaws. A labrum above and one below are similar to another animal's upper and lower lips. In an insect with a sucking mouth function, the mandibles, maxillae, labrum, and labium are modified in such a way that they constitute a tube through which liquid such as water, blood, or flower nectar can be drawn. In a butterfly or moth, this coiled drinking tube is called the proboscis because of its resemblance, in miniature, to the trunk of an elephant or a very large nose. Composed chiefly of modified maxillae fitted together, the insect's proboscis can be flexed and extended to reach nectar deep in a flower. In mosquitoes or aphids, mandibles and maxillae are modified to sharp stylets with which the insect can drill through surfaces like human or vegetable skin membranes to reach juice. In a housefly, the expanding labium forms a spongelike mouth pad that it can use to stamp over the surface of food, sopping up food particles and juices.

Insects, the most numerous creatures on our planet, are also the most adaptable. They require little food because they are small. They easily find shelter and protection in small crevices in trees and surface geological formations. Species of insects can evolve quickly because of their rapid reproduction cycle; they live in every climate, some making their homes in the frozen Arctic regions and many others choosing the humid, warm, and nutrient-rich rain forest environment. An active part of the natural food cycle, insects provide nutrition for animals and devour waste products of other life forms.

23. What is the best title for this passage?

Ⓐ An Insect's Environment
Ⓑ The Structure of an Insect
Ⓒ Grasshoppers and Beetles
Ⓓ The Stages of Life of an Insect

24. Look at the word subdivided in the passage. Click on the word or phrase in the **bold** text that is closest in meaning to subdivided.

Beginning

The body of an adult insect is subdivided into three sections, including a head, a three-segment thorax, and segmented abdomen. Ordinarily, the thorax bears three pairs of legs and a single or double pair of wings. The vision of most adult insects is specialized through two large compound eyes and multiple simple eyes.

Features of an insect's mouth parts are used in classifying insects into types. Biting mouth parts, called mandibles, such as the mouth parts found in grasshoppers and beetles, are common among insects. Behind the mandibles are located the maxillae, or lower jaw parts, which serve to direct food into the mouth between the jaws. A labrum above and one below are similar to another animal's upper and lower lips. In an insect with a sucking mouth function, the mandibles, maxillae, labrum, and labium are modified in such a way that they constitute a tube through which liquid such as water, blood, or flower nectar can be drawn. In a butterfly or moth, this coiled drinking tube is called the proboscis because of its resemblance, in miniature, to the trunk of an elephant or a very large nose. Composed chiefly

---

25. How are insects classified?

Ⓐ By the environment in which they live
Ⓑ By the food they eat
Ⓒ By the structure of the mouth
Ⓓ By the number and type of wings

26. The word common in paragraph 2 is closest in meaning to

Ⓐ normal
Ⓑ rare
Ⓒ important
Ⓓ necessary

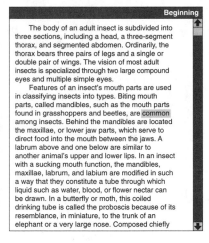

Beginning

The body of an adult insect is subdivided into three sections, including a head, a three-segment thorax, and segmented abdomen. Ordinarily, the thorax bears three pairs of legs and a single or double pair of wings. The vision of most adult insects is specialized through two large compound eyes and multiple simple eyes.

Features of an insect's mouth parts are used in classifying insects into types. Biting mouth parts, called mandibles, such as the mouth parts found in grasshoppers and beetles, are common among insects. Behind the mandibles are located the maxillae, or lower jaw parts, which serve to direct food into the mouth between the jaws. A labrum above and one below are similar to another animal's upper and lower lips. In an insect with a sucking mouth function, the mandibles, maxillae, labrum, and labium are modified in such a way that they constitute a tube through which liquid such as water, blood, or flower nectar can be drawn. In a butterfly or moth, this coiled drinking tube is called the proboscis because of its resemblance, in miniature, to the trunk of an elephant or a very large nose. Composed chiefly

---

27. The author compares labrum and labium to

Ⓐ an upper and lower lip
Ⓑ mandibles
Ⓒ maxillae
Ⓓ jaws

28. What is the proboscis?

Ⓐ Nectar
Ⓑ A tube constructed of modified maxillae
Ⓒ A kind of butterfly
Ⓓ A kind of flower

29. Which of the following have mandibles and maxillae that have been modified to sharp stylets?

    Ⓐ Grasshoppers
    Ⓑ Butterflies
    Ⓒ Mosquitoes
    Ⓓ Houseflies

30. The phrase drill through in paragraph 2 could best be replaced by

    Ⓐ penetrate
    Ⓑ saturate
    Ⓒ explore
    Ⓓ distinguish

More Available

the maxillae, or lower jaw parts, which serve to direct food into the mouth between the jaws. A labrum above and one below are similar to another animal's upper and lower lips. In an insect with a sucking mouth function, the mandibles, maxillae, labrum, and labium are modified in such a way that they constitute a tube through which liquid such as water, blood, or flower nectar can be drawn. In a butterfly or moth, this coiled drinking tube is called the proboscis because of its resemblance, in miniature, to the trunk of an elephant or a very large nose. Composed chiefly of modified maxillae fitted together, the insect's proboscis can be flexed and extended to reach nectar deep in a flower. In mosquitoes or aphids, mandibles and maxillae are modified to sharp stylets with which the insect can drill through surfaces like human or vegetable skin membranes to reach juice. In a housefly, the expanding labium forms a spongelike mouth pad that it can use to stamp over the surface of food, sopping up food particles and juices.
    Insects, the most numerous creatures on our planet, are also the most adaptable. They require

31. The word it in paragraph 2 refers to

    Ⓐ pad
    Ⓑ food
    Ⓒ housefly
    Ⓓ mouth

More Available

the maxillae, or lower jaw parts, which serve to direct food into the mouth between the jaws. A labrum above and one below are similar to another animal's upper and lower lips. In an insect with a sucking mouth function, the mandibles, maxillae, labrum, and labium are modified in such a way that they constitute a tube through which liquid such as water, blood, or flower nectar can be drawn. In a butterfly or moth, this coiled drinking tube is called the proboscis because of its resemblance, in miniature, to the trunk of an elephant or a very large nose. Composed chiefly of modified maxillae fitted together, the insect's proboscis can be flexed and extended to reach nectar deep in a flower. In mosquitoes or aphids, mandibles and maxillae are modified to sharp stylets with which the insect can drill through surfaces like human or vegetable skin membranes to reach juice. In a housefly, the expanding labium forms a spongelike mouth pad that it can use to stamp over the surface of food, sopping up food particles and juices.
    Insects, the most numerous creatures on our planet, are also the most adaptable. They require

32. The following sentence can be added to the passage.

   > **Although some insects, like the cockroach, have remained essentially unchanged for eons, most insects adapt readily to changing environmental conditions.**

   Where would it best fit in the passage?

   Click on the square (■) to add the sentence to the passage.

   Scroll the passage to see all of the choices.

   End

   proboscis can be flexed and extended to reach nectar deep in a flower. In mosquitoes or aphids, mandibles and maxillae are modified to sharp stylets with which the insect can drill through surfaces like human or vegetable skin membranes to reach juice. In a housefly, the expanding labium forms a spongelike mouth pad that it can use to stamp over the surface of food, sopping up food particles and juices.

   ■Insects, the most numerous creatures on our planet, are also the most adaptable. They require little food because they are small.■ They easily find shelter and protection in small crevices in trees and surface geological formations. ■ Species of insects can evolve quickly because of their rapid reproduction cycle; they live in every climate, some making their homes in the frozen Arctic regions and many others choosing the humid, warm, and nutrient-rich rain forest environment. An active part of the natural food cycle, insects provide nutrition for animals and devour waste products of other life forms.■

33. What is the purpose of this passage?

   (A) To complain
   (B) To persuade
   (C) To entertain
   (D) To inform

The protozoans, minute aquatic creatures, each of which consists of a single cell of protoplasm, constitute a classification of the most primitive forms of animal life. The very name *protozoan* indicates the scientific understanding of the animals. *Proto-* means first or primitive, and *zoa* refers to animal. They are fantastically diverse, but three major groups may be identified on the basis of their motility. The Mastigophora have one or more long tails that they use to propel themselves forward. The Ciliata, which use the same basic means for locomotion as the Mastigophora, have a larger number of short tails. The Sarcodina, which include amoebae, float or row themselves about on their crusted bodies.

In addition to their form of movement, several other features discriminate among the three groups of protozoans. For example, at least two nuclei per cell have been identified in the Ciliata, usually a large nucleus that regulates growth but decomposes during reproduction, and a smaller one that contains the genetic code necessary to generate the large nucleus.

Chlorophyll, which is the green substance encountered in plants, is found in the bodies of some protozoans, enabling them to make some of their own food from water and carbon dioxide. Protozoans are not considered plants but animals, because unlike pigmented plants to which some protozoans are otherwise almost identical, they do not live on simple organic compounds. Their cell demonstrates all of the major characteristics of the cells of higher animals, such as eating, breathing, and reproducing.

Many species of protozoans collect into colonies, physically connected to one another and responding uniformly to outside stimulae. Current research into this phenomenon along with investigations carried out with advanced microscopes may necessitate a redefinition of what constitutes protozoans, even calling into question the basic premise that they have only one cell. Nevertheless, with the current data available, almost 40,000 species of protozoans have been identified. No doubt, as technology improves methods of observation, better models of classification of these simple single cells will be proposed.

34. With what topic is the passage primarily concerned?

Ⓐ Colonies of protozoans
Ⓑ Mastigophora
Ⓒ Motility in protozoans
Ⓓ Characteristics of protozoans

35. The word minute in paragraph 1 could best be replaced by

Ⓐ very common
Ⓑ very fast
Ⓒ very old
Ⓓ very small

36. What is protoplasm?

Ⓐ A class of protozoan
Ⓑ The substance that forms the cell of a protozoan
Ⓒ A primitive animal similar to a protozoan
Ⓓ An animal that developed from a protozoan

37. Look at the word motility in the passage. Click on the word or phrase in the **bold** text that is closest in meaning to motility.

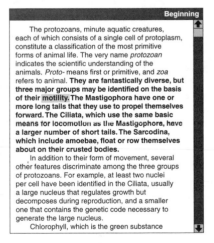

Beginning

The protozoans, minute aquatic creatures, each of which consists of a single cell of protoplasm, constitute a classification of the most primitive forms of animal life. The very name *protozoan* indicates the scientific understanding of the animals. *Proto-* means first or primitive, and *zoa* refers to animal. They are fantastically diverse, but three major groups may be identified on the basis of their motility. The Mastigophora have one or more long tails that they use to propel themselves forward. The Ciliata, which use the same basic means for locomotion as the Mastigophora, have a larger number of short tails. The Sarcodina, which include amoebae, float or row themselves about on their crusted bodies.

In addition to their form of movement, several other features discriminate among the three groups of protozoans. For example, at least two nuclei per cell have been identified in the Ciliata, usually a large nucleus that regulates growth but decomposes during reproduction, and a smaller one that contains the genetic code necessary to generate the large nucleus.

Chlorophyll, which is the green substance

38. What does the author mean by the statement They are fantastically diverse, but three major groups may be identified on the basis of their motility?

Ⓐ The three major groups are unique in that they all move in the same manner.
Ⓑ Everything we know about the protozoans is tied into their manner of movement.
Ⓒ The manner of movement is critical when classifying the three major groups of protozoans.
Ⓓ Mobility in the protozoans is insignificant.

Beginning

The protozoans, minute aquatic creatures, each of which consists of a single cell of protoplasm, constitute a classification of the most primitive forms of animal life. The very name *protozoan* indicates the scientific understanding of the animals. *Proto-* means first or primitive, and *zoa* refers to animal. They are fantastically diverse, but three major groups may be identified on the basis of their motility. The Mastigophora have one or more long tails that they use to propel themselves forward. The Ciliata, which use the same basic means for locomotion as the Mastigophora, have a larger number of short tails. The Sarcodina, which include amoebae, float or row themselves about on their crusted bodies.

In addition to their form of movement, several other features discriminate among the three groups of protozoans. For example, at least two nuclei per cell have been identified in the Ciliata, usually a large nucleus that regulates growth but decomposes during reproduction, and a smaller one that contains the genetic code necessary to generate the large nucleus.

Chlorophyll, which is the green substance

39. To which class of protozoans do the amoebae belong?

Ⓐ Mastigophora
Ⓑ Ciliata
Ⓒ Sarcodina
Ⓓ Motility

40. What is the purpose of the large nucleus in the Ciliata?

Ⓐ It generates the other nucleus.
Ⓑ It contains the genetic code for the small nucleus.
Ⓒ It regulates growth.
Ⓓ It reproduces itself.

41. Why are protozoans classified as animals?

Ⓐ They do not live on simple organic compounds.
Ⓑ They collect in colonies.
Ⓒ They respond uniformly to outside stimulae.
Ⓓ They may have more than one cell.

42. The word they in paragraph 3 refers to

Ⓐ protozoans
Ⓑ microscopes
Ⓒ investigations
Ⓓ colonies

More Available

In addition to their form of movement, several other features discriminate among the three groups of protozoans. For example, at least two nuclei per cell have been identified in the Ciliata, usually a large nucleus that regulates growth but decomposes during reproduction, and a smaller one that contains the genetic code necessary to generate the large nucleus.

Chlorophyll, which is the green substance encountered in plants, is found in the bodies of some protozoans, enabling them to make some of their own food from water and carbon dioxide. Protozoans are not considered plants but animals, because unlike pigmented plants to which some protozoans are otherwise almost identical, they do not live on simple organic compounds. Their cell demonstrates all of the major characteristics of the cells of higher animals, such as eating, breathing, and reproducing.

colonies, physically connected to one another and responding uniformly to outside stimulae. Current research into this phenomenon along with investigations carried out with advanced

43. Click on the sentence in paragraph 4 that brings into question the current belief that protozoans are single celled.

Paragraph 4 is marked with an arrow (→).

> End
>
> some protozoans, enabling them to make some of their own food from water and carbon dioxide. Protozoans are not considered plants but animals, because unlike pigmented plants to which some protozoans are otherwise almost identical, they do not live on simple organic compounds. Their cell demonstrates all of the major characteristics of the cells of higher animals, such as eating, breathing, and reproducing.
> → Many species of protozoans collect into colonies, physically connected to one another and responding uniformly to outside stimulae. Current research into this phenomenon along with investigations carried out with advanced microscopes may necessitate a redefinition of what constitutes protozoans, even calling into question the basic premise that they have only one cell. Nevertheless, with the current data available, almost 40,000 species of protozoans have been identified. No doubt, as technology improves methods of observation, better models of classification of these simple single cells will be proposed.

44. The word uniformly in paragraph 4 is closest in meaning to

Ⓐ in the same way
Ⓑ once in a while
Ⓒ all of a sudden
Ⓓ in the long run

> End
>
> some protozoans, enabling them to make some of their own food from water and carbon dioxide. Protozoans are not considered plants but animals, because unlike pigmented plants to which some protozoans are otherwise almost identical, they do not live on simple organic compounds. Their cell demonstrates all of the major characteristics of the cells of higher animals, such as eating, breathing, and reproducing.
> Many species of protozoans collect into colonies, physically connected to one another and responding uniformly to outside stimulae. Current research into this phenomenon along with investigations carried out with advanced microscopes may necessitate a redefinition of what constitutes protozoans, even calling into question the basic premise that they have only one cell. Nevertheless, with the current data available, almost 40,000 species of protozoans have been identified. No doubt, as technology improves methods of observation, better models of classification of these simple single cells will be proposed.

45. Which of the following statements is NOT true of protozoans?

Ⓐ There are approximately 40,000 species.
Ⓑ They are the most primitive forms of animal life.
Ⓒ They have a large cell and a smaller cell.
Ⓓ They are difficult to observe.

To check your answers for Model Test 3, refer to the Answer Key on pages 371–372. For an explanation of the answers, refer to the Explanatory Answers for Model Test 3 on pages 399–409.

Writing Section Model Test 3

When you take a Model Test, you should use one sheet of paper, both sides. Time each Model Test carefully. After you have read the topic, you should spend 30 minutes writing. For results that would be closest to the actual testing situation, it is recommended that an English teacher score your test, using the guidelines on page 234 of this book.

Many people have learned a foreign language in their own country; others have learned a foreign language in the country in which it is spoken. Give the advantages of each and support your viewpoint.

Notes

Model Test 4
Computer-Assisted TOEFL

Section 1:
Listening

The Listening section of the test measures the ability to understand conversations and talks in English. You will use headphones to listen to the conversations and talks. While you are listening, pictures of the speakers or other information will be presented on your computer screen. There are two parts to the Listening section, with special directions for each part.

On the day of the test, the amount of time you will have to answer all of the questions will appear on the computer screen. The time you spend listening to the test material will not be counted. The listening material and questions about it will be presented only one time. You will not be allowed to take notes or have any paper at your computer. You will both see and hear the questions before the answer choices appear. You can take as much time as you need to select an answer; however, it will be to your advantage to answer the questions as quickly as possible. You may change your answer as many times as you want before you confirm it. After you have confirmed an answer, you will not be able to return to the question.

Before you begin working on the Listening section, you will have an opportunity to adjust the volume of the sound. You will not be able to change the volume after you have started the test.

QUESTION DIRECTIONS—Part A

In Part A of the Listening section, you will hear short conversations between two people. In some of the conversations, each person speaks only once. In other conversations, one or both of the people speak more than once. Each conversation is followed by one question about it.

Each question in this part has four answer choices. You should click on the best answer to each question. Answer the questions on the basis of what is stated or implied by the speakers.

1. What will the woman probably do?

   (A) Have a party.
   (B) Attend the International Students' Association.
   (C) Go to work.
   (D) Get some rest.

2. What will the speakers probably do?

   (A) Leave immediately.
   (B) Watch the game on TV.
   (C) Start to play.
   (D) Eat a sandwich.

3. What did the man do after he lost his passport?

   (A) He went to see the foreign student advisor.
   (B) He went to Washington.
   (C) He wrote to the Passport Office.
   (D) He reported it to the Passport Office.

4. What does the woman suggest the man do?

   (A) Ask Dr. Tyler to clarify the assignment.
   (B) Show a preliminary version to Dr. Tyler.
   (C) Let her see the first draft before Dr. Tyler sees it.
   (D) Talk to some of the other students in Dr. Tyler's class.

5. What does the woman mean?

   (A) Dr. Clark is a good teacher.
   (B) Statistics is a boring class.
   (C) Two semesters of statistics are required.
   (D) The students do not like Dr. Clark.

6. What are the speakers discussing?

   (A) A teacher.
   (B) A textbook.
   (C) An assignment.
   (D) A movie.

7. What had the man assumed about the woman?

   (A) She was Sally Harrison's cousin.
   (B) She was Sally Harrison's sister.
   (C) She was Sally Harrison's friend.
   (D) She was Sally Harrison.

8. What is the woman's problem?

   (A) The desk drawer won't open.
   (B) The pen is out of ink.
   (C) She cannot find her pen.
   (D) She is angry with the man.

9. What does the man imply about John?

   (A) John is usually late.
   (B) John will be there at eight-thirty.
   (C) John will not show up.
   (D) John is usually on time.

10. What does the man mean?

   (A) The results of the tests are not available.
   (B) The experiment had unexpected results.
   (C) He has not completed the experiment yet.
   (D) It is taking a lot of time to do the experiment.

11. What does the man imply about Barbara?

    (A) She does not put much effort in her studies.
    (B) She is very likable.
    (C) She prefers talking to the woman.
    (D) She has a telephone.

12. What does the man suggest the woman do?

    (A) See the doctor.
    (B) Get another job.
    (C) Go to the counter.
    (D) Buy some medicine.

13. What does the woman mean?

    (A) She will try her best.
    (B) She has to save her money.
    (C) She is still undecided.
    (D) She needs an application.

14. What does the woman mean?

    (A) The man must stop working.
    (B) There is a little more time.
    (C) The test is important.
    (D) It is time for the test.

15. What does the man imply?

    (A) The woman's roommate took a different class.
    (B) The book is very expensive.
    (C) The textbook may have been changed.
    (D) The course is not offered this semester.

16. What does the woman imply?

    (A) Sally may get a bike for Christmas.
    (B) Sally already has a bike like that one.
    (C) Sally likes riding a bike.
    (D) Sally may prefer a different gift.

17. What does the woman suggest that the man do?

    (A) Take a break.
    (B) Go to work.
    (C) Do the other problems.
    (D) Keep trying.

QUESTION DIRECTIONS—Part B

In Part B of the Listening section, you will hear several longer conversations and talks. Each conversation or talk is followed by several questions. The conversations, talks, and questions will not be repeated.

The conversations and talks are about a variety of topics. You do not need special knowledge of the topics to answer the questions correctly. Rather, you should answer each question on the basis of what is stated or implied by the speakers in the conversations or talks.

For most of the questions, you will need to click on the best of four possible answers. Some questions will have special directions. The special directions will appear in a box on the computer screen.

18. What is the topic under discussion?

    (A) Whether to introduce the metric system in the United States.
    (B) How the metric system should be introduced in the United States.
    (C) Which system is better— the English system or the metric system.
    (D) How to convert measurements from the English system to the metric system.

19. What changes in measurement in the United States have the students observed?

    (A) Now the weather on radio and TV is reported exclusively in metrics.
    (B) Road signs have miles marked on them, but not kilometers.
    (C) Both the English system and the metric system are being used on signs, packages, and in weather reports.
    (D) Grocery stores use only metrics for their packaging.

20. What was Professor Baker's opinion?

    (A) He thought that a gradual adoption would be better for everyone.
    (B) He thought that only metrics should be used.
    (C) He thought that only the English system should be used.
    (D) He thought that adults should use both systems, but that children should be taught only the metric system.

21. Which word best describes Professor Baker's attitude toward his students?

    (A) Unfriendly.
    (B) Patronizing.
    (C) Uninterested.
    (D) Cooperative.

22. What is the talk mainly about?

    (A) Private industry.
    (B) Advances in medicine.
    (C) Space missions.
    (D) Technological developments.

23. Which of the advances listed are NOT mentioned as part of the technology developed for space missions?

    (A) Contact lenses.
    (B) Cordless tools.
    (C) Food packaging.
    (D) Ultrasound.

24. According to the speaker, why did NASA develop medical equipment?

    (A) To monitor the condition of astronauts in spacecraft.
    (B) To evaluate candidates who wanted to join the space program.
    (C) To check the health of astronauts when they returned from space.
    (D) To test spacecraft and equipment for imperfections.

25. Why does the speaker mention archeology?

    (A) Archaeologists and astronauts were compared.
    (B) Astronauts made photographs of the earth later used by archaeologists.
    (C) Archaeologists have used advances in medical technology developed for astronauts.
    (D) Space missions and underwater missions are very similar.

26. Why did the student want to see the professor?

    (A) To give him a note from another student.
    (B) To ask for an excused absence from class.
    (C) To get notes from a class that she had missed.
    (D) To make an appointment for help in a class.

27. What is the student's problem?

    (A) She cannot see the slides and videos from her seat.
    (B) Her friend's notes are difficult to read.
    (C) She has been absent from class too often.
    (D) Her family needs her help next week.

28. What does the professor offer to do?

    (A) Ask another student to take notes for the woman.
    (B) Meet with the woman to clarify the classes she will miss.
    (C) Make an appointment for the woman with another professor.
    (D) Repeat the lecture for the woman.

29. What is the professor's attitude in this conversation?

    (A) Disinterested.
    (B) Helpful.
    (C) Appreciative.
    (D) Confused.

30. What is the main purpose of this talk?

    (A) Transportation on the Pacific Coast.
    (B) History of California.
    (C) Orientation to San Francisco.
    (D) Specifications of the Golden Gate Bridge.

31. According to the speaker, what was the settlement called before it was renamed San Francisco?

    (A) Golden Gate.
    (B) San Francisco de Asis Mission.
    (C) Military Post Seventy-six.
    (D) Yerba Buena.

32. According to the speaker, what happened in 1848?

    (A) Gold was discovered.
    (B) The Transcontinental Railroad was completed.
    (C) The Golden Gate Bridge was constructed.
    (D) Telegraph communications were established with the East.

33. How long is the Golden Gate Bridge?

    (A) Eighteen miles.
    (B) 938 feet.
    (C) One mile.
    (D) Between five and six miles.

34. What does the lecturer mainly discuss?

   Ⓐ Transcendentalism.
   Ⓑ Puritanism.
   Ⓒ Ralph Waldo Emerson.
   Ⓓ Nature.

35. During which century did the literary movement develop?

   Ⓐ Seventeenth century.
   Ⓑ Eighteenth century.
   Ⓒ Nineteenth century.
   Ⓓ Twentieth century.

36. According to the speaker, what did the Puritans do?

   Ⓐ They stressed the importance of the individual.
   Ⓑ They supported the ideals of the Transcendental Club.
   Ⓒ They believed that society was more important than the individual.
   Ⓓ They established a commune at Brook Farm.

37. What is *Walden*?

   Ⓐ A book by Emerson.
   Ⓑ A history of Puritanism.
   Ⓒ A novel by Nathaniel Hawthorne.
   Ⓓ A book by Thoreau.

38. What is the purpose of this conversation?

   Ⓐ The man is looking for help with his research.
   Ⓑ The man is applying for a teaching position.
   Ⓒ The man is being trained to give library orientation.
   Ⓓ The man is interviewing for a job in the library.

39. Who is the man?

   Ⓐ A teacher.
   Ⓑ A librarian.
   Ⓒ A graduate student.
   Ⓓ A computer programmer.

40. What does the man need to do when he is not working?

   Ⓐ Take a few days off.
   Ⓑ Begin his own research.
   Ⓒ Write his dissertation.
   Ⓓ Take classes.

41. When would the man be available?

   Ⓐ After he graduates.
   Ⓑ When he completes his dissertation.
   Ⓒ After work and on his days off.
   Ⓓ Immediately.

42. Which two requirements are considered when mounting a solar collector on a roof?

Click on 2 answers.

   Ⓐ The angle of the collector.
   Ⓑ The thickness of the glass.
   Ⓒ The direction of the exposure.
   Ⓓ The temperature of the air.

43. Identify the fan in the solar heating system.

44. What problem does the professor point out?

    Ⓐ Solar heating is very expensive.
    Ⓑ The sun may not be available every day.
    Ⓒ Solar storage systems are too small.
    Ⓓ The sun does not supply enough energy without other power sources.

45. Why does the professor mention the project to place solar modules in orbit?

    Ⓐ It has the potential to generate cheap power.
    Ⓑ It is a research project that he is working on.
    Ⓒ It is the same basic principle he has been explaining.
    Ⓓ It is an example of a very complex model of a solar heating system.

46. What is the purpose of this conversation?

    Ⓐ The man wants to apply for a tutoring position.
    Ⓑ The man needs to arrange for tutoring.
    Ⓒ The man is looking for a friend who works at the Tutoring Center.
    Ⓓ The woman is tutoring the man.

47. For which course does the man want a tutor?

    Ⓐ Literature.
    Ⓑ Math.
    Ⓒ French.
    Ⓓ Composition.

48. How much will the tutoring cost?

    Ⓐ Five dollars an hour.
    Ⓑ Four dollars a session.
    Ⓒ Whatever the student can afford.
    Ⓓ There is no fee for the sessions.

49. When will the tutoring session begin?

    Ⓐ Tuesday morning.
    Ⓑ Thursday morning.
    Ⓒ Tuesday afternoon.
    Ⓓ Thursday afternoon.

50. What should the man bring to his tutoring session?

    Ⓐ A check for five dollars.
    Ⓑ Books and notes.
    Ⓒ His class schedule.
    Ⓓ A composition.

Section 2:
Structure

This section measures the ability to recognize language that is appropriate for standard written English. There are two types of questions in this section.

In the first type of question, there are incomplete sentences. Beneath each sentence, there are four words or phrases. You will choose the one word or phrase that best completes the sentence.

Clicking on a choice darkens the oval. After you click on **Next** and **Confirm Answer**, the next question will be presented.

The second type of question has four underlined words or phrases. You will choose the one underlined word or phrase that must be changed for the sentence to be correct.

Clicking on an underlined word or phrase will darken it. After you click on **Next** and **Confirm Answer**, the next question will be presented.

1. Based on the premise that light was composed of color, the Impressionists came to the conclusion --------------- not really black.

   - (A) which was that shadows
   - (B) was shadows which
   - (C) were shadows
   - (D) that shadows were

2. --------------- a parliamentary system, the prime minister must be appointed on the basis of the distribution of power in the parliament.

   - (A) The considered
   - (B) To be considered
   - (C) Considering
   - (D) Considers

3. Interest <u>in</u> automatic data
   (A)
   processing has grown rapid
   (B) (C)
   <u>since</u> the first large calculators
   (D)
   were introduced in 1950.

4. Vaslav Nijinsky <u>achieved</u> world
   (A)
   recognition <u>as</u> both <u>a dancer</u>
   (B)   (C)
   <u>as well as</u> a choreographer.
   (D)

5. --------------- of the play
   Mourning Becomes Electra
   introduces the cast of characters and hints at the plot.

   - (A) The act first
   - (B) Act one
   - (C) Act first
   - (D) First act

6. The plants that <u>they</u> <u>belong to</u>
   (A)   (B)
   the family of ferns <u>are</u> quite
   (C)
   varied in <u>their</u> size and structure.
   (D)

7. --------------- acid, salt, and sometimes water, is formed.

   - (A) a base will react
   - (B) a base reacts
   - (C) a base is reacting
   - (D) the reaction of a base

8. Columbus Day is celebrated on
   <u>(A)</u>   <u>(B)</u>
   the twelve of October because
   <u>(C)</u>   <u>(D)</u>
   on that day in 1492, Christopher
   Columbus first landed in the
   Americas.

9. One of the most influence
          <u>(A)</u>   <u>(B)</u>
   newspapers in the U.S. is
                          <u>(C)</u>
   The New York Times, which is
   widely distributed throughout
   <u>(D)</u>
   the world.

10. Weathering -------------- the
    action whereby surface rock is
    disintegrated or decomposed.

    (A) it is
    (B) is that
    (C) is
    (D) being

11. Coastal and inland waters
    are inhabited not only by fish but
    <u>(A)</u>   <u>(B)</u>
    also by such sea creature as
          <u>(C)</u>   <u>(D)</u>
    shrimps and clams.

12. Economists have tried
    to discourage the use of the
    <u>(A)</u>   <u>(B)</u>
    phrase "underdeveloped nation"
    and encouraging the more
        <u>(C)</u>   <u>(D)</u>
    accurate phrase "developing
    nation" in order to suggest an
    ongoing process.

13. A gas like propane will
            <u>(A)</u>
    combination with water
    <u>(B)</u>
    molecules in a saline solution
    to form a solid called a hydrate.
    <u>(C)</u>   <u>(D)</u>

14. The people of Western Canada
    have been considering
    -------------- themselves from
    the rest of the provinces.

    (A) to separate
    (B) separated
    (C) separate
    (D) separating

15. Although it cannot be proven,
                <u>(A)</u>   <u>(B)</u>
    presumable the expansion of the
    <u>(C)</u>
    universe will slow down as
    it approaches a critical radius.
    <u>(D)</u>

16. A City University professor
    reported that he discovers a
                      <u>(A)</u>
    vaccine that has been 80 percent
          <u>(B)</u>
    effective in reducing the
             <u>(C)</u>
    instances of tooth decay among
                              <u>(D)</u>
    small children.

17. When they have been frightened,
                  <u>(A)</u>   <u>(B)</u>
    as, for example, by an electrical
                      <u>(C)</u>
    storm, dairy cows may refuse
    giving milk.
    <u>(D)</u>

18. Although Margaret Mead had
    several assistants during her
    long investigations of Samoa,
    the bulk of the research was
    done by -------------- alone.

    (A) herself
    (B) she
    (C) her
    (D) hers

19. Miami, Florida, is among the
    ⒶⒶ
    few cities in the United States
    that has been awarded official
    Ⓑ   Ⓒ
    status as bilingual municipalities.
           Ⓓ

20. Fertilizers are used primarily to
               Ⓐ   Ⓑ
    enrich soil and increasing yield.
          Ⓒ   Ⓓ

21. -------------- war correspondent,
    Hemingway used his
    experiences for some of his most
    powerful novels.
    Ⓐ But a
    Ⓑ It is a
    Ⓒ While
    Ⓓ A

22. If the ozone gases of the
    atmosphere did not filter out the
                   Ⓐ
    ultraviolet rays of the sun, life
    as we know it would not have
    Ⓑ   Ⓒ
    evolved on earth.
          Ⓓ

23. Thirty-eight national sites are
    known as parks, another eighty-
    two as monuments, and
    -------------- .

    Ⓐ the another one hundred
       seventy-eight as historical
       sites
    Ⓑ the other one hundred
       seventy-eight as historical
       sites
    Ⓒ seventy-eight plus one
       hundred more as historical
       sites
    Ⓓ as historical sites one
       hundred seventy-eight

24. When he was a little boy, Mark
             Ⓐ
    Twain would walk along the
          Ⓑ
    piers, watch the river boats,
           Ⓒ
    swimming and fish in the
    Ⓓ
    Mississippi, much like his
    famous character, Tom Sawyer.

25. Almost all books have a few
    Ⓐ
    errors in them in spite of the care
                  Ⓑ
    taken to check its proof pages
    Ⓒ   Ⓓ
    before the final printing.

Section 3: Reading

This section measures the ability to read and understand short passages similar in topic and style to those that students are likely to encounter in North American universities and colleges. This section contains reading passages and questions about the passages. There are several different types of questions in this section.

In the Reading section, you will first have the opportunity to read the passage.

You will use the scroll bar to view the rest of the passage.

When you have finished reading the passage, you will use the mouse to click on **Proceed**. Then the questions about the passage will be presented. You are to choose the one best answer to each question. Answer all questions about the information in a passage on the basis of what is stated or implied in that passage.

Most of the questions will be multiple-choice questions. To answer these questions you will click on a choice below the question.

To answer some questions, you will click on a word or phrase.

To answer some questions, you will click on a sentence in the passage.

To answer some questions, you will click on a square to add a sentence to the passage.

   The computer screens for selected questions in the Reading section have been printed in this book to provide you with orientation to the format of the Computer-Based TOEFL. Use the screen to find the place in the original reading passage that corresponds to the question you are answering.

Precipitation, commonly referred to as rainfall, is a measure of the quantity of atmospheric water in the form of rain, hail, or snow that reaches the ground. The average annual precipitation over the whole of the United States is thirty-six inches per year. It should be understood, however, that all precipitation is not measured equally. For example, a foot of snow does not equal a foot of precipitation. According to the general formula for computing the precipitation of snowfall, ten inches of snow equals one inch of precipitation. In upper New York State, for example, where there is typically a large amount of snowfall every winter, a hundred inches of snow in one year would be recorded as only ten inches of precipitation. On the other hand, rain is rain. Forty inches of rain would be recorded as forty inches of precipitation. The total annual precipitation for an area with forty inches of rain and one hundred inches of snow would be recorded as fifty inches of precipitation.

The amount of precipitation that an area receives is a combined result of several factors, including location, altitude, proximity to the sea, and the direction of prevailing winds. Most of the precipitation in the United States is brought originally by prevailing winds from the Pacific Ocean, the Gulf of Mexico, the Atlantic Ocean, and the Great Lakes. Because these prevailing winds generally come from the west, the Pacific Coast receives more annual precipitation than the Atlantic Coast. Along the Pacific Coast itself, however, altitude causes some diversity in rainfall. The mountain ranges of the United States especially the Rocky Mountain Range and the Appalachian Mountain Range, influence the amount of precipitation in the areas to the windward and leeward sides of these ranges. East of the Rocky Mountains, the annual precipitation is substantially less than that west of the Rocky Mountains. The precipitation north of the Appalachian Mountains averages 40 percent less than that south of the Appalachian Mountains. As air currents from the oceans move over land, the air must rise to pass over the mountains. The air cools, and the water that is held in the clouds falls as rain or snow on the ascending side of the mountains. The air, therefore, is much drier on the other side of the mountains.

1. What does this passage mainly discuss?

   (A) Precipitation
   (B) Snowfall
   (C) New York State
   (D) A general formula

2. Which of the following is another word that is often used in place of precipitation?

   (A) Humidity
   (B) Wetness
   (C) Rainfall
   (D) Rain-snow

3. The term *precipitation* includes

   (A) only rainfall
   (B) rain, hail, and snow
   (C) rain, snow, and humidity
   (D) rain, hail, and humidity

4. What is the average annual rainfall in inches in the United States?

   (A) Thirty-six inches
   (B) Thirty-eight inches
   (C) Forty inches
   (D) Forty-two inches

5. If a state has 40 inches of snow in a year, by how much does this increase the annual precipitation?

   (A) By two feet
   (B) By four inches
   (C) By four feet
   (D) By 40 inches

6. The phrase proximity to in paragraph 2 is closest in meaning to

   (A) communication with
   (B) dependence on
   (C) nearness to
   (D) similarity to

More Available

The total annual precipitation for an area with forty inches of rain and one hundred inches of snow would be recorded as fifty inches of precipitation.

The amount of precipitation that an area receives is a combined result of several factors, including location, altitude, proximity to the sea, and the direction of prevailing winds. Most of the precipitation in the United States is brought originally by prevailing winds from the Pacific Ocean, the Gulf of Mexico, the Atlantic Ocean, and the Great Lakes. Because these prevailing winds generally come from the west, the Pacific Coast receives more annual precipitation than the Atlantic Coast. Along the Pacific Coast itself, however, altitude causes some diversity in rainfall. The mountain ranges of the United States, especially the Rocky Mountain Range and the Appalachian Mountain Range, influence the amount of precipitation in the areas to the windward and leeward sides of these ranges. East of the Rocky Mountains, the annual precipitation is substantially less than that west of the Rocky Mountains. The precipitation north of the Appalachian Mountains averages 40 percent less than that south of the

7. Click on the sentence in paragraph 2 that identifies the origins of most of the precipitation in the United States.

Paragraph 2 is marked with an arrow (→).

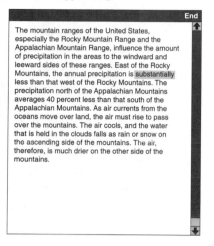

8. Where is the annual precipitation highest?

  Ⓐ The Atlantic Coast
  Ⓑ The Great Lakes
  Ⓒ The Gulf of Mexico
  Ⓓ The Pacific Coast

9. Which of the following was NOT mentioned as a factor in determining the amount of precipitation that an area will receive?

  Ⓐ Mountains
  Ⓑ Latitude
  Ⓒ The sea
  Ⓓ Wind

10. The word substantially in paragraph 2 could best be replaced by

  Ⓐ fundamentally
  Ⓑ slightly
  Ⓒ completely
  Ⓓ apparently

End

The mountain ranges of the United States, especially the Rocky Mountain Range and the Appalachian Mountain Range, influence the amount of precipitation in the areas to the windward and leeward sides of these ranges. East of the Rocky Mountains, the annual precipitation is substantially less than that west of the Rocky Mountains. The precipitation north of the Appalachian Mountains averages 40 percent less than that south of the Appalachian Mountains. As air currents from the oceans move over land, the air must rise to pass over the mountains. The air cools, and the water that is held in the clouds falls as rain or snow on the ascending side of the mountains. The air, therefore, is much drier on the other side of the mountains.

11. The word that in paragraph 2 refers to

  Ⓐ decreases
  Ⓑ precipitation
  Ⓒ areas
  Ⓓ mountain ranges

End

The mountain ranges of the United States, especially the Rocky Mountain Range and the Appalachian Mountain Range, influence the amount of precipitation in the areas to the windward and leeward sides of these ranges. East of the Rocky Mountains, the annual precipitation is substantially less than that west of the Rocky Mountains. The precipitation north of the Appalachian Mountains averages 40 percent less than that south of the Appalachian Mountains. As air currents from the oceans move over land, the air must rise to pass over the mountains. The air cools, and the water that is held in the clouds falls as rain or snow on the ascending side of the mountains. The air, therefore, is much drier on the other side of the mountains.

During the nineteenth century, women in the United States organized and participated in a large number of reform movements, including movements to reorganize the prison system, improve education, ban the sale of alcohol, grant rights to people who were denied them, and, most importantly, free slaves. Some women saw similarities in the social status of women and slaves. Women like Elizabeth Cady Stanton and Lucy Stone were not only feminists who fought for the rights of women but also fervent abolitionists who fought to do away with slavery. These brave people were social leaders who supported the rights of both women and blacks. They were fighting against a belief that voting should be tied to land ownership, and because land was owned by men, and in some cases by their widows, only those who held the greatest stake in government, that is the male landowners, were considered worthy of the vote. Women did not conform to the requirements.

A number of male abolitionists, including William Lloyd Garrison and Wendell Phillips, also supported the rights of women to speak and to participate equally with men in antislavery activities. Probably more than any other movement, abolitionism offered women a previously denied entry into politics. They became involved primarily in order to better their living conditions and improve the conditions of others. However, they gained the respect of those they convinced and also earned the right to be considered equal citizens.

When the civil war between the North and the South ended in 1865, the Fourteenth and Fifteenth Amendments to the Constitution adopted in 1868 and 1870 granted citizenship and suffrage to blacks but not to women. Discouraged but resolved, feminists worked tirelessly to influence

more and more women to demand the right to
vote. In 1869, the Wyoming Territory had yielded
to demands by feminists, but the states on the
East Coast resisted more stubbornly than before.
A women's suffrage bill had been presented to
every Congress since 1878, but it continually
failed to pass until 1920, when the Nineteenth
Amendment granted women the right to vote.

12. With what topic is the passage primarily concerned?

    Ⓐ The Wyoming Territory
    Ⓑ The Fourteenth and Fifteenth Amendments
    Ⓒ Abolitionists
    Ⓓ Women's suffrage

13. The word ban in paragraph 1 most nearly means to

    Ⓐ encourage
    Ⓑ publish
    Ⓒ prohibit
    Ⓓ limit

> **Beginning**
>
> During the nineteenth century, women in the United States organized and participated in a large number of reform movements, including movements to reorganize the prison system, improve education, ban the sale of alcohol, grant rights to people who were denied them, and, most importantly, free slaves. Some women saw similarities in the social status of women and slaves. Women like Elizabeth Cady Stanton and Lucy Stone were not only feminists who fought for the rights of women but also fervent abolitionists who fought to do away with slavery. These brave people were social leaders who supported the rights of both women and blacks. They were fighting against a belief that voting should be tied to land ownership, and because land was owned by men, and in some cases by their widows, only those who held the greatest stake in government, ▓▓▓▓ ▓▓ ▓▓▓ ▓▓▓▓ ▓▓▓▓ worthy of the vote. Women did not conform to the requirements.
>
> A number of male abolitionists, including William Lloyd Garrison and Wendell Phillips, also supported the rights of women to speak and to

14. Click on the sentence in paragraph 1 that explains the relationship between voting and property.

Paragraph 1 is marked with an arrow (→).

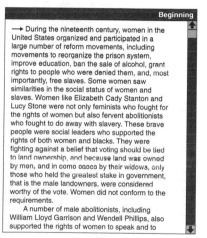

> **Beginning**
>
> → During the nineteenth century, women in the United States organized and participated in a large number of reform movements, including movements to reorganize the prison system, improve education, ban the sale of alcohol, grant rights to people who were denied them, and, most importantly, free slaves. Some women saw similarities in the social status of women and slaves. Women like Elizabeth Cady Stanton and Lucy Stone were not only feminists who fought for the rights of women but also fervent abolitionists who fought to do away with slavery. These brave people were social leaders who supported the rights of both women and blacks. They were fighting against a belief that voting should be tied to land ownership, and because land was owned by men, and in some cases by their widows, only those who held the greatest stake in government, that is the male landowners, were considered worthy of the vote. Women did not conform to the requirements.
>
> A number of male abolitionists, including William Lloyd Garrison and Wendell Phillips, also supported the rights of women to speak and to

15. The word primarily in paragraph 2 is closest in meaning to

   (A) above all
   (B) somewhat
   (C) finally
   (D) always

More Available

the rights of women but also fervent abolitionists who fought to do away with slavery. These brave people were social leaders who supported the rights of both women and blacks. They were fighting against a belief that voting should be tied to land ownership, and because land was owned by men, and in some cases by their widows, only those who held the greatest stake in government, that is the male landowners, were considered worthy of the vote. Women did not conform to the requirements.

A number of male abolitionists, including William Lloyd Garrison and Wendell Phillips, also supported the rights of women to speak and to participate equally with men in antislavery activities. Probably more than any other movement, abolitionism offered women a previously denied entry into politics. They became involved primarily in order to better their living conditions and improve the conditions of others. However, they gained the respect of those they convinced and also earned the right to be considered equal citizens.

When the civil war between the North and the

16. Look at the word improve in the passage. Click on the word or phrase in the **bold** text that is closest in meaning to improve.

More Available

rights of both women and blacks. They were fighting against a belief that voting should be tied to land ownership, and because land was owned by men, and in some cases by their widows, only those who held the greatest stake in government, that is the male landowners, were considered worthy of the vote. Women did not conform to the requirements.

A number of male abolitionists, including William Lloyd Garrison and Wendell Phillips, also supported the rights of women to speak and to participate equally with men in antislavery activities. **Probably more than any other movement, abolitionism offered women a previously denied entry into politics. They became involved primarily in order to better their living conditions and improve the conditions of others. However, they gained the respect of those they convinced and also earned the right to be considered equal citizens.**

When the civil war between the North and the South ended in 1865, the Fourteenth and Fifteenth Amendments to the Constitution adopted in 1868 and 1870 granted citizenship and suffrage to

17. What had occurred shortly after the Civil War?

   (A) The Wyoming Territory was admitted to the Union.
   (B) A women's suffrage bill was introduced in Congress.
   (C) The eastern states resisted the end of the war.
   (D) Black people were granted the right to vote.

18. The word suffrage in paragraph 3 could best be replaced by which of the following?

   (A) pain
   (B) citizenship
   (C) freedom from bondage
   (D) the right to vote

End

abolitionism offered women a previously denied entry into politics. They became involved primarily in order to better their living conditions and improve the conditions of others. However, they gained the respect of those they convinced and also earned the right to be considered equal citizens.

When the civil war between the North and the South ended in 1865, the Fourteenth and Fifteenth Amendments to the Constitution adopted in 1868 and 1870 granted citizenship and suffrage to blacks but not to women. Discouraged but resolved, feminists worked tirelessly to influence more and more women to demand the right to vote. In 1869, the Wyoming Territory had yielded to demands by feminists, but the states on the East Coast resisted more stubbornly than before. A women's suffrage bill had been presented to every Congress since 1878, but it continually failed to pass until 1920, when the Nineteenth Amendment granted women the right to vote.

19. The word it in paragraph 3 refers to

  Ⓐ bill
  Ⓑ Congress
  Ⓒ Nineteenth Amendment
  Ⓓ vote

20. What does the Nineteenth Amendment guarantee?

  Ⓐ Voting rights for blacks
  Ⓑ Citizenship for blacks
  Ⓒ Voting rights for women
  Ⓓ Citizenship for women

21. When were women allowed to vote throughout the United States?

  Ⓐ After 1866
  Ⓑ After 1870
  Ⓒ After 1878
  Ⓓ After 1920

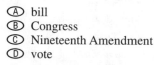

End

abolitionism offered women a previously denied entry into politics. They became involved primarily in order to better their living conditions and improve the conditions of others. However, they gained the respect of those they convinced and also earned the right to be considered equal citizens.

When the civil war between the North and the South ended in 1865, the Fourteenth and Fifteenth Amendments to the Constitution adopted in 1868 and 1870 granted citizenship and suffrage to blacks but not to women. Discouraged but resolved, feminists worked tirelessly to influence more and more women to demand the right to vote. In 1869, the Wyoming Territory had yielded to demands by feminists, but the states on the East Coast resisted more stubbornly than before. A women's suffrage bill had been presented to every Congress since 1878, but it continually failed to pass until 1920, when the Nineteenth Amendment granted women the right to vote.

The *Acacia*, a genus of trees and shrubs of the *mimosa* family that originated in Australia, has long been used there in building simple mud and stick structures. The *acacia* is called a wattle in Australia, and the structures are said to be made of daub and wattle. The *acacia* is actually related to the family of plants known as *legumes* that includes peas, beans, lentils, peanuts, and pods with beanlike seeds. Some *acacias* actually produce edible crops. Other *Acacia* varieties are valued for the sticky resin, called gum arabic or gum acacia, used widely in medicines, foods, and perfumes, for the dark dense wood prized for making pianos, or for the bark, rich in tannin, a dark, acidic substance used to cure the hides of animals, transforming them into leather.

Nearly five hundred species of *Acacia* have been analyzed, identified, categorized, and proven capable of survival in hot and generally arid parts of the world; however, only a dozen of the three hundred Australian varieties thrive in the southern United States. Most *acacia* imports are low spreading trees, but of these, only three flower, including the *Bailey Acacia* with fernlike silver leaves and small, fragrant flowers arranged in rounded clusters, the *Silver Wattle*, similar to the *Bailey Acacia*, which grows twice as high, and the squat *Sydney Golden Wattle*, bushy with broad, flat leaves, showy bright yellow blossoms, and sharp spined twigs. Another variety, the *Black Acacia*, also called the *Blackwood*, has dark green foliage and unobtrusive blossoms. Besides being a popular ornamental tree, the *Black Acacia* is considered valuable for its dark wood, which is used in making furniture, as well as highly prized musical instruments.

The *Acacia's* unusual custom of blossoming in February has been commonly attributed to its Australian origins, as if the date and not the quality of light made the difference for a tree in its flowering cycle. In the Southern Hemisphere, the seasons are reversed, and February, which is wintertime in the United States, is summertime in Australia. Actually, however, the pale, yellow blossoms appear in August in Australia. Whether growing in the Northern or Southern Hemisphere, the lovely *acacia* blossoms in winter.

22. With which of the following topics is the passage primarily concerned?

    (A) The *Black Acacia*
    (B) Characteristics and varieties of the *Acacia*
    (C) Australian varieties of the *Acacia*
    (D) The use of *Acacia* wood in ornamental furniture

23. Look at the word prized in the passage. Click on the word or phrase in the **bold** text that is closest in meaning to prized.

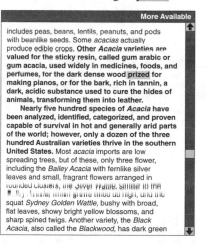

includes peas, beans, lentils, peanuts, and pods with beanlike seeds. Some *acacias* actually produce edible crops. **Other *Acacia* varieties are valued for the sticky resin, called gum arabic or gum acacia, used widely in medicines, foods, and perfumes, for the dark dense wood prized for making pianos, or for the bark, rich in tannin, a dark, acidic substance used to cure the hides of animals, transforming them into leather.**
    Nearly five hundred species of *Acacia* have been analyzed, identified, categorized, and proven capable of survival in hot and generally arid parts of the world; however, only a dozen of the three hundred Australian varieties thrive in the southern United States. Most *acacia* imports are low spreading trees, but of these, only three flower, including the *Bailey Acacia* with fernlike silver leaves and small, fragrant flowers arranged in rounded clusters, the *Silver Wattle*, similar to the *Bailey Acacia*, which grows twice as high, and the squat *Sydney Golden Wattle*, bushy with broad, flat leaves, showy bright yellow blossoms, and sharp spined twigs. Another variety, the *Black Acacia*, also called the *Blackwood*, has dark green

24. How many species of *Acacia* grow well in the southern United States?

    (A) Five hundred
    (B) Three hundred
    (C) Twelve
    (D) Three

25. The word thrive in paragraph 2 is closest in meaning to which of the following?

    (A) grow well
    (B) are found
    (C) were planted
    (D) can live

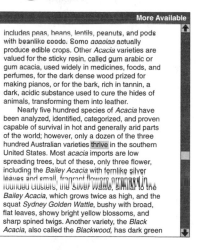

includes peas, beans, lentils, peanuts, and pods with beanlike seeds. Some *acacias* actually produce edible crops. Other *Acacia* varieties are valued for the sticky resin, called gum arabic or gum acacia, used widely in medicines, foods, and perfumes, for the dark dense wood prized for making pianos, or for the bark, rich in tannin, a dark, acidic substance used to cure the hides of animals, transforming them into leather.
    Nearly five hundred species of *Acacia* have been analyzed, identified, categorized, and proven capable of survival in hot and generally arid parts of the world; however, only a dozen of the three hundred Australian varieties thrive in the southern United States. Most *acacia* imports are low spreading trees, but of these, only three flower, including the *Bailey Acacia* with fernlike silver leaves and small, fragrant flowers arranged in rounded clusters, the *Silver Wattle*, similar to the *Bailey Acacia*, which grows twice as high, and the squat *Sydney Golden Wattle*, bushy with broad, flat leaves, showy bright yellow blossoms, and sharp spined twigs. Another variety, the *Black Acacia*, also called the *Blackwood*, has dark green

26. The word these in paragraph 2 refers to

    Ⓐ United States
    Ⓑ varieties
    Ⓒ species
    Ⓓ trees and shrubs

More Available

includes peas, beans, lentils, peanuts, and pods with beanlike seeds. Some *acacias* actually produce edible crops. Other *Acacia* varieties are valued for the sticky resin, called gum arabic or gum acacia, used widely in medicines, foods, and perfumes, for the dark dense wood prized for making pianos, or for the bark, rich in tannin, a dark, acidic substance used to cure the hides of animals, transforming them into leather.

    Nearly five hundred species of *Acacia* have been analyzed, identified, categorized, and proven capable of survival in hot and generally arid parts of the world; however, only a dozen of the three hundred Australian varieties thrive in the southern United States. Most *acacia* imports are low spreading trees, but of these, only three flower, including the *Bailey Acacia* with fernlike silver leaves and small, fragrant flowers arranged in rounded clusters, the *Silver Wattle*, similar to the *Bailey Acacia*, which grows twice as high, and the squat *Sydney Golden Wattle*, bushy with broad, flat leaves, showy bright yellow blossoms, and sharp spined twigs. Another variety, the *Black Acacia*, also called the *Blackwood*, has dark green

---

27. According to this passage, the *Silver Wattle*

    Ⓐ is squat and bushy
    Ⓑ has unobtrusive blossoms
    Ⓒ is taller than the *Bailey Acacia*
    Ⓓ is used for making furniture

28. In paragraph 2, the word flat most nearly means

    Ⓐ smooth
    Ⓑ pretty
    Ⓒ pointed
    Ⓓ short

More Available

includes peas, beans, lentils, peanuts, and pods with beanlike seeds. Some *acacias* actually produce edible crops. Other *Acacia* varieties are valued for the sticky resin, called gum arabic or gum acacia, used widely in medicines, foods, and perfumes, for the dark dense wood prized for making pianos, or for the bark, rich in tannin, a dark, acidic substance used to cure the hides of animals, transforming them into leather.

    Nearly five hundred species of *Acacia* have been analyzed, identified, categorized, and proven capable of survival in hot and generally arid parts of the world; however, only a dozen of the three hundred Australian varieties thrive in the southern United States. Most *acacia* imports are low spreading trees, but of these, only three flower, including the *Bailey Acacia* with fernlike silver leaves and small, fragrant flowers arranged in rounded clusters, the *Silver Wattle*, similar to the *Bailey Acacia*, which grows twice as high, and the squat *Sydney Golden Wattle*, bushy with broad, flat leaves, showy bright yellow blossoms, and sharp spined twigs. Another variety, the *Black Acacia*, also called the *Blackwood*, has dark green

---

29. The word showy in paragraph 2 could best be replaced by

    Ⓐ strange
    Ⓑ elaborate
    Ⓒ huge
    Ⓓ fragile

More Available

includes peas, beans, lentils, peanuts, and pods with beanlike seeds. Some *acacias* actually produce edible crops. Other *Acacia* varieties are valued for the sticky resin, called gum arabic or gum acacia, used widely in medicines, foods, and perfumes, for the dark dense wood prized for making pianos, or for the bark, rich in tannin, a dark, acidic substance used to cure the hides of animals, transforming them into leather.

    Nearly five hundred species of *Acacia* have been analyzed, identified, categorized, and proven capable of survival in hot and generally arid parts of the world; however, only a dozen of the three hundred Australian varieties thrive in the southern United States. Most *acacia* imports are low spreading trees, but of these, only three flower, including the *Bailey Acacia* with fernlike silver leaves and small, fragrant flowers arranged in rounded clusters, the *Silver Wattle*, similar to the *Bailey Acacia*, which grows twice as high, and the squat *Sydney Golden Wattle*, bushy with broad, flat leaves, showy bright yellow blossoms, and sharp spined twigs. Another variety, the *Black Acacia*, also called the *Blackwood*, has dark green

30. Which of the following *Acacias* has the least colorful blossoms?

    (A) *Bailey Acacia*
    (B) *Sydney Golden Wattle*
    (C) *Silver Wattle*
    (D) *Black Acacia*

31. Which of the following would most probably be made from a *Black Acacia* tree?

    (A) A flower arrangement
    (B) A table
    (C) A pie
    (D) Paper

32. When do *Acacia* trees bloom in Australia?

    (A) February
    (B) Summer
    (C) August
    (D) Spring

33. The following sentence can be added to the passage.

    Some *acacias* are popular in landscaping because of their graceful shapes, lacey foliage, and fragrant blossoms.

    Where would it best fit in the passage?

    Click on the square (■) to add the sentence to the passage.

    Scroll the passage to see all of the choices.

Beginning

The *Acacia*, a genus of trees and shrubs of the *mimosa* family that originated in Australia, has long been used there in building simple mud and stick structures. ■ The acacia is called a wattle in Australia, and the structures are said to be made of daub and wattle. ■ The acacia is actually related to the family of plants known as *legumes* that includes peas, beans, lentils, peanuts, and pods with beanlike seeds. Some *acacias* actually produce edible crops. ■ Other *Acacia* varieties are valued for the sticky resin, called gum arabic or gum acacia, used widely in medicines, foods, and perfumes, for the dark dense wood prized for making pianos, or for the bark, rich in tannin, a dark, acidic substance used to cure the hides of animals, transforming them into leather. ■

Nearly five hundred species of *Acacia* have been analyzed, identified, categorized, and proven capable of survival in hot and generally arid parts of the world; however, only a dozen of the three hundred Australian varieties thrive in the southern United States. Most *acacia* imports are low spreading trees, but of those, only three flower, including the *Bailey Acacia* with fernlike silver

In 1626, Peter Minuit, governor of the Dutch settlements in North America known as New Amsterdam, negotiated with Canarsee chiefs for the purchase of Manhattan Island for merchandise valued at sixty guilders or about $24.12. He purchased the island for the Dutch West India Company.

The next year, Fort Amsterdam was built by the company at the extreme southern tip of the island. Because attempts to encourage Dutch immigration were not immediately successful, offers, generous by the standards of the era, were extended throughout Europe. Consequently, the settlement became the most heterogeneous of the North American colonies. By 1637, the fort had expanded into the village of New Amsterdam, other small communities had grown up around it, including New Haarlem and Stuyvesant's Bouwery, and New Amsterdam began to prosper, developing characteristics of religious and linguistic tolerance unusual for the times. By 1643, it was reported that eighteen different languages could be heard in New Amsterdam alone.

Among the multilingual settlers was a large group of English colonists from Connecticut and Massachusetts who supported the English King's claim to all of New Netherlands set out in a charter that gave the territory to his brother James, Duke of York. In 1644, when the English sent a formidable fleet of warships into the New Amsterdam harbor, Dutch governor Peter Stuyvesant surrendered without resistance.

When the English acquired the island, the village of New Amsterdam was renamed New York in honor of the Duke. By the onset of the Revolution, New York City was already a bustling commercial center. After the war, it was selected as the first capital of the United States. Although the government was eventually moved, first to

Philadelphia and then to Washington, D.C., New York maintained its status. It became a haven for pirates who conspired with leading merchants to exchange supplies for their ships in return for a share in the plunder. As a colony, New York exchanged many agricultural products for English manufactured goods. In addition, trade with the West Indies prospered. Three centuries after his initial trade with the Native Americans, Minuit's tiny investment was worth more than seven billion dollars.

34. Which of the following would be the best title for this passage?

   Ⓐ A History of New York City
   Ⓑ An Account of the Dutch Colonies
   Ⓒ A Biography of Peter Minuit
   Ⓓ The First Capital of the United States

35. What did the Native Americans receive in exchange for their island?

   Ⓐ Sixty Dutch guilders
   Ⓑ $24.12 U.S.
   Ⓒ Goods and supplies
   Ⓓ Land in New Amsterdam

36. Where was New Amsterdam located?

   Ⓐ In Holland
   Ⓑ In North America
   Ⓒ On the island of Manhattan
   Ⓓ In India

37. What does the author mean by the statement Because attempts to encourage Dutch immigration were not immediately successful, offers, generous by the standards of the era, were extended throughout Europe?

   Ⓐ Other Europeans were given opportunities to immigrate to the new world after a slow response by the Dutch.
   Ⓑ Since the Dutch immigration was so successful, opportunities were provided for the Europeans to immigrate to the new world also.
   Ⓒ The Dutch took advantage of opportunities to immigrate to Europe instead of to the new world.
   Ⓓ Immigration to the new world required that the Dutch and other Europeans wait until opportunities were available.

> **Beginning**
>
> In 1626, Peter Minuit, governor of the Dutch settlements in North America known as New Amsterdam, negotiated with Canarsee chiefs for the purchase of Manhattan Island for merchandise valued at sixty guilders or about $24.12. He purchased the island for the Dutch West India Company.
>
> The next year, Fort Amsterdam was built by the company at the extreme southern tip of the island. Because attempts to encourage Dutch immigration were not immediately successful, offers, generous by the standards of the era, were extended throughout Europe. Consequently, the settlement became the most heterogeneous of the North American colonies. By 1637, the fort had expanded into the village of New Amsterdam, other small communities had grown up around it, including New Haarlem and Stuyvesant's Bouwery, and New Amsterdam began to prosper, developing characteristics of religious and linguistic tolerance unusual for the times. By 1643, it was reported that eighteen different languages could be heard in New Amsterdam alone.
>
> Among the multilingual settlers was a large

38. The word heterogeneous in paragraph 2 could best be replaced by

   Ⓐ liberal
   Ⓑ renowned
   Ⓒ diverse
   Ⓓ prosperous

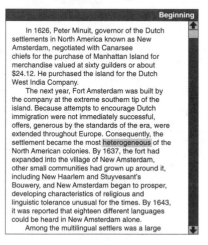

> **Beginning**
>
> In 1626, Peter Minuit, governor of the Dutch settlements in North America known as New Amsterdam, negotiated with Canarsee chiefs for the purchase of Manhattan Island for merchandise valued at sixty guilders or about $24.12. He purchased the island for the Dutch West India Company.
>
> The next year, Fort Amsterdam was built by the company at the extreme southern tip of the island. Because attempts to encourage Dutch immigration were not immediately successful, offers, generous by the standards of the era, were extended throughout Europe. Consequently, the settlement became the most heterogeneous of the North American colonies. By 1637, the fort had expanded into the village of New Amsterdam, other small communities had grown up around it, including New Haarlem and Stuyvesant's Bouwery, and New Amsterdam began to prosper, developing characteristics of religious and linguistic tolerance unusual for the times. By 1643, it was reported that eighteen different languages could be heard in New Amsterdam alone.
>
> Among the multilingual settlers was a large

39. Why were so many languages spoken in New Amsterdam?

   Ⓐ The Dutch West India Company was owned by England.
   Ⓑ The Dutch West India Company allowed freedom of speech.
   Ⓒ The Dutch West India Company recruited settlers from many different countries in Europe.
   Ⓓ The Indians who lived there before the Dutch West India Company purchase spoke many languages.

40. Look at the word his in the passage. Click on the word or phrase in the **bold** text that his refers to.

More Available

extended throughout Europe. Consequently, the settlement became the most heterogeneous of the North American colonies. By 1637, the fort had expanded into the village of New Amsterdam, other small communities had grown up around it, including New Haarlem and Stuyvesant's Bouwery, and New Amsterdam began to prosper, developing characteristics of religious and linguistic tolerance unusual for the times. By 1643, it was reported that eighteen different languages could be heard in New Amsterdam alone.

Among the multilingual settlers was a large group of English colonists from Connecticut and Massachusetts who supported the English King's claim to all of New Netherlands set out in a charter that gave the territory to his brother James, Duke of York. In 1644, when the English sent a formidable fleet of warships into the New Amsterdam harbor, Dutch governor Peter Stuyvesant surrendered without resistance.

When the English acquired the island, the village of New Amsterdam was renamed New York in honor of the Duke. By the onset of the Revolution, New York City was already a bustling

41. The word formidable in paragraph 3 is closest in meaning to

Ⓐ powerful
Ⓑ modern
Ⓒ expensive
Ⓓ unexpected

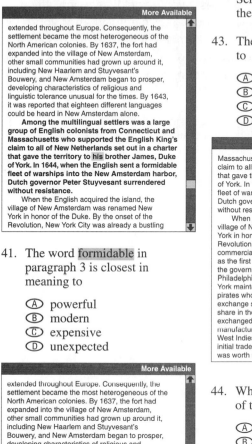

More Available

extended throughout Europe. Consequently, the settlement became the most heterogeneous of the North American colonies. By 1637, the fort had expanded into the village of New Amsterdam, other small communities had grown up around it, including New Haarlem and Stuyvesant's Bouwery, and New Amsterdam began to prosper, developing characteristics of religious and linguistic tolerance unusual for the times. By 1643, it was reported that eighteen different languages could be heard in New Amsterdam alone.

Among the multilingual settlers was a large group of English colonists from Connecticut and Massachusetts who supported the English King's claim to all of New Netherlands set out in a charter that gave the territory to his brother James, Duke of York. In 1644, when the English sent a formidable fleet of warships into the New Amsterdam harbor, Dutch governor Peter Stuyvesant surrendered without resistance.

When the English acquired the island, the village of New Amsterdam was renamed New York in honor of the Duke. By the onset of the Revolution, New York City was already a bustling

42. Click on the paragraph that explains the reason for renaming New Amsterdam.

Scroll the passage to see all of the paragraphs.

43. The word it in paragraph 4 refers to

Ⓐ Revolution
Ⓑ New York City
Ⓒ the island
Ⓓ the first capital

End

Massachusetts who supported the English King's claim to all of New Netherlands set out in a charter that gave the territory to his brother James, Duke of York. In 1644, when the English sent a formidable fleet of warships into the New Amsterdam harbor, Dutch governor Peter Stuyvesant surrendered without resistance.

When the English acquired the island, the village of New Amsterdam was renamed New York in honor of the Duke. By the onset of the Revolution, New York City was already a bustling commercial center. After the war, it was selected as the first capital of the United States. Although the government was eventually moved, first to Philadelphia and then to Washington, D.C., New York maintained its status. It became a haven for pirates who conspired with leading merchants to exchange supplies for their ships in return for a share in the plunder. As a colony, New York exchanged many agricultural products for English manufactured goods. In addition, trade with the West Indies prospered. Three centuries after his initial trade with the Indians, Minuit's tiny investment was worth more than seven billion dollars.

44. Which city was the first capital of the new United States?

Ⓐ New Amsterdam
Ⓑ New York
Ⓒ Philadelphia
Ⓓ Washington

45. On what date was Manhattan valued at $7 billion?

Ⓐ 1626
Ⓑ 1726
Ⓒ 1656
Ⓓ 1926

To check your answers for Model Test 4, refer to the Answer Key on pages 372–373. For an explanation of the answers, refer to the Explanatory Answers for Model Test 4 on pages 410–420.

Writing Section Model Test 4

When you take a Model Test, you should use one sheet of paper, both sides. Time each Model Test carefully. After you have read the topic, you should spend 30 minutes writing. For results that would be closest to the actual testing situation, it is recommended that an English teacher score your test, using the guidelines on page 234 of this book.

> In your opinion, what is the best way to choose a marriage partner? Use specific reasons and examples why you think this approach is best.

Notes

ANSWER KEYS FOR THE TOEFL REVIEW EXERCISES AND MODEL TESTS

ANSWER KEY—EXERCISES FOR STRUCTURE

Patterns

Problem		Part A	Part B	
Problem	1	(A)	(A)	have
Problem	2	(C)	(A)	to evolve
Problem	3	(D)	(B)	smoking
Problem	4	(D)	(B)	permitting
Problem	5	(C)	(A)	saw
Problem	6	(A)	(B)	turns *or* will turn
Problem	7	(A)	(C)	will have to pay *or* may have to pay
Problem	8	(A)	(C)	unless they complete
Problem	9	(D)	(B)	be used
Problem	10	(B)	(A)	be
Problem	11	(B)	(B)	for making *or* to make
Problem	12	(C)	(C)	measured
Problem	13	(A)	(A)	It is believed
Problem	14	(D)	(C)	will have succeeded
Problem	15	(B)	(B)	is losing
Problem	16	(B)	(D)	should be discontinued
Problem	17	(A)	(D)	for them
Problem	18	(A)	(A)	which
Problem	19	(C)	(C)	eight or ten computers
Problem	20	(C)	(A)	Religion
Problem	21	(B)	(A)	Space
Problem	22	(C)	(A)	Progress
Problem	23	(B)	(C)	pieces of equipment
Problem	24	(C)	(A)	Spelling *or* To spell
Problem	25	(B)	(A)	~~It is~~
Problem	26	(A)	(A)	The philosophy
Problem	27	(D)	(B)	no
Problem	28	(C)	(A)	Most of *or* Almost all of
Problem	29	(C)	(A)	Sex education

Problem		*Part A*	*Part B*	
Problem	30	(A)	(B)	four-stage
Problem	31	(A)	(B)	so expensive
Problem	32	(B)	(B)	the same
Problem	33	(C)	(D)	like
Problem	34	(A)	(B)	differ from *or* are different from
Problem	35	(C)	(A)	as much as
Problem	36	(A)	(A)	more than
Problem	37	(C)	(C)	as many as
Problem	38	(C)	(B)	most
Problem	39	(C)	(B)	worse
Problem	40	(C)	(A)	the more intense
Problem	41	(A)	(B)	like that of England
Problem	42	(B)	(B)	besides
Problem	43	(C)	(C)	because
Problem	44	(D)	(D)	also easy to install
Problem	45	(B)	(D)	complete
Problem	46	(D)	(C)	the plane is
Problem	47	(B)	(B)	does the same major league baseball team win
Problem	48	(C)	(A)	since 1930
Problem	49	(C)	(B)	as a whole
Problem	50	(B)	(B)	that

Style

Problem		*Part A*	*Part B*	
Problem	1	(C)	(C)	were
Problem	2	(C)	(B)	gave
Problem	3	(B)	(B)	enables
Problem	4	(C)	(A)	is
Problem	5	(B)	(A)	There are
Problem	6	(D)	(D)	its
Problem	7	(B)	(C)	their
Problem	8	(B)	(A)	Having designed
Problem	9	(D)	(C)	find
Problem	10	(C)	(B)	to develop
Problem	11	(B)	(D)	to use as currency

Problem		Part A	Part B	
Problem	12	**(B)**	**(B)**	rapidly
Problem	13	**(B)**	**(A)**	an old one *or* an ancient one
Problem	14	**(C)**	**(A)**	✖
Problem	15	**(B)**	**(A)**	raised
Problem	16	**(C)**	**(A)**	lies
Problem	17	**(B)**	**(B)**	sits
Problem	18	**(B)**	**(C)**	do
Problem	19	**(A)**	**(B)**	depends on
Problem	20	**(B)**	**(B)**	differ

ANSWER KEY—EXERCISES FOR READING

Problem 1. Previewing

A black hole is a region of space created by the total gravitational collapse of matter. It is so intense that nothing, not even light or radiation, can escape. In other words, it is a one-way surface through which matter can fall inward but cannot emerge.

Some astronomers believe that a black hole may be formed when a large star collapses inward from its own weight. So long as they are emitting heat and light into space, stars support themselves against their own gravitational pull with the outward thermal pressure generated by heat from nuclear reactions deep in their interiors. But if a star eventually exhausts its nuclear fuel, then its unbalanced gravitational attraction could cause it to contract and collapse. Furthermore, it could begin to pull in surrounding matter, including nearby comets and planets, creating a black hole.

The topic is black holes.

Problem 2. Reading for Main Ideas

For more than a century, despite attacks by a few opposing scientists, Charles Darwin's theory of evolution by natural selection has stood firm. Now, however, some respected biologists are beginning to question whether the theory accounts for major develop-

<u>ments such as the shift from water to land habitation</u>. Clearly, evolution has not proceeded steadily but has progressed by radical advances. Recent research in molecular biology, particularly in the study of DNA, provides us with a new possibility. Not only environmental changes but also genetic codes in the underlying structure of DNA could govern evolution.

The main idea is that biologists are beginning to question Darwin's theory.
A good title would be "Questions about Darwin's Theory."

Problem 3. Using Contexts for Vocabulary

1. *To auction* means to sell.
2. *Proprietor* means an owner.
3. *Formerly* means in the past.
4. *To sample* means to try or to taste.
5. *Royalty* means payment.

Problem 4. Scanning for Details

To prepare for a career in engineering, a student must begin planning in high school. Mathematics and science should form the core curriculum. For example, in a school where sixteen credit hours are required for high school graduation, four should be in mathematics, one each in chemistry, biology, and physics. The remaining credits should include four in English and at least three in the humanities and social sciences. The average entering freshman in engineering should have achieved at least a 2.5 grade point average on a 4.0 scale in his or her high school. Although deficiencies can be corrected during the first year, the student who needs additional work should expect to spend five instead of four years to complete a degree.

1. What is the average grade point for an entering freshman in engineering?

2.5

2. When should a student begin planning for a career in engineering?

in high school

3. How can a student correct deficiencies in preparation?

by spending five years

4. How many credits should a student have in English?

four

5. How many credits are required for a high school diploma?

sixteen

Problem 5.   Making Inferences

When an acid is dissolved in water, the acid molecule divides into two parts, a hydrogen ion and another ion. An ion is an atom or a group of atoms which has an electrical charge. The charge can be either positive or negative. If hydrochloric acid is mixed with water, for example, it divides into hydrogen ions and chlorine ions.

A strong acid ionizes to a great extent, but a weak acid does not ionize so much. The strength of an acid, therefore, depends on how much it ionizes, not on how many hydrogen ions are produced. It is interesting that nitric acid and sulfuric acid become greatly ionized whereas boric acid and carbonic acid do not.

1. What kind of acid is sulfuric acid?

a strong acid ionizes to a great extent, and sulfuric acid becomes greatly ionized.
Conclusion: Sulfuric acid is a strong acid.

2. What kind of acid is boric acid?

a weak acid does not ionize so much and boric acid does not ionize greatly.
Conclusion: Boric acid is a weak acid.

Problem 6. Identifying Exceptions

All music consists of two elements—expression and design. Expression is inexact and subjective, and may be enjoyed in a personal or instinctive way. Design, on the other hand is exact and must be analyzed objectively in order to be understood and appreciated. The folk song, for example, has a definite musical <u>design which relies on simple repetition</u> with a <u>definite beginning and ending</u>. A folk song generally consists of one stanza of music repeated for each stanza of verse.

Because of their communal, and usually <u>uncertain origin</u>, folk songs are often popular verse set to music. They are not always recorded, and tend to be passed on in a kind of musical version of oral history. Each singer revises and perfects the song. In part as a consequence of this continuous revision process, most folk songs are almost perfect in their construction and design. A particular singer's interpretation of the folk song may provide an interesting expression, but the simple design that underlies the song itself is stable and enduring.

1. All of the following are true of a folk song EXCEPT
✓ There is a clear start and finish.
✓ The origin is often not known.
   The design may change in the interpretation.
✓ Simple repetition is characteristic of its design.

Problem 7. Locating References

The National Road, also known as the Cumberland Road, was constructed in the early 1800s to provide transportation between the established commercial areas of the East and
Line Northwest Territory. By 1818, <u>the road</u> had reached Wheeling,
(5) West Virginia, 130 miles from (its) point of origin in Cumberland, Maryland. The cost was a monumental thirteen thousand dollars per mile.

Upon reaching the Ohio River, the National Road became one of the major trade routes to the western states and territo-
(10) ries, providing Baltimore with a trade advantage over neighboring cities. In order to compete, New York state authorized the construction of <u>the Erie Canal</u>, and Philadelphia initiated a transportation plan to link (it) with Pittsburgh. Towns along the

rivers, canals, and the new National Road became important trade centers.

1. The word "its" in line 5 refers to *the road.*

2. The word "it" in line 13 refers to *the canal.*

Problem 8. Referring to the Passage

In September of 1929, traders experienced <u>a lack of confidence in the stock market's ability to continue its phenomenal rise. Prices fell. For many inexperienced investors,</u>
Line <u>the drop produced a panic.</u> They had all their money tied up in
(5) the market, and they were pressed to sell before the prices fell even lower. Sell orders were coming in so fast that the ticker tape at the New York Stock Exchange could not accommodate all the transactions.

To try to reestablish confidence in the market, a power-
(10) ful group of New York bankers agreed to pool their funds and purchase stock above current market values. Although the buy orders were minimal, they were counting on their reputations to restore confidence on the part of the smaller investors, thereby affecting the number of sell orders. On Thursday, October
(15) 24, Richard Whitney, the Vice President of the New York Stock Exchange and a broker for the J.P. Morgan Company, made the effort on their behalf. <u>Initially, it appeared to have been successful</u>, then, on the following Tuesday, the crash began again and accelerated. By 1932, stocks were worth only twenty per-
(20) cent of their value at the 1929 high. The results of the crash had extended into every aspect of the economy, causing a long and painful depression, referred to in American history as the Great Depression.

1. Where in the passage does the author refer to the reason for the stock market crash? *Lines 1-4.*

2. Where in the passage does the author suggest that there was a temporary recovery in the stock market? *Lines 17-18.*

ANSWER KEY—MODEL TESTS

Model Test 1—Computer-Assisted TOEFL

Section 1: Listening

1. **(C)**	10. **(C)**	19. **(C)**	28. **(B)**	37. **(B)**	46. **(A)**
2. **(A)**	11. **(B)**	20. **(B)**	29. **(A)**	38. **(B)**	47. **(B)**
3. **(C)**	12. **(A)**	21. **(B)**	30. **(A)**	39. **(A)**	48. **(C)**
4. **(A)**	13. **(C)**	22. **(C)**	31. **(C)**	40. **(C)(D)**	49. **(B)**
5. **(A)**	14. **(B)**	23. **(B)**	32. **(A)**	41. **(B)**	50. **(B)**
6. **(B)**	15. **(C)**	24. **(D)**	33. **(C)**	42. **(A)**	
7. **(D)**	16. **(C)**	25. **(C)**	34. **(A)**	43. **(A)(C)**	
8. **(C)**	17. **(C)**	26. **(C)**	35. **(C)**	44. **(B)**	
9. **(D)**	18. **(D)**	27. **(D)**	36. **(C)**	45. **(C)**	

Section 2: Structure

1. **(B)**	6. **(B)**	10. **(B)**	14. **(C)**	18. **(A)**	22. **(D)**
2. **(C)**	7. **(B)**	11. **(C)**	15. **(C)**	19. **(A)**	23. **(B)**
3. **(A)**	8. **(A)**	12. **(A)**	16. **(D)**	20. **(B)**	24. **(D)**
4. **(D)**	9. **(A)**	13. **(D)**	17. **(A)**	21. **(D)**	25. **(A)**
5. **(C)**					

Section 3: Reading

1. (**B**)	16. (**D**)	34. (**B**)
2. (**B**)	17. (**C**)	35. (**B**)
3. (**D**)	18. (**A**)	36. (**D**)
4. (**A**)	19. (**B**)	37. (**A**)
5. **sentence 6,**	20. **award**	38. (**C**)
paragraph 1	21. (**C**)	39. **large**
6. (**A**)	22. **generally**	40. (**B**)
7. (**B**)	23. (**D**)	41. (**A**)
8. (**B**)	24. (**A**)	42. (**B**)
9. (**C**)	25. (**B**)	43. (**B**)
10. (**A**)	26. (**D**)	44. **sentence 2,**
11. (**B**)	27. (**B**)	**paragraph 3**
12. (**A**)	28. (**B**)	45. (**C**)
13. (**B**)	29. (**C**)	
14. (**B**)	30. (**C**)	
15. "**. . . invented**	31. **brilliant tricks**	
dynamite.	32. **purpose**	
When he read . . ."	33. (**B**)	

Model Test 2—Computer-Assisted TOEFL

Section 1: Listening

1. (**B**)	14. (**C**)	27. (**C**)	40. (**A**)
2. (**D**)	15. (**A**)	28. (**B**)	41. (**C**)
3. (**D**)	16. (**B**)	29. (**D**)	42. (**C**)
4. (**B**)	17. (**B**)	30. (**B**)	43. (**A**)
5. (**D**)	18. (**B**)	31. (**C**)	44. (**A**)(**B**)
6. (**A**)	19. (**A**)	32. (**D**)	45. (**C**)
7. (**B**)	20. (**A**)	33. (**C**)	46. (**C**)(**D**)
8. (**A**)	21. (**C**)	34. (**D**)	47. (**B**)
9. (**C**)	22. (**B**)	35. (**B**)	48. (**C**)
10. (**A**)	23. (**C**)	36. (**A**)(**B**)	49. (**B**)(**A**)(**C**)
11. (**B**)	24. (**B**)	37. (**C**)	50. (**A**)
12. (**D**)	25. (**B**)	38. (**B**)	
13. (**D**)	26. (**D**)	39. (**D**)	

Section 2: Structure

1. (A)	6. (B)	11. (B)	16. (C)	21. (A)
2. (A)	7. (A)	12. (A)	17. (C)	22. (A)
3. (C)	8. (C)	13. (A)	18. (C)	23. (B)
4. (D)	9. (A)	14. (B)	19. (A)	24. (B)
5. (C)	10. (A)	15. (D)	20. (C)	25. (B)

Section 3: Reading

1. (A)	17. (D)	32. sentence 4, paragraph 3
2. (C)	18. signs	33. damage
3. (A)	19. (B)	34. ". . . solids or liquids. One objection . . ."
4. (A)	20. (C)	
5. (D)	21. ". . . a rude noise. Gestures such as . . ."	35. (A)
6. (A)		36. (D)
7. (D)	22. (B)	37. (B)
8. data	23. interaction	38. (A)
9. (C)	24. (D)	39. (A)
10. problems	25. (D)	40. (C)
11. sentence 2, paragraph 2	26. (D)	41. (B)
	27. (B)	42. (C)
12. (C)	28. (B)	43. sentence 3, paragraph 1
13. (D)	29. (C)	
14. sentence 4, paragraph 1	30. (A)	44. tamed
	31. (C)	45. (A)
15. (A)		
16. (B)		

Model Test 3—Computer-Assisted TOEFL

Section 1: Listening

1. (A)	14. (A)	27. (B)	40. (B)
2. (C)	15. (C)	28. (B)	41. (A)
3. (C)	16. (A)	29. (B)	42. (D)
4. (A)	17. (B)	30. (A)	43. (A)
5. (A)	18. (D)	31. (C)	44. (B)
6. (A)	19. (B)	32. (B)	45. (B)
7. (C)	20. (B)	33. (B)	46. (C)
8. (C)	21. (C)	34. (D)	47. (D)
9. (D)	22. (B)	35. (C)	48. (D)
10. (B)	23. (C)	36. (B)	49. (A)(C)
11. (A)	24. (C)	37. (A)	50. (A)
12. (A)	25. (A)	38. (B)(C)	
13. (D)	26. (A)	39. (C)(B)(D)(A)	

Section 2: Structure

1. (C)	6. (A)	11. (C)	16. (C)	21. (C)
2. (B)	7. (C)	12. (B)	17. (B)	22. (A)
3. (A)	8. (D)	13. (B)	18. (B)	23. (C)
4. (B)	9. (C)	14. (B)	19. (A)	24. (A)
5. (B)	10. (A)	15. (D)	20. (A)	25. (D)

Section 3: Reading

1. **(A)**
2. **(D)**
3. **(C)**
4. **(D)**
5. **very successful**
6. **(A)**
7. **(C)**
8. **(D)**
9. **sentence 4, paragraph 2**
10. **(C)**
11. **(C)**
12. **(A)**
13. **(B)**
14. **(C)**
15. **(C)**
16. **(D)**
17. **(D)**
18. **(C)**
19. **(A)**
20. **devastating**
21. **earthquakes**
22. **(D)**
23. **(B)**
24. **segmented**
25. **(C)**
26. **(A)**
27. **(A)**
28. **(B)**
29. **(C)**
30. **(A)**
31. **(C)**
32. **". . . other life forms. Although some insects . . ."**
33. **(D)**
34. **(D)**
35. **(D)**
36. **(B)**
37. **locomotion**
38. **(C)**
39. **(C)**
40. **(C)**
41. **(A)**
42. **(A)**
43. **sentence 4, paragraph 1**
44. **(A)**
45. **(C)**

Model Test 4—Computer-Assisted TOEFL

Section 1: Listening

1. **(C)**
2. **(A)**
3. **(A)**
4. **(B)**
5. **(D)**
6. **(C)**
7. **(B)**
8. **(C)**
9. **(A)**
10. **(B)**
11. **(A)**
12. **(D)**
13. **(A)**
14. **(A)**
15. **(C)**
16. **(D)**
17. **(A)**
18. **(B)**
19. **(C)**
20. **(D)**
21. **(D)**
22. **(D)**
23. **(A)**
24. **(D)**
25. **(B)**
26. **(B)**
27. **(D)**
28. **(B)**
29. **(B)**
30. **(C)**
31. **(D)**
32. **(A)**
33. **(C)**
34. **(A)**
35. **(C)**
36. **(C)**
37. **(D)**
38. **(D)**
39. **(C)**
40. **(C)**
41. **(D)**
42. **(A)(C)**
43. **(B)**
44. **(B)**
45. **(C)**
46. **(B)**
47. **(D)**
48. **(D)**
49. **(C)**
50. **(B)**

Section 2: Structure

1. **(D)**	6. **(A)**	11. **(D)**	16. **(A)**	21. **(D)**
2. **(B)**	7. **(B)**	12. **(C)**	17. **(D)**	22. **(A)**
3. **(C)**	8. **(C)**	13. **(B)**	18. **(C)**	23. **(B)**
4. **(D)**	9. **(B)**	14. **(D)**	19. **(C)**	24. **(D)**
5. **(B)**	10. **(C)**	15. **(C)**	20. **(D)**	25. **(D)**

Section 3: Reading

1. **(A)**
2. **(C)**
3. **(B)**
4. **(A)**
5. **(B)**
6. **(C)**
7. **sentence 2, paragraph 2**
8. **(D)**
9. **(B)**
10. **(A)**
11. **(B)**
12. **(D)**
13. **(C)**
14. **sentence 5, paragraph 1**
15. **(A)**
16. **better**
17. **(D)**
18. **(D)**
19. **(A)**
20. **(C)**
21. **(D)**
22. **(B)**
23. **valued**
24. **(C)**
25. **(A)**
26. **(B)**
27. **(C)**
28. **(A)**
29. **(B)**
30. **(D)**
31. **(B)**
32. **(C)**
33. **". . . fragrant blossoms. Other *Acacia* . . ."**
34. **(A)**
35. **(C)**
36. **(B)**
37. **(A)**
38. **(C)**
39. **(C)**
40. **the English King's**
41. **(A)**
42. **sentence 1, paragraph 4**
43. **(B)**
44. **(B)**
45. **(D)**

EXPLANATORY
ANSWERS FOR THE
TOEFL MODEL TESTS

Model Test 1—Computer Assisted TOEFL

Section 1: Listening

1. **(C)** Since the man says that there aren't any seats left, it must be concluded that he has to stand when he takes the bus to school. Choice (B) refers to the woman's suggestion, not to the man's response. Choices (A) and (D) are not mentioned and may not be concluded from information in the conversation.

2. **(A)** *Who cares* means that it isn't important (that her advisor might be offended). Choices (B), (C), and (D) are not mentioned and may not be concluded from information in the conversation.

3. **(C)** Because the woman says that the invitation sounds "great," and she thanks the man for asking her, it must be concluded that she would go out with the man on another occasion. Choice (A) contradicts the fact that she responds so positively while refusing the invitation. Choices (B) and (D) contradict the fact that she has plans to attend a lecture.

4. **(A)** *In good shape* is an idiomatic expression that means the item is in good condition. Choice (B) contradicts the fact that the man thinks the bike is new, and that the woman says it is in good shape. Choice (C) contradicts the fact that the speakers are talking about a bike that is able to be seen. Choice (D) contradicts the fact that the woman got the bike almost five years ago.

5. **(A)** The man says that he would rather have something cold. Choices (B), (C), and (D) refer to what the man likes, not to what he wants.

6. **(B)** ". . . it isn't too far to walk [to the shopping center]." Choice (A) contradicts the fact that he is already giving the woman information about the shopping center. Choices (C) and (D) are alternative possibilities that the man mentions before making his suggestion.

7. **(D)** Since the man says that he is just checking the schedule now, it must be concluded that he has not registered yet. Choice (A) contradicts the fact that he is checking the schedule for a class. Choices (B) and (C) are not mentioned and may not be concluded from information in the conversation.

8. **(C)** To *not mind* is an idiomatic expression that means the speaker will not be bothered by an activity or situation. Choices (A), (B), and (D) are not paraphrases of the expression.

9. **(D)** "She'd better see someone at the Counseling Center." Choices (A), (B), and (C) are not mentioned and may not be concluded from information in the conversation.

10. **(C)** *Please go on* is an idiomatic expression that means the speaker wants the other person to continue. Choices (A), (B), and (D) are not paraphrases of the expression.

11. **(B)** Since the man apologizes for going ahead of the woman in line, he will most probably allow her to go ahead of him. Choice (A) contradicts the fact that it is the man, not the woman, who apologizes. Choice (C) contradicts the fact that he has already apologized. Choice (D) is not mentioned and may not be concluded from information in the conversation.

12. **(A)** *Not again* is an idiomatic expression that means the speaker is impatient with some kind of repeated behavior or activity. Choice (C) contradicts the fact that she does not know about the party until the man informs her. Choices (B) and (D) are not mentioned and may not be concluded from information in the conversation.

13. **(C)** *That's too bad* is an idiomatic expression that means the speaker is sorry about the news. Choice (D) contradicts the fact that the man thought the professor would give the woman an extension. Choices (A) and (B) are not mentioned and may not be concluded from information in the conversation.

14. **(B)** Since the man says that they should have left already, it must be concluded that they are late. Choice (A) is not likely because of the woman's suggestion that they make a call. Choices (C) and (D) are not mentioned and may not be concluded from information in the conversation.

15. **(C)** Since the woman says that she has her rent paid until the 15th, she will probably stay where she is living until the 15th. The reference to half a month in Choice (A) refers to the fact that the woman already has her rent paid until the 15th, not to what she will do. Choice (B) contradicts the fact that the woman, not the man, is planning to move. Choice (D) contradicts the fact that the woman mentions having her rent paid.

16. **(C)** Since the man expresses surprise, it must be concluded that he thought she had not taken the placement test. Choice (A) contradicts the fact that the man was surprised. Choices (B) and (D) are not mentioned and may not be concluded from information in the conversation.

17. **(C)** To *catch cold* is an idiomatic expression that means to get sick. Choices (A), (B), and (D) are not paraphrases of the expression, and may not be concluded from information in the conversation.

18. **(D)** "I need your technical writing class. . . . In that case, I'll sign an override for you." Choice (A) contradicts the fact that he went early to registration. Choice (B) contradicts the fact that his advisor signed his course request. Choice (C) contradicts the fact that the course will not be taught until fall semester.

19. **(C)** ". . . I'll sign an override. . . . Take this form back to the registration area and they'll get you in." Choice (D) refers to something that the professor tells Mike to do, not to something that Mike wants the professor to do. Choices (A) and (B) are not mentioned and may not be concluded from information in the conversation.

20. **(B)** ". . . I can't graduate without your class." Choice (A) contra-

dicts the fact that he plans to graduate in the spring. Choices (C) and (D) are not mentioned and may not be concluded from information in the conversation.

21. **(B)** ". . . I'll sign an override for you." Choice (A) refers to the suggestion that the professor makes at the beginning of the conversation, not to what he actually decides to do. Choices (C) and (D) are not mentioned and may not be concluded from information in the conversation.

22. **(C)** ". . . background music, more commonly known as MUZAK." Choice (A) is one kind of MUZAK, but it contradicts the fact that MUZAK can be upbeat songs, too. Choice (B) is one place where MUZAK is played, but it contradicts the fact that MUZAK can be played in the workplace and the supermarket, too. Choice (D) contradicts the fact that MUZAK is more than a pleasant addition to the environment.

23. **(B)** "In one survey, overall productivity increased by thirty percent, although five to ten percent is the average." Choice (D) refers to one survey, not to the average. Choices (A) and (C) are not mentioned and may not be concluded from information in the talk.

24. **(D)** ". . . stimulus progression . . . starts with a slow, soft song . . . and builds up . . . to an upbeat song . . . programmed . . . when people are generally starting to tire." Choice (A) refers to the first stage of stimulus progression, not to the total progression. Choices (B) and (C) refer to varieties of MUZAK, not to stimulus progression.

25. **(C)** "In supermarkets, slow music can influence shoppers to walk slower and buy more." Choice (D) contradicts the fact that it can influence shoppers to buy more. Choices (A) and (B) are not mentioned and may not be concluded from information in the talk.

26. **(C)** ". . . Community College offers a series of video telecourses to meet the needs of students who prefer to complete coursework in their homes." Choices (A) and (B) are secondary themes used to develop the main theme of the talk. Choice (D) is not mentioned and may not be concluded from information in the conversation.

27. **(D)** "Some telecourses will also be broadcast on KCC-TV's 'Sun-Up Semester.'" Choice (A) contradicts the fact that students should call the Community College Distance Learning Program to register. Choice (C) contradicts the fact that a listing of courses is printed in the television guide. Choice (B) is not mentioned and may not be concluded from information in the conversation.

28. **(B)** "To register for a telecourse, phone the Community College. . . ." Choice (A) contradicts the fact that the program is designed to meet the needs of students who are not able to come to campus. Choices (C) and (D) are not mentioned and may not be concluded from information in the conversation.

29. **(A)** ". . . you can use either an 800 telephone number or an e-mail address to contact your instructor." Choices (B), (C), and (D) are not mentioned and may

not be concluded from information in the conversation.

30. **(A)** "I thought I had a cold, but it was mono. . . . It's a virus. . . ." The word *joke* in Choice (C) refers to the phrase *no joke* which means something that isn't funny. Choice (D) is mentioned but is not the main topic of the conversation. Choice (B) is not mentioned and may not be concluded from information in the conversation.

31. **(C)** "I had to drop out last semester." Choices (A) and (B) are probably true, but they caused her problem; they were not the problem. Choice (D) contradicts the fact that she had to withdraw last semester, not this semester.

32. **(A)** "A lot of college students get it [mono]." The word *joke* in Choice (C) refers to the phrase *no joke* which means something that isn't funny. Choices (B) and (D) are not mentioned and may not be concluded from information in the conversation.

33. **(C)** ". . . if you get sick . . . you'll end up with an extra semester. . . . so you might as well slow down." The woman warns the man that he will have to drop out of school if he gets sick, but she does not advise him to drop out as in Choice (A). Choices (B) and (D) contradict the fact that the woman suggests that the man slow down.

34. **(A)** "I would like to outline the development of the Sapir-Whorf Hypothesis concerning the relationship between language and culture." Choices (B), (C), and (D) are secondary themes that are used to develop the main theme of the lecture.

35. **(C)** "In 1936, he [Whorf] wrote 'An American Indian Model of the Universe,' which explored the implications of the Hopi verb system. . . ." Choice (A) refers to historical linguistics, not to the languages that Whorf used in his research. Choices (B) and (D) are not mentioned and may not be concluded from information in the talk.

36. **(C)** ". . . 'linguistic relativity' which states, at least as a hypothesis, that the grammar of a man's language influences the manner in which he understands reality and behaves with respect to it." Choice (D) contradicts the fact that grammar influences cultural behavior. Choices (A) and (B) are not mentioned and may not be concluded from information in the talk.

37. **(B)** ". . . it [linguistic relativity] came to be called the Sapir-Whorf Hypothesis." Choice (A) is incomplete because it does not include the name of Whorf. Choice (C) includes the name of Boas, who contributed to the hypothesis but was not named in it. Choice (D) refers to a paper written by Whorf regarding the Hopi verb system, not to linguistic relativity.

38. **(B)** "Let's begin our discussion today by defining acid rain." Choices (A), (C), and (D) are all secondary points of discussion that are used to develop the main topic of the discussion.

39. **(A)** ". . . Acid rain is . . . sulfur dioxide and nitrogen oxide [that] combine with water vapor and form sulfuric acid and nitric acid." Choice (C) refers to the result of acid rain, not to a

definition of it. Choice (D) contradicts the fact that it is sulfur dioxide and nitrogen oxide, not just sulfur, that combines with water vapor. Choice (B) is not mentioned and may not be concluded from information in the discussion.

40. **(C) (D)** "Acidity . . . has all but eliminated . . . fish populations . . . in the Great Lakes. . . . [and] rain has caused a chemical change in the soil. . . . Plants don't get the nutrients they need. . . ." Choices (A) and (B) are not mentioned and may not be concluded from information in the discussion.

41. **(B)** ". . . Air Quality Accord . . . to establish limits for the amount of acidic deposits that may flow across international boundaries." Choice (A) refers to the result of the legislation, not to the conditions of it. Choice (C) contradicts the fact that the problem of automobile emissions is a larger challenge to governments and their agencies. Choice (D) contradicts the fact that the fuels are lower in sulfur, but some sulfur still remains in the fuels.

42. **(A)** "There are three main types of bacteria. . . ." Choices (B), (C), and (D) are all secondary points of discussion that are used to develop the main topic of discussion.

43. **(B) (C)** "Bacteria is the name for a very large group of one-celled microscopic organisms. . . . bacteria reproduce very rapidly. . . ." Choice (B) contradicts the fact that, for the most part, bacteria live harmlessly on the skin, in the mouth, and in the intestines. Choice (D) is not men-

tioned and may not be concluded from information in the lecture.

44. **(B)** Visual B is the slide for the cocci bacteria. Visual A is the slide for the bacilli bacteria. Visual C is the slide for the spirilla bacteria.

45. **(C)** "Bacterial cells resemble the cells of other life forms. . . ." Choice (A) contradicts the fact that bacteria cells resemble the cells of other life forms. Choices (B) and (D) are true, but they are not the reasons that bacteria are being used in research studies.

46. **(A)** "It [the class] was supposed to be offered at three o'clock . . . the time has been changed. . . ." Choice (B) contradicts the fact that the man has a job in the morning that conflicts with his class schedule. Choice (C) contradicts the fact that the man has a student loan. Choice (D) contradicts the fact that the man is already a sociology major.

47. **(B)** "I have to be a full-time student in order to qualify for my student loan." Choice (D) contradicts the fact that the courses are electives. Choices (A) and (C) are not mentioned and may not be concluded from information in the lecture.

48. **(C)** "Dr. Brown teaches Soc 560. . . . I've been trying to take a class with her. . . ." Choice (A) contradicts the fact that it is an elective, not a required course. Choice (B) contradicts the fact that it has been changed to nine in the morning. Choice (D) contradicts the fact that both courses are sociology classes.

49. **(B)** ". . . when I scheduled that class, it was supposed to be

offered at three o'clock . . . but . . . the time has been changed. . . ." Choice (A) contradicts the fact that the man is trying to register for classes. Choice (C) contradicts the fact that the man already has a student loan. Choice (D) contradicts the fact that the man is a sociology major, and he is trying to add a sociology class.

50. **(B)** ". . . tell Dr. Brown what happened when you see her in class." Choices (A), (C), and (D) contradict the fact that he will tell Dr. Brown what happened when he goes to her class.

Section 2: Structure

1. **(B)** A cardinal number is used after a noun. *The* is used with an ordinal number before a noun. Choice (A) is incomplete because there is no verb after *who*. Choices (C) and (D) are redundant.

2. **(C)** *But also* is used in correlation with the inclusive *not only*. Choice (B) would be used in correlation with *both*. Choices (A) and (D) are not used in correlation with another inclusive.

3. **(A)** A past form in the condition requires either *would* or *could* and a verb word in the result. Because the past form *planted* is used in the condition, *will* should be *would* in the result.

4. **(D)** In order to refer to an *increase* in the rate of inflation, *rises* should be used. *To raise* means to move to a higher place. *To rise* means to increase.

5. **(C)** A form of *have* with someone such as *General Lee* and a verb word expresses a causative. Choice (A) is an infinitive, not a

verb word. Choice (B) is a participle. Choice (D) is an *-ing* form.

6. **(B)** Ideas after exclusives should be expressed by parallel structures. *To hunt* should be *in hunting* to provide for parallelism with the phrase *in planting*.

7. **(B)** *Effect on* is a prepositional idiom. *In* should be *on*.

8. **(A)** *Because* is used before a subject and verb to introduce cause. Choices (B), (C), and (D) are not accepted for statements of cause.

9. **(A)** The word order for a passive sentence is a form of BE followed by a participle. *Call* should be *called*.

10. **(B)** *Form* should be *formation*. Although both are nouns derived from verbs, the *-ation* ending is needed here. *Form* means the structure. *Formation* means the process of forming over time.

11. **(C)** For scientific results, a present form in the condition requires a present or future form in the result. Choices (A), (B), and (D) are not conditional statements.

12. **(A)** Ideas in a series should be expressed by parallel structures. Only *to sell* in Choice (A) provides for parallelism with the infinitive *to increase*. Choices (B), (C), and (D) are not parallel.

13. **(D)** Because it is a prepositional phrase, *as grass* should be *like grass*. *As* functions as a conjunction. *Like* functions as a preposition.

14. **(C)** Ideas in a series should be expressed by parallel structures. *It is* should be deleted to provide for parallelism with the adjectives *interesting*, *informative*, and *easy*.

15. **(C)** Activities of the dead logically establish a point of view in the past. *Lives* should be *lived* in order to maintain the point of view.

16. **(D)** In contrary-to-fact clauses, *were* is the only accepted form of the verb BE. Choices (A), (B), and (C) are forms of the verb BE, but they are not accepted in contrary-to-fact clauses.

17. **(A)** The anticipatory clause *it is generally believed that* introduces a subject and verb, *Java Man . . . is*. In Choices (B) and (C) the verb *is* is repeated. Choice (D) may be used as a subject clause preceding a main verb, not preceding a subject and verb. "That it is generally believed that Java Man, who lived before the first Ice Age, is the first manlike animal *is* the result of entries in textbooks" would also be correct.

18. **(A)** A verb word must be used in a clause after an impersonal expression. *Is not* should be *not be* after the impersonal expression *it is essential*.

19. **(A)** *Who* should be *whom* because it is the complement of the clause *many people consider*. *Who* functions as a subject. *Whom* functions as a complement.

20. **(B)** Only Choice (B) may be used with a noncount noun such as *money*. Choices (A), (C), and (D) may be used with count nouns.

21. **(D)** *By* expresses means before an *-ing* form. *Refine* should be *refining* after the preposition *by*.

22. **(D)** There must be agreement between pronoun and antecedent. *Their* should be *its* to agree with the singular antecedent *atmosphere*.

23. **(B)** Most adverbs of manner are formed by adding *-ly* to adjectives. *Broad* should be *broadly* to qualify the manner in which the speaking was done.

24. **(D)** An adjective clause modifies a noun in the main clause. *That provides food* modifies *the one*. Choice (A) is a subject and verb without the clause marker *that*. Choice (B) is a clause marker *that* with an *-ing* form, not a verb. Choice (C) is a verb without a clause marker.

25. **(A)** Plural count nouns are used after a number or a reference to a number of items. *Term* should be *terms*.

Section 3: Reading

1. **(B)** "The Process of Photosynthesis" is the best title because it states the main idea of the passage. The other choices are secondary ideas which are used to develop the main idea. Choice (A) describes the process in the form of an equation. In Choice (C), the parts of plants are named because of their roles in the process. Choice (D) is one of the products of the process.

2. **(B)** ". . . the green parts of plants use carbon dioxide from the atmosphere and release oxygen to it. Oxygen is the product of the reaction." The water referred to in Choice (A) and the carbon referred to in Choice (C) are used in photosynthesis, but neither one is mentioned as occurring in excess as a result of the process. Choice (D) refers to the natural substance in the chloroplasts of

plants, not to a chemical combination of carbon dioxide and water.

3. **(D)** "These exchanges are the opposite of those that occur in respiration." Choices (A), (B), and (C) refer to processes which occur in photosynthesis, not to processes which are the opposite.

4. **(A)** ". . . radiant energy from the sun is stored as chemical energy." In Choice (B), it is water, not energy from the sun, which is conducted from the xylem to the leaves. Choice (C) contradicts the fact that energy from the sun is the source of the chemical energy used in decomposing carbon dioxide and water. Choice (D) is incorrect because it is oxygen, not energy, that is released one to one for each molecule of carbon dioxide used.

5. "Except for the usually small percentage used in respiration, the oxygen released in the process diffuses out of the leaf into the atmosphere through stomates." Quotation from sentence 6, paragraph 1.

6. **(A)** In the context of this passage, stored is closest in meaning to retained. Choices (B), (C), and (D) are not accepted definitions of the word.

7. **(B)** "The products of their decomposition [carbon dioxide and water] are recombined into a new compound, which is successively built up into more and more complex substances." Choices (A), (C), and (D) would change the meaning of the sentence.

8. **(B)** In the context of this passage, successively is closest in meaning to in a sequence. Choices (A),

(C), and (D) are not accepted definitions of the word.

9. **(C)** "At the same time, a balance of gases is preserved in the atmosphere." Energy from the sun, referred to in Choice (A), and carbon dioxide, referred to in Choice (B), are used in the process of photosynthesis, not produced as a result of it. Choice (D) is not mentioned and may not be concluded from information in the passage.

10. **(A)** Choices (B), (C), and (D) are mentioned in sentences 6 and 7, paragraph 1. Water, not oxygen, is absorbed by the roots.

11. **(B)** The other choices are secondary ideas that are used to develop the main idea, "the Nobel Prizes." Choices (A), (C), and (D) are historically significant to the discussion.

12. **(A)** "The Nobel Prizes . . . were made available by a fund bequeathed for that purpose . . . by Alfred Bernhard Nobel." Because of the reference to *bequeath*, it must be concluded that Nobel left money in a will. In Choice (B), Nobel was the founder of the prizes, not a recipient. Choice (C) refers to the place where Nobel was born, not to where he is living now. Since Nobel has bequeathed funds, it must be concluded that he is dead and could not serve as chairman of a committee as in Choice (D).

13. **(B)** In the context of this passage, will refers to a legal document Choices (A), (C), and (D) are not accepted definitions of the word in this context.

14. **(B)** "The Nobel Prizes, awarded annually . . ." Because of the reference to *annually*, it must be

concluded that the prizes are awarded once a year. Choices (A), (C), and (D) are not mentioned and may not be concluded from information in the passage.

15. "According to the legend, Nobel's death had been erroneously reported in a newspaper, and the focus of the obituary was the fact that Nobel had invented dynamite. When he read this objective summary of his life [the obituary], the great chemist, it is said, decided that he wanted his name to be remembered for something more positive and humanitarian than inventing an explosive that was a potential weapon." The connection between these two sentences is the reference to "the obituary."

16. **(D)** In the context of this passage, outstanding could best be replaced by exceptional. Choices (A), (B), and (C) are not accepted definitions of the word.

17. **(C)** "The Nobel Prizes [are] awarded annually for distinguished work in chemistry, physics, physiology or medicine, literature, and international peace." Since there is no prize for music, a composer, in Choice (C) would not be eligible for an award. Choice (A) could be awarded a prize for literature. Choice (B) would be awarded a prize for medicine. Choice (D) could be awarded a prize for peace.

18. **(A)** Choice (A) is a restatement of the sentence referred to in the passage. To *administer* means to oversee or to manage. Choices (B), (C), and (D) would change the meaning of the original sentence.

19. **(B)** "The awards are . . . presented . . . on December 10 . . . on the anniversary of his [Alfred Nobel's] death." Choice (A) is incorrect because it is a tribute to Nobel, not to the King of Sweden. Choice (D) contradicts the fact that the Nobel Foundation, not the Central Bank of Sweden, administers the trust. Choice (C) is not mentioned and may not be concluded from information in the passage.

20. In the context of this passage, the word award is closest in meaning to prize. No other words or phrases in the **bold** text are close to the meaning of the word prize.

21. **(C)** The other choices are secondary ideas that are used to develop the main idea, "the development of opera." Choices (A), (B), and (D) are historically significant to the discussion.

22. In the context of this passage, the word generally is closest in meaning to usually. No other words or phrases in the **bold** text are close to the meaning of the word usually.

23. **(D)** "The usually accepted date for the beginning of opera as we know it is 1600." Choice (A) refers to Greek tragedy, the inspiration for modern opera. Choices (B) and (C) are not mentioned and may not be concluded from information in the passage.

24. **(A)** "Although stage plays have been set to music since the era of the ancient Greeks, when the dramas of Sophocles and Aeschylus were accompanied by lyres and flutes, the usually accepted date for the beginning of opera as we know it [the opera] is 1600." Choices (B), (C), and (D) would

change the meaning of the sentence.

25. **(B)** "... composer Jacopo Perí produced his famous *Euridice*, generally considered to be the first opera." Choice (A) refers to the form of musical story that inspired Perí, not to the opera that he wrote. Choice (C) refers to the wife of Henry IV for whose marriage the opera was written, not to the title of the opera. Choice (D) refers to the group of musicians who introduced the opera form, not to the title of an opera written by them.

26. **(D)** "As part of the celebration of the marriage of King Henry IV ... Jacopo Perí produced his famous *Euridice*." Choice (A) contradicts the fact that *Euridice* was produced in Florence, the native city of King Henry's wife and the place where the wedding was celebrated. Choice (B) refers to Greek tragedy, not to modern opera. Choice (C) is improbable because *Euridice* has become so famous.

27. **(B)** "... a group of Italian musicians called the Camerata began to revive the style of musical story that had been used in Greek tragedy." In Choice (A), musicians in the Camerata were Italian, not Greek. Choice (C) contradicts the fact that the center of the Camerata was Florence, Italy. King Henry IV referred to in Choice (D) was a patron of opera, but the name given to his court was not mentioned and may not be concluded from information in the passage.

28. **(B)** In the context of this passage, revive could best be replaced

by resume. Choices (A), (C), and (D) are not accepted definitions of the word.

29. **(C)** In the context of this passage, plots is closest in meaning to stories. Choices (A), (B), and (D) are not accepted definitions of the word.

30. **(C)** "They called their compositions *opera in musica* or musical works. It is from this phrase that the word 'opera' is borrowed." Choice (A) refers to the origin of the plots for opera, not to the term. Choice (B) contradicts the fact that the Camerata was a group of Italian musicians. Choice (D) refers to the composer of the first opera.

31. "Composers gave in to the demands of singers, writing many operas that were little more than a succession of brilliant tricks for the voice, designed to showcase the splendid voices of the singers who had requested them [brilliant tricks]." Other choices would change the meaning of the sentence.

32. In the context of this passage, the word purpose is closest in meaning to function. No other words or phrases in the **bold** text are close to the meaning of the word function.

33. **(B)** The author's main purpose is to describe the nature of sunspots. Choice (A) contradicts the fact that there is no theory that completely explains sunspots. Choices (C) and (D) are important to the discussion, and provide details that support the main idea.

34. **(B)** In the context of this passage, controversial is closest in mean-

ing to open to debate. Choices (A), (C), and (D) are not accepted definitions of the word.

35. **(B)** ". . . great storms on the surface of the sun hurl streams of solar particles into the atmosphere." *Storms* refer to disturbances of wind. Choice (A) contradicts the fact that great storms have been identified as the cause of particles being hurled into space. In Choice (C), there are storms, not rivers on the surface of the sun. Choice (D) refers to what happens as a result of the particles being hurled into space.

36. **(D)** In the context of this passage, particles refers to small pieces of matter. Choices (A), (B), and (C) are not accepted definitions of the word.

37. **(A)** ". . . streams of solar particles [are hurled] into the atmosphere." Because of the reference to *particles*, it must be concluded that the matter is very small. Choices (B), (C), and (D) are not mentioned and may not be concluded from information in the passage.

38. **(C)** Choice (C) is a restatement of the sentence referred to in the passage. The fact that the cooler sunspots may account for their color means that the color could be affected by the cooler temperature.

39. In the context of this passage, the word large is most opposite in meaning to tiny. No other words or phrases in the **bold** text are opposite in meaning to the word tiny.

40. **(B)** "About five percent of the spots are large enough so that

they [the spots] can be seen without instruments; consequently, observations of sunspots have been recorded for several thousand years." Choices (A), (C), and (D) would change the meaning of the sentence.

41. **(A)** In the context of this passage, consequently could best be replaced by as a result. Choices (B), (C), and (D) are not accepted definitions of the word.

42. **(B)** "Sunspots . . . tend to occur in pairs." Choices (A) and (C) refer to possibilities for arrangements, but not to the configuration in which sunspots usually occur. Choice (D) is not mentioned in the range of numbers for sunspots, from one to more than one hundred. The number *one thousand* refers to the number of years sunspots have been recorded, not to the number in a configuration.

43. **(B)** ". . . several models attempt to relate the phenomenon [of sunspots] to magnetic fields along the lines of longitude from the north and south poles of the sun." Choice (A) is incorrect because the magnetic fields are on the sun, not the Earth. Choice (C) is incorrect because the storms are on the sun, not on the Earth. Choice (D) contradicts the fact that several models attempt to relate sunspots to magnetic fields.

44. "About 5 percent of all sunspots are large enough so that they can be seen from Earth without instruments; consequently, observations of sunspots have been recorded for thousands of years." Quotation from sentence 2, paragraph 3.

45. **(C)** ". . . the controversial sunspot theory." Because the theory is controversial, it must be concluded that it is subject to disagreement. Choice (B) contradicts the fact that the theory is controversial. Choices (A) and (D) are not mentioned and may not be concluded from information in the passage.

Model Test 2—Computer-Assisted TOEFL

Section 1: Listening

1. **(B)** *You don't mean it* is an idiomatic expression that means the speaker is surprised. Choice (C) contradicts the fact that the man is surprised by the large turn out. Choices (A) and (D) are not mentioned and may not be concluded from information in the conversation.

2. **(D)** Since the woman points out the sign on the door, she implies that the man should look at it. Choices (A), (B), and (C) are not mentioned and may not be concluded from information in the conversation.

3. **(D)** Since the woman expressed interest in and enthusiasm for the opportunity to do a project for extra credit, it must be concluded that she intends to do one. Choice (A) contradicts the fact that the woman is already taking a class from Professor Wilson. Choice (C) contradicts the fact that the reference to "extra" is to extra credit, not to an extra class. Choice (B) is not mentioned and may not be concluded from information in the conversation.

4. **(B)** Listen carefully for the distinction between the words *angry* and *hungry*. Because the woman says that Paul would tell them if he were angry, it must be concluded that Paul would tell them if there were a problem. In choices (A) and (C), the word *angry* is confused with the word *hungry*. Choice (B) refers to what the woman, not the man, thinks about Paul.

5. **(D)** Since the woman says that there were a couple of As, it must be concluded that several other students received A grades. Choice (B) contradicts the fact that she refers to other As, implying that she received one. Choices (A) and (C) are not mentioned and may not be concluded from information in the conversation.

6. **(A)** Since the man says that the clock is fast, it must be concluded that the woman still has time to study. Choice (B) contradicts the fact that there is only a half hour left. Choice (D) contradicts the fact that the man knows the clock is fast. Choice (C) is not mentioned and may not be con-

cluded from information in the conversation.

7. **(B)** *To not agree more* means to agree very much. Choices (A) and (D) misinterpret the phrase *couldn't agree more* as a negative. Choice (C) is not mentioned and may not be concluded from information in the conversation.

8. **(A)** The man says that he has to go to class. Choice (B) refers to what the woman, not the man, is going to do. Choices (C) and (D) are not mentioned and may not be concluded from information in the conversation.

9. **(C)** *Meaning to* is an idiomatic expression that means intention on the part of the speaker. To "get back with" someone means to return a call or otherwise communicate. Choice (B) contradicts the fact that a message was left on the machine. Choice (D) contradicts the fact that the man acknowledges the message. Choice (A) is not mentioned and may not be concluded from information in the conversation.

10. **(A)** To be *out* is an idiomatic expression that means to be absent. Choices (B), (C), and (D) are not paraphrases of the expression, and may not be concluded from information in the conversation.

11. **(B)** "Check with the secretary before going in . . ." Choice (A) contradicts the fact that the woman has already given him directions to the Math Department. Choice (C) contradicts the fact that the woman tells him to check with the secretary first. Choice (D) is not mentioned and may not be concluded from information in the conversation.

12. **(D)** Since Tom is often absent, and there is doubt that he will be present for the final exam, it must be concluded that Tom is not very responsible. Choices (A), (B), and (C) are not mentioned and may not be concluded from information in the conversation.

13. **(D)** *Are we still on* is an idiomatic expression that is used to confirm a date. Choice (C) refers to the woman's feelings, not to the man's feelings. Choices (A) and (B) are not mentioned and may not be concluded from information in the conversation.

14. **(C)** Since the woman must have the course to graduate and Dr. Collin's section is closed, she will probably enroll in the section marked "staff." Choice (A) contradicts the fact that Dr. Collin's section is closed. Choice (B) contradicts the fact that the woman is distressed because she is planning to graduate soon. Choice (D) contradicts the fact that she needs the course to graduate and is more interested in the course than in the instructor.

15. **(A)** Since the woman says that it takes six weeks to receive the score, she implies that the man should wait for the results to be mailed. Choice (B) refers to the man's plan, not to the woman's suggestion. Choice (C) contradicts the fact that the man has already taken the test and is waiting for the score. Choice (D) contradicts the fact that the woman tells him not to worry.

16. **(B)** To *make the most of* something is an idiomatic expression that means to take advantage of an opportunity. Choices (A), (C), and (D) are not paraphrases of the

expression and may not be concluded from information in the
conversation.

17. **(B)** To *take care of something*
is an idiomatic expression that
means to be responsible for it.
Choices (A), (C), and (D) are not
paraphrases of the expression and
may not be concluded from information in the conversation.

18. **(B)** "Did you understand that experiment that Bill mentioned in
the group presentation?" Choices
(A), (C), and (D) are not mentioned and may not be concluded from information in the
discussion.

19. **(A)** ". . . since there is no air
resistance on the moon, it is
the ideal environment for the
experiment." Choice (B) refers
to the fact that the moon has a
lower gravitational acceleration,
not that there is no gravitational
acceleration. Choices (C) and (D)
are true, but they are not the
reason the moon is an ideal
environment.

20. **(A)** ". . . much easier . . . to lift
the hammer on the moon . . .
because of the moon's lower
rate of gravitational acceleration." Choice (B) is true, but it is
not the reason it is easier to lift the
hammer on the moon. Choices
(C) and (D) are not mentioned and
may not be concluded from information in the discussion.

21. **(C)** "I really liked the presentation." Choice (A) refers to information about the hammer, not
to the entire presentation. Choice
(B) contradicts the fact that she
liked the presentation. Choice
(D) is not mentioned and may not
be concluded from information in
the discussion.

22. **(B)** "It [the video] was about
stress." Choices (A), (C), and (D)
are secondary themes used to
develop the main theme of the
video.

23. **(C)** "They said that women
usually don't get the same level
of care that men do. . . ." Choice
(D) contradicts the fact that the
heart attacks suffered by women
are likely to be more serious.
Choices (A) and (B) are not
mentioned and may not be concluded from information in the
conversation.

24. **(B)** "Really it was [good]."
Choice (A) contradicts the fact
that he explains the video to the
woman. Choice (C) contradicts
the fact that he encourages the
woman to view it. Choice (D)
contradicts the fact that he was
surprised by the report on the
number of women who have
heart attacks.

25. **(B)** "It's on reserve in the library.
. . ." Choice (A) refers to the fact
that the man and woman have
already discussed the video tape,
not to what the woman will do.
Choice (C) contradicts the fact
that tapes on reserve cannot be
checked out. Choice (D) refers to
what the woman will do after she
sees the video.

26. **(D)** Elizabeth Barrett Browning
is the main topic of this lecture.
Choices (A), (B), and (C) are secondary topics that are used to
develop the main topic of the
lecture.

27. **(C)** "In part because the sovereign was a woman, there was
great support for a movement to
break with the tradition of a male
Poet Laureate." Choice (A) contradicts the fact that Elizabeth

Barrett was not married at the time that she was considered for the title of Poet Laureate. Choice (B) contradicts the fact that *Sonnets from the Portuguese* was not published at the time that she was considered for the title. Choice (D) is not mentioned and may not be concluded from information in the talk.

28. **(B)** "... she married Robert Browning, himself a gifted poet, and they fled to Florence, Italy." The place in Choice (C) refers to the title of one of Elizabeth's most famous works, *Sonnets from the Portuguese*, not to a place where she lived. The place in Choice (D) refers to the country where she lived before, not after her marriage. Choice (A) is not mentioned and may not be concluded from information in the talk.

29. **(D)** "*Aurora Leigh*, her longest work, appeared in 1856, only five years before her death in 1861." Choice (A) refers to the date when Elizabeth Barrett was suggested to replace the Poet Laureate, not to the date of her death. Choice (B) refers to the date when her son was born, one year before she published her collected works in 1850. Choice (C) refers to the date when *Aurora Leigh* was published, five years before her death.

30. **(B)** The contributions of biology to medicine are the main topic of this lecture. Choices (A), (C), and (D) are secondary topics that are used to develop the main topic of the lecture.

31. **(C)** "Hippocrates ... began ... to apply scientific method to the problems of diagnosis and the

treatment of diseases. . . . he kept careful records of symptoms and treatments." Choice (A) refers to the work of Aristotle, not Hippocrates. Choice (B) refers to the work of Sir Joseph Lister. Choice (D) refers to a theory that Hippocrates discarded in favor of the scientific method, not to his work.

32. **(B)** "Because of his great contribution to the field, Aristotle has been called the father of biology." Choice (A) refers to the father of modern medicine, not to the father of biology. Choice (C) refers to the author of *Materia Medica*. Choice (D) refers to the physician who established the science of immunization.

33. **(C)** "... the English physician and anatomist William Harvey discovered a mechanism for the circulation of the blood in the body." Choice (A) refers to a contribution by Louis Pasteur, not by William Harvey. Choice (B) refers to a contribution by Edward Jenner. Choice (D) refers to a reference book that was a contribution by Dioscorides.

34. **(D)** "... gangs have been prevalent for much longer than I had assumed. I was so surprised." The number in Choice (A) is true, but it was not what surprised the student. Choice (C) contradicts the fact that not much has changed over the years. Choice (B) is not mentioned and may not be concluded from information in the discussion.

35. **(B)** "... Joan Moore, indicated that gang behavior is probably caused by normal adolescent insecurities. . . ." Choice (A) refers to a similar form of behavior, but

not to the cause of gang activity. Choice (C) refers to the neighborhoods where gang activity takes place, but it is not the cause of gang activity. Choice (D) is not mentioned and may not be concluded from information in the discussion.

36. **(A) (B)** ". . . a gang member will be recognizable because of gang-related tattoos, clothing. . . ." The phrase *research studies* in Choice (D) refers to the research reported in the discussion, not to ways that gang members are identified. Choice (C) is not mentioned and may not be concluded from information in the discussion.

37. **(C)** "They [women] are viewed as more of a support system. . . ." Choice (A) contradicts the fact that women are not considered members of gangs. Choice (D) contradicts the fact that women are part of the extended social group of a gang. Choice (B) is not mentioned and may not be concluded from information in the discussion.

38. **(B)** "I have a problem with my schedule." Choice (A) contradicts the fact that Mary really likes her job. Choice (D) contradicts the fact that she is a work-study employee. Choice (C) is not mentioned and may not be concluded from information in the conversation.

39. **(D)** "I have a required class at nine o'clock on Monday, Wednesday, and Friday." The phrase *every day* in Choice (A) refers to her work schedule, not to her class schedule. The phrase *ten-thirty on Monday* in Choice (C) refers to the time she will report to work, not to the time

for her class. Choice (B) is not mentioned and may not be concluded from information in the conversation.

40. **(A)** ". . . you could come in at ten-thirty and work until two-thirty. . . ." Choice (B) contradicts the fact that she will continue to work four hours a day. Choice (D) contradicts the fact that he changes her work schedule. Choice (C) is not mentioned and may not be concluded from information in the conversation.

41. **(C)** "You're a work-study employee, and that means . . . you can study on the job as long as the work is done first." Choice (A) is true, but it is not a complete definition of a work-study employee. Choices (B) and (D) are not mentioned and may not be concluded from information in the conversation.

42. **(C)** ". . . we have developed several techniques for building more earthquake-resistant structures." Choices (A), (B), and (D) are all mentioned in the lecture, but they are secondary ideas used to develop the main topic of the lecture.

43. **(A)** "Walls can also be reinforced, using cross-bracing." Choice (B) refers to a structure in the center of a building. Choice (D) refers to a device positioned below the building. Choice (C) is not mentioned and may not be concluded from information in the lecture.

44. **(A) (B)** "Most . . . base isolators . . . are made of . . . layers of steel and synthetic rubber." Choice (C) refers to construction material, but not to material used in base

isolators. Choice (D) refers to fill dirt.

45. **(C)** ". . . fill dirt can lose its bearing strength . . . and the buildings constructed on it can . . . disappear into the Earth." Choice (A) refers to the characteristics of a moat, not to those of fill dirt. Choice (B) refers to the techniques for building earthquake-resistant structures. The phrase *shock waves* in Choice (D) refers to the advantage of rubber, not to a characteristic of fill dirt.

46. **(C) (D)** "The most common [vein patterns] are the pinnate and the palmate." Choices (A) and (B) refer to vein patterns, but they are not the most common vein patterns.

47. **(B)** ". . . a pinnate leaf has one large central vein called the midrib . . . that extends the full length of the leaf." Choice (A) contradicts the fact that the pinnate leaf, not the midrib, is one of the major classifications. Choice (C) contradicts the fact that the midrib is a central vein in the pinnate, not the parallel leaf. Choice (D) is not mentioned and may not be concluded from information in the lecture.

48. **(C)** "A good way to remember this classification [palmate] is to think of the palm of your hand." Choices (A) and (B) are both true, but he did not use the visual in the explanation as a memory aid. The phrase *lab manual* in Choice (D) refers to a reference for the lab activity, not to a way to remember the classification.

49. **(B)** Pinnate **(A)** Palmate **(C)** Parallel

50. **(A)** ". . . work with your lab partner to classify the veining of each leaf." The word *fifty-two* in Choice (C) refers to the page number in the lab manual, not to the number of pages to read. Choices (B) and (D) are not mentioned and may not be concluded from information in the lecture.

Section 2: Structure

1. **(A)** In some dependent clauses, the clause marker is the subject of the dependent clause. *Which* refers to *the soybeans* and is the subject of the verb *can be used*. Choices (B) and (D) do not have clause markers. Choice (C) is a clause marker that refers to a person, not to *soybeans*.

2. **(A)** Only Choice (A) may be used with a count noun like *species* and a number. Choices (C) and (D) may be used with noncount nouns. Choice (B) may be used with count nouns without a number. "As many species of finch have been identified" would also be correct.

3. **(C)** The verb *had* establishes a point of view in the past. *Serves* should be *served* in order to maintain the point of view.

4. **(D)** There must be agreement between subject and verb. *Produce* should be *produces* to agree with the singular subject *a thunderhead*.

5. **(C)** When the degree of one quality, *the price*, is dependent upon the degree of another quality, *the demand*, two comparatives are required, each of which must be preceded by *the*. Choice (A) is a comparative, but it is not preceded by *the*. Choices (B) and (D) are not accepted comparative forms.

6. **(B)** *The same like* is a combination of *the same as* and *like*. *Like* should be *as* in the phrase with *the same*.

7. **(A)** *Despite of* is a combination of *despite* and *in spite of*. Either *despite* or *in spite of* should be used.

8. **(C)** *So* is used with an adjective to express cause. Choice (A) may be used before a noun, not before an adjective such as *big*. Choices (B) and (D) may not be used to express cause before a clause of result such as *that there are four time zones*. "The United States is very big" would be correct without the clause of result.

9. **(A)** Ideas in a series should be expressed by parallel structures. Only Choice (A) has three parallel *-ing* forms. Choices (B), (C), and (D) are not parallel.

10. **(A)** *Behave* should be *behavior*. *Behave* is a verb. *Behavior* is a noun.

11. **(B)** *Whom* should be *who* because it is the subject of the verb *is*. *Whom* functions as a complement. *Who* functions as a subject.

12. **(A)** *Such as* is commonly used to introduce an example.

13. **(A)** An introductory verbal phrase should immediately precede the noun that it modifies. Only Choice (A) provides a noun that could be logically modified by the introductory verbal phrase *upon hatching*. *Swimming, the knowledge*, and *how to swim* could not logically *hatch* as would be implied by Choices (B), (C), and (D).

14. **(B)** Comparative forms are usually followed by *than*. *Highest* in Choices (A) and (C) may be used to compare more than two decks.

Choice (D) correctly compares *this deck* with *any other one*, but *that*, not *than*, follows the comparative.

15. **(D)** A verb word must be used in a clause after the verb *to insist*. *Will not smoke* should be *not smoke*.

16. **(C)** *Invent* should be *invention*. *Invent* is a verb. *Invention* is a noun.

17. **(C)** *Calcium* is the subject of the verb *is*. Choice (A) may be used with the word *that*. Choice (B) may be used as a subject clause preceding a main verb. Choice (D) may be used preceding a subject and verb. "It is calcium *that* is necessary for the development of strong bones and teeth." "That calcium is necessary for the development of strong bones and teeth *is* known," and "Although calcium is necessary for strong bones and teeth, *other minerals are* also important" would also be correct.

18. **(C)** *Larger* should be *largest*. Because there are more than two masses of nerve tissue in the human body, a superlative form must be used.

19. **(A)** *Like* is a preposition. *Alike* should be *like*.

20. **(C)** *Capable of* is a prepositional idiom. *To perform* should be *of performing*.

21. **(A)** For scientific results, a present form in the condition requires a present or future form in the result. Only Choice (A) introduces a conditional.

22. **(A)** Repetition of the subject by a subject pronoun is redundant. *It* should be deleted.

23. **(B)** A negative phrase introduces inverted order. *Not until* requires

an auxiliary verb, subject, and main verb. In Choice (A) there is no auxiliary. In Choices (C) and (D), there is no subject and no auxiliary.

24. **(B)** The verb phrase *to approve of* requires an *-ing* form in the complement. *-Ing* forms are modified by possessive pronouns. Choices (A) and (D) are infinitives, not *-ing* forms. Choice (C) is an *-ing* form, but it is modified by a subject, not a possessive pronoun.

25. **(B)** *Commonly* should be *common*. *Commonly* is an adverb. *Common* is an adjective.

Section 3: Reading

1. **(A)** The other choices are secondary ideas that are used to develop the main idea, "Technological Advances in Oceanography." Choices (B), (C), and (D) are important to the discussion, and provide details that support the main idea.

2. **(C)** In the context of this passage, sluggish is closest in meaning to slow moving. Choices (A), (B), and (D) are not accepted definitions of the word.

3. **(A)** "Because of undersea pressure that affected their speech organs, communication among divers was difficult or impossible." Choices (B), (C), and (D) are not mentioned and may not be concluded from information in the passage.

4. **(A)** "Direct observations of the ocean floor are made not only by divers but also by deep-diving submarines." Choices (B), (C), and (D) contradict the fact that observations are made by deep-diving submarines as well as by divers.

5. **(D)** "Direct observations of the ocean floor are made . . . by deep-diving submarines." Choice (A) contradicts the fact that some of the vehicles are manned. Choice (B) refers to the divers, not to the undersea vehicles. Choice (C) contradicts the fact that undersea vehicles have overcome some of the limitations of divers.

6. **(A)** In the context of this passage, cruise could best be replaced by travel at a constant speed. Choices (B), (C), and (D) are not accepted definitions of the word.

7. **(D)** "Radio-equipped buoys can be operated by remote control in order to transmit information back to the land-based laboratories." Choices (A), (B), and (C) are not mentioned and may not be concluded from information in the passage.

8. In the context of this passage, the word data is closest in meaning to information. No other words or phrases in the **bold** text are close to the meaning of the word information.

9. **(C)** Choices (A), (B) and (D) are mentioned in sentences 8 and 9, paragraph 1. (C) refers to computers, not to satellites.

10. "Some of humankind's most serious problems, especially those [problems] concerning energy and food, may be solved with the help of observations made possible by this new technology." Other choices would change the meaning of the sentence.

11. "Some of humankind's most serious problems, especially

those concerning energy and food, may be solved with the help of observations made possible by this new technology." Quotation from sentence 2, paragraph 2.

12. **(C)** "Communication" is the best title because it states the main idea of the passage. The other choices are all examples of communication that provide details in support of the main idea.

13. **(D)** "Whereas speech is the most advanced form of communication. . . ." Choice (A) contradicts the fact that there are many ways to communicate without speech including signals, signs, symbols, and gestures. Choice (B) is incorrect because the advances are dependent upon speech; speech is not dependent upon the advances. Choice (C) is not mentioned and may not be concluded from information in the passage.

14. "For instance, the function of any signal is to impinge upon the environment in such a way that it attracts attention, as for example, the dots and dashes that can be applied in a telegraph circuit." Quotation from sentence 4, paragraph 1.

15. **(A)** In the context of this passage, impinge upon is closest in meaning to intrude. Choices (B), (C), and (D) are not accepted definitions of the word.

16. **(B)** "The basic function of a signal is to impinge upon the environment in such a way that it [the signal] attracts attention, as, for example, the dots and dashes of a telegraph circuit." Choices (A), (C), and (D) would change the meaning of the sentence.

17. **(D)** In the context of this passage, potential could best be replaced by possibility. Choices (A), (B), and (C) are not accepted definitions of the word.

18. "Less adaptable to the codification of words, signs also contain agreed upon meaning; that is, they [signs] convey information in and of themselves [the signs]." Other choices would change the meaning of the sentence.

19. **(B)** In the context of this passage, intricate could best be replaced by complicated. Choices (A), (C), and (D) are not accepted definitions of the word.

20. **(C)** ". . . applauding in a theater provides performers with an auditory symbol." A telegraph circuit was cited as an example of Choice (A). A stop sign and a barber pole were cited as examples of Choice (B). Waving and handshaking were cited as examples of Choice (D).

21. "A loud smacking of the lips after a meal can be either a kinesthetic and auditory symbol of approval and appreciation, or simply a rude noise. Gestures such as waving and handshaking also communicate certain cultural messages." The connection between the two sentences is the reference to cultural symbols and cultural messages. The second sentence with the word *also* must be mentioned after the first sentence.

22. **(B)** ". . . means of communication intended to be used for long distances and extended periods are based upon speech. Radio, television, and telephone are only a few." Choices (A), (C), and (D) are not mentioned and may not be concluded from information in the passage.

23. In the context of this passage, the word interaction is closest in meaning to communication. No other words or phrases in the **bold** text are close to the meaning of the word communication.

24. **(D)** Choices (A), (B), and (C) are important to the discussion and provide details that support the primary topic, "the content, form, and effects of fertilizer."

25. **(D)** In the context of this passage, essential could best be replaced by required. Choices (A), (B), and (C) are not accepted definitions of the word.

26. **(D)** Since the last number in the formula represents the percentage content of potash, and since the last number is the smallest, it must be concluded that potash has the smallest percentage content. Choice (A) refers to the number 4 in the formula. Choices (B) and (C) are the substances found in phosphoric acid which refers to the number 8 in the formula.

27. **(B)** Since the content of nitrogen is represented by the first number in the formula, it must be concluded that there is 5 percent nitrogen in the fertilizer. The number in Choice (A) refers to the quantity of numbers in the formula. The percentage in Choice (C) refers to potash. The percentage in Choice (D) refers to phosphoric acid.

28. **(B)** In the context of this passage, designate could best be replaced by specify. Choices (A), (C), and (D) are not accepted definitions of the word.

29. **(C)** "Recently, liquids have shown an increase in popularity. . . ." Choice (A) refers to a form

of fertilizers that used to be used, but was found to be less convenient, not to a form that is more popular than ever. Choices (B) and (D) contradict the fact that solids in the shape of chemical granules are easy to store and apply.

30. **(A)** "Formerly, powders were also used, but these [powders] were found to be less convenient than either solids or liquids." Choices (B), (C), and (D) would change the meaning of the sentence.

31. **(C)** In the context of this passage, convenient is closest in meaning to easy to use. Choices (A), (B), and (D) are not accepted definitions of the word.

32. "Accumulations of chemical fertilizer in the water supply accelerate the growth of algae and, consequently, may disturb the natural cycle of life, contributing to the death of fish." Quotation from sentence 4, paragraph 3.

33. In the context of this passage, the word damage is closest in meaning to harm. No other words or phrases in the **bold** text are close to the meaning of the word harm.

34. "Formerly, powders were also used, but these were found to be less convenient than either solids or liquids. One objection to powders was their propensity to become solid chunks if the bags got damp." The connection between the two sentences is the reference to "powders." The first sentence is a general sentence, and the second sentence is an example.

35. **(A)** The other choices are secondary ideas that are used to develop the main idea, "the

evolution of the horse." Choices (B), (C), and (D) are significant steps in the evolution.

36. **(D)** Choices (A), (B), and (C) are mentioned in sentence 3, paragraph 1. The Miocene Age is the earliest historical period mentioned in the passage.

37. **(B)** In the context of this passage, instigated could best be replaced by caused. Choices (A), (C), and (D) are not accepted definitions of the word.

38. **(A)** Choice (A) is a restatement of the sentence referred to in the passage. Since horses appeared 60 million years ago and humans appeared two million years ago, it must be concluded that horses appeared long before human beings.

39. **(A)** ". . . a horse crossed . . . from Alaska into the grasslands of Europe." Because of the reference to *grasslands*, it must be concluded that the hipparions migrated to Europe to feed in developing grasslands. Choice (B) contradicts the fact that the European colonists brought horses to North America where the species had become extinct. Choice (D) contradicts the fact that the evolution of the horse has been recorded from its beginnings through all of its evolutionary stages.

40. **(C)** ". . . smaller than the hipparion, the anchitheres was completely replaced by it." Choice (A) refers to the very early form of the horse, not to the hipparion. Choice (B) contradicts the fact that the hipparion was a more highly evolved form than the anchitheres. Choice (D) contradicts the fact that the hipparion was about the size of a small pony.

41. **(B)** "Less developed and smaller than the hipparion, the anchitheres was completely replaced by it [the hipparion]." Choices (A), (C), and (D) would change the meaning of the sentence.

42. **(C)** In the context of this passage, extinct is closest in meaning to nonexistent. Choices (A), (B), and (D) are not accepted definitions of the word.

43. "Fossil finds provide us not only with detailed information about the horse itself, but also with valuable insights into the migration of herds, and even evidence for speculation about the climatic conditions that could have instigated such migratory behavior." Quotation from sentence 3, paragraph 1.

44. In the context of this passage, tamed is closest in meaning to domesticated. No other words or phrases in the **bold** text are close to the meaning of the word domesticated.

45. **(A)** "At the beginning of the Pliocene Age, a horse . . . crossed . . . into the grasslands of Europe. The horse was the hipparion. . . . The hipparion encountered . . . the anchitheres, which had previously invaded Europe . . . probably during the Miocene Period." Because the anchitheres invaded Europe during the Miocene and was already there when the hipparion arrived in the Pliocene, it must be concluded that the Miocene Period was prior to the Pliocene Period. By the Pleistocene referred to in Choices (B) and (C), the anchitheres and the hipparion had become extinct. Therefore, the Pleistocene Period must have been after both the Miocene and the Pliocene.

Model Test 3—Computer-Assisted TOEFL

Section 1: Listening

1. **(A)** Since the woman agrees with the man, it must be concluded that she will not go home for spring vacation. Choice (C) contradicts the fact that she will be graduating in May. Choices (B) and (D) are not mentioned and may not be concluded from information in the conversation.

2. **(C)** From the reference to *the assignment for Monday*, it must be concluded that the speakers are talking about homework. Choices (A), (B), and (D) are all mentioned in the conversation in reference to the assignment.

3. **(C)** *Cramming* is an idiomatic expression that means studying a lot, especially just before a test. Choices (A), (B), and (D) contradict the fact that the man is confident about being ready for the test.

4. **(A)** Since the man says that he needs a book for an English course, it must be concluded that he will buy the textbook. Choice (C) contradicts the fact that he is already in the bookstore. Choice (D) contradicts the fact that he needs a book for the course. Choice (B) is not mentioned and may not be concluded from information in the conversation.

5. **(A)** To *turn someone off* is an idiomatic expression that means the speaker does not like something or someone. Choice (D) contradicts the fact that the woman does not like the class. Choice (C) contradicts the fact that the woman thinks Professor Collins is a great person. Choice (B) is not mentioned and may not be concluded from information in the conversation.

6. **(A)** To *not put off* is an idiomatic expression that means to stop postponing. Choices (B) and (C) contradict the fact that the woman has not made an appointment yet. Choice (D) is not mentioned and may not be concluded from information in the conversation.

7. **(C)** To be *used to something* is an idiomatic expression that means to be accustomed to something. Choices (A), (B), and (D) are not paraphrases of the expression and may not be concluded from information in the conversation.

8. **(C)** To *get caught up* is an idiomatic expression that means to bring work or assignments up to date. Choice (B) contradicts the fact that the man says he knows what time it is. Choices (A) and (D) are not mentioned and may not be concluded from information in the conversation.

9. **(B)** To *pass* is an idiomatic expression that means to lose a turn. Choices (A), (B), and (C) are not paraphrases of the expression and may not be concluded from information in the conversation.

10. **(B)** To *look into something* is an idiomatic expression that means

to investigate. Choice (A) refers to the woman's conclusion, not to the man's intention. Choices (C) and (D) are not mentioned and may not be concluded from information in the conversation.

11. **(A)** To *get mixed up* is an idiomatic expression that means to become confused. Choice (C) contradicts the fact that the man understands the lectures. Choices (B) and (D) are not mentioned and may not be concluded from information in the conversation.

12. **(A)** To *turn in* is an idiomatic expression that means to submit. "Ahead of time" means early. Choice (C) contradicts the fact that she wants to turn in the paper before it is due. Choice (D) contradicts the fact that she is ready to turn the paper in. Choice (B) is not mentioned and may not be concluded from information in the conversation.

13. **(D)** "You have to take it [the class] in order to graduate." Choice (A) refers to the man's attitude, not to the woman's opinion. Choice (B) contradicts the fact that the class is required for graduation. Choice (C) is not mentioned and may not be concluded from information in the conversation.

14. **(A)** ". . . the T.A. said to get into a study group and quiz each other." Choice (B) refers to the type of exam that they will be given, not to the T.A.'s suggestion. Choice (C) refers to quizzes, but the T.A. suggests that they "quiz each other," which means to ask each other questions. Choice (D) contradicts the fact that the professor recommends studying alone, not in a group.

15. **(C)** Since the woman goes to get a pen, it must be concluded that she will sign the form. Choice (A) contradicts the fact that the woman says he doesn't need an appointment. Choice (B) refers to the pen that the woman, not the man, will use. Choice (D) contradicts the fact that the man is asked to wait for the woman.

16. **(A)** "I'd better make one more draft." A "draft" is a revision of written work. Choice (D) refers to the man's suggestion, not to what the woman is going to do. Choices (B) and (C) are not mentioned and may not be concluded from information in the conversation.

17. **(B)** "That's what I thought [that the computer . . . scheduled for the fifth]." Choice (C) refers to the woman's original statement, not to her final conclusion. Choice (D) contradicts the fact that payments are still due. Choice (A) refers to an error made by the woman, not the computer.

18. **(D)** ". . . I need three letters of recommendation. Would you be willing to write me one?" Choice (A) contradicts the fact that Betty is already in the professor's seminar class. Choice (C) refers to additional information that the professor gives to Betty, not to the purpose of her call. Choice (B) is not mentioned and may not be concluded from information in the conversation.

19. **(B)** "I think you are an excellent candidate for graduate school." Choice (A) contradicts the fact that Betty is already taking the seminar. Choice (D) contradicts the fact that the professor does

not recall the deadline for applications. Choice (C) is not mentioned and may not be concluded from information in the conversation.

20. **(B)** "The committee meets on April 30." Choices (A) and (D) refer to the person who will receive the letter, not to who will make the decision. Choice (C) refers to the person who will make a recommendation.

21. **(C)** "The committee meets on April 30, so all the materials must be submitted before then." Choice (A) contradicts the fact that the materials must be submitted before April 30. Choices (B) and (D) are not mentioned and may not be concluded from information in the conversation.

22. **(B)** Because the speaker is introduced as a professor of history and discusses trade during the eighteenth century, it must be concluded that he is a professor of history. It is not as probable that the lecturers mentioned in Choices (A), (C), and (D) would discuss this topic.

23. **(C)** "To maintain this favorable balance of trade, England went to fantastic lengths to keep secret the advanced manufacturing processes . . ." Choice (D) contradicts the fact that it was the colony (America), not England, that stole the plans. Choices (A) and (B) are not mentioned and may not be concluded from information in the talk.

24. **(C)** "Determined to take nothing in writing, Slater memorized the intricate designs for all the machines in an English textile mill. . . ." Choices (A) and (B) contradict the fact that Slater, in part-

nership with Brown, opened a mill in the United States in the state of Rhode Island. Choice (D) contradicts the fact that he took nothing in writing.

25. **(A)** ". . . in part as a result of Slater and Brown, America had changed from a country of small farmers and craftsmen to an industrial nation. . . ." Choices (B), (C), and (D) are not mentioned and may not be concluded from information in the talk.

26. **(A)** "I understand that I can reserve textbooks for next semester." Choice (B) is true, but it is a comment, not the purpose of the conversation. Choice (C) contradicts the fact that the faculty member, not the woman, orders books for the whole class. Choice (D) is not mentioned and may not be concluded from information in the conversation.

27. **(B)** "This semester I couldn't get two of my books until three weeks into the semester. . . ." Choice (C) contradicts the fact that he received his books three weeks after the semester started. Choice (D) refers to this semester, not last semester. Choice (A) is not mentioned and may not be concluded from information in the conversation.

28. **(B)** "Just fill out one of these forms. . . . Then pay for your books . . . and we'll place the order." Choice (A) is true but refers to ordering books for the whole class. Choices (C) and (D) are not mentioned and may not be concluded from information in the conversation.

29. **(B)** "We'll call you as soon as they [the books] come in." Choice (C) refers to the student's

question about receiving his books, but is not how he will know when the books arrive. The word *form* in Choice (A) refers to the system for ordering books, not to the way to know that books have arrived. Choice (D) is not mentioned and may not be concluded from information in the conversation.

30. **(A)** "So many different kinds of writing have been called essays, it is difficult to define exactly what an essay is." Choices (B), (C), and (D) are secondary themes used to develop a definition of the essay.

31. **(C)** ". . . four characteristics that are true of most essays." Choices (A), (B), and (D) are secondary themes used to develop the main theme of the talk.

32. **(B)** ". . . an essay [is] a short, prose composition with a personal viewpoint that discusses one topic." Choice (B) contradicts the fact that an essay is written in prose, not poetry. Choices (A), (C), and (D) are all included in the definition.

33. **(B)** ". . . let's brainstorm some topics for your first essay assignment." Choices (A), (C), and (D) are not mentioned and may not be concluded from information in the conversation.

34. **(D)** The main purpose of this talk is to summarize Jefferson's life. Choices (A), (B), and (C) are secondary themes in the life of Jefferson.

35. **(C)** "Although Jefferson was a Republican, he at first tried to cooperate with Alexander Hamilton, a Federalist. . . ." Choice (A) refers to Jefferson's

opinion of Hamilton's political affiliation. Choice (B) refers to Hamilton, not Jefferson. Choice (D) is not mentioned and may not be concluded from information in the talk.

36. **(B)** "He [Jefferson] and Federalist Aaron Burr received an identical vote, but the Republican Congress elected to approve Jefferson as president." Choice (A) contradicts the fact that Jefferson and Burr received an identical vote. Choices (C) and (D) are not mentioned and may not be concluded from information in the conversation.

37. **(A)** "Thomas Jefferson was a statesman, a diplomat, an author, and an architect. . . . Not a gifted public speaker, he was most talented as a literary draftsman." Choices (B), (C), and (D) are all mentioned as attributes of Jefferson.

38. **(B) (C)** "They [fossils] are occasionally preserved in ice, but most have been buried in mud or sand . . . at the bottom . . . of water. . . ." Choice (A) refers to a place where fossils are occasionally preserved, not the most usual place. Choice (D) refers to the location of the mud and sand, under water.

39. **(C) (B) (D) (A)** ". . . animals and plants must be buried quickly . . . mineral-rich water soaks into the . . . plant or animal . . . minerals in the water dissolve the original organism, leaving a fossil mold."

40. **(B)** ". . . the internal features of the organism are not preserved. . . ." Choice (A) contradicts the fact that the shapes of fragile

feathers and fur are preserved. The word *minerals* in Choice (C) refers to a part of the process, not to what is lost in the process. Choice (D) contradicts the fact that the mold is left.

41. **(A)** "The location of fossils in layers of . . . sedimentary rock shows . . . the order in which they were buried, that is, their relative ages." Choice (B) is true, but it is not the reason that the layers are important to the fossil record. Choice (C) contradicts the fact that the mineral water dissolves the organisms. Choice (D) contradicts the fact that plants and animals buried in the same layers of rock lived at approximately the same time.

42. **(D)** ". . . I thought I would [graduate] automatically." Choice (A) contradicts the fact that the student believes he has completed all of the course work for graduation. Choice (B) contradicts the fact that he has enough hours to graduate. Choice (C) is true, but does not explain why the man did not apply for graduation.

43. **(A)** "The requirements are . . . in the catalog . . ." Choice (B) contradicts the fact that the man has to explain how he selected his courses. Choice (C) contradicts the fact that the man did not have a program of study. Choice (D) contradicts the fact that the man did not have an advisor.

44. **(B)** "The first thing we need to do is to assign you an advisor . . ." Choice (A) contradicts the fact that the man may have taken the required courses. Choice (C) contradicts the fact that the man

referred to the requirements in the catalog. Choice (D) contradicts the fact that the man has his latest transcript with him.

45. **(B)** ". . . if you . . . failed to take a critical course, then you may not be eligible for graduation." Choice (A) contradicts the fact that the man is told that he has enough hours to graduate. Choice (C) contradicts the fact that the woman will try to get the man in to see someone that day. Choice (D) is not mentioned and may not be concluded from information in the conversation.

46. **(C)** Since this is a linguistics class, "the articles were written by linguists. . . ." Choices (A), (B), and (D) are subjects that are referred to in the discussion, but they are not the class in which the discussion takes place.

47. **(D)** "A standard dialect is the dialect that is selected as the educational model." Choice (B) contradicts the fact that all dialects of a language are of equal value. Choice (C) is true of all dialects, but it is not the definition of a standard dialect. Choice (A) is not mentioned and may not be concluded from information in the discussion.

48. **(D)** ". . . from a linguistic point of view, all dialects of a language are of equal value." Choice (A) contradicts the fact that the accents taught with standard grammar may be regional accents. Choice (B) contradicts the fact that the school may teach a standard dialect with a regional accent. Choice (C) contradicts the fact that several major dialect regions have been identified.

49. **(A) (C)** "Standard English has a common grammar and vocabulary. These [grammar and vocabulary] are the basic building blocks of a dialect." Choice (B) refers to accent, not dialect. Choice (D) is not mentioned and may not be concluded from information in the discussion.

50. **(A)** "Some accents are associated with a higher socioeconomic class, and therefore tend to be the preferred standard accent in schools." Choice (B) contradicts the fact that the prestige of a social group makes a dialect more desirable. Choice (D) refers to the linguistic perspective of accents, not the sociological perspective. Choice (C) is not mentioned and may not be concluded from information in the discussion.

Section 2: Structure

1. **(C)** *Most* is used before a noncount noun to express a quantity that is larger than half the amount. A singular verb follows the noncount noun. Choice (A) does not have a verb. In Choice (B), the verb is before, not after the noun. In Choice (D), *the* is used before *most*.

2. **(B)** An adjective is used before *enough* to express sufficiency. In Choice (A), *goodly* is ungrammatical. The adverbial form of the adjective *good* is *well*. In Choice (C), *as* is unnecessary and incorrect. In Choice (D), the adjective is used after, not before *enough*.

3. **(A)** *Responsible for* is a prepositional idiom. *Responsible the* should be *responsible for the*.

4. **(B)** A form of BE is used with the participle in passive sentences. *Practice* should be *practiced*.

5. **(B)** There must be agreement between pronoun and antecedent. *Which* should be *who* to refer to the antecedent *Shirley Temple Black*. *Which* refers to things. *Who* refers to persons.

6. **(A)** *The* can be used before a noncount noun that is followed by a qualifying phrase. *Population* should be *the population* before the qualifying phrase *of the Americas*.

7. **(C)** An adjective clause modifies a noun in the main clause. *That the earliest cultures evolved* modifies *the way*. Choice (A) is a clause marker *that* and a noun. Choice (B) is a verb and a noun. Choice (D) is a clause marker *which* and a noun.

8. **(D)** Comparative forms are usually followed by *than*. After the comparative *more reasonable, as* should be *than*.

9. **(C)** *There* introduces inverted order, but there must still be agreement between subject and verb. *Has been* should be *have been* to agree with the plural subject *two major factions*.

10. **(A)** In order to refer to occupying a place on the battlefields, *lain* should be used. *To lay* means to put in a place, and the participle is *laid*. *To lie* means to occupy a place, and the participle is *lain*.

11. **(C)** A sentence has a subject and a verb. Choice (A) is redundant because the subject pronoun *it* is used consecutively with the subject *calculus*. Choice (B) has the marker *that* to introduce a main clause. Choice (D) is redundant

because it has a verb that replaces the main verb *can reduce*.

12. **(B)** Subject-verb order and a negative verb with *either* expresses negative agreement. Negative agreement with *neither* requires verb-subject order and an affirmative verb. In Choice (A), verb-subject order is reversed. In Choice (C), verb-subject order is reversed, and *neither* is used at the beginning, not at the end of the clause. In Choice (D) *either*, not *neither*, is used with verb-subject order and an affirmative verb. "Neither does Mexico" would also be correct.

13. **(B)** *Large* should be *largest*. Because there were more than two ethnic groups, a superlative form must be used.

14. **(B)** The determiner *a* is used before a singular count noun. *Results* should be *result*.

15. **(D)** A sentence has a subject and a verb. Choice (A) does not have a verb. Choices (B) and (C) introduce a main clause subject and verb.

16. **(C)** The anticipatory clause *it is accepted that* introduces a subject and verb, *the formation ... began*. Choices (A), (B), and (D) are incomplete and ungrammatical.

17. **(B)** When the degree of one quality, *the heat*, is dependent upon the degree of another quality, *the humidity*, two comparatives are used, each preceded by *the*. *The worst* should be *the worse* because it is a comparative.

18. **(B)** A dependent clause modifies an independent clause. *Which are* should be *are* to provide a verb for the subject *statistical data*, of the independent clause.

19. **(A)** The word order for a passive sentence is a form of BE followed by a participle. Only Choice (A) has the correct word order. Choice (B) does not have a BE form. Choice (C) has a HAVE, not a BE form. Choice (D) is a present tense verb, not BE followed by a participle.

20. **(A)** *Despite of* is a combination of *despite* and *in spite of*. Either *despite* or *in spite of* should be used.

21. **(C)** Subject-verb order is used in the clause after a question word connector such as *how much*. In Choice (A), subject-verb order is reversed. In Choice (B), the auxiliary *does* is unnecessary and incorrect. In Choice (D), the verb *are* is repetitive. "The Consumer Price Index lists how much every car *is*" would also be correct.

22. **(A)** Because it is a prepositional phrase, in a comparison *as every nation* should be *like every nation*. *As* functions as a conjunction. *Like* functions as a preposition.

23. **(C)** A logical conclusion about the past is expressed by *must have* and a participle. Choices (A), (B), and (D) are not logical because they imply that the theater will act to restore itself.

24. **(A)** The verb *thought* establishes a point of view in the past. *Will* should be *would* in order to maintain the point of view.

25. **(D)** Ideas in a series should be expressed by parallel structures. *To plant* should be *planting* to provide for parallelism with the -*ing* forms *plowing* and *rotating*.

Section 3: Reading

1. **(A)** "Webster's Work" is the best title because it states the main idea of the passage. Choice (B) is incorrect because Webster's dictionaries represent only part of the work referred to in the passage. Choices (C) and (D) are mentioned briefly in the discussion, but are not the most important topics.

2. **(D)** In the context of this passage, inadequate could best be replaced by unsatisfactory Choices (A), (B), and (C) are not accepted definitions of the word.

3. **(C)** ". . . he discovered how inadequate the available schoolbooks were for the children of a new and independent nation. . . . In response to the need for truly American textbooks, Webster published *A Grammatical Institute of the English Language*." Choice (A) is a result of having written *A Grammatical Institute*, not a reason for writing it. Choice (B) contradicts the fact that British books were available, but not appropriate. Choice (D) is not mentioned and may not be concluded from information in the passage.

4. **(D)** ". . . *The American Spelling Book* . . . provided him with a considerable income for the rest of his life." Choices (A), (B), and (C) are all publications by Webster, but the income afforded by each is not mentioned and may not be concluded from information in the passage.

5. In the context of this passage, popular is closest in meaning to the phrase very successful. No other words or phrases in the **bold** text are close to the meaning of the word popular.

6. **(A)** In the context of this passage, considerable is closest in meaning to large. Choices (B), (C), and (D) are not accepted definitions of the word.

7. **(C)** "Published . . . in 1828, *An American Dictionary of the English Language* has become the recognized authority for usage. . . ." Choice (A) refers to the date that Webster finished his study of English and began writing the dictionary. Choice (B) refers to the date that Webster began work on the dictionary. Choice (D) refers to the date that Webster finished writing the dictionary, not to the date that it was published.

8. **(D)** "Webster's purpose in writing it [the dictionary] was to demonstrate that the American language was developing distinct meanings, pronunciations, and spellings from those of British English." Choices (A), (B), and (C) would change the meaning of the sentence.

9. "Webster's purpose in writing it [an American dictionary] was to demonstrate that the American language was developing distinct meanings, pronunciations, and spellings from those of British English." Quotation from sentence 4, paragraph 2.

10. **(C)** In the context of this passage, distinct is closest in meaning to different. Choices (A), (B), and (D) are not accepted definitions.

11. **(C)** "He [Webster] is responsible for advancing the form color . . . instead of colour." Choices (A),

(B), and (D) are British English spellings.

12. **(A)** Choice (A) is the author's main purpose because the passage refers to the San Andreas Fault specifically. The general information referred to in Choices (B), (C), and (D) is not mentioned and may not be concluded from information in the passage.

13. **(B)** "The San Andreas Fault is a fracture at the congruence of two major plates of the Earth's crust." Choice (A) refers to the plates, not to the fracture. Choices (C) and (D) refer to the results of the movement along the fracture, not to the fault.

14. **(C)** In the context of this passage, originates could best be replaced by begins. Choices (A), (B), and (D) are not accepted definitions of the word.

15. **(C)** "Its western side always moves north in relation to its eastern side." Choices (A), (B), and (D) contradict the fact that the western side always moves north, not in any other direction.

16. **(D)** "Its western side always moves north in relation to its [the fault's] eastern side." Choices (A), (B), and (C) would change the meaning of the sentence.

17. **(D)** intermittent means occasional. Choices (A), (B), and (C) are not accepted definitions of the word.

18. **(C)** "Tremors are not unusual along the San Andreas Fault. . . . Choice (B) contradicts the fact that tremors are not unusual. Choices (A) and (D) are not mentioned and may not be concluded from information in the passage.

19. **(A)** "Californians have long anticipated the recurrence of what they refer to as the 'Big One,' a chain reaction of destructive earthquakes. . . ." Choices (B), (C), or (D) would change the meaning of the sentence.

20. In the context of this passage, devastating is closest in meaning to destructive. No other words or phrases in the **bold** text are close to the meaning of the word destructive.

21. "Californians have long anticipated the recurrence of what they refer to as the 'Big One,' a chain reaction of destructive earthquakes that would measure near 8 on the Richter scale, similar in intensity to those [earthquakes] that occurred in 1857 and 1906." Other choices would change the meaning of the sentence.

22. **(D)** ". . . the San Andreas Fault . . . runs north in an irregular line. . . ." The word *uneven* in Choice (D) means irregular. Choice (A) contradicts the fact that the line is irregular. Choices (B) and (C) are not mentioned and may not be concluded from information in the passage.

23. **(B)** "The Structure of an Insect" is the best title because it states the main idea of the passage. Choice (C) is a secondary idea that is used to develop the main idea. Choices (A) and (D) are not mentioned and may not be concluded from information in the passage.

24. In the context of this passage, the word segmented is closest in meaning to subdivided. No other words or phrases in the **bold** text

are close to the meaning of the word subdivided.

25. **(C)** "Features of the mouth parts are very helpful in classifying the many kinds of insects." Choices (A), (B), and (D) are discussed, but not as a basis for classification.

26. **(A)** In the context of this passage, the word normal is closest in meaning to common. Choices (B), (C), and (D) are not accepted definitions of the word.

27. **(A)** "A labrum above and a labium below are similar to an upper and lower lip." Choice (B) is compared to Choice (D). Choice (C) is discussed, but not compared to anything.

28. **(B)** "...the coiled drinking tube ...called the proboscis... [is] composed...of modified maxillae." Choice (A) refers to food, not to the proboscis that is used in reaching it. Choices (C) and (D) are not mentioned and may not be concluded from information in the passage.

29. **(C)** "In a mosquito or an aphid, mandibles and maxillae are modified to sharp stylets." The insect referred to in choice (A) has mandibles similar to jaws, not sharp stylets. The insect referred to in Choice (B) has a proboscis. The insect referred to in Choice (D) has a spongelike mouth pad.

30. **(A)** In the context of this passage, drill through could best be replaced by penetrate. Choices (B), (C), and (D) are not accepted definitions of the phrase.

31. **(C)** "In a housefly, the expanding labium forms a spongelike mouth pad that it [the housefly] can use to stamp over the surface of food." Choices (A), (B), and (D) would change the meaning of the sentence.

32. "An active part of the natural food cycle, insects provide nutrition for animals and devour waste products of other life forms. Although some insects, like the cockroach, have remained essentially unchanged for eons, most insects adapt readily to changing environmental conditions." The connection between the two sentences occurs on the paragraph level. The first sentence in the paragraph introduces the idea that insects are adaptable, and the four sentences that follow provide examples. The inserted sentence is a conclusion that reinforces the first sentence.

33. **(D)** Because the passage is a statement of scientific facts written from an objective point of view, it must be concluded that the purpose is to inform. Choices (A) and (B) are improbable because the passage is not written from a subjective point of view. Choice (C) is improbable because of the scientific content.

34. **(D)** The primary topic is the characteristics of protozoans. Choices (A), (B), and (C) are important to the discussion and provide details that support the primary topic.

35. **(D)** In the context of this passage, minute could best be replaced by very small. Choices (A), (B), and (C) are not accepted definitions of the word.

36. **(B)** "The protozoans ... [consist] of a single cell of protoplasm. ...." Choices (A), (C), and (D) contradict the fact that the cell of a protozoan is composed of protoplasm.

37. In the context of this passage, locomotion is closest in meaning to motility. No other words or phrases in the **bold** text are close to the meaning of the word motility.

38. **(C)** Choice (C) is a restatement of the sentence referred to in the passage. *Motility* means the manner of movement. Choices (A), (B), and (D) would change the meaning of the original sentence.

39. **(C)** "The Sarcodina, which include amoebae. . . ." Choices (A) and (B) refer to two other groups of protozoans that do not include amoebae. Choice (D) refers to the basis of classification for the three major groups of protozoans.

40. **(C)** ". . . a large nucleus that regulates growth but decomposes during reproduction . . ." Choice (A) refers to the small, not the large, nucleus. Choice (B) contradicts the fact that the small nucleus contains the genetic code for the large nucleus. Choice (D) contradicts the fact that the large nucleus decomposes during reproduction.

41. **(A)** "Protozoans are considered animals because . . . they do not live on simple organic compounds." Choices (B) and (C) refer to characteristics of some protozoans, not to a reason why they are considered animals. Choice (D) contradicts the fact that they have only one cell, although current research is calling that into question.

42. **(A)** "Current research into this phenomenon along with investigations carried out with advanced microscopes may necessitate a redefinition of what constitutes a protozoan, even calling into question the basic premise that they [protozoans] have only one cell." Choices (B), (C), and (D) would change the meaning of the sentence.

43. "They are fantastically diverse, but three major groups may be identified on the basis of their motility." Quotation from sentence 4, paragraph 1.

44. **(A)** In the context of this passage, uniformly is closest in meaning to in the same way. Choices (B), (C), and (D) are not accepted definitions of the word.

45. **(C)** Choice (A) is mentioned in sentence 3, paragraph 4. Choice (B) is mentioned in sentence 1, paragraph 1. Choice (D) is mentioned in sentence 4, paragraph 4. Protozoans consist of a single cell, although in the case of Ciliata, the cell may have a larger nucleus and a smaller nucleus.

Model Test 4—Computer-Assisted TOEFL

Section 1: Listening

1. **(C)** *I wish I could* is an idiomatic expression that means the speaker would like to but is not able to do something. Choice (A) refers to a party that the Association, not the woman, will have. Choice (B) refers to what the woman would like to do, not to what she will probably do. Choice (D) is not mentioned and may not be concluded from information in the conversation.

2. **(A)** Since they have just enough time to get there, it must be concluded that they will leave immediately. Choices (B), (C), and (D) are not mentioned and may not be concluded from information in the conversation.

3. **(A)** The man said that he went to see the foreign student advisor. Choice (D) refers to what the advisor did, not to what the man did himself. The Passport Office is in Washington, D.C., but Choices (B) and (C) are not mentioned and may not be concluded from information in the conversation.

4. **(B)** "I'd write a rough draft and ask Dr. Tyler to look at it." A "rough draft" is a preliminary version. Choice (C) contradicts the fact that the woman says to show the draft to Dr. Tyler, not to her. Choices (A) and (D) are not mentioned and may not be concluded from information in the conversation.

5. **(D)** To *put up with* is an idiomatic expression that means to tolerate. It must be concluded that the students do not like Dr. Clark. Choices (A), (B), and (C) are not paraphrases of the expression, and may not be concluded from information in the conversation.

6. **(C)** The references to a *textbook* and a *movie* in Choices (B) and (D) relate to the assignment for the class. Choice (A) is not mentioned and may not be concluded from information in the conversation.

7. **(B)** Since the man asks whether the woman is Sally Harrison's sister, it must be concluded that he assumed the women were sisters. Choice (A) refers to who the woman is, not to the man's assumption. Choices (C) and (D) contradict the fact that the woman is Sally Harrison's cousin.

8. **(C)** Since the woman says that she can't find her pen, it must be concluded that finding her pen is the problem. Choices (A), (B), and (D) are not mentioned and may not be concluded from information in the conversation.

9. **(A)** Because John agreed to arrive at eight-thirty but the man estimates that he won't arrive until nine o'clock, or one half-hour later, it must be concluded that John is usually late. Choice (B) refers to the time when John

agreed to arrive, not to a conclusion that the man wants us to make. Choice (C) contradicts both the fact that John had agreed to come and the fact that the man estimates John's arrival at nine o'clock. Choice (D) contradicts the fact that the man estimates John's arrival one half-hour after he has agreed to arrive.

10. **(B)** ". . . it didn't turn out quite like I thought it would." Choice (A) contradicts the fact that the man knows how it turned out. Choice (C) contradicts the fact that the man says the experiment is finished. Choice (D) is not mentioned and may not be concluded from information in the conversation.

11. **(A)** Since the man expresses exasperation about the woman's attention to her classes, he implies that she does not put much effort in her studies. Choice (D) is true, but it is not what the man implies by his comment. Choices (B) and (C) are not mentioned and may not be concluded from information in the conversation.

12. **(D)** ". . . I'd try some over-the-counter medication. . . ." Choice (A) refers to the woman's plan, not to the man's suggestion. Choice (B) refers to the idiom "do the job" which means to cure. Choice (C) refers to the place to buy nonprescription medicine [over the counter], not to the man's suggestion.

13. **(A)** To *give it all you've got* is an idiomatic expression that means to try your best. Choices (B), (C), and (D) are not paraphrases of the expression and may not be concluded from information in the conversation.

14. **(A)** Since the woman denies the man's request for a few more minutes, it must be concluded that the man must stop working on the test. Choice (B) contradicts the fact that the man cannot have a few more minutes to finish. Choice (D) contradicts the fact that the test is in progress, not about to start. Choice (C) is not mentioned and may not be concluded from information in the conversation.

15. **(C)** Since the man thinks they are using a different book this semester, he implies that the textbook may have been changed. Choice (D) contradicts the fact that they are discussing plans for this semester. Choices (A) and (B) are not mentioned and may not be concluded from information in the conversation.

16. **(D)** Since the woman questions whether Sally would like a bike, she implies that Sally may prefer a different gift. Choice (A) refers to the man's idea, not to the woman's comment. Choices (B) and (C) are not mentioned and may not be concluded from information in the conversation.

17. **(A)** ". . . get some rest and try it again later." Choices (B) and (D) contradict the fact that the woman recommends rest. Choice (C) is not mentioned and may not be concluded from information in the conversation.

18. **(B)** ". . . the question is not whether the metric system should be introduced in the United States, but rather, how it should be introduced." Choice (A) contradicts the fact that the question is not whether the metric system should be introduced. Choices

(C) and (D) are not mentioned and may not be concluded from information in the discussion.

19. **(C)** "They [cans and packages] are marked in both ounces and grams. . . . And the weather reporters on radio and TV give the temperature readings in both degrees Fahrenheit and degrees Celsius now. . . . Some road signs have the distances marked in both miles and kilometers. . . ." Choice (A) contradicts the fact that the temperature readings are in both degrees Fahrenheit and degrees Celsius. Choice (B) contradicts the fact that the road signs have distances marked in both miles and kilometers. Choice (D) contradicts the fact that cans and packages are marked in both ounces and grams.

20. **(D)** "I [Professor Baker] agree that a gradual adoption is better for those of us who have already been exposed to the English system of measurement. But I would favor teaching only metrics in the elementary schools." Choice (A) refers to the woman's suggestion, not to Professor Baker's opinion. The opinions expressed in Choices (B) and (C) arc not mentioned and may not be concluded from information in the discussion.

21. **(D)** Because Professor Baker invites a free exchange of ideas and does not criticize his students, it must be concluded that he is cooperative. The words in Choices (A), (B), and (C) do not describe Professor Baker's manner in the conversation.

22. **(D)** ". . . an extensive research effort, which, in cooperation with private industry, has transferred technology to the international marketplace." Choices (A), (B), and (C) are secondary themes used to develop the main theme of the talk.

23. **(A)** "Hundreds of everyday products can be traced back to the space mission, including cordless electric tools, airtight food packaging. . . . ultrasound. . . ." Choice (A) is not mentioned and may not be concluded from information in the talk.

24. **(D)** "First used to detect flaws in spacecraft, ultrasound is now standard equipment in almost every hospital. . . ." Choice (A) refers to implants and pacemakers, not to ultrasound. Choices (B) and (C) are not mentioned and may not be concluded from information in the conversation.

25. **(B)** ". . . archaeologists have been able to explore the earth . . . cities . . . have been located . . . and the sea floor has been mapped using photographs from outer space." Choices (A), (C), and (D) are not mentioned and may not be concluded from information in the conversation.

26. **(B)** "Is there any way you could give me an excused absence. . . ." The word *note* in Choice (A) refers to the notes that Beverly plans to borrow from her friend Gloria, not to a note she has for the professor. Choice (C) contradicts the fact that she never misses class. Choice (D) is not mentioned and may not be concluded from information in the conversation.

27. **(D)** "I have a family emergency, and I am needed at home for at least a week." Choice (A) contra-

dicts the fact that Beverly sits in front to see better. Choice (B) refers to the professor's concern, not to the student's problem. Choice (C) contradicts the fact that the professor says she never misses class.

28. **(B)** "If you need some clarification, I can meet with you for a few minutes before class on Monday." Choice (A) contradicts the fact that the woman has already arranged to borrow notes from her friend, Gloria. Choices (C) and (D) are not mentioned and may not be concluded from information in the conversation.

29. **(B)** "You're very welcome. And I hope that everything goes well for you at home." Choice (A) contradicts the fact that the professor spends so much time talking with Beverly. Choice (C) describes the woman's attitude, not that of the professor. The word *confused* in Choice (D) refers to the professor's comment about how difficult it can be to understand someone else's notes, not to his attitude.

30. **(C)** The speaker discusses the history, economy, and landmarks of San Francisco. Choices (A), (B), and (D) are secondary themes used to support the main purpose of the talk, an orientation to the City of San Francisco.

31. **(D)** "... the name was changed from Yorba Buena to San Francisco." Choice (A) refers to the name of the bridge, not a settlement. Choice (B) refers to a mission established before Yerba Buena was settled. Choice (C) refers to a military post established before the settlement of Yerba Buena.

32. **(A)** "... in 1848, with the discovery of gold, the population grew to ten thousand." Choice (B) refers to what happened in 1869, not 1848. Choice (C) refers to what happened in 1937. Choice (D) refers to what happened in 1862.

33. **(C)** "The bridge, which is more than one mile long, spans the harbor from San Francisco to Marin County...." Choice (A) refers to the length of the Port of San Francisco, not to the length of the Golden Gate Bridge. Choice (B) refers to the altitude of the city. The number in Choice (D) refers to the number of tons of cargo handled at the Port of San Francisco every year.

34. **(A)** "Today we will discuss Transcendentalism...." Choices (B), (C), and (D) are secondary themes that are used to develop the main theme of the lecture.

35. **(C)** "Today we will discuss Transcendentalism, which is a philosophical and literary movement that developed in New England in the early nineteenth century." Choices (A), (B), and (D) are not mentioned and may not be concluded from information in the talk.

36. **(C)** "This group [the Transcendental Club] was the advance guard of a reaction against the rigid Puritanism of the period, especially insofar as it emphasized society at the expense of the individual." Choices (A) and (D) refer to the Transcendental Club, not to the Puritans. Choice (B) contradicts the fact that the Transcendental Club reacted against the Puritans.

37. **(D)** "Thoreau built a small cabin along the shores of Walden Pond . . . he published an account of his experiences in *Walden*. . . ." Choices (A), (B), and (C) are not mentioned and may not be concluded from information in the talk.

38. **(D)** "Do you have any experience working in a library?" Choice (A) contradicts the fact that the man does his own research in the library and knows how to use most of the search equipment. The phrase *teaching position* in Choice (B) refers to a job that the man had before he came back to school, not to a position that he is applying for now. The phrase *library orientation* in Choice (C) refers to one of the responsibilities of the position that the man is applying for, not to training that he is receiving now.

39. **(C)** "I am working toward my doctorate at the University. . . ." Choice (A) contradicts the fact that he was a teacher before he came back to school, not now. Choice (B) contradicts the fact that he has never been an employee in a library. The word *computer* in Choice (D) refers to the type of library searches that the students need to do for their term papers, not to the man's background.

40. **(C)** "I'm writing my dissertation. . . . I plan to do that [write my dissertation] after work and on my days off." Choice (B) contradicts the fact that he has most of his own research finished. Choice (D) contradicts the fact that he is not taking any classes now. Choice (A) is not mentioned and may not be concluded from information in the conversation.

41. **(D)** ". . . when could you start? Right away!" Choices (A) and (B) contradict the fact that he will complete his dissertation after work and on his days off, and he will graduate after the dissertation is complete. Choice (C) refers to when he will write his dissertation, not to when he will be available for work.

42. **(A) (C)** ". . . a solar collector is mounted . . . at a . . . steep angle . . . with a southern exposure." Choices (B) and (D) are not mentioned and may not be concluded from information in the lecture.

43. **(B)** Choice (A) is a solar collector. Choice (C) is a backup heater. Choice (D) is the space under the collector.

44. **(B)** ". . . one of the problems with solar heat is the intermittent nature of solar radiation as an energy source. Especially in climates where the sun does not shine regularly. . . ." Choices (A), (C), and (D) are not mentioned as problems and may not be concluded from information in the lecture.

45. **(C)** "The principle [of the solar orbit system] would be basically the same as that of the much simpler model that I showed you." Choice (A) contradicts the fact that the system is costly. Choice (B) contradicts the fact that he identifies scientists as those involved in working on the project and does not include himself. Choice (D) is true, but it is not the reason that the professor mentioned the project.

46. **(B)** ". . . is this where I request a tutor?" Choice (A) contradicts the fact that the man asks for a tutor, not for a position. Choice

(D) contradicts the fact that the woman is helping the man to arrange for tutoring. Choice (C) is not mentioned and may not be concluded from information in the conversation.

47. **(D)** "Which course do you need help in? English . . . Composition. . . ." The word *literature* in Choice (A) refers to a question that the woman asked, not to the course that the man needs help in. Choice (B) refers to the course that Janine was tutored for, not to the course for which the man needs a tutor. Choice (C) refers to the other course that Janine tutors in, not to the course that the man will receive tutoring in.

48. **(D)** "This is a free service. . . ." Choices (A), (B), and (C) contradict the fact that the tutoring is a free service.

49. **(C)** ". . . should I just come back on Tuesday at four? Yes." Choices (A) and (B) refer to the times for the man's classes. Choice (D) refers to one of the times for which the man scheduled tutoring, but not the first session.

50. **(B)** ". . . bring your books . . . a syllabus, your class notes. . . ." Choice (A) contradicts the fact that the service is free. The word *composition* in Choice (D) refers to the course in which the man will receive tutoring, not to an essay that he should bring to his tutoring session. Choice (C) is not mentioned and may not be concluded from information in the conversation.

Section 2: Structure

1. **(D)** A dependent clause modifies an independent clause. Choice (A) has two clause markers,

which and *that*. Choice (B) is a verb followed by a noun and a clause marker. Choice (C) does not have a clause marker.

2. **(B)** A passive infinitive is used to express purpose. Choice (A) is a noun. Choice (C) is an *-ing* form. Choice (D) is a present verb.

3. **(C)** Most adverbs of manner are formed by adding *-ly* to adjectives. *Rapid* should be *rapidly* to qualify the manner in which automatic data processing has grown.

4. **(D)** *As well as* should be *and*, which is used in correlation with *both*.

5. **(B)** A cardinal number is used after a noun. *The* is used with an ordinal number before a noun. In Choices (A) and (C) an ordinal number is used after, not before a noun. Choice (D) is incomplete because it does not include *the* before the ordinal number.

6. **(A)** Repetition of the subject by a subject pronoun is redundant. *They* should be deleted.

7. **(B)** *As soon as* is an idiom that introduces a limit of time. The phrase *as soon as* is followed by a noun and a simple present verb. Choice (A) is a modal and a verb word, not a simple present verb. Choice (D) is a noun. Choice (C) uses a present but not a simple present form.

8. **(C)** Because dates require ordinal numbers, *twelve* should be *twelfth*.

9. **(B)** *Influence* should be *influential*. *Influence* is a noun. *Influential* is an adjective.

10. **(C)** *Weathering* is the subject of the verb *is*. Choices (A) and (B) are redundant and indirect. Choice (D) is an *-ing* form, not a verb.

11. **(D)** *Such as* introduces the example *shrimps and clams*, which

must refer to a plural antecedent. *Sea creature* should be *sea creatures.*

12. **(C)** Ideas in a series should be expressed by parallel structures. *Encouraging* should be *to encourage* to provide for parallelism with the infinitive *to discourage.*

13. **(B)** *Combination* should be *combine. Combination* is a noun. *Combine* is a verb.

14. **(D)** The verb *to consider* requires an *-ing* form in the complement. Choice (A) is an infinitive, not an *-ing* form. Choice (B) is a participle. Choice (C) is a verb word.

15. **(C)** *Presumable* should be *presumably. Presumable* is an adjective. *Presumably* is an adverb.

16. **(A)** The verb *reported* establishes a point of view in the past. *Discovers* should be *discovered* in order to maintain the point of view.

17. **(D)** Because the verb *refuse* requires an infinitive in the complement, *giving* should be *to give.*

18. **(C)** Object pronouns are used after prepositions such as *by.* Choice (A) is a reflexive pronoun, not an object pronoun. Choices (B) and (D) are possessive pronouns. "The work was done *by herself*" without the repetitive word *alone* would also be correct.

19. **(C)** There must be agreement between subject and verb. *Has* should be *have* to agree with the plural subject *the few cities.*

20. **(D)** Ideas in a series should be expressed by parallel structures. *Increasing* should be *to increase* to provide for parallelism with the infinitive *to enrich.*

21. **(D)** An appositive does not require connectors or an additional subject. Choices (A) and (C) include connecting conjunctions. Choice (B) is an anticipatory *it* clause, not an appositive.

22. **(A)** *Would have* and a participle in the result requires *had* and a participle in the condition. Because *would not have evolved* is used in the result, *did not filter out* should be *had not filtered out* in the condition.

23. **(B)** Consecutive order must be maintained, along with parallel structure.

24. **(D)** Ideas in a series should be expressed by parallel structures. *Swimming* should be *swim* to provide for parallelism with the verb words *walk, watch,* and *fish.*

25. **(D)** There must be agreement between pronoun and antecedent. *Its* should be *their* to agree with the plural antecedent *books.*

Section 3: Reading

1. **(A)** The other choices are secondary ideas that are used to develop the main idea, "precipitation." Choices (B), (C), and (D) provide details and examples.

2. **(C)** "Precipitation [is] commonly referred to as rainfall." Choices (A), (B), and (D) are not mentioned and may not be concluded from information in the passage.

3. **(B)** "Precipitation, commonly referred to as rainfall, is a measure of the quantity of water in the form of either rain, hail, or snow." Choice (A) is incomplete because it does not include hail and snow. Humidity referred to in Choices (C) and (D) is not mentioned and may not be con-

cluded from information in the passage.

4. **(A)** "The average annual precipitation over the whole of the United States is thirty-six inches." Choice (B) refers to the formula for computing precipitation, not to the annual rainfall over the United States. Choice (C) refers to the amount of rain recorded in New York State, not in the United States. Choice (D) refers to the total annual precipitation recorded in New York State.

5. **(B)** "A general formula for computing the precipitation of snowfall is that ten inches of snow is equal to one inch of precipitation." Forty inches of snow divided by 10 inches per one inch of precipitation is four inches, or one-third foot. Choices (A), (C), and (D) may not be computed on the basis of the formula in the passage.

6. **(C)** In the context of this passage, proximity to is closest in meaning to nearness to. Choices (A), (B), and (D) are not accepted definitions of the phrase.

7. "Most of the precipitation in the United States is brought originally by prevailing winds from the Pacific Ocean, the Gulf of Mexico, the Atlantic Ocean, and the Great Lakes." Quotation from sentence 2, paragraph 2.

8. **(D)** ". . . the Pacific Coast receives more annual precipitation than the Atlantic Coast." Choices (A), (B), and (C) refer to the prevailing winds, not to the highest annual precipitation.

9. **(B)** Choice (A) is mentioned in sentence 5, paragraph 1. Choices (C) and (D) are mentioned in sentence 1, paragraph 2. Choice (B)

is not mentioned and may not be concluded from information in the passage.

10. **(A)** In the context of this passage, substantially could best be replaced by fundamentally. Choices (B), (C), and (D) are not accepted definitions of the word.

11. **(B)** "East of the Rocky Mountains, the annual precipitation decreases substantially from that [precipitation] west of the Rocky Mountains." Choices (A), (C), and (D) would change the meaning of the sentence.

12. **(D)** Choices (A), (B), and (C) are important to the discussion, and provide details that support the main topic, "women's suffrage."

13. **(C)** In the context of this passage, ban most nearly means to prohibit. Choices (A), (B), and (D) are not accepted definitions of the word.

14. "They were fighting against a belief that voting should be tied to land ownership, and because land was owned by men, and in some cases by their widows, only those who held the greatest stake in government, that is the male landowners, were considered worthy of the vote." Quotation from sentence 5, paragraph 1.

15. **(A)** In the context of this passage, primarily is closest in meaning to above all. Choices (B), (C), and (D) are not accepted definitions of the word.

16. In the context of this passage, better is closest in meaning to improve. No other words or phrases in the **bold** text are close to the meaning of the word improve.

17. **(D)** "When the Civil War ended . . . the Fifteenth Amendment . . .

granted . . . suffrage to blacks. . . ." *Suffrage* means the right to vote. Choice (B) contradicts the fact that the bill was presented to Congress in 1878, not immediately after the Civil War. Choice (C) refers to the fact that the eastern states resisted the women's suffrage bill, not the end of the Civil War. Choice (A) is not mentioned and may not be concluded from information in the passage.

18. **(D)** *Suffrage* means the right to vote; the exercise of such a right. Choice (A) is a definition of the word *suffering*, not *suffrage*. Choices (B) and (C) are related to the word *suffrage*, but they are not accepted definitions of it.

19. **(A)** "A women's suffrage bill had been presented to every Congress since 1878 but it [the bill] continually failed to pass until 1920, when the Nineteenth Amendment granted women the right to vote." Choices (B), (C), and (D) would change the meaning of the sentence.

20. **(C)** ". . . the Nineteenth Amendment granted women the right to vote." Choice (A) refers to the Fifteenth, not the Nineteenth Amendment. Choice (B) refers to the Fourteenth Amendment. Choice (D) is not mentioned and may not be concluded from information in the passage.

21. **(D)** ". . . 1920 when the Nineteenth Amendment granted women the right to vote." Choice (A) refers to the date when the Civil War ended. Choice (B) refers to the date when the Fifteenth Amendment was adopted granting blacks, not women, the right to vote. Choice (C) refers to

the date when the bill to grant women the right to vote was presented to Congress, not to the date that it was passed and became law.

22. **(B)** The other choices are secondary topics that are used to develop the primary topic, "characteristics and varieties of the *Acacia*." Choices (A), (C), and (D) are important details and examples.

23. In the context of this passage, valued is closest in meaning to prized. No other words or phrases in the **bold** text are close to the meaning of the word prized.

24. **(C)** "Only about a dozen of the three hundred Australian varieties grow well in the southern United States." Choice (A) refers to the number of species identified, not to the number that grow well in the United States. Choice (B) refers to the number of species that grow well in Australia, not in the southern United States. Choice (D) refers to the number of species that have flowers, not to the total number of species that grow well in the southern United States.

25. **(A)** In the context of this passage, thrive is closest in meaning to the phrase grow well. Choices (B), (C), and (D) are not accepted definitions of the word.

26. **(B)** "Although nearly five hundred species of *Acacia* have been identified, only about a dozen of the three hundred Australian varieties grow well in the southern United States, and of these [varieties], only three are flowering." Choices (A), (C), and (D) would change the meaning of the sentence.

27. **(C)** "The *Silver Wattle*, although very similar to the *Bailey Acacia*, grows twice as high." Choice (A) refers to the *Sydney Golden Wattle*, not to the *Silver Wattle*. Choices (B) and (D) refer to the *Black Acacia*.

28. **(A)** In the context of this passage, flat most nearly means smooth. Choices (B), (C), and (D) are not accepted definitions of the word.

29. **(B)** In the context of this passage, showy could best be replaced by elaborate. Choices (A), (C), and (D) are not accepted definitions of the word.

30. **(D)** "...the *Black Acacia* or *Blackwood*, has dark green leaves and unobtrusive blossoms." The species referred to in Choices (A), (B), and (C) have fragrant clusters of yellow flowers.

31. **(B)** "... the *Black Acacia* is valuable for its dark wood which is used in making cabinets and furniture." Choices (A), (C), and (D) are not mentioned and may not be concluded from information in the passage.

32. **(C)** "...the pale yellow blossoms appear in August in Australia." Choice (A) refers to the month that the *Acacia* blooms in the United States, not in Australia. Choices (B) and (D) refer to the reversal of seasons in the northern and southern hemispheres, but not to the blossoming of the *Acacia*.

33. "Some acacias are popular in landscaping because of their graceful shapes, lacey foliage, and fragrant blossoms. Other *Acacia* varieties are valued for the sticky resin, called gum Arabic or gum acacia, used widely in medicines, foods, and perfumes, for the dark dense wood prized for making pianos, or for the bark, rich in tannin, a dark, acidic substance used to cure the hides of animals, transforming them into leather." The connection between the two sentences occurs in the first words—*Some* and *Other*, which determine consecutive order.

34. **(A)** "A History of New York City" is the best title because it states the main idea of the passage. Choices (C) and (D) are details used to develop the main idea. Choice (B) is not specific enough.

35. **(C)** "Peter Minuit ... negotiated with Indian chiefs for the purchase of Manhattan Island for merchandise...." Choices (A) and (B) refer to the value of the merchandise, not to what the Native Americans received. Choice (D) refers to where the Dutch settlements were located.

36. **(B)** "... Dutch settlements in North America known as New Amsterdam...." Choice (C) refers to the location of the land that was purchased from the Native Americans. Choices (A) and (D) are not mentioned and may not be concluded from information in the passage.

37. **(A)** Choice (A) is a restatement of the sentence in the passage. Since offers were extended throughout Europe, it must be assumed that other Europeans were given opportunities to immigrate.

38. **(C)** In the context of this passage, heterogeneous could best be replaced by diverse. Choices (A), (B), and (D) are not accepted definitions of the word.

39. **(C)** ". . . offers, generous by the standards of the era, were extended throughout Europe. Consequently, the settlement became the most heterogeneous of the North American colonies." Choice (A) contradicts the fact that it was New Amsterdam, not the Dutch West India Company, that the English acquired. Choices (B) and (D) are not mentioned and may not be concluded from information in the passage.

40. "Among the multilingual settlers was a large group of English colonists from Connecticut and Massachusetts who supported the English King's claim to all of New Netherlands set out in a charter that gave the territory to his [the English King's] brother James, Duke of York." Other choices would change the meaning of the sentence.

41. **(A)** In the context of this passage, formidable is closest in meaning to powerful. Choices (B), (C), and (D) are not accepted definitions of the word.

42. "When the English acquired the island, the village of New Amsterdam was renamed New York in honor of the Duke." Quotation from sentence 1, paragraph 4.

43. **(B)** "After the war, it [New York] was selected as the first capital of the United States." Choices (A), (C), and (D) would change the meaning of the sentence.

44. **(B)** "After the war, it [New York] was selected as the first capital of the United States." Choice (A) refers to the former name for New York, which had already been changed when it became the first capital. Choices (C) and (D) refer to cities that became the capital after New York.

45. **(D)** "Three centuries after his initial trade . . . Minuit's tiny investment was worth more than seven billion dollars." Choice (A) refers to the date that the Dutch purchased Manhattan Island from the Native Americans. Choice (B) refers to the date one century after the purchase. Choice (C) refers to the date three decades after the purchase.

SCORE ESTIMATES

Important Background Information

It is not possible for you to determine the exact score that you will receive on the TOEFL. There are three reasons why this is true. First, the testing conditions on the day of your official TOEFL will affect your score. If you are in an uncomfortable room, if there are noisy distractions, if you are upset because you almost arrived late for the test, or if you are very nervous, then these factors can affect your score. The administration of a Model Test is more controlled. You will probably not be as stressed when you take one of the tests in this book. Second, the Model Tests in the book are designed to help you practice the most frequently tested item types on the official TOEFL. Because they are constructed to teach as well as to test, there is more repetition in Model Tests than there is on official TOEFL tests. Tests that are not constructed for exactly the same purposes are not exactly comparable. Third, the TOEFL scores received by the same student will vary from one official Computer-Based TOEFL examination to another official Computer-Based TOEFL examination by as many as 20 points, even when the examinations are taken on the same day. In testing and assessment, this is called a standard error of measurement. Therefore, a TOEFL score cannot be predicted precisely even when two official tests are used.

But, of course, you would like to know how close you are to your goal. To do that, you can use the following procedure to estimate your TOEFL score. An estimate is an approximation. In this case, it is a range of scores.

Score Correspondence Procedure

1. Use the charts on the following pages to determine your percentage scores for each section of the TOEFL.
2. Determine the total percentage score for the TOEFL.
   Listening Section = one third the total
   Structure Section = one sixth the total
   Reading Section = one third the total
   Writing Section = one sixth the total
3. Use the Score Correspondence Table to estimate an official TOEFL score.

Listening Section

Number Correct	Percentage Score
50	100
49	98
48	96
47	94
46	92
45	90
44	88
43	86
42	84
41	82
40	80
39	78
38	76
37	74
36	72
35	70
34	68
33	66
32	64
31	62
30	60
29	58
28	56
27	54
26	52
25	50
24	48
23	46
22	44
21	42
20	40
19	38
18	36
17	34
16	32
15	30
14	28
13	26
12	24
11	22
10	20
9	18
8	16
7	14
6	12
5	10
4	8
3	6
2	4
1	2
0	0

Structure Section

Number Correct	Percentage Score
25	100
24	96
23	92
22	88
21	84
20	80
19	76
18	72
17	68
16	64
15	60
14	56
13	52
12	48
11	44
10	40
9	36
8	32
7	28
6	24
5	20
4	16
3	12
2	8
1	4
0	0

Reading Section

Number Correct	Percentage Score
45	100
44	98
43	96
42	93
41	91
40	89
39	87
38	84
37	82
36	80
35	78
34	76
33	73
32	71
31	69
30	67
29	64
28	62
27	60
26	58
25	56
24	53
23	51
22	49
21	47
20	44
19	42
18	40
17	38
16	36
15	33
14	31
13	29
12	27
11	24
10	22
9	20
8	18
7	16
6	13
5	11
4	9
3	7
2	4
1	2
0	0

Writing Section

Scaled Score	Percentage Score
6.0	100
5.5	92
5.0	84
4.5	76
4.0	68
3.5	60
3.0	52
2.5	44
2.0	36
1.5	28
1.0	20
0	0

Score Correspondence Table

Model Test Percentage Scores	Computer-Based TOEFL Score Ranges	Paper-Based TOEFL Score Ranges
100	287–300	660–677
95	273–283	640–657
90	260–270	620–637
85	250–260	600–617
80	237–247	580–597
75	220–233	560–577
70	207–220	540–557
65	190–203	520–537
60	173–187	500–517
55	157–170	480–497
50	140–153	460–477
45	123–137	440–457
40	110–123	420–437
35	97–107	400–417
30	83–93	380–397
25	70–80	360–377
20	60–70	340–357
15	47–57	320–337
10	40–47	310–317
5		
0		

Progress Chart   Percentage Scores

Model Test	Listening $\frac{1}{3}$	Structure $\frac{1}{6}$	Reading $\frac{1}{3}$	Writing $\frac{1}{6}$	=	Total	=	Score Ranges
One								
Two								
Three								
Four								

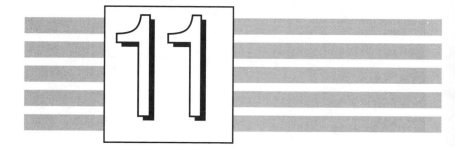

TRANSCRIPT FOR THE LISTENING SECTIONS OF THE TOEFL MODEL TESTS

The following is the transcript for the Listening sections for the TOEFL Model Tests included in this book. Note that the Listening sections always appear as Section 1 of the examinations.

When you take the Model Tests in this book as a preliminary step in your preparation for the actual examination, you should use either the compact disk that supplements this book or the CD-ROM that supplements the larger version of this book, *Barron's How to Prepare for the TOEFL*. If you use a CD-ROM, you will see visuals on your computer screen. If you use a compact disk, you will hear the audio, but you will not see the visuals.

If you have someone read the TOEFL transcript to you, be sure that he or she understands the timing sequences. The reader should work with a stopwatch or with a regular watch with a second hand in order to keep careful track of the timed pauses between questions. The total amount of time for each section is noted on the Model Tests. Be sure that the reader speaks clearly and at a moderately paced rate. For results that would be closest to the actual testing situation, it is recommended that three persons be asked to read, since some of the Listening Sections include dialogues.

Model Test 1
Computer-Assisted TOEFL

Section 1:
Listening

The Listening section of the test measures the ability to understand conversations and talks in English. On the actual TOEFL exam, you will use headphones to listen to the conversations and talks. While you are listening, pictures of the speakers or other information will be presented on your computer screen. There are two parts to the Listening section, with special directions for each part.

On the day of the test, the amount of time you will have to answer all of the questions will appear on the computer screen. The time you spend listening to the test material will not be counted. The listening material and questions about it will be presented only one time. You will not be allowed to take notes or have any paper at your computer. You will both see and hear the questions before the answer choices appear. You can take as much time as you need to select an answer; however, it will be to your advantage to answer the questions as quickly as possible. You may change your answer as many times as you want before you confirm it. After you have confirmed an answer, you will not be able to return to the question.

Before you begin working on the Listening section, you will have an opportunity to adjust the volume of the sound. You will not be able to change the volume after you have started the test.

QUESTION DIRECTIONS—Part A

In Part A of the Listening section, you will hear short conversations between two people. In some of the conversations, each person speaks only once. In other conversations, one or both of the people speak more than once. Each conversation is followed by one question about it.

Each question in this part has four answer choices. You should click on the best answer to each question. Answer the questions on the basis of what is stated or implied by the speakers.

1. Woman: If I were you I'd take the bus to school. Driving in that rush-hour traffic is terrible.
   Man: But by the time the bus gets to my stop, there aren't any seats left.
   Narrator: What is the man's problem?

2. Woman: I'd like to take Dr. Sullivan's section of Physics 100, but my advisor is teaching it too, and I don't want her to be offended.
   Man: Who cares?
   Woman: Well, I don't want to get on her bad side.
   Man: I wouldn't worry about it.
   Narrator: What does the man mean?

3. Man: Let's go to the dance at the Student Center on Friday.
   Woman: Sounds great, but I'm going to a lecture. Thanks for asking me though.
   Narrator: What does the woman imply?

4. Man: That's a nice bike.
   Woman: I got it almost five years ago.
   Man: You did? It looks new.
   Woman: Yes, it's still in really good shape.
   Narrator: What does the woman mean?

5. Woman: Would you like some hot coffee or tea?
   Man: I like them both, but I'd rather have something cold.
   Narrator: What does the man want to drink?

6. Woman: How can I get to the shopping center from here? Not the
                   one on campus. The one downtown.
   Man: You can take a bus or a taxi, but it isn't too far to walk.
   Narrator: What does the man suggest the woman do?

7. Man: Have you found a class yet?
   Woman: I'm just checking the schedule now.
   Narrator: What can be inferred about the man?

8. Woman: Do you mind if I turn on the radio for a while?
   Man: No, I don't mind.
   Narrator: What does the man mean?

9. Man: I'm worried about Anna. She's really been depressed
                   lately. All she does is stay in her room all day.
   Woman: That sounds serious. She'd better see someone at the
                   Counseling Center.
   Narrator: What does the woman suggest Anna do?

10. Woman: If you have a few minutes, I'd like to talk with you about
                   my project.
    Man: Please go on.
    Narrator: What does the man mean?

11. Woman: Excuse me. I was in line here first.
    Man: Oh, I'm sorry. I didn't realize that you were waiting.
    Narrator: What will the man probably do?

12. Man: The neighbors are going to have another party.
    Woman: Not again!
    Narrator: What does the woman imply?

13. Man: You mean Dr. Franklin said you couldn't have an
                   extension?
    Woman: He said it was not his policy.
    Man: Really?
    Woman: Yes, so now I have to work over the holiday weekend.
    Narrator: What had the man assumed?

14. Man: We really should have left already.
    Woman: Maybe we can get there on time if we run. Hurry.
    Narrator: What problem do the man and woman have?

15. Man: Have you moved out of your apartment yet?
    Woman: No. I'm paid up until the 15th.
    Narrator: What is the woman probably going to do?

16. Woman: Mary Anne took the math placement test.
    Man: So, she *finally* did it!
    Narrator: What had the man assumed about Mary Anne?

17. Woman:	Where have you been? I haven't seen you in class all week.
Man:	I caught cold, so I stayed in.
Narrator:	What does the man mean?

QUESTION DIRECTIONS—Part B

In Part B of the Listening section, you will hear several longer conversations and talks. Each conversation or talk is followed by several questions. The conversations, talks, and questions will not be repeated.

The conversations and talks are about a variety of topics. You do not need special knowledge of the topics to answer the questions correctly. Rather, you should answer each question on the basis of what is stated or implied by the speakers in the conversations or talks.

For most of the questions, you will need to click on the best of four possible answers. Some questions will have special directions. The special directions will appear in a box on the computer screen.

Narrator:	Listen to a conversation with a professor.
Man:	Professor Day, may I see you for a minute?
Woman:	Sure. Come on in, Mike. What's the matter?
Man:	I've got a problem.
Woman:	Okay.
Man:	I need your technical writing class. And, I knew I had to have it so I went early to registration, but by the time I got to the front of the line, it was closed. See, my advisor signed my course request and everything. I was just too far back in the line.
Woman:	That's a big class already, Mike. If it's closed, that means I have fifty students in it.
Man:	I'm not surprised. It's supposed to be a really good class.
Woman:	Can't you take it next year? We offer it every fall.
Man:	Well, that's the problem. I'm supposed to be graduating this spring. But, of course, I can't graduate without your class.
Woman:	I see. In that case, I'll sign an override for you. It looks like there will be fifty-one. Take this form back to the registration area and they'll get you in.
Man:	Thanks, Professor Day. I really appreciate this!

Now get ready to answer the questions

Narrator:	18. What is Mike's problem?
	19. What does Mike want Professor Day to do?

20. What does Mike say about graduation?

21. What does Professor Day decide to do?

Narrator: Listen to a talk by a business instructor.

Today's lecture is about the effects of background music on employee performance and retail sales. As you know, every day millions of people in offices and factories around the world do their work to the accompaniment of background music, more commonly known as MUZAK. But did you know that MUZAK is more than a pleasant addition to the environment? Studies show that this seemingly innocent background music can be engineered to control behavior. In fact, MUZAK can improve employee performance by reducing stress, boredom, and fatigue. In one survey, overall productivity increased by thirty percent, although five to ten percent is the average.

The key to MUZAK's success is something called stimulus progression, which means quite simply that the background music starts with a slow, soft song that is low in stimulus value and builds up gradually to an upbeat song that is high in stimulus value. The fastest, loudest sounds are programmed for about ten-thirty in the morning and two-thirty in the afternoon when people are generally starting to tire.

Besides employee performance, MUZAK can increase sales. In supermarkets, slow music can influence shoppers to walk slower and buy more. In restaurants, fast music can cause customers to eat quickly so that the same number of tables may be used to serve more people during peak times such as the lunch hour.

> Now get ready to answer the questions

Narrator: 22. What is MUZAK?

23. What is the average increase in productivity when MUZAK is introduced?

24. What is stimulus progression?

25. How does MUZAK influence sales in supermarkets?

Narrator: Listen to a public service announcement.

Community College understands that everyone who wants to attend college will not be able to come to campus. So, as part of the Distance Learning Program, Community College offers a series of video telecourses to meet the needs of students who prefer to complete coursework in their homes, at their convenience.

These telecourses are regular college credit classes taught on video-cassette tapes by a Community College professor. To use the materials for the course, you will need your own VHS-type VCR player. Some tele-courses will also be broadcast on KCC7-TV's "Sun-Up Semester." This program airs from six o'clock in the morning to seven-thirty, Monday through Friday, and a complete listing of courses is printed in your regular television guide.

To register for a telecourse, phone the Community College Distance Learning Program at 782-6394. The course syllabus, books, and video-tapes will be available at the Community College bookstore. During the first week of classes, your instructor will contact you to discuss the course and answer any questions you might have about the course requirements. Then, throughout the rest of the semester, you can use either an 800 tele-phone number or an e-mail address to contact your instructor.

> Now get ready to answer the questions

Narrator:	26. What is this announcement mainly about?
	27. Why does the speaker mention the "Sun-Up Semester"?
	28. How can students register for a course?
	29. How can students contact the instructor?
Narrator:	Listen to part of a conversation between two friends on campus.
Donna:	Hi, Bill.
Bill:	Hi, Donna. Where have you been? I haven't seen you for weeks.
Donna:	I know. I had to drop out last semester. I thought I had a cold, but it was mono.
Bill:	I'm sorry to hear that. What is mono anyway?
Donna:	It's a virus, actually, that attacks your immune system. You really become susceptible to it when you stay up late, stress out, and get run down. It was my own fault. I just kept going, studying late. I didn't get enough rest. You know the story.
Bill:	Wow! All too well. I'm surprised that we all don't have it.
Donna:	A lot of college students do get it. In fact, it is jokingly called the "college disease." I can tell you though, it's no joke.
Bill:	So how are you now?
Donna:	I'm still tired. But I learned my lesson though. This semester I'm taking twelve hours, and I'm not pushing myself so hard.

Bill:	Good for you. I'm taking twenty-one hours. Sometimes I just don't know why I put so much pressure on myself. If I took one more semester to finish my program, then I wouldn't be so overloaded.
Donna:	Listen, if you get sick like I did, you'll have to drop out and you'll end up with an extra semester anyway. So you might as well slow down.
Bill:	True. Well, it's something to think about. Take care of yourself, Donna.
Donna:	I will. You, too.

> Now get ready to answer the questions

Narrator:	30. What is the main topic of this conversation?
	31. What was the woman's problem?
	32. Why is mono called the "college disease"?
	33. What advice does the woman give the man?
Narrator:	Listen to a talk by a college professor.

When Edward Sapir was teaching at Yale, Benjamin Lee Whorf enrolled in his class. Whorf was recognized for his investigations of the Hopi language, including his authorship of a grammar book and a dictionary. Even in his early publications, it is clear that he was developing the theory that the very different grammar of Hopi might indicate a different manner of conceiving and perceiving the world on the part of the native speaker of Hopi.

In 1936, he wrote "An American Indian Model of the Universe," which explored the implications of the Hopi verb system with regard to the Hopi conception of space and time.

Whorf is probably best known for his article "The Relation of Habitual Thought and Behavior to Language" and for the three articles that appeared in 1941 in the *Technology Review*

In these articles, he proposed what he called the principle of "linguistic relativity," which states, at least as a hypothesis, that the grammar of a language influences the manner in which the speaker understands reality and behaves with respect to it.

Since the theory did not emerge until after Whorf had begun to study with Sapir, and since Sapir had most certainly shared in the development of the idea, it came to be called the Sapir-Whorf Hypothesis.

> Now get ready to answer the questions

Narrator:	34. What central theme does the lecture examine?
	35. Which languages did Whorf use in his research?
	36. According to the lecturer, what is linguistic relativity?
	37. What is another name for linguistic relativity?

Narrator:	Listen to part of a class discussion in an environmental science class.
Dr. Green:	Let's begin our discussion today by defining acid rain. Joanne?
Joanne:	Acid rain is, uh, pollution that results when sulfur dioxide and nitrogen oxide mix with the water vapor in the atmosphere.
Dr. Green:	Good. But why do we call it acid rain, then?
Joanne:	Oh, well, sulfur dioxide and nitrogen oxide combine with water vapor and form sulfuric acid and nitric acid.
Dr. Green:	And the acid corrodes the environment?
Joanne:	It does. According to the book, acid reaches the Earth as rain, sleet, snow, fog, or even mist, but we call all of these various forms of pollution acid rain.
Dr. Green:	Exactly right. Now, who can explain how the sulfur dioxide and nitrogen oxide are introduced into the atmosphere in the first place? Ted?
Ted:	Fossil fuels, mostly. Right?
Dr. Green:	Right. Could you elaborate on that a little?
Ted:	Sure. The fossil fuels can be the result of natural events such as volcanic eruptions or forest fires, but most of the time, they are introduced into the atmosphere by industrial processes like the smelting of metals or the burning of oil, coal, and gas.
Dr. Green:	Anything else we should add to that? Yes, Joanne?
Joanne:	Dr. Green, I think it's important to mention the extent of the damage to areas like the Great Lakes.
Dr. Green:	Good point, Joanne. Acidity in the water and on the shorelines has all but eliminated some of the fish populations once found in the Great Lakes region along the United States-Canadian border. Any other damaging effects?
Ted:	I'm an agriculture major, Dr. Green, so I am more familiar with the large concentrations of acids that have been deposited in the soil around the Great Lakes.
Dr. Green:	And what has happened to the vegetation in that region?

Ted:	Well, the rain has caused a chemical change in the soil, which is absorbed by the roots of plants. The plants don't get the nutrients they need, and as a consequence, they die, and uh . . .
Dr. Green:	Yes?
Ted:	And it just occurred to me that acid rain is having an adverse effect not only on the environment but also on the economy, especially forestry and agriculture.
Dr. Green:	Excellent deduction. Now, let me give you the good news. In the Great Lakes region that was mentioned in our book, an Air Quality Accord was signed by Canada and the United States about ten years ago to establish limits for the amount of acidic deposits that may flow across international boundaries. Since then, many companies on both sides of the border have installed equipment that limits sulfur dioxide emissions, and some have even changed to fuels that are lower in sulfur content.
Ted:	Excuse me. Isn't it automobile emission that accounts for a high percentage of the nitrogen oxide?
Dr. Green:	Yes, it is, Ted. And that problem presents a somewhat larger challenge to the governments and their agencies.

> Now get ready to answer the questions

Narrator: 38. What is the topic of this discussion?

39. What is acid rain?

40. In which two ways has the environment been damaged along the Great Lakes?

41. What are the conditions of the Air Quality Accord?

Narrator: Listen to part of a lecture in a microbiology class.

Bacteria is the common name for a very large group of one-celled microscopic organisms that, we believe, may be the smallest, simplest, and perhaps even the very first form of cellular life that evolved on Earth. Because they are so small, bacteria must be measured in microns, with one micron measuring about 0.00004 inches long. Most bacteria range from about 0.1 microns to 4 microns wide and 0.2 microns to 50 microns long. So you can understand that they are observable only under a microscope.

There are three main types of bacteria, which are classified according to their shape. The slides that I am going to show you are photographic enlargements of bacteria that I observed under the microscope in the lab earlier today. This slide is an example of bacilli.

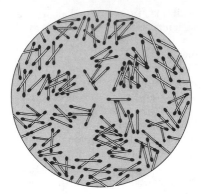

The bacilli are a group of bacteria that occur in the soil and air. As you can see, they are shaped like rods, and if you were to see them in motion, they would be rolling or tumbling under the microscope. These bacilli are largely responsible for food spoilage.

The next slide is a very different shape of bacteria.

It is referred to as the cocci group, and it tends to grow in chains. This example is of the common streptococci that causes strep throat.

Finally, let's look at the spiral-shaped bacteria called the spirilla. They look a little like corkscrews, and they are responsible for a number of diseases in humans.

Some species of bacteria do cause diseases, but for the most part, bacteria live harmlessly on the skin, in the mouth, and in the intestines. In fact, bacteria are very helpful to researchers. Bacterial cells resemble the cells of other life forms in many ways, and may be studied to give us insights. For example, we have a major research project in genetics in progress here at the University. Since bacteria reproduce very rapidly, we are using them to determine how certain characteristics are inherited.

> Now get ready to answer the questions

Narrator: 42. What is the topic of this lecture?

43. Which two characteristics are common in bacteria?

44. Which of the following slides contain cocci bacteria?

45. Why are bacteria being used in the research study at the University?

Narrator: Listen to part of a conversation between a student and an academic advisor on campus.

Man: Dr. Kelly, do you have a minute?
Dr. Kelly: Sure. Come in.
Man: Thanks. I need to talk with you about my sociology class.
Dr. Kelly: Let's see, that would be Sociology 530 with Dr. Brown.
Man: Right. The problem is that when I scheduled that class, it was supposed to be offered at three o'clock in the afternoon, Tuesdays and Thursdays, but for some reason the time has been changed to nine in the morning. Since I work mornings, I can't take it at that time.
Dr. Kelly: I see. Well, would you like to drop the class?
Man: Yes, but I also need to pick up another class. I have to be a full-time student in order to qualify for my student loan.

Dr. Kelly:	So you need at least twelve hours. And you need afternoon classes.
Man:	That's right. Or evening classes.
Dr. Kelly:	Did you have anything in mind?
Man:	Yes. I was considering Sociology 560 or 570. I thought I'd get your opinion.
Dr. Kelly:	Either one will fit into your program since you are a Soc major, and they are both electives. Too bad you can't get a required course.
Man:	I know, but they all seem to be offered in the morning.
Dr. Kelly:	Okay, then. Which one is the most interesting to you?
Man:	I'm interested in both of them, but I was thinking since Dr. Brown teaches Soc 560, I might prefer that one. I've been trying to take a class with her because I hear that she is an excellent professor.
Dr. Kelly:	Good. The class is open, and I'll just sign that drop-add form for you to drop 530 and add 560. You can just tell Dr. Brown what happened when you see her in class.
Man:	Okay. Thanks a lot, Dr. Kelly. I really appreciate it.
Dr. Kelly:	Don't mention it.

> Now get ready to answer the questions

Narrator:

46. What is the purpose of this conversation?

47. Why does the man need to take at least twelve hours?

48. Why does the man prefer Sociology 560?

49. What will Dr. Kelly do?

50. What will the man probably do after the conversation?

Model Test 2
Computer-Assisted TOEFL

Section 1:
Listening

The Listening section of the test measures the ability to understand conversations and talks in English. On the actual TOEFL exam, you will use headphones to listen to the conversations and talks. While you are listening, pictures of the speakers or other information will be presented on your computer screen. There are two parts to the Listening section, with special directions for each part.

On the day of the test, the amount of time you will have to answer all of the questions will appear on the computer screen. The time you spend listening to the test material will not be counted. The listening material and questions about it will be presented only one time. You will not be allowed to take notes or have any paper at your computer. You will both see and hear the questions before the answer choices appear. You can take as much time as you need to select an answer; however, it will be to your advantage to answer the questions as quickly as possible. You may change your answer as many times as you want before you confirm it. After you have confirmed an answer, you will not be able to return to the question.

Before you begin working on the Listening section, you will have an opportunity to adjust the volume of the sound. You will not be able to change the volume after you have started the test.

QUESTION DIRECTIONS—Part A

In Part A of the Listening section, you will hear short conversations between two people. In some of the conversations, each person speaks only once. In other conversations, one or both of the people speak more than once. Each conversation is followed by one question about it.

Each question in this part has four answer choices. You should click on the best answer to each question. Answer the questions on the basis of what is stated or implied by the speakers.

1. Man: How many did you have for the orientation?
   Woman: Well, let me see. Fifty had registered, but everyone didn't show up. I believe that we had twenty-five from the Middle East and at least fifteen from Latin America.
   Man: You don't mean it!
   Narrator: What had the man assumed?

2. Man: Excuse me. Could you tell me when Dr. Smith has office hours?
   Woman: Not really, but there's a sign on the door I think.
   Narrator: What does the woman imply that the man should do?

3. Man: I heard that Professor Wilson will let you do a project for extra credit.
   Woman: That's great! I could use some.
   Narrator: What is the woman probably going to do?

4. Man: Is Paul angry?
   Woman: If he were, he'd tell us.
   Narrator: What does the woman say about Paul?

5. Man: I heard you got an A on the final exam. I think you're the only one who did!

   Woman: Not really. There were a couple of other As.

   Narrator: What does the woman mean?

6. Woman: Oh, no. It's five o'clock already and I haven't finished studying for the quiz in Dr. Taylor's class.

   Man: Don't worry. That clock is half an hour fast.

   Narrator: What problem does the woman have?

7. Man: It's much better to wait until tomorrow to go. Don't you agree?

   Woman: Yes. I couldn't agree more.

   Narrator: What does the woman mean?

8. Man: I have to go to class because I have a test, but if I could, I'd go with you to the movie.

   Woman: That's too bad. I wish that you could come along.

   Narrator: What is the man going to do?

9. Woman: I left a message on your answering machine a couple of days ago.

   Man: Yes. I've been meaning to get back with you.

   Narrator: What does the man mean?

10. Man: I think it's my turn.

    Woman: Sorry you had to wait so long. One of the other secretaries is out today.

    Narrator: What does the woman mean?

11. Man: Could you please tell me what room Dr. Robert Davis is in?

    Woman: Yes, he's in the Math Department on the fourth floor. Check with the secretary before going in, though.

    Narrator: What does the woman suggest that the man do?

12. Man: Tom wasn't in class again today!

    Woman: I know. I wonder whether he'll show up for the final exam.

    Narrator: What can be inferred about Tom?

13. Man: Hey, Kathy.

    Woman: Hi Ted. How are you doing?

    Man: Fine. Are we still on for tonight?

    Woman: I'm looking forward to it.

    Narrator: What does the man mean?

14. Woman: So the course *is* closed. This is terrible! I have to have it to graduate.

| Man: | You're okay. Just Dr. Collin's section is closed. There's another section that's still open, but nobody knows who's teaching it. It's marked "staff." |
| Narrator: | What will the woman probably do? |

15.
Woman:	What's wrong?
Man:	I still haven't received my score on the GMAT test. Maybe I should call to check on it.
Woman:	Don't worry so much. It takes at least six weeks to receive your score.
Narrator:	What does the woman think that the man should do?

16.
Man:	You've been doing a lot of traveling, haven't you?
Woman:	Yes. We want to make the most of our time here.
Narrator:	What does the woman mean?

17.
Woman:	Did you get your tickets?
Man:	I talked to Judy about it, and she took care of it for me.
Narrator:	What does the man mean?

QUESTION DIRECTIONS—Part B

In Part B of the Listening section, you will hear several longer conversations and talks. Each conversation or talk is followed by several questions. The conversations, talks, and questions will not be repeated.

The conversations and talks are about a variety of topics. You do not need special knowledge of the topics to answer the questions correctly. Rather, you should answer each question on the basis of what is stated or implied by the speakers in the conversations or talks.

For most of the questions, you will need to click on the best of four possible answers. Some questions will have special directions. The special directions will appear in a box on the computer screen.

Narrator:	Listen to part of a conversation between two classmates on a college campus.
Man:	Did you understand that experiment that Bill mentioned in the group presentation?
Woman:	The one about free fall?
Man:	Right. The one that illustration in the module
Woman:	Sure. The astronaut held a hammer in one hand and a feather in the other. Then he dropped them at the same time . . .
Man:	. . . and both of them hit the ground at the same time.
Woman:	Yes. So that proves Galileo's theory that all objects fall at the same rate in the absence of air resistance.
Man:	Okay. That was the part that was missing for me. The part about air resistance.

Woman:	Oh. Well, since there is no air resistance on the moon, it is the ideal environment for the experiment.
Man:	That makes sense.
Woman:	Actually, the part that surprised me was how much easier it is to lift the hammer on the moon than it is on Earth because of the moon's lower rate of gravitational acceleration.
Man:	But didn't they say that it was just as difficult to push the hammer along the surface when it fell?
Woman:	Right again. Because gravity only governs vertical motion like lifting, but not horizontal motion like pushing.
Man:	Thanks for going over this with me.
Woman:	You're welcome. I really liked the presentation. I think the group did a good job.

> Now get ready to answer the questions

Narrator:	18. What are the man and woman talking about?
	19. Why is the moon an ideal environment for the experiment?
	20. Why was it easier to lift the hammer on the moon?
	21. How did the woman feel about the presentation?
Narrator:	Listen to a conversation between two college students.
Man:	What did you think about the video we were supposed to watch for Professor Stephen's class?
Woman:	I didn't see it. Was it good?
Man:	Really it was. It was about stress.
Woman:	How to relieve stress?
Man:	Not really. More the effects of stress on the national health.
Woman:	Oh.
Man:	But it was interesting, though.
Woman:	Really?
Man:	Yes. I think they said that one out of nine women age forty-five through sixty-five will have a heart attack.
Woman:	I'm surprised at that.
Man:	I was, too. Oh, another thing. They said that women usually don't get the same level of care that men do, so the heart attack is likely to be more serious.
Woman:	Why is that?
Man:	Because many members of the medical profession still think of a heart attack as a male problem, so they don't recognize the symptoms in their women patients.

Woman:	Well, it does sound like an interesting video. I'm going to try to see it before class next time so I'll be ready for the discussion.
Man:	It's on reserve in the library, so you can't check it out, but you can use one of the viewing rooms. It's only an hour long.

> Now get ready to answer the questions

Narrator:	22. What was the video about?
	23. What did the students learn about women?
	24. How did the man feel about the video?
	25. What will the woman probably do?
Narrator:	Listen to a lecture by an English intructor.

The romance and marriage of Elizabeth Barrett to Robert Browning inspired some of the greatest love poems written in the English language. Elizabeth, without a doubt the greatest woman poet of the Victorian period, was born in Durham County, England, in 1806. Her first important publication was *The Seraphim and Other Poems*, which appeared in 1838.

By 1843, she was so widely recognized that her name was suggested to replace the late Poet Laureate as the official national poet of England. In part because the sovereign was a woman, there was great support for a movement to break with the tradition of a male Poet Laureate. Nevertheless, she lost the competition to William Wordsworth.

A short time later, she married Robert Browning, himself a gifted poet, and they fled to Florence, Italy. A play, *The Barretts of Wimpole Street*, recounts their confrontation with Elizabeth's father and their eventual elopement against his wishes.

While living in Florence, their only son was born. A year later, in 1850, Elizabeth published her collected works, along with a volume of new poems entitled *Sonnets from the Portuguese*, so named because her husband often called her his "Portuguese." *Aurora Leigh*, her longest work, appeared in 1856, only five years before her death in Italy in 1861.

Now get ready to answer the questions

Narrator: 26. What is the main topic of this lecture?

27. According to the lecturer, what was one reason that Elizabeth Barrett was considered for the title of Poet Laureate?

28. Where did Elizabeth and Robert Browning live after their elopement?

29. When did Elizabeth Barrett Browning die?

Narrator: Listen to a lecture by a biology instructor.

Today's lecture will include the most outstanding achievements in biology as it relates to the medical sciences.

Early in Greek history, Hippocrates began to study the human body and to apply scientific method to the problems of diagnosis and the treatment of diseases. Unlike other physicians of his time, he discarded the theory that disease was caused by the gods. Instead, he kept careful records of symptoms and treatments, indicating the success or failure of the patient's cure. He has been recognized as the father of modern medicine.

About a century later, Aristotle began a scientific study of plants and animals, classifying more than five hundred types on the basis of body structure. Because of his great contribution to the field, Aristotle has been called the father of biology.

By the first century A.D., Dioscorides had collected a vast amount of information on plants, which he recorded in the now famous *Materia Medica*, a book that remained an authoritative reference among physicians for fifteen hundred years.

During the Middle Ages, scientific method was scorned in favor of alchemy. Thus, medicine and biology had advanced very little from the time of the ancients until the seventeenth century when the English physician and anatomist William Harvey discovered a mechanism for the circulation of the blood in the body.

Now get ready to answer the questions

Narrator: 30. What is the main topic of this lecture?

31. What was Hippocrates' greatest contribution to medicine?

32. Who is known as the father of biology?

33. What was the contribution made to medicine by William Harvey?

Narrator:	Listen to part of a class discussion in a sociology class.
Dr. Jackson:	Last class, I asked you to locate some articles about gang activity. Let's just go around the table and share what we found. Tracy, will you begin please?
Tracy:	Okay. Actually, I did a search of sociological studies on gang activity, and I found that gangs have been prevalent for much longer than I had assumed. I was so surprised. For some reason, I thought that gang activity was a fairly recent phenomenon, but actually, one of the largest studies was carried out by Thrasher in 1936.
Dr. Jackson:	Good. Good. I'm pleased that you did that. Thrasher's study is a classic research investigation. Can you summarize the findings?
Tracy:	Sure. First, I should say that the study included more than 1300 gangs with more than 25,000 members. According to Thrasher, a gang is a group that may form spontaneously, but after that, will integrate through conflict and violence. Over time, a spirit of solidarity and an attachment to a local territory form. What is most interesting, besides the long history of gangs in the United States, is the fact that not much has changed over the years. And, oh yes, gang behavior seems pretty similar even across cultures.
Dr. Jackson:	That is interesting.
Bill:	Dr. Jackson, may I go next? I have just a brief comment that seems to fit in here.
Dr. Jackson:	Please.
Bill:	Well, another classic study, much later, about 1987 or 8, I think, by Joan Moore, indicated that gang behavior is probably caused by normal adolescent insecurities—the desire for peer approval, respect, support, acceptance, and, in some cases, protection, if the neighborhood is perceived as dangerous. It seems that gangs take the place of the more childish and acceptable cliques that develop in high school.
Sandy:	Is it my turn? Well, I looked up the definitions of gang members by police departments and law enforcement agencies. According to the California Youth Gang Task Force, for example, a gang member will be recognizable because of gang-related tattoos, clothing, and paraphernalia like scarves and hats that identify a particular gang, and allow others to confirm that the wearer has a right to be on the gang's turf. And, to follow up on Tracy's comments about the history of gangs, these criteria have been in place for a long time.

Dr. Jackson:	Good job. So far, what I am hearing, though, refers to male gang membership. What about females? Did anyone find any research on their role in gang activity?
Bill:	I did. Although there are a few girl gangs, females are generally not considered members of the male-dominated gang. They are viewed as more of a support system, and an extended social group—friends and girlfriends to party with.
Sandy:	That's what I found, too.

Now get ready to answer the questions

Narrator:	34. What was surprising about Thrasher's study?
	35. According to the study by Moore, what causes gang activity?
	36. In which two ways are gang members identified by law enforcement authorities?
	37. What is the role of women in gangs?
Narrator:	Listen to part of a conversation between a student and a professor in the professor's office.
Mary:	Dr. Brown, could I speak with you for a minute?
Dr. Brown:	Sure, Mary. Come in.
Mary:	I'm afraid I have a problem.
Dr. Brown:	Oh?
Mary:	You see, I really like my job here.
Dr. Brown:	That's good. Because we really like having you here.
Mary:	Thank you. But the problem is I won't be able to work here next semester. You see, I have a problem with my schedule at school.
Dr. Brown:	Well, what exactly is the problem?
Mary:	I have a required class at nine o'clock on Monday, Wednesday, and Friday.
Dr. Brown:	Oh. Okay. Remind me what your hours are here.
Mary:	I work from nine to one every day. Which has been great, because I have been able to schedule all my classes in the afternoon, until now.
Dr. Brown:	I see. When does the class end?
Mary:	It's a three-hour class, so it meets for an hour three times a week.
Dr. Brown:	So you're finished at ten.
Mary:	Yes. And it would take me half an hour to get here after class, so you see, I would be an hour and a half late on those days.

Dr. Brown:	Well, we need someone four hours a day. But, how about this—you could come in at ten-thirty on Monday, Wednesday, and Friday, and work until two-thirty on those days. That would give you a fairly late lunch, but if that's not a problem for you, then we can do it.
Mary:	That would be great. So I'd just keep my regular hours on Tuesday and Thursday then.
Dr. Brown:	Right. Listen, Mary. You're a work-study employee, and that means that you have two responsibilities—to work and to study. We know that. As long as you put in the hours to get the job done, we expect to fit your work hours around your school schedule. And don't forget, you can study on the job as long as the work is done first.

Now get ready to answer the questions

Narrator:	38. What is Mary's problem?
	39. When is Mary's class next semester?
	40. How does Dr. Brown resolve the problem?
	41. What is a work-study employee?
Narrator:	Listen to part of a lecture in an engineering class.

In recent years, we have developed several techniques for building more earthquake-resistant structures. For relatively small buildings, all we have to do is bolt the buildings to their foundations and provide some support walls.

These walls are referred to as shear walls in your textbook. They are made of reinforced concrete, and by that I mean concrete with steel rods embedded in it. This not only strengthens the structure but also diminishes the forces that tend to shake a building during a quake. In addition to the shear walls that surround a building, shear walls can be situated in the center of a building around an elevator shaft or a stairwell. This is really an excellent reinforcement. It is commonly known as a shear core, and it, too, contains reinforced concrete.

Walls can also be reinforced, using a technique called cross-bracing. Imagine steel beams that cross diagonally from the ceiling to the floor of each story in a building. Before the walls are finished, you can see a vertical row of steel x's on the structure.

Besides steel reinforcements, engineers have also devised base isolators, which are positioned below the building to absorb the shock of the sideways shaking that can undermine a building and cause it to collapse. Most of the base isolators that are currently being used are made of alternating layers of steel and synthetic rubber. The steel is for strength, but the rubber absorbs shock waves. In higher buildings, a moat of flexible materials allows the building to sway during seismic activity.

The combination of a reinforced structure and flexible materials has been proven to reduce earthquake damage. But even these engineering techniques are insufficient if the building has been constructed on filled ground. Soil used in fill dirt can lose its bearing strength when subjected to the shock waves of an earthquake, and the buildings constructed on it can literally disappear into the Earth.

In areas where earthquakes are known to occur, understanding the terrain and using the techniques we have discussed today can greatly reduce property damage, and can save lives as well.

Now get ready to answer the questions

Narrator: 42. What is the topic of this lecture?

43. Which technique is used to reinforce walls?

44. Which two materials are used in base isolators?

45. What happens to fill dirt during an earthquake?

Narrator: Listen to part of a lecture in a botany lab. The lab assistant is talking about leaves.

Food and water are carried throughout leaves by their veins. Today we will be looking at some examples of the main types of vein patterns in leaves. The most common are the pinnate and the palmate. This is a pinnate leaf, which is characteristic of trees like the beech and birch that you see outside this building on campus.

Remember that a pinnate leaf has one large central vein called the midrib, with large veins branching off on each side of it. The midrib extends the full length of the leaf.

Notice how different this leaf is. This is an example of a palmate leaf from a maple tree. A good way to remember this classification is to think of the palm of your hand. In a palmate leaf, there are several main veins of about equal size that originate at the base of the leaf and extend out to the edge of the leaf like fingers.

A few very narrow leaves are neither pinnate nor palmate. This leaf of grass for example has a parallel pattern.

Several veins extend themselves from the base of the blade to the tip, as you can see here.

Needle leaves are so small that they only have one, or occasionally two, veins in the center of the needle. I don't have a good slide of a needle leaf, but there is a drawing in your lab manual for you to refer to.

Now, I'd like you to turn to chapter three in the manual, and use page fifty-two as a reference for your lab activity. You will find twenty leaves in a plastic bag on your lab table. Please work with your lab partner to classify the veining of each leaf.

> Now get ready to answer the questions

Narrator: 46. Which two types represent the most common vein patterns in leaves?

47. According to the lecturer, what is a midrib?

48. How does the lab assistant help students remember the palmate classification?

49. Match the leaves with their vein patterns.

50. What will the students probably do after the short lecture?

Model Test 3
Computer-Assisted TOEFL

Section 1:
Listening

The Listening section of the test measures the ability to understand conversations and talks in English. On the actual TOEFL exam, you will use headphones to listen to the conversations and talks. While you are listening, pictures of the speakers or other information will be presented on your computer screen. There are two parts to the Listening section, with special directions for each part.

On the day of the test, the amount of time you will have to answer all of the questions will appear on the computer screen. The time you spend listening to the test material will not be counted. The listening material and questions about it will be presented only one time. You will not be allowed to take notes or have any paper at your computer. You will both see and hear the questions before the answer choices appear. You can take as much time as you need to select an answer; however, it will be to your advantage to answer the questions as quickly as possible. You may change your answer as many times as you want before you confirm it. After you have confirmed an answer, you will not be able to return to the question.

Before you begin working on the Listening section, you will have an opportunity to adjust the volume of the sound. You will not be able to change the volume after you have started the test.

QUESTION DIRECTIONS— Part A

In Part A of the Listening section, you will hear short conversations between two people. In some of the conversations, each person speaks only once. In other conversations, one or both of the people speak more than once. Each conversation is followed by one question about it.

Each question in this part has four answer choices. You should click on the best answer to each question. Answer the questions on the basis of what is stated or implied by the speakers.

1. Man: It doesn't make any sense for us to go home for spring vacation now.
   Woman: Especially since we'll be graduating in May.
   Narrator: What does the woman mean?

2. Man: Could you please explain the assignment for Monday, Miss Smith?
   Woman: Certainly. Read the next chapter in your textbook and come to class prepared to discuss what you've read.
   Narrator: What are the speakers talking about?

3. Woman: Are you ready for this?
   Man: I should be. I've been cramming for the past three days.
   Narrator: What does the man mean?

4. Man: I need a book for English two-twenty-one.
   Woman: All of the textbooks are on the shelves in the back of the store.
   Narrator: What will the man probably do?

5. Man: You're in my economics class, aren't you?
   Woman: Yes. I'm not an economics major, though.
   Man: So, what do you think of Professor Collins?
   Woman: I think he's a great person, but the class just turns me off.
   Narrator: What does the woman mean?

6. Man: Have you made an appointment with Dr. Peterson's T.A. yet?
   Woman: No. And I really can't put it off anymore.
   Narrator: What will the woman probably do?

7. Woman: How do you like American food?
   Man: I'm used to it now.
   Narrator: What does the man mean?

8. Woman: Are you still studying? It's two o'clock in the morning.
   Man: I know. I just can't seem to get caught up.
   Narrator: What does the man mean?

9. Man: It's your turn to call the names on the list if you want to.
   Woman: I think I'll pass this time.
   Narrator: What is the woman going to do?

10. Woman: I'm pretty sure that the deadline for applications has passed.
    Man: Why don't you let me look into it for you?
    Narrator: What does the man mean?

11. Man: This is the first time I've had to get a tutor.
    Woman: What seems to be the problem?

| Man: | Well, I understand the lectures but I get mixed up when I try to read the book. |
| Narrator: | What does the man mean? |

12. | Man: | The paper isn't due until next week. |
| Woman: | Yes, I know. But I wanted to turn it in ahead of time if that's all right. |
| Narrator: | What does the woman mean? |

13. | Man: | I can't stand this class! |
| Woman: | Well, you might as well get used to it. You have to take it in order to graduate. |
| Narrator: | What does the woman say about the class? |

14. | Woman: | How are you going to get ready for an oral final? |
| Man: | The professor said we should study alone, but the T.A. said to get into a study group and quiz each other. |
| Narrator: | What did the T.A. suggest the students do? |

15. | Man: | I need an advisor's signature on my course request form. Could I make an appointment, please? |
| Woman: | Oh, well, you don't need to make an appointment. Just wait here. I'll get a pen. |
| Narrator: | What is the woman going to do? |

16. | Woman: | Thanks for reading my paper. |
Man:	Sure. This copy looks good. Why don't you just hand it in?
Woman:	No, I'd better make one more draft.
Narrator:	What is the woman going to do?

17. | Woman: | Your loan payment is due on the first. Oh, sorry, the computer has you scheduled for the fifth. |
| Man: | That's good. That's what I thought. |
| Narrator: | What had the man assumed about the loan payment? |

QUESTION DIRECTIONS—Part B

In Part B of the Listening section, you will hear several longer conversations and talks. Each conversation or talk is followed by several questions. The conversations, talks, and questions will not be repeated.

The conversations and talks are about a variety of topics. You do not need special knowledge of the topics to answer the questions correctly. Rather, you should answer each question on the basis of what is stated or implied by the speakers in the conversations or talks.

For most of the questions, you will need to click on the best of four possible answers. Some questions will have special directions. The special directions will appear in a box on the computer screen.

Narrator:	Listen to a conversation between a student and a professor.
Woman:	Hello, Professor Hayes. I'm Betty Peterson. I'm in your senior seminar this semester.
Man:	Oh, yes, Betty. How are you?
Woman:	Just fine, thanks. I'm here because I'm applying for graduate school, and I need three letters of recommendation. Would you be willing to write me one?
Man:	Why yes, Betty. I'd be happy to. I think you are an excellent candidate for graduate school. Are you applying here or to another university?
Woman:	Here. That's why I think your letter is so important. Everyone on the selection committee knows and respects you.
Man:	Let's see, Dr. Warren is the chair of that committee, isn't she?
Woman:	Yes. So, if you would just write the letter to her, that would be great.
Man:	Okay. And when do you need this? I don't recall the deadline for applications.
Woman:	The committee meets on April 30, so all the materials must be submitted before then.
Man:	All right. I'll send it directly to her office.
Woman:	Thank you. I really appreciate it.
Man:	You're welcome. Glad to do it.

Now get ready to answer the questions

Narrator:	18. Why did Betty see Professor Hayes?
	19. What does Professor Hayes think about Betty?
	20. Who will decide whether Betty is accepted to the program?
	21. When does Betty need to submit all her materials?
Narrator:	Listen to a lecture by a history professor.

I know that this is probably a digression from the topic of today's lecture, but it is worth noting that although England no longer ruled her former colonies after the eighteenth century, she controlled trade with them by selling products so cheaply that it was not possible for the new countries to manufacture and compete with English prices. To maintain this favorable balance of trade, England went to fantastic lengths to keep secret the advanced manufacturing processes upon which such a monopoly depended.

Enterprising Americans made all kinds of ingenious attempts to smuggle drawings for the most modern machines out of England, but it was an Englishman, Samuel Slater, who finally succeeded.

Although textile workers were forbidden to emigrate, Slater traveled to the United States in secret. Determined to take nothing in writing, he memorized the intricate designs for all the machines in an English textile mill, and in partnership with Moses Brown, a Quaker merchant, recreated the mill in Rhode Island.

Forty-five years later, in part as a result of the initial model by Slater and Brown, America had changed from a country of small farmers and craftsmen to an industrial nation in competition with England.

> Now get ready to answer the questions

Narrator:	22. Who is the speaker?
	23. According to the speaker, how did England control trade in the eighteenth century?
	24. What did Samuel Slater do?
	25. What happened as a result of the Slater-Brown partnership?
Narrator:	Listen to part of a conversation between a student and an employee in the bookstore on campus.
Man:	Hi. I understand that I can reserve textbooks for next semester.
Woman:	That's right. If you know what courses you will be taking, we can have your order waiting for you the week before classes start.
Man:	Great! This semester I couldn't get two of my books until three weeks into the semester because you ran out of them before I made it to the bookstore.
Woman:	That has been a problem for a lot of students, and that's why we are trying this system. If we know that you want them, we can order books right away instead of waiting until faculty members place their orders for the whole class.
Man:	What do I have to do?
Woman:	Just fill out one of these forms. Be sure that you include both the course number and the section number for each course because different instructors may not be using the same books. Then pay for your books at the register, and we'll place the order.

Man:	Then do I just stop by the bookstore at the beginning of the semester?
Woman:	There's a space for your phone number on the form. We'll call you as soon as they come in. Sometimes we get them before the end of the current semester.
Man:	That would be great. Then I could take them home with me over the break to get a head start on the reading.
Woman:	Quite a few students do that now.

Now get ready to answer the questions

Narrator: 26. What is the purpose of this conversation?

                  27. What was the man's problem last semester?

                  28. How can the man order books?

                  29. How will the man know that the books have arrived?

Narrator: Listen to a talk by a college instructor in an English class.

So many different kinds of writing have been called essays, it is difficult to define exactly what an essay is. Perhaps the best way is to point out four characteristics that are true of most essays. First, an essay is about one topic. It does not start with one subject and digress to another and another. Second, although a few essays are long enough to be considered a small book, most essays are short. Five hundred words is the most common length for an essay. Third, an essay is written in prose, not poetry. True, Alexander Pope did call two of his poems essays, but that word is part of a title, and after all, the "Essay on Man" and the "Essay on Criticism" really are not essays at all. They are long poems. Fourth, and probably most important, an essay is personal. It is the work of one person whose purpose is to share a thought, idea, or point of view. Let me also state here that since an essay is always personal, the term "personal essay" is redundant. Now, taking into consideration all of these characteristics, perhaps we can now define an essay as a short, prose composition that has a personal viewpoint that discusses one topic. With that in mind, let's brainstorm some topics for your first essay assignment.

Now get ready to answer the questions

Narrator: 30. What is the instructor defining?

                  31. What is the main point of the talk?

32. According to the talk, which of the characteristics are NOT true of an essay?

33. What will the students probably do as an assignment?

Narrator: Listen to a talk by a guest speaker in a history class.

Not a gifted public speaker, Thomas Jefferson was most talented as a literary draftsman. Sent to Congress by the Virginia Convention in 1775, he was elected to the committee to draft a declaration of independence from England. Although John Adams and Benjamin Franklin also served on the committee, the composition of the Declaration of Independence belongs indisputably to Jefferson. In 1779, Jefferson was elected governor of the state of Virginia, an office he held until Congress appointed him to succeed Franklin as U.S. minister to France. Upon returning to Washington, he accepted the position of secretary of state.

Although Jefferson was a Republican, he at first tried to cooperate with Alexander Hamilton, a Federalist who was first among President Washington's advisors. When he concluded that Hamilton was really in favor of a monarchy, hostility between the two men sharpened.

Having served as vice-president in John Adams' administration, Jefferson ran for president in the election of 1800. He and Federalist Aaron Burr received an identical vote, but the Republican Congress elected to approve Jefferson as president. The most outstanding accomplishment of his administration was the purchase of the Louisiana Territory from France in 1803. He was easily re-elected in 1804. When he left office four years later, he returned here to Monticello, where he promoted the formation of a liberal university for Virginia.

Now get ready to answer the questions

Narrator: 34. What is the main purpose of this talk?

35. Jefferson was a member of which political group?

36. How did Jefferson become president?

37. According to the lecturer, what was it that Jefferson was NOT?

Narrator: Listen to part of a lecture on geology.

Fossils are the remains of organisms that have been preserved. Some of the most common fossils are shells, skeletons, leaves, and insects. They are occasionally preserved in ice, but most have been buried in mud or sand that collects at the bottom of bodies of water, especially lakes, swamps, and oceans. In order for fossils to form, the animals and plants must be buried quickly; otherwise, the organisms will disintegrate. If they are buried in loose sediment, the soft tissues will begin to decay. But the harder structures such as bones and shells will remain intact for much longer. After years of pressure from the layers of sediment above them, the lower layers of sediment turn into rock, encapsulating the organisms.

There are several different mineral processes that continue the fossilization of organisms in the sedimentary rocks. A few plants and animals become fossilized after mineral-rich water soaks into the pores and openings in the hard tissues of the plant or animal. In these fossils, the original body of the organism is strengthened by the infusion of mineral deposits, and every detail of the organism is preserved. But in most fossils, the minerals in the water dissolve the original organism, leaving a fossil mold. Minerals continue to be deposited in the mold at the same time, a process that results in the replacement of the living organism by a mineral deposit of exactly the same shape. In the casts of these molds, the internal features of the organism are not preserved, but the outer structure is accurate in every detail. Sometimes the fine shapes of even very fragile feathers and fur are preserved by mineral replacement.

Although the fossil record is incomplete, the composite of fossil findings chronicles the forms of life that existed at various periods in the past. In a sense the fossil record is a history of life. The location of fossils in layers of undisturbed sedimentary rock shows not only which groups of organisms lived at approximately the same time but also indicates the order in which they were buried, that is, their relative ages. Plants and animals on the lower layers are presumed to be older than those buried after them in the layers above.

> Now get ready to answer the questions

Narrator: 38. What are the two most common places where fossils may be found?

39. The professor briefly explains a process. Summarize the process by putting the events in order.

40. What is lost in the process of replacement?

41. Why are the layers of sedimentary rock important to the fossil record?

Narrator: Listen to part of a conversation between a student and a secretary on campus.

Woman:	Let me see if I understand this. You have completed all of your course work for graduation.
Man:	Right.
Woman:	But you didn't apply to graduate.
Man:	Right.
Woman:	But you want to graduate this semester.
Man:	Yes, and I thought I would, automatically. I mean, I didn't understand that I had to do anything.
Woman:	Who is your advisor?
Man:	I'm not sure. I have been sort of advising myself.
Woman:	You have?
Man:	It's not that hard. The requirements are all spelled out in the catalog, and I have just been taking the required courses, and keeping track of all my grades. Here's my latest transcript, and as you can see, I've got all the credits I need.
Woman:	So you don't even have a signed program of study.
Man:	Not signed, no. But I have a program of study. I used the program in the catalog.
Woman:	I know. But I am talking about a form that is filed by your advisor.
Man:	No, I don't have that.
Woman:	Okay. The first thing we need to do is to assign you an advisor to go over all your transcripts and help you create a program of study.
Man:	How long will that take?
Woman:	We'll try to get you in to see someone today. If you really have been able to take all the requirements, then there shouldn't be anything missing from the program and your advisor can sign it and also help you apply for graduation. But if you have misread the catalog or failed to take a critical course, then you may not be eligible for graduation. All I can tell you right now is that you have enough hours to graduate, but only an academic advisor can verify that you have completed the correct course work.
Man:	Oh no. You mean I might not graduate?
Woman:	I don't know. Let's make that appointment and go from there.

Now get ready to answer the questions

Narrator:	42. Why didn't the man apply for graduation?
	43. How did the man select his courses?

44. What does the woman suggest?

45. What is the man's problem?

Narrator:	Listen to part of a class discussion about American English.
Dr. Wilson:	Because the United States is so large, and has such a diverse population, several major dialect regions have been identified. The question is whether there is one universally acceptable standard of American English. Any thoughts?
Laura:	Dr. Wilson? I know that the two articles we read both argued that no dialect is inherently better than any other. Isn't that right?
Dr. Wilson:	Yes, I would say so. Since this is a linguistics class, the articles were written by linguists, and from a linguistic point of view, all dialects of a language are of equal value.
Laura:	Okay. And that is because all dialects can express everything that is necessary for a language community to communicate.
Dr. Wilson:	Precisely. But, I think you are going somewhere with this argument.
Laura:	I am. All dialects are linguistically equal, but are they equal socially? In other words, aren't some dialects more well-respected than others?
Dr. Wilson:	Interesting observation. In fact, your comment anticipates our assignment for the next class period when we will discuss standard dialects. For now, let me just say that, although there are several definitions of a standard dialect, the definition that we will use for our class is this: A standard dialect is the dialect that is selected as the educational model.
Laura:	Does that mean that the dialect of the schools is the standard?
Dr. Wilson:	Exactly.
Vicki:	Now I have a question.
Dr. Wilson:	Okay.
Vicki:	In different regions of the country, the pronunciation is very different, so the schools in each of these regions would have a different standard dialect. Isn't there a standard for the whole country?
Dr. Wilson:	Indeed, there is. Standard English has a common grammar and vocabulary. These are the basic building blocks of a dialect. The pronunciation is an accent, not a dialect. So the accent may be regional, but as long as the grammar and vocabulary are standard, the school is teaching the standard American English dialect with, let's say, a Southern accent or a New York accent.

Vicki:	So an accent is different from a dialect?
Dr. Wilson:	Technically, yes. However, certain accents tend to attach themselves to particular dialects.
Laura:	Oh, I see. So there is a standard accent, too, then.
Dr. Wilson:	Some linguists would say no, there isn't. But a number of sociologists would answer your question in a different way. Some accents are associated with a higher socioeconomic class and, therefore, tend to be the preferred standard accent in schools.
Laura:	I think I understand. There isn't anything inherently better about any dialect or accent, but the prestige of the social group that uses it makes some more desirable than others, so they are chosen for the language of the schools, and become the standard.
Dr. Wilson:	Well said.

Now get ready to answer the questions

Narrator:
46. In which class would this discussion probably take place?

47. According to the discussion, what is the definition of a standard dialect?

48. What is the linguistic perspective put forward in the articles that were assigned?

49. Which two linguistic components arc included in a dialect?

50. What do sociologists tell us about accents?

Model Test 4
Computer-Assisted TOEFL

Section 1:
Listening

The Listening section of the test measures the ability to understand conversations and talks in English. On the actual TOEFL exam, you will use headphones to listen to the conversations and talks. While you are listening, pictures of the speakers or other information will be presented on your computer screen. There are two parts to the Listening section, with special directions for each part.

On the day of the test, the amount of time you will have to answer all of the questions will appear on the computer screen. The time you spend listening to the test material will not be counted. The listening material and questions about it will be presented only one time. You will not be allowed to take notes or have any paper at your computer. You will both see and hear the questions before the answer choices appear. You can take as much time as you need to select an answer; however, it will be to your advantage to answer the questions as quickly as possible. You may change your answer as many times as you want before you confirm it. After you have confirmed an answer, you will not be able to return to the question.

Before you begin working on the Listening section, you will have an opportunity to adjust the volume of the sound. You will not be able to change the volume after you have started the test.

QUESTION DIRECTIONS—Part A

In Part A of the Listening section, you will hear short conversations between two people. In some of the conversations, each person speaks only once. In other conversations, one or both of the people speak more than once. Each conversation is followed by one question about it.

Each question in this part has four answer choices. You should click on the best answer to each question. Answer the questions on the basis of what is stated or implied by the speakers.

1. Man: The International Students' Association is having a party Saturday night. Can you come or do you have to work at the hospital?
   Woman: I wish I could.
   Narrator: What will the woman probably do?

2. Woman: I think that the game starts at eight.
   Man: Good. We have just enough time to get there.
   Narrator: What will the speakers probably do?

3. Woman: What did you do after you lost your passport?
   Man: I went to see the foreign student advisor, and he reported it to the Passport Office in Washington.
   Narrator: What did the man do after he lost his passport?

4. Man: I'm not sure what Dr. Tyler wants us to do.
   Woman: If I were you, I'd write a rough draft and ask Dr. Tyler to look at it.
   Narrator: What does the woman suggest the man do?

5. Man: Dr. Clark is the only one teaching statistics this term.
   Woman: You mean we have to put up with her for another semester?
   Narrator: What does the woman mean?

6. Woman: Did we have an assignment for Monday? I don't have anything written down.

    Man: Nothing to read in the textbook, but we have to see a movie and write a paragraph about it.

    Narrator: What are the speakers discussing?

7. Man: Excuse me. Are you Sally Harrison's sister?

    Woman: No, I'm not. I'm her cousin.

    Narrator: What had the man assumed about the woman?

8. Woman: I can't find my pen. It was right here on the desk yesterday and now it's gone. Have you seen it?

    Man: Yes. I put it in the desk drawer.

    Narrator: What is the woman's problem?

9. Woman: When is John coming?

    Man: Well, he said he'd be here at eight-thirty, but if I know him, it will be at least nine o'clock.

    Narrator: What does the man imply about John?

10. Woman: How is your experiment coming along?

    Man: It's finished, but it didn't turn out quite like I thought it would.

    Narrator: What does the man mean?

11. Woman: Barbara sure likes to talk on the phone.

    Man: If only she liked her classes as well!

    Narrator: What does the man imply about Barbara?

12. Man: What's the matter?

    Woman: My allergies are really bothering me. I guess I'll have to go to the doctor.

    Man: If I were you, I'd try some over-the-counter medications first. They usually do the job.

    Narrator: What does the man suggest the woman do?

13. Man: What did you decide about the scholarship? Did you fill out the application?

    Woman: I'm going to give it all I've got.

    Narrator: What does the woman mean?

14. Woman: Please pass your papers in.

    Man: Could I have a few more minutes to finish?

    Woman: I'm afraid not. It's a timed test.

    Narrator: What does the woman mean?

15. Man: Dr. Taylor's class is supposed to be really good.

    Woman: The best part is I can use my roommate's book.

    Man: I'm not so sure about that. I think they're using a different book this semester.

    Narrator: What does the man imply?

16. Man: I'm going to get Sally a bike for Christmas.
  Woman: Are you sure she'd like one?
  Narrator: What does the woman imply?

17. Man: I just can't get the answer to this problem! I've been
         working on it for three hours.
  Woman: Maybe you should get some rest and try it again later.
  Narrator: What does the woman suggest that the man do?

QUESTION DIRECTIONS—Part B

In Part B of the Listening section, you will hear several longer conversations and talks. Each conversation or talk is followed by several questions. The conversations, talks, and questions will not be repeated.

The conversations and talks are about a variety of topics. You do not need special knowledge of the topics to answer the questions correctly. Rather, you should answer each question on the basis of what is stated or implied by the speakers in the conversations or talks.

For most of the questions, you will need to click on the best of four possible answers. Some questions will have special directions. The special directions will appear in a box on the computer screen.

Narrator: Listen to a class discussion.

Baker: It seems to me that the question is not whether the metric system should be introduced in the United States, but rather, how it should be introduced.
Woman: I think that it should be done gradually to give everyone enough time to adjust.
Man: Yes. Perhaps we could even have two systems for a while. I mean, we could keep the English system and use metrics as an optional system.
Woman: That's what they seem to be doing. When you go to the grocery store, look at the labels on the cans and packages. They are marked in both ounces and grams.
Man: Right. I've noticed that too. And the weather reporters on radio and TV give the temperature readings in both degrees Fahrenheit and degrees Celsius now.
Woman: Some road signs have the distances marked in both miles and kilometers, especially on the interstate highways. What do you think, Professor Baker?
Baker: Well, I agree that a gradual adoption is better for those of us who have already been exposed to the English system of measurement. But I would favor teaching only metrics in the elementary schools.
Man: I see your point. It might be confusing to introduce two systems at the same time.

Now get ready to answer the questions

Narrator: 18. What is the topic under discussion?

19. What changes in measurement in the United States have the students observed?

20. What was Professor Baker's opinion?

21. Which word best describes Professor Baker's attitude toward his students?

Narrator: Listen to part of a lecture in a science class.

Since the National Aeronautics and Space Administration was established in 1961, NASA has been engaged in an extensive research effort, which, in cooperation with private industry, has transferred technology to the international marketplace. Hundreds of everyday products can be traced back to the space mission, including cordless electrical tools, airtight food packaging, water purification systems, and even scratch coating for eyeglasses.

In addition, many advances in medical technology can be traced back to NASA laboratories. First used to detect flaws in spacecraft, ultrasound is now standard equipment in almost every hospital for diagnosis and assessment of injuries and disease; equipment first used by NASA to transmit images from space to Earth is used to assist in cardiac imaging, and lasers first used to test satellites are now used in surgical procedures. Under-the-skin implants for the continuous infusion of drugs, and small pacemakers to regulate the heart were originally designed to monitor the physical condition of astronauts in space.

Finally, with the help of images that were obtained during space missions, and NASA technology, archaeologists have been able to explore the earth. Cities lost under desert sands have been located and rediscovered, and the sea floor has been mapped using photographs from outer space.

Now get ready to answer the questions

Narrator: 22. What is the talk mainly about?

23. Which of the advances listed are NOT mentioned as part of the technology developed for space missions?

24. According to the speaker, why did NASA develop medical equipment?

25. Why does the speaker mention archaeology?

Narrator: Listen to part of a conversation between a student and a professor in the professor's office.

Beverly: Oh, Dr. Williams. I expected to leave you a note since this is not one of your office hours. But I would really appreciate a few minutes of your time. I'm Beverly Jackson, and I'm in your two o'clock political science class.

Dr. Williams: Yes, Beverly. I remember you. You always sit in the front.

Beverly: I do. I really like the class, and I want to be able to see all the slides and videos.

Dr. Williams: Good, so what can I do for you?

Beverly: I'm hoping you can help me. I have a family emergency, and I am needed at home for at least a week. That means I'll have to miss your Wednesday and Friday class, but I'm sure that I can be back by class on Monday.

Dr. Williams: Oh.

Beverly: I know that attendance is part of the evaluation, and I want to get a good grade in the class. Is there any way you could give me an excused absence or something so it won't bring my grade down? I would be happy to do extra work to make up the time.

Dr. Williams: Oh, don't worry about that, Beverly. You never miss class, and I'm sure you have a very good reason to be absent this time. I'll be glad to give you an excused absence for Wednesday and Friday. Is there anything else I can do?

Beverly: Not really. I have already arranged to get the notes from Gloria Hayes. She and I always study together.

Dr. Williams: Fine. Well, when you get back, and you read Gloria's notes, let me know if there is anything you don't understand. Sometimes it's hard to understand someone else's notes. If you need some clarification, I can meet with you for a few minutes before class on Monday.

Beverly: That's very nice of you, Dr. Williams. I'll call to set up an appointment, if I need to. But I think I'll be okay with the notes. Thanks for the excused absence.

Dr. Williams: You're very welcome. And I hope that everything goes well for you at home.

Beverly: Thank you, Dr. Williams. I really appreciate it.

Now get ready to answer the questions

Narrator: 26. Why did the student want to see the professor?

27. What is the student's problem?

28. What does the professor offer to do?

29. What is the professor's attitude in this conversation?

Narrator: Listen to part of a talk in a history class.

The first permanent settlement was made in San Francisco in 1776, when a Spanish military post was established on the end of that peninsula. During the same year, some Franciscan Fathers founded the Mission San Francisco de Asis on a hill above the post. A trail was cleared from the military post to the mission, and about halfway between the two, a station was established for travelers called *Yerba Buena*, which means "good herbs."

For thirteen years the village had fewer than one hundred inhabitants. But in 1848, with the discovery of gold, the population grew to ten thousand. That same year, the name was changed from Yerba Buena to San Francisco.

By 1862 telegraph communications linked San Francisco with eastern cities, and by 1869, the first transcontinental railroad connected the Pacific coast with the Atlantic seaboard. Today San Francisco has a population of almost three million. It is the financial center of the West, and serves as the terminus for trans-Pacific steamship lines and air traffic. The port of San Francisco, which is almost eighteen miles long, handles between five and six million tons of cargo annually.

If you travel to San Francisco, you will see the most identifiable landmark, the Golden Gate Bridge. The bridge, which is more than one mile long, spans the harbor from San Francisco to Marin County and the Redwood Highway. It was completed in 1937 at a cost of thirty-two million dollars and is still one of the largest suspension bridges in the world.

Now get ready to answer the questions

Narrator: 30. What is the main purpose of this talk?

31. According to the speaker, what was the settlement called before it was renamed San Francisco?

32. According to the speaker, what happened in 1848?

33. How long is the Golden Gate Bridge?

Narrator: Listen to a talk by an English professor.

Transcendentalism began with the formation in 1836 of the Transcendental Club in Boston, Massachusetts, by a group of artists and writers. This group advanced a reaction against the rigid Puritanism of the period, especially insofar as it emphasized society at the expense of the individual.

One of the most distinguished members of the club was Ralph Waldo Emerson, who served as editor of the literary magazine *Dial.* His writing stressed the importance of the individual. In one of his best-known essays, "Self-Reliance," he appealed to intuition as a source of ethics, asserting that people should be the judge of their own actions, without the rigid restrictions of society.

From 1841 to 1843, Emerson entertained in his home the naturalist and author Henry David Thoreau, who also became a member of the Transcendental Club. Probably more than any other member, he demonstrated by his lifestyle the ideas that the group advanced. He preferred to go to jail rather than to pay taxes to the federal government for a war of which he did not approve.

Upon leaving Emerson's home, Thoreau built a small cabin along the shores of Walden Pond near Concord, Massachusetts, where he lived alone for two years. Devoting himself to the study of nature and to writing, he published an account of his experiences in *Walden*, a book that is generally acknowledged as the most original and sincere contribution to literature by the Transcendentalists.

> Now get ready to answer the questions

Narrator: 34. What does the lecturer mainly discuss?

35. During which century did this literary movement develop?

36. According to the lecturer, what did the Puritans do?

37. What is *Walden?*

Narrator: Listen to part of a conversation between a student and a librarian.

Woman: Do you have any experience working in a library?

Man:	No, not as an employee. But I am working toward my doctorate at the University, and I have spent a great deal of time doing my own research in the library. I'm finishing my dissertation now.
Woman:	So you are familiar with the electronic search equipment?
Man:	Yes, I am. I used several databases for my review of the literature in my dissertation, and I know how to use most of the search equipment that you have here, because this is where I am doing most of my own research.
Woman:	Good. Can you think of anything else that would qualify you for the job?
Man:	Yes. I like helping students. My undergraduate degree was in education, and I was a high school teacher for twelve years before I came back to school. The ad says that you want someone to show new students how to do computer searches for their term papers, and I think that my teaching experience would be very useful.
Woman:	Good, good. But what about the hours? If you are working on your dissertation, will you be able to work? This job requires twenty hours of your time per week, and the hours are not regular. You see, in addition to helping students one-on-one, we make appointments for faculty to bring their classes to the library for orientation before they make their first term paper assignments.
Man:	That sounds very interesting. I feel that I can handle a job now. I have most of my own research finished, and I'm writing my dissertation. I plan to do that after work and on my days off.
Woman:	So you aren't taking any classes now?
Man:	No. That's another advantage I have. I can schedule my time around the appointments.
Woman:	And if you are the successful candidate, when could you start?
Man:	Right away!

> Now get ready to answer the questions

Narrator:	38. What is the purpose of this conversation?
	39. Who is the man?
	40. What does the man need to do when he is not working?
	41. When would the man be available?
Narrator:	Listen to part of a lecture on solar heating.

In general, solar heating requires a solar collector, a water or air distribution system, and a storage system. Most of the time, a solar collector is mounted on the roof of a building at a somewhat steep angle, positioned with a southern exposure. In the hot water system that I am going to show you, the collector is a glass plate with another plate under it, and an air space between the two, through which water can be pumped. I think it will make more sense when you see the model, so let's look at it now.

Notice that water that has been heated by the sun is pumped in closely positioned tubes through the space between the plates. The hot water is then pumped to a storage tank, and warmed air is circulated to the other side of the building with a fan. You will also see a backup heater in this system, usually a conventional furnace, because only about 20 to 30 percent of the solar energy can actually be used in this design. The supply air moves across the space to be heated, and enters the return air exchanger where it rises and, with exposure to the sun, begins heating again to raise the temperature of the water in the tubes below. So, the process begins again.

Of course, one of the problems with solar heat is the intermittent nature of solar radiation as an energy source. Especially in climates where the sun does not shine regularly, it just isn't a feasible option without large, and often complex, storage systems. However, scientists are now working on a project to place solar modules in orbit around the Earth, where energy generated by the sun could be converted to microwaves and beamed to antennas for conversion to electric power. It is estimated that such a system, although costly and somewhat cumbersome, could potentially generate as much power as five large nuclear power plants. The principle would be basically the same as that of the much simpler model that I showed you. A solar collector, an air distribution center, and a storage system would be required. So if you understand the model here, you can understand even the most complex solar heating unit.

> Now get ready to answer the questions

Narrator:	42. Which two requirements are considered when mounting a solar collector on a roof?
	43. Identify the fan in the solar heating system.
	44. What problem does the professor point out?
	45. Why does the professor mention the project to place solar modules in orbit?
Narrator:	Listen to part of a conversation between a student and a secretary in the Tutoring Center.
Man:	Excuse me, is this where I request a tutor?
Woman:	Yes, it is. Which course do you need help in?
Man:	English.
Woman:	English language or literature?
Man:	Composition really. I seem to have a hard time figuring out how to write my essays.
Woman:	Oh. Well, we have some excellent tutors for that.
Man:	My grades are really good in math and science, but I can't figure out how to organize my writing.
Woman:	When would you be able to come in for tutoring? Do you have classes in the afternoon?
Man:	Just on Monday, Wednesday, and Friday. I only have morning classes on Tuesday and Thursday.
Woman:	Good. Some of our best tutors for English work in the afternoon. I could set you up with Janine on Tuesdays and Thursdays at four o' clock if you want.
Man:	Is the tutoring session an hour long?
Woman:	Yes. You would be finishing up about five.
Man:	Okay. I could do that. And, uh, how much will that cost?
Woman:	Oh, I thought you knew. This is a free service for our students.
Man:	It is? No, I wasn't aware of that.
Woman:	Actually, a lot of students who receive tutoring come back and serve as tutors once they get squared away themselves.
Man:	That's really a great system.

Woman:	Janine needed some tutoring in math a few years ago, as I recall, and now she helps us in English composition and French.
Man:	So, should I just come back on Tuesday at four?
Woman:	Yes. I have your name down. Just check in with me when you get here, and I'll take you over to Janine's table. And, bring your books for the class that you need help in, along with a syllabus, your class notes, and anything that might help your tutor to understand the course requirements.
Man:	Thank you so much. I'll see you Tuesday, then.

> Now get ready to answer the questions

Narrator:	46. What is the purpose of this conversation?
	47. For which course does the man want a tutor?
	48. How much will the tutoring cost?
	49. When will the tutoring session begin?
	50. What should the man bring to his tutoring session?

NOTES

BARRON'S UPDATED TEST PREPARATION TOOLS FOR THE CURRENT TOEFL® TEST

Test of English as a Foreign Language

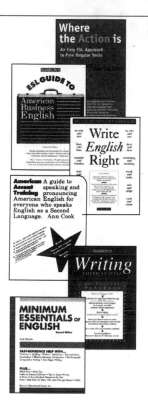

Barron's TOEFL
Compact Disk

The compact disk in the back of this book can be used in your compact disk player to provide the audio for two of the TOEFL model tests. You should hear audio only. If you want to simulate the Computer-Based TOEFL, with both audio and visuals, you need a CD-ROM, not a compact disk. The CD-ROM is available from Barron's Educational Series, Inc. The CD-ROM has four model tests on it.

Telephone: 800-645-3476
FAX: 631-434-3723
E-mail: customer.service@barronseduc.com
Web site: *http://www.barronseduc.com*